A CANADIAN WRITER'S REFERENCE

Third Edition

Diana Hacker

Prince George's Community College

BEDFORD/ST. MARTIN'S   BOSTON ◆ NEW YORK

For Bedford/St. Martin's

Executive Editor: Leasa Burton
Developmental Editors: Michelle Clark, Nelina Backman
Senior Production Editor: Anne Noonan
Senior Production Supervisor: Catherine Hetmansky
Marketing Manager: Richard Cadman
Editorial Assistant: Amy Hurd
Production Assistant: Kerri Cardone
Copy Editors: Barbara G. Flanagan, Dawn Hunter
Text Design: Claire Seng-Niemoeller
Cover Design: Night & Day Design
Composition: Monotype Composition Company, Inc.
Printing and Binding: R.R. Donnelley & Sons Company

President: Joan E. Feinberg
Editorial Director: Denise B. Wydra
Editor in Chief: Karen S. Henry
Director of Marketing: Karen Melton Soeltz
Director of Editing, Design, and Production: Marcia Cohen
Managing Editor: Elizabeth M. Schaaf

Library of Congress Control Number: 2002102537

For information, write: Bedford/St. Martin's, 75 Arlington Street, Boston, MA 02116 USA   (617-399-4000)

ISBN: 0–312–41683–0

ACKNOWLEDGMENTS

Nelson W. Aldrich Jr., from *Old Money: The Mythology of America's Upper Class.* Copyright ©1988 by Nelson W. Aldrich Jr. Published by Alfred A. Knopf, Inc.

The American Heritage Dictionary of the English Language, from the entry "regard." Copyright ©1996 by Houghton Mifflin Company. Reprinted by permission from *The American Heritage Dictionary of the English Language,* Third Edition.

Acknowledgments and copyrights are continued at the back of the book on page 466, which constitutes an extension of the copyright page. It is a violation of the law to reproduce these selections by any means whatsoever without the written permission of the copyright holder.

How to use this book

A Canadian Writer's Reference has been carefully designed to save you time. As you can see, the book lies flat, making it easy to consult while you are revising and editing a draft. And the book's twelve section dividers will lead you — in most cases very quickly — to the information you need.

Here are brief descriptions of the book's major reference aids, followed by a chart summarizing the content of the book's companion Web site.

The menu system. The main menu inside the front cover displays the book's contents as briefly and simply as possible. Each of the twelve sections in the main menu leads you to a colour-coded tabbed divider, on the back of which you will find a more detailed menu.

Let's say you have a question about the proper use of commas between items in a series. Your first step is to scan the main menu, where you will find the comma listed as the first item under section P (Punctuation). Next flip the book open to the red tabbed divider marked P. Now consult the detailed menu for the precise subsection (P1-c) and the exact page number.

The index. If you aren't sure what topic to choose from the main menu, consult the index at the back of the book. For example, you may not realize that the issue of whether to use *has* or *have* is a matter of subject-verb agreement (G1 on the main menu). In that case, simply look up "*has* vs. *have*" in the index and you will be directed to specific pages and given a cross-reference to the general topic of subject-verb agreement.

The Glossary of Usage. When in doubt about the correct use of a particular word (such as *affect* and *effect, among* and *between,* or *hopefully*), flip to section W1 and consult the alphabetically arranged glossary for the word in question. If the word you are looking for isn't in the Glossary of Usage, try the index instead. For example, you won't find an entry for "*I* vs. *me*" in the glossary because the issue is too complicated for a short glossary entry. The index, however, will take you straight to the pages you need.

The directories to documentation models. When you are writing a research paper, there is no need to memorize all of the technical details about handling citations or constructing a list of the works you have cited. Instead, you can rely on one of the book's directories to documentation models. If you are using the Modern Language Association (MLA) system of documentation, flip the book open to the tabbed section marked MLA to find the appropriate directory. If you are using the American Psychological Association (APA) or the *Chicago* (CMS) system, flip to the tabbed section marked APA/CMS.

List of ESL boxes. If you are a nonnative speaker of English, you will find most of the ESL (English as a second language) advice in the tabbed section marked T (for ESL Trouble Spots). Other ESL advice appears in boxed ESL notes throughout *A Canadian Writer's Reference.* For quick reference, a list of ESL notes is given near the end of the book, after the index and before the revision symbols.

Revision symbols. Some instructors mark student papers with the codes given on the main menu or detailed menus, such as S1 or G3-c. If your instructor uses standard revision symbols instead, consult the list on the very last page of the book, right before the endpapers.

Detailed menu (inside the back cover). A menu more detailed than the main menu appears inside the back cover.

Companion Web site. The following chart describes resources for students that appear on the book's companion Web site at <www.dianahacker.com/writersref>. The electronic exercises (more than one hundred sets on writing, grammar, and research) can be used for self-study. After answering each exercise item, you receive specific feedback for correct and incorrect answers; you do not need to wait until the end of an exercise set to know how you are doing.

ON THE WEB

Throughout *A Canadian Writer's Reference,* Third Edition, On the Web boxes direct you to relevant resources on the book's companion Web site.

Simply go to **www.dianahacker.com/writersref** and click on

▶ **Electronic Writing Exercises**
Interactive exercises on topics such as choosing a thesis statement and conducting a peer review

▶ **Electronic Grammar Exercises**
Interactive exercises on grammar, style, and punctuation

▶ **Electronic Research Exercises**
Interactive exercises on topics such as integrating quotations and documenting sources in MLA, APA, and CMS (*Chicago*) styles

▶ **Language Debates**
Mini-essays by Diana Hacker that explore controversial issues of grammar and usage, such as split infinitives

▶ **Links Library**
Carefully selected and annotated links to additional online resources for every part of the book

▶ **Model Papers**
Annotated sample papers in MLA, APA, CMS (*Chicago*), and CBE styles

▶ **Research and Documentation Online**
Advice on finding sources and up-to-date guidelines for documenting print and online sources in MLA, APA, CMS (*Chicago*), and CBE styles

▶ **Additional Resources**
Print-format exercises for practice; "Looking at Yourself as a Writer" charts that encourage reflection

Tutorials

The following tutorials will give you practice using the book's menu system, the index, the Glossary of Usage, and the directory to the MLA documentation models. Answers to all tutorials appear on pages xi–xiii.

TUTORIAL 1   Using the menu system

Each of the following "rules" violates the principle it expresses. Using the menu system, find the section in *A Canadian Writer's Reference* that explains the principle. Then fix the problem. Examples:

> *has*
> A verb ~~have~~ to agree with its subject. *G1*
>   ^
>
> *Tutors in*
> ~~In~~ the writing centre/ ~~they~~ say that vague pronoun reference is
> ^
>
> unacceptable. *G3-b*

1. Each pronoun must agree with their antecedent.
2. About sentence fragments. You should avoid them.
3. Its important to use apostrophe's correctly.
4. Watch out for *-ed* endings that have been drop from verbs.
5. Discriminate careful between adjectives and adverbs.
6. Be alert for irregular verbs that have came to you in the wrong form.
7. If your sentence begins with a long introductory word group use a comma to separate the word group from the rest of the sentence.
8. Don't write a run-on sentence, you must connect independent clauses with a comma and a coordinating conjunction or with a semicolon.
9. A writer must be careful not to shift your point of view.
10. When dangling, watch your modifiers.

TUTORIAL 2   Using the index

Assume that you have written the following sentences and want to know the answers to the questions in brackets. Use the index at the back of the book to locate the information you need, and edit the sentences if necessary.

1. Each of the candidates have agreed to participate in tonight's debate. [Does the subject *Each* agree with *have* or with *has*?]
2. We had intended to go surfing but spent most of our vacation lying on the beach. [Should I use *lying* or *laying*?]
3. We only looked at two houses before buying the house of our dreams. [Is *only* in the right place?]
4. In Saudi Arabia it is considered ill mannered for you to accept a gift. [Is it okay to use *you* to mean "anyone in general"?]
5. Joanne picked up several bottles of maple syrup for her sister and me. [Should I write *for her sister and I*?]

TUTORIAL 3 Using the menu system or the index

Imagine that you are in the following situations. Using either the menu system or the index, find the information you need.

1. You are Ray Farley, a community college student who has been out of high school for ten years. You recall learning to punctuate items in a series by putting a comma between all items except the last two. In your college readings, however, you have noticed that most writers use a comma between all items. You're curious about the current rule. What does *A Canadian Writer's Reference* tell you?
2. You are Maria Sanchez, an honours student working in your university's writing centre. Mike Lee, who speaks English as a second language, has come to you for help. He is working on a rough draft that contains a number of problems involving the use of articles *(a, an,* and *the)*. You know how to use articles, but you aren't able to explain the rules on their correct use. Which section of *A Canadian Writer's Reference* will you and Mike Lee consult?
3. You are John Pell, engaged to marry Jane Dalton. In a note to Jane's parents, you have written, "Thank you for giving Jane and myself such a generous contribution toward our honeymoon trip to Hawaii." You wonder if you should write *Jane and I* or *Jane and me* instead. What does *A Canadian Writer's Reference* tell you?
4. You are Selena Young, a supervisor of co-op students at a housing agency. Two of your students, Jake Gill and Susan Green, have writing problems involving *-s* endings on verbs. Gill tends to drop *-s* endings; Green tends to add them where they don't belong. You suspect that both problems stem from dialects spoken at home.

    Susan and Jake are in danger of losing their jobs because your boss thinks that anyone who writes "the tenant refuse" or "the landlords agrees" is beyond hope. You disagree. Susan and Jake are more intelligent than your boss supposes, and they have asked for your help. Where in *A Canadian Writer's Reference* can they find the rules they need?

5. You are Joe Thompson, a first-year college student. Your friend Samantha, who has completed two years of college, seems to enjoy correcting your English. Just yesterday she corrected your sentence "I felt badly about her death" to "I felt bad about her death." You're sure you've heard many educated persons, including professors, say "I felt badly." Upon consulting *A Canadian Writer's Reference,* what do you discover?

TUTORIAL 4   Using the Glossary of Usage

Consult the Glossary of Usage (section W1) to see if the italicized words are used correctly. Then edit any sentences containing incorrect usage. Example:

an

The pediatrician gave my daughter ~~a~~ injection for her allergy.

1. The *amount* of horses a warrior had in his possession indicated the wealth of his family.
2. This afternoon I plan to *lie* out in the sun and work on a tan.
3. That is the most *unique* floral arrangement I have ever seen.
4. Changing attitudes *toward* alcohol have *effected* the beer industry.
5. Jenny *should of* known better than to attempt that dive.
6. Everyone in our office is *enthused* about this project.
7. George and Pat are selling *there* house because now that *their* children are grown, *their* planning to move to Arizona.
8. Most sleds are pulled by no *fewer* than two dogs and no more than ten.
9. It is the nature of *mankind* to think wisely and act foolishly.
10. Dr. Newman and *myself* have agreed to arrange the party.

TUTORIAL 5   Using the directory to MLA works cited models

Assume that you have written a short research paper on the growth of gambling operations on American Indian reservations. You have cited the following sources in your paper, using MLA documentation, and you are ready to type your list of works cited. Flip the book open to the tabbed section marked MLA Papers and use the MLA directory to locate the appropriate models. Then write a correct entry for each source and arrange the entries in a properly formatted list of works cited. *Note:* Do not number the entries in a list of works cited.

A book by Jeff Benedict entitled *Without Reservation: The Making of America's Most Powerful Indian Tribe and the World's Largest Casino.* The book was published in New York by Harper in 2000.

An article by Jerry Useem entitled "The Big Game: Have American Indians Found Their New Buffalo?" from the biweekly magazine *Fortune.* The article appears on nonconsecutive pages beginning with page 22 of the October 2, 2000, issue of the magazine.

An e-mail with the subject line "Casinos on reservations in the Northeast," sent to you by Helen Codoga on April 10, 2001.

A journal article by Susan Johnson entitled "From Wounded Knee to Capitol Hill." The article appears in *State Legislatures,* which is paginated by issue. The volume number is 24, the issue number is 9, and the year is 1998. You found this article using the InfoTrac database *Expanded Academic ASAP* at the University of Pittsburgh library on April 6, 2001.

A short Web document entitled "Tribal Gaming Myths and Facts" written by the National Indian Gaming Association and published in 2000 on the group's Web site at http://www.indiangaming.org/info/pr/myths.shtml. You found the document on April 4, 2001.

A radio segment entitled "Indian Gaming" from the program *All Things Considered* hosted by Robert Siegel. The program was produced by National Public Radio on March 5, 2001. You listened to the program on WDUQ in Pittsburgh.

Answers to Tutorial 1

1. Each pronoun must agree with its antecedent. (G3-a)
2. You should avoid sentence fragments. (G5)
3. It's important to use apostrophes correctly. (P5-c and P5-e)
4. Watch out for *-ed* endings that have been dropped from verbs. (G2-d)
5. Discriminate carefully between adjectives and adverbs. (G4)
6. Be alert for irregular verbs that have come to you in the wrong form. (G2-a)
7. If your sentence begins with a long introductory word group, use a comma to separate the word group from the rest of the sentence. (P1-b)
8. Don't write a run-on sentence; you must connect independent clauses with a comma and a coordinating conjunction or with a semicolon. (G6)
9. A writer must be careful not to shift his or her [*not* their] point of view. *Or* Writers must be careful not to shift their point of view. (S4-a)
10. Watch out for dangling modifiers. (S3-e)

Answers to Tutorial 2

1. The index entry *"each"* mentions that the word is singular, so you might not need to look further to realize that *has* [not *have*] is correct. The first page reference leads you to section G1-e, which explains in more detail why *has* is correct.
2. The index entry *"lie, lay"* takes you to the Glossary of Usage and to section G2-b, where you will learn that *lying* (meaning "reclining or resting on a surface") is correct.
3. Look up *"only"* and you will be directed to section S3-a, which explains that limiting modifiers such as *only* should be placed before the words they modify. The sentence should read *We looked at only two houses before buying the house of our dreams.*
4. Looking up *"you,* inappropriate use of*"* leads you to the Glossary of Usage and section G3-b, both of which explain that *you* should not be used to mean "anyone in general." You can revise the sentence by using *a person* or *one* instead of *you,* or you can restructure the sentence completely: *In Saudi Arabia, accepting a gift is considered ill mannered.*
5. The index entries *"I* vs. *me"* and *"me* vs. *I"* take you to section G3-c, which explains why *me* is correct.

Answers to Tutorial 3

1. Section P1-c notes that although usage varies, most experts advise using a comma between all items in a series—to prevent possible misreadings or ambiguities. To find this section, Ray Farley would probably use the menu system.
2. Maria Sanchez and Mike Lee would consult section T1, on articles. This section is easy to locate on the main menu.
3. Section G3-c explains why *Jane and me* is correct. To find section G3-c, John Pell could use the menu system if he knew to look under "Problems with pronouns." Otherwise, he could look up *"I* vs. *me"* in the index. Pell could also look up *"myself"* in the index or he could consult the Glossary of Usage, where a cross-reference would direct him to section G3-c.
4. Selena Young's employees could turn to sections G1 and G2-c for help. Young could use the menu system to find these sections if she knew to look under "Subject-verb agreement" or "Other problems with verbs." If she wasn't sure about the grammatical terminology, she could look up *"-s,* as verb ending" or "Verbs, *-s* form of*"* in the index.
5. Section G4-b explains why "I felt bad about her death" is correct. To find section G4-b, Joe Thompson could use the menu system if he knew that *bad* versus *badly* is a choice between an adjective and an adverb. Otherwise he could look up *"bad, badly"* in the index or the Glossary of Usage.

Answers to Tutorial 4

1. The *number* of horses a warrior had in his possession indicated the wealth of his family.
2. Correct
3. That is the most *unusual* floral arrangement I have ever seen.
4. Changing attitudes *toward* alcohol have *affected* the beer industry.
5. Jenny *should have* known better than to attempt that dive.
6. Everyone in our office is *enthusiastic* about this project.
7. George and Pat are selling *their* house because now that *their* children are grown, *they're* planning to move to Arizona.
8. Correct
9. It is *human* nature to think wisely and act foolishly.
10. Dr. Newman and *I* have agreed to arrange the party.

Answers to Tutorial 5

Benedict, Jeff. Without Reservation: The Making of America's Most Powerful Indian Tribe and the World's Largest Casino. New York: Harper, 2000.

Codoga, Helen. "Casinos on reservations in the Northeast." E-mail to the author. 10 Apr. 2001.

"Indian Gaming." All Things Considered. Host Robert Siegel. Natl. Public Radio. WDUQ, Pittsburgh. 5 Mar. 2001.

Johnson, Susan. "From Wounded Knee to Capitol Hill." State Legislatures 24.9 (1998). Expanded Academic ASAP. InfoTrac. U of Pittsburgh Lib. 6 Apr. 2001.

National Indian Gaming Association. "Tribal Gaming Myths and Facts." 2000. 4 Apr. 2001 <http://www.indiangaming.org/info/pr/myths.shtml>.

Useem, Jerry. "The Big Game: Have American Indians Found Their New Buffalo?" Fortune 2 Oct. 2000: 22+.

Preface for instructors

When Bedford and I invented the quick-reference format—with its main menu, tabbed dividers, and lie-flat binding—more than ten years ago, we had no idea that *A Writer's Reference* would become so popular (or so widely imitated). My goals were more modest. I hoped that the format and the title would send a clear message: *A Writer's Reference* is meant to be consulted as needed; it is not a set of grammar lessons to be studied in a vacuum. I also hoped that the book would support and promote modern pedagogy, which places students' own texts at the centre of writing instruction. These hopes have been realized: Instructors across the country tell me that their students can and do use the book on their own, keeping it flipped open next to their computers.

Like the book itself, this preface is organized for quick reference. It has three main parts: What's new, below; What's the same, page xvi; and What's on the companion Web site, page xvii.

What's new

Most of my revisions respond to technological change. In addition to updating the book for the digital age, I have improved the sections on critical thinking and made the book more useful for writers across the curriculum. Here, briefly, are some highlights.

Integration of the book with its companion Web site. Because most students are now working online, I've extended my book beyond its paper covers by linking it explicitly to its Web site. Throughout the book, On the Web boxes take students to locations on the Web site where they will find a variety of supplements to the book: model papers, essays called Language Debates, Research and Documentation Online, a links library, and more than one hundred electronic exercises on writing, grammar, and research. Because the Web site is an extension of the book, I have written nearly all of its content myself. For more about these Web features, see pages xvii–xix.

Updated advice on finding and evaluating sources. With the help of reference librarian Barbara Fister, I have revised the sections on finding and evaluating sources with the awareness that the library and the Web now depend on one another. I encourage students to enter the Web through a library's portal or another "juried" venue that ensures some sort of quality control. Also, I emphasize the need for evaluation throughout the research process — from choosing a search engine or database to selecting reliable sources to reading those sources.

The sections on finding and evaluating sources are more cross-curricular than before: They are now illustrated with examples linked to the topics of the book's MLA, APA, and CMS (*Chicago*) papers.

Discipline-specific rhetorical advice for MLA, APA, and CMS (Chicago) styles in colour-coded sections. Handbook advice on drafting a thesis, avoiding plagiarism, and integrating sources has traditionally been illustrated only with MLA examples. To make the third edition of *A Canadian Writer's Reference* more useful for students writing APA and CMS papers, I now present discipline-specific advice on these important matters in three colour-coded sections. Students in social science or history classes no longer need to "translate" the examples, mentally replacing MLA's in-text citations with APA's quite different in-text citations or with CMS's notes. In all three sections, examples are tied to topics appropriate to each discipline.

Expanded MLA guidelines, especially for Web sources. Because many Web sources have corporate or unknown authors and because most lack stable page numbers, I now pay special attention to authorship and pagination in my presentation of MLA's in-text citations. It is easier for students to document both print and Web sources if they focus on a clear first step: identifying the author of a source. Once students grasp that the author's name links an in-text citation to an entry in the list of works cited, they can better understand the intricacies of MLA style: how to handle multiple authors, for example, or corporate authors or unknown authors. As for the issue of page numbers, I explain the MLA guidelines, along with their implications, in more detail than before.

The works cited models now cover a wider range of multimedia and Web sources because students are relying more heavily on such sources in their papers.

New sample papers. A new MLA paper that advocates regulating the use of cell phones while driving is paired with a paper opposing such regulation; the second paper appears on the book's companion Web site. Each paper draws on both print and electronic sources.

Pages of a new CMS paper appear in the book. The full version of the paper is posted on the companion Web site.

Revised advice on constructing and evaluating arguments. The section on argument devotes more attention to audience and the need to build credibility. A new section on evaluating arguments shows students how argumentative tactics, such as generalizing and appealing to emotions, can work either to build or to undermine a writer's credibility.

More attention to writing in online environments. The section on document design includes new advice about creating scannable and online résumés as well as updated and expanded advice about designing Web sites.

What's the same

Although technology has led to a number of changes in the book, many of the book's features will be familiar to users of the previous edition. The features that have most contributed to the book's success are detailed in this section.

Colour-coded main menu and tabbed dividers. The main menu points unmistakably to teal, red, black, and white sets of tabbed dividers, making it easy for students to identify and flip to the section they need. The documentation sections are now also colour-coded: red for MLA, teal for APA, and blue for CMS.

A user-friendly index. In the index of the fifth edition, I include the letter of the tabbed section (in boldface) before the page number of the indexed word, such as G: 151 or P: 234–35. That way users can flip directly to the correct tabbed divider, such as G (for Grammatical sentences) or P (for Punctuation), before tracking down the page number.

The index (which I write myself) helps students find what they are looking for even if they don't know grammatical terminology. When facing a choice between *I* and *me,* for example, students may not know to look up "Case" or even "Pronoun case." They are more likely to look up "*I*" or "*me,*" so I have included index entries for "*I* vs. *me"* and *"me* vs. *I."* Similar user-friendly entries appear throughout the index.

Four-colour page design, still uncluttered. Rules and hand-edited sentences continue to be highlighted in a single colour (red) so that students can scan for quick answers, reading as much or as little of the text as they need. Charts and boxes appear consistently in red and tan, making them easy to find and, just as important, easy to skip.

Quick-reference charts. Many of the charts in *A Canadian Writer's Reference* help students review for common problems in their own writing, such as fragments and subject-verb agreement. Other charts summarize important material: a checklist for global revision, strategies for avoiding sexist language, guidelines for evaluating Web sites, and so on.

Grammar checker boxes. As you have no doubt discovered, students sometimes produce strange errors because they have taken the advice of a grammar checker without thinking first. And many students believe that once they have run their text through a grammar checker, their problems are over.

To discover the capabilities and limits of current grammar checkers, I have run a large bank of exercise sentences (many containing errors), along with some student drafts, through two commonly used programs. The results, summarized in boxes throughout the book, show that grammar checkers help with some but by no means all of the typical problems in a draft.

Help for culturally diverse students. More than ten years ago, I was the first handbook author to write a special section for students who speak English as a second (or third or fourth) language. Over the years, I have expanded the section and added a number of ESL boxes throughout the book. ESL students are of course my primary audience in these sections, but many instructors and tutors who work with culturally diverse students have also found this material helpful.

What's on the companion Web site

Language Debates. The companion Web site's Language Debates are brief essays in which I explore controversial issues of grammar and usage, such as split infinitives, by citing experts and weighing their arguments. The inspiration for these essays came from e-mails I've received from student users of my books: queries about passive verbs, *that* versus *which,* and so on. My goal in the Language Debates is to encourage such students to think about the rationales for a rule and then make their own rhetorical decisions.

Electronic grammar exercises. I have nearly doubled the number of grammar exercises on the book's companion Web site — from six hundred to about one thousand items. As always, I have played an active role in creating the exercises and writing the feedback for correct and incorrect responses.

Most of the exercises are scorable. Exercises that call for editing are not scorable because answers may vary; these exercises, on topics such as parallelism or dangling modifiers, which have a rhetorical dimension, are labelled "edit and compare." They ask students to edit sentences and compare their versions with possible revisions.

Electronic research and writing exercises. Using material from pencil-and-paper research exercises that I put together for my own students, I have created scorable electronic exercises on matters such as avoiding plagiarism, integrating sources, and using MLA, APA, and CMS documentation. Many students have a hard time understanding these matters just by reading the book; when they work through a couple of exercises, I've found, they begin to grasp the issues. At the very least, they can't tell me later that they had no idea copying was wrong!

To accompany section C, Composing and revising, I've written a few electronic exercises on thesis statements, peer review, point of view, transitions, and the like. These too are scorable.

Links library. Throughout the book, students are directed to relevant portions of a links library on the companion Web site. For example, from the companion site students can go to resources such as online writing centres, tutorials on creating Web sites, and online libraries.

Model papers. Model papers for MLA, APA, CMS (*Chicago*), and CBE styles illustrate both the design and content of researched writing. Annotations highlight important points about each paper's style, content, and method of documentation.

Research and Documentation Online. As its title suggests, this online resource (available at <www.dianahacker.com/resdoc>) helps students conduct research and document their sources. Reference librarian Barbara Fister has updated her advice on finding sources and has provided new links to resources in a variety of disciplines, and she continues to maintain the research portion of the site. My role has been to update guidelines for documenting print and on-line sources in MLA, APA, CMS, and CBE styles.

The instructor site. Accessible from the student site and at <www.dianahacker.com/writersref/instructor>, this password-protected Web site provides a portal for retrieving student exercise results. In addition, it includes the following electronic diagnostic tests and downloadable, print-format ancillaries:

> *Exercises to Accompany A* WRITER'S REFERENCE (and password-protected answer key)
>
> *Developmental Exercises to Accompany A* WRITER'S REFERENCE (and password-protected answer key)
>
> *Quiz Masters,* quizzes on key topics in the book (and password-protected answer key)

Ancillary package

Both print and electronic ancillaries are available for students and instructors. Ancillaries support both *A Writer's Reference,* Fifth Edition, and *A Canadian Writer's Reference,* Third Edition.

PRINT RESOURCES

Research and Documentation in the Electronic Age, Third Edition

Exercises to Accompany A WRITER'S REFERENCE (with answer key)

Developmental Exercises to Accompany A WRITER'S REFERENCE (with answer key)

Writing about Literature Supplement to Accompany A WRITER'S REFERENCE

NEW MEDIA RESOURCES

An Electronic Writer's Reference 6.0 (available on CD-ROM for Windows and Macintosh)

A Writer's Reference companion Web site (see the On the Web box on p. vii)

Acknowledgments

No author can possibly anticipate the many ways in which a variety of students might respond to a text: Where might students be confused? How much explanation is enough? What is too intimidating? Do the examples appeal to a range of students? Are the examples free of stereotypes? To help me answer such questions, more than forty professors contributed useful insights based on their varied experiences in the classroom.

For their commentary on the newest edition of *A Writer's Reference* and on the Diana Hacker Web sites, I am grateful to a group of perceptive reviewers:

Dorothy Arnett, Central Missouri State University
Connie Austin, Azusa Pacific University
Shane Borrowman, Gonzaga University
Donna M. Campbell, Gonzaga University
Deany M. Cheramie, Xavier University of Louisiana
Matthew DeVoll, Washington University
Virginia Elkins, University of Cincinnati
Michael W. George, Ohio Northern University
Carol Howard, Warren Wilson College
Jeffrey Nelson, The University of Alabama in Huntsville
Diann Mason, Paris Junior College
Victoria McClure, South Plains College
Arlo Stoltenberg, North Iowa Area Community College
Thomas C. Thompson, The Citadel
Stephen Wilhoit, University of Dayton
Mark Wollaeger, Vanderbilt University

For helping me to see the strengths and deficiencies of the previous edition, thanks go to the many instructors who took the time to answer a detailed questionnaire: Ralph Batie, Oregon Institute of Technology; Johannes D. Bergmann, George Mason University; Matt Bolinder, Boston College; Christopher K. Brooks, Wichita State University; Lyt Burris, Grand Rapids Community College; Stephen A. Calatrello, Calhoun Community College; Murray Callaway, University of Maine; Jill Chadwick, Calhoun Community College; Deborah Coxwell Teague, Florida State University; Janis Banks Fisher, Valley College; Deborah Fleming, Ashland University; Patrick Houlihan, Albuquerque Technical Vocational Institute; Glenda James, Calhoun Community College; Danell Jones, The College Board; Todd McCann, Bay de Noc Community College; Michael Moghtader, University of New Mexico; Harry V. Moore,

Calhoun Community College; Jeffrey Nelson, The University of Alabama in Huntsville; Tennyson L. O'Donnell, Syracuse University; Cherie Parsons, Malone College; Roland Rowe, University of New Mexico; Dawn Reno, Lake City Community College; Mark Roberts, Cal Poly, San Luis Obispo; Cheryl W. Ruggiero, Virginia Polytechnic Institute and State University; Lynette M. Sandley, Samford University; David Sharpe, Ohio University; Beth Shelton, Paris Junior College; Jean Sorensen, Grayson County College; Barbara Wenner, University of Cincinnati; Carla Wilson, Columbia College Chicago; Judy Worman, Dartmouth College.

Writing a handbook is truly a collaborative effort. Librarian Barbara Fister helped me reorganize the research sections and bring them up to date (no small feat). William Peirce assisted with the sections on argument, and Lloyd Shaw helped me improve the research sections. For the book's companion Web site, Carolyn Lengel has created several well-written grammar exercises on a variety of interesting topics, and Wanda Van Goor authored the popular *Developmental Exercises to Accompany A WRITER'S REFERENCE.*

I am indebted to the students whose essays appear in the book or on its companion Web site: Ned Bishop, Angela Daly, Andrew Knutson, Dan Larson, Paul Levi, Margaret Peel, Karen Shaw, and Matt Watson — not only for permission to use their work but for allowing me to adapt it for pedagogical purposes as well. My thanks also go to the students who granted me permission to use their paragraphs: Connie Hailey, Kathleen Lewis, Margaret Smith, Margaret Stack, and David Warren.

Several talented editors have contributed to the book. Leasa Burton and Nelina Backman directed the project, both the book and its companion Web site, with spirited good humour; their understanding of technology proved invaluable as we worked to keep pace with changing realities in the classroom. Ellen Thibault provided me with a wealth of useful materials as I revised the book's research sections, and Sara Eaton contributed to the book's companion Web site, especially its links library. Editorial assistant Christine Turnier-Vallecillo has helped me field e-mail queries in a professional manner, and she has handled other matters too numerous to mention. This team — Leasa, Nelina, Ellen, Sara, and Christine — worked under the adroit leadership of editor in chief Karen Henry, who stepped in occasionally to help me solve especially thorny rhetorical problems.

Book editor Anne Noonan has expertly steered the book through production under impossible deadlines with the help of Kerri Cardone and Kendra LeFleur and under the direction of managing editor Elizabeth Schaaf. Designer Claire Seng-Niemoeller has retained the clean, uncluttered look of the book's pages while adding new visuals and colour-coded sections on MLA, APA, and CMS papers. Copy editor Barbara Flanagan has once again brought grace and consistency to the final manuscript, and copy editor Dawn Hunter has helped tremendously in bringing Canadian content and conventions to the new edition.

I would also like to thank marketing manager Richard Cadman and director of marketing Karen Melton Soeltz for promoting my book so enthusiastically and for helping to guide its revision in light of the needs of instructors and their students.

Special thanks are due to publishers Chuck Christensen and Joan Feinberg. Nearly twenty years ago Chuck took a chance on an unknown community college instructor with an inexplicable urge to write a handbook. I am deeply grateful to him for giving me this opportunity. In retrospect, I suppose Chuck knew that almost anyone could learn to write a handbook under the guidance of Joan Feinberg. Certainly a better teacher-editor could not have been found. Chuck retired at the end of 2001, and Joan has become president of Bedford/St. Martin's, a position she richly deserves.

Finally, for their support and encouragement, a note of thanks goes to my husband, Robert Hacker; to the families of Greg and Joyce Tarvin, Jeff and Eileen Hacker, Jack and Chris Dougherty, and Steve and Peggy Shearer; to Robbie Wallin, Austin Nichols, Kate Miller, Jessica Webner, Rima Koyler, Greg Krakower, Betty Renshaw, Bill Fry, John Bodnar, Sandra Kurtinitis, Joanne Amberson, Margaret Van de Ree, Joyce Neff, Christine McMahon, Mary Multer Greene, and Joan Naake; to the English department at Prince George's Community College; and to the many students over the years who have taught me that errors, a natural by-product of the writing process, are simply problems waiting to be solved.

Diana Hacker
Prince George's Community College

C

Composing
and Revising

C

Composing and Revising

Since it's not possible to think about everything all at once, most experienced writers handle a piece of writing in stages. Roughly speaking, those stages are planning, drafting, and revising. You should generally move from planning to drafting to revising, but be prepared to circle back to earlier stages whenever the need arises.

C1

Planning

C1-a Assess the writing situation.

Begin by taking a look at the writing situation in which you find yourself. The key elements of the writing situation include your subject, the sources of information available to you, your purpose, your audience, and constraints such as length, document design, review sessions, and deadlines.

It is unlikely that you will make final decisions about all of these matters until later in the writing process—after a first draft, for example. Nevertheless, you can save yourself time by thinking about as many of them as possible in advance. For a quick checklist, see page 4.

ESL

What counts as good writing varies from culture to culture and even among groups within cultures. In some situations, you will need to become familiar with the writing styles—such as direct or indirect, personal or impersonal, plain or embellished—that are valued by the culture or discourse community for which you are writing.

C1-b Experiment with techniques for exploring ideas.

Instead of just plunging into a first draft, experiment with one or more techniques for exploring your subject—perhaps listing, clustering, asking questions, freewriting, annotating texts, or simply talking and listening. Whatever technique you turn to, the goal is the same: to generate a wealth of ideas. At this early stage of the writing process, you should aim for quantity, not necessarily quality, of ideas. If an idea proves to be off the point, trivial, or too far-fetched, you can always throw it out later.

Checklist for assessing the writing situation

SUBJECT

— Has a subject (or a range of possible subjects) been given to you, or are you free to choose your own?

— Why is your subject worth writing about?

— How broadly should you cover the subject? Do you need to narrow it to a more specific topic (because of length restrictions, for instance)?

— How detailed should your coverage be?

SOURCES OF INFORMATION

— Where will your information come from: Personal experience? Direct observation? Interviews? Questionnaires? Reading?

— If your information comes from reading, what sort of documentation is required?

PURPOSE

— Why are you writing: To inform readers? To persuade them? To entertain them? To call them to action? Some combination of these?

AUDIENCE

— Who are your readers? How well informed are they about your subject?

— How interested and attentive are they likely to be? Will they resist any of your ideas?

— What is your relationship to them: Employee to supervisor? Citizen to citizen? Expert to novice? Scholar to scholar?

— How much time are they willing to spend reading?

LENGTH AND DOCUMENT DESIGN

— Do you have any length specifications? If not, what length seems appropriate, given your purpose and audience?

— Must you use a particular design for your document? If so, do you have guidelines or examples that you can consult?

REVIEWERS AND DEADLINES

— Who will be reviewing your draft in progress: Your instructor? A writing centre tutor? Your classmates? A friend? Someone in your family?

— What are your deadlines? How much time will you need to allow for the various stages of writing, including typing and proofreading the final draft?

ON THE WEB

For an electronic exercise on considering purpose and audience, go to **www.dianahacker.com/writersref**

and click on ▶ **Electronic Writing Exercises**
                      ▶ **E-ex C1–1**

ON THE WEB

For links to online writing labs and other resources that will help you with the writing process, go to **www.dianahacker.com/writersref**

and click on ▶ **Links Library**
                      ▶ **Composing and Revising**

Listing

You might begin by simply listing ideas, putting them down in the order in which they occur to you—a technique sometimes known as *brainstorming*. Here, for example, is a list one writer jotted down as she was preparing to write a literature paper on the short story "The Chrysanthemums" by John Steinbeck. Notice that some items in the list pose questions for further thought.

Elisa's gardening clothes—"a man's black hat," "clodhopper shoes," a dress "covered by a big corduroy apron," "heavy leather gloves"—not very feminine.

The words "strong," "strength," "power," "powerful," "energy" keep popping up in connection with Elisa and her gardening. Why?

Conversation about her chrysanthemums makes Elisa come alive. Her talk with the pots-and-pans repairman about growing chrysanthemums is sexually charged—her "eyes grew alert and eager," she "shook out her dark pretty hair," "She looked deep into his eyes," "Her breast swelled passionately."

Is she attracted to the travelling repairman or just his way of life? She envies his freedom to sleep outdoors in his wagon: "I wish women could do such things." She wistfully watches him leave: "That's a bright direction. There's a glowing there."

Repairman has pride in his work—mending pots and pans and sharpening knives and scissors. Seems indifferent to

Elisa's pride in her gardening. Characters have their own agendas.

Bathtub scene after repairman leaves—awakened sexuality, romance, beauty.

What do chrysanthemums symbolize? Beauty? Femininity? Source of pride? Strength? All of the above?

Elisa sees chrysanthemums tossed into ditch. Disillusion. She is left "crying weakly—like an old woman."

The ideas appear here as they occurred to the writer on her first and second readings of the story. Later, when she drafted her paper, she rearranged them, clustered them under general categories, deleted some, and added others. In other words, she treated her initial list as a source of ideas and a springboard to new ideas, not as a formal outline.

Clustering

Unlike listing, the technique of clustering highlights relationships among ideas. To cluster ideas, write your topic in the center of a sheet of paper, draw a circle around it, and surround that circle with related ideas connected to it with lines. If some of the satellite ideas lead to more specific clusters, write them down as well. The writer of the following cluster diagram was exploring ideas for an essay on home uses for computers.

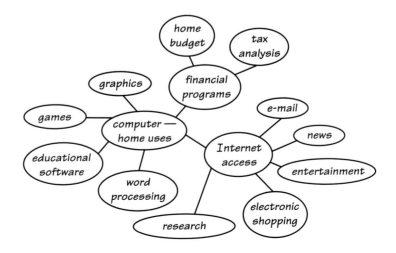

Asking questions

By asking relevant questions, you can generate many ideas — and you can make sure that you have adequately surveyed your subject. When gathering material for a story, journalists routinely ask themselves Who? What? When? Where? Why? and How? In addition to helping journalists get started, these questions ensure that they will not overlook an important fact: the date of a prospective summit meeting, for example, or the exact location of a burglary.

Whenever you are writing about events, whether current or historical, the journalist's questions are one way to get started. One student, whose subject was the reaction in 1915 to D. W. Griffith's silent film *The Birth of a Nation,* began exploring her topic with this set of questions:

> *Who* objected to the film?
>
> *What* were the objections?
>
> *When* were the protests first voiced?
>
> *Where* were protests most strongly expressed?
>
> *Why* did protesters object to the film?
>
> *How* did protesters make their views known?

In the academic world, scholars often generate ideas with specific questions related to their discipline: one set of questions for analyzing short stories, another for evaluating experiments in social psychology, still another for reporting field experiences in anthropology. If you are writing in a particular discipline, try to discover the questions that scholars typically explore. These are frequently presented in textbooks as checklists.

Freewriting

In its purest form, freewriting is simply nonstop writing. You set aside ten minutes or so and write whatever comes to you, without pausing to think about word choice, spelling, or even meaning. If you get stuck, you can write about being stuck, but you should keep your pencil moving. The point is to loosen up, relax, and see what happens. Even if nothing much happens, you have lost only ten minutes. It's more likely, though, that something interesting will emerge on paper — perhaps an eloquent sentence, an honest expression of feeling, or a line of thought worth exploring.

Annotating texts

When you write about reading, one of the best ways to explore ideas is to mark up the text—on the pages themselves if you own the work, on photocopies if you don't. Here, for example, are two paragraphs from an essay by philosopher Michael Tooley as one student annotated them.

Why is the American policy debate not focused more intensely on the relative merits or demerits of our current approach to drugs and of possible alternatives to it? The lack of discussion of this issue is rather striking, given that America has the most serious drug problem in the world, that alternatives to a prohibitionist approach are under serious consideration in other countries, and that the grounds for reconsidering our current approach are, I shall argue, so weighty. . . .

But the subject has been discussed.

I guess he's for legalizing drugs. Why doesn't he say so?

True? How is he defining "drug problem"?

I want to turn in detail to perhaps the two most important reasons for reconsidering our current drug policy: first, the difficulty of providing any adequate justification for the restrictions that prohibitive laws place on people's liberty; and second, the enormous social and personal costs associated with a prohibitionist approach.

Biased language?

This first reason seems off the point. Is it really worth half of our attention?

Aren't there important aspects of the subject that he's ignoring?

Talking and listening

The early stages of the writing process need not be lonely. Many writers begin a writing project by brainstorming ideas in a group, debating a point with friends, or engaging in conversation with a professor.

Some writers "virtually converse" by exchanging ideas through e-mail, by joining an Internet chat group, or by following a mailing list discussion. If you are part of a networked classroom, you may be encouraged to exchange ideas with your classmates and instructor in an electronic workshop. One advantage of engaging in such discussions is that while you are "talking" you are actually writing. That writing might prove useful later. For example, a student who participated in the chat pictured on page 9 was able to cut and paste some of her own words into an essay.

Talking can be a good way to get to know your audience. If you're planning to write a narrative, for instance, you can test its dramatic effect on a group of friends. Or if you hope to advance a

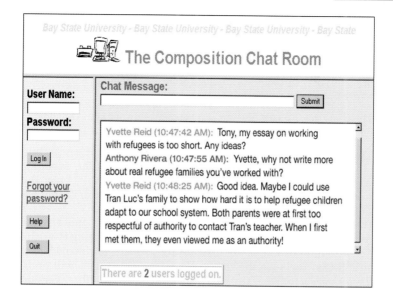

certain argument, you can try it out on listeners who hold a different view.

As you have no doubt discovered, conversation can deepen and refine your ideas before you even begin to set them down on paper. Our first thoughts are not necessarily our wisest thoughts; by talking and listening to others we can all stretch our potential as thinkers and as writers.

C1-c Settle on a tentative focus.

As you explore your subject, you will begin to see possible ways of focusing your material. At this point, try to settle on a tentative central idea. The more complex your subject, the more your initial focus will change as your drafts evolve.

For many types of writing, the central idea can be asserted in one sentence, a generalization preparing readers for the supporting details that will follow. Such a sentence, which often appears in the opening paragraph, is called a *thesis* (see also C2-a). A successful thesis—like the following, all taken from articles in popular magazines—points both the writer and the reader in a definite direction.

Much maligned and the subject of unwarranted fears, most bats are harmless and highly beneficial.

Geometric forms known as fractals may have a profound effect on how we view the world, not only in art and film but in many branches of science and technology, from astronomy to economics to predicting the weather.

There are some earth phenomena you can count on, but the magnetic field, some say, is not one of them.

The thesis sentence usually contains a key word or controlling idea that limits its focus. The preceding sentences, for example, prepare for essays that focus on the *beneficial* aspects of bats, the *effect* of fractals on how we view the world, and the unreliable aspects of the earth's *magnetic field.*

It's a good idea to formulate a thesis early in the writing process, perhaps by jotting it on scratch paper, by putting it at the head of a rough outline, or by attempting to write an introductory paragraph that includes the thesis. Your tentative thesis will probably be less graceful than the thesis you include in the final version of your essay. Here, for example, is one student's early effort:

Although they both play percussion instruments, drummers and percussionists are very different.

The thesis that appeared in the final draft of the student's paper was more polished:

Two types of musicians play percussion instruments—drummers and percussionists—and they are as different as Rymes with Orange and the Hamilton Philharmonic.

Don't worry too soon about the exact wording of your thesis, however, because your main point may change as you refine your ideas. For a more detailed discussion of the thesis, see C2-a.

C1-d Sketch a tentative plan.

Once you have generated some ideas and formulated a tentative thesis, you may want to sketch an informal outline. Informal outlines can take many forms. Perhaps the most common is simply the preliminary thesis followed by a list of major supporting ideas.

Hawaii is losing its cultural identity.

— pure-blooded Hawaiians increasingly rare
— native language diluted
— natives forced off ancestral lands
— little emphasis on native culture in schools
— customs exaggerated and distorted by tourism

Clustering diagrams, often used to generate ideas, can also serve as rough outlines (see p. 6). And if you began by jotting down a list of ideas (see pp. 5–6), you may be able to turn the list into a rough outline by crossing out some ideas, adding others, and numbering the ideas to create a logical order.

When to use a formal outline

Early in the writing process, rough outlines have advantages over formal ones: They can be produced more quickly, they are more obviously tentative, and they can be revised more easily should the need arise. However, a formal outline may be useful later in the writing process, especially if your subject matter is complex.

The following formal outline brought order to the research paper on U.S. cell phone use and driving that appears in MLA-5b. Notice that the thesis is an important part of the outline. Everything else in the outline supports it, directly or indirectly.

Thesis: States must regulate use of cell phones on the road because drivers using phones are seriously impaired and because laws on negligent and reckless driving are not sufficient to punish offenders.

I. Drivers distracted by cell phones are seriously impaired.
   A. Cell phones have been a factor in traffic deaths.
   B. Expert testimony, public opinion, and even cartoons suggest that driving while phoning is dangerous.
   C. Scientific research confirms the dangers of using phones while driving.

II. Laws on negligent and reckless driving are not adequate.
   A. Under state laws, drivers distracted by phones can receive light punishment even when they have caused fatal accidents.
   B. When certain kinds of driver behavior are especially dangerous, we draft special laws making them illegal; phoning in a moving vehicle should be no exception.

III. In the United States, state legislatures must take the responsibility for passing laws regulating the use of cell phones in moving vehicles.
- A. Many other countries have passed legislation regulating use of car phones, but the U.S. government leaves such matters to the states.
- B. Although some counties and towns in the United States have restricted use of cell phones on the road, local laws are not likely to have the impact of state laws.
- C. Because of mounting public awareness of the dangers of driving while phoning, state legislators must begin to take the problem seriously; the time for legislation has arrived.

Guidelines for constructing an outline

1. Put the thesis at the top.

2. Make items at the same level of generality as parallel as possible (see S1).

3. Use sentences unless phrases are clear.

4. Use the conventional system of numbers and letters for the levels of generality.

    I.
        A.
        B.
            1.
            2.
                a.
                b.
    II.

5. Always use at least two subdivisions for a category, since nothing can be divided into fewer than two parts.

6. Limit the number of major sections in the outline; if the list of roman numerals begins to look like a laundry list, find some way of clustering the items into a few major categories with more subcategories.

7. Be flexible; in other words, be prepared to change your outline as your drafts evolve.

C2

Drafting

As you rough out an initial draft, keep your planning materials — lists, diagrams, outlines, and so on — close at hand. In addition to helping you get started, such notes and blueprints will encourage you to keep moving. Writing tends to flow better when it is drafted relatively quickly, without many starts and stops.

For most kinds of writing, an introduction announces a main idea, several body paragraphs develop it, and a conclusion drives it home. You can begin drafting, however, at any point. For example, if you find it difficult to introduce a paper that you have not yet written, you can draft the body first and save the introduction for later.

C2-a For most types of writing, draft an introduction that includes a thesis.

For most writing tasks, your introduction will be a paragraph of 50 to 150 words. Perhaps the most common strategy is to open the paragraph with a few sentences that engage the reader and to conclude it with a statement of the essay's main point. The sentence stating the main point is called a *thesis*. (See also C1-c.) In the following examples, the thesis has been italicized.

> To the Australian aborigines, the Dreamtime was the time of creation. It was then that the creatures of the earth, including man, came into being. There are many legends about that mystical period, but unfortunately the koala does not fare too well in any of them. *Slow-witted though it is in life, the koala is generally depicted in myth and folklore as a trickster and a thief.*
> —Roger Caras, "What's a Koala?"

> Credit card companies love to extend credit to college students, especially those just out of high school. Ads for credit cards line campus bulletin boards, flash across commercial Web sites for students, and get stuffed into shopping bags at college bookstores. Why do the companies market their product so vigorously to a population that lacks a substantial credit history and often has no steady source of income? The answer is that significant profits can

be earned through high interest rates and assorted penalties and fees. *By granting college students liberal lending arrangements, credit card companies often hook them on a cycle of spending that can ultimately lead to financial ruin.*

—Matt Watson, student

Ideally, the sentences leading to the thesis should hook the reader, perhaps with one of the following:

a startling statistic, an unusual fact, or a vivid example

a paradoxical statement

a quotation or bit of dialogue

a question

an analogy

a joke or an anecdote

Such hooks are particularly important when you cannot assume your reader's interest in the subject. Hooks are less necessary in scholarly essays and other writing aimed at readers with a professional interest in the subject.

Although the thesis frequently appears at the end of the introduction, it can just as easily appear at the beginning. Much work-related writing, in which a straightforward approach is most effective, commonly begins with the thesis.

Flex-time scheduling, which has proved its effectiveness at the National Library of Canada, should be introduced on a trial basis at the main branch of the Kamloops Public Library. By offering flexible work hours, the library can boost employee morale, cut down on absenteeism, and expand its hours of operation.

—David Warren, library employee

For some types of writing, it may be difficult or impossible to express the central idea in a thesis sentence; or it may be unwise or unnecessary to put a thesis sentence in the essay itself. A personal narrative, for example, may have a focus too subtle to be distilled in a single sentence, and such a sentence might ruin the story. Strictly informative writing, like that found in many business memos, may be difficult to summarize in a thesis. In such instances, do not try to force the central idea into a thesis sentence. Instead, think in terms of an overriding purpose, which may or may not be stated directly.

Characteristics of an effective thesis

A thesis states a claim that will be supported in the body of a paper; it tells readers what to expect as they read on. To be effective, a thesis must be a generalization, not a fact; limited in scope, not too broad; and sharply focused, not too vague.

Because a thesis must prepare readers for facts and details, it cannot itself be a fact. It must always be a generalization demanding proof or further development.

> **TOO FACTUAL**   The polygraph was developed by Dr. John A. Larson in 1921.

> **REVISED**   Because the polygraph has not been proved reliable, even under the most controlled conditions, its use by employers should be banned.

Although a thesis must be a generalization, it must not be *too* general. You will need to narrow the focus of any thesis that you cannot adequately develop in the space allowed. Unless you were writing a book or a very long research paper, the following thesis would be too broad.

> **TOO BROAD**   Many drugs are now being used successfully to treat mental illnesses.

You would need to restrict the thesis, perhaps like this:

> **REVISED**   Despite its risks and side effects, Prozac is an effective treatment for depression.

Finally, a thesis should be sharply focused, not too vague. Beware of any thesis containing a fuzzy, hard-to-define word such as *interesting, good,* or *disgusting.*

> **TOO VAGUE**   Many of the songs played on station CXQP are disgusting.

The word *disgusting* is needlessly vague. To sharpen the focus of this thesis, the writer should be more specific.

> **REVISED**   Of the songs played on station CXQP, all too many depict sex crudely, sanction the beating or rape of women, or foster gang violence.

In the process of making a too-vague thesis more precise, you may find yourself outlining the major sections of your paper, as in the preceding example, which prepares readers for a three-part criticism of the songs played on CXQP. This technique, known as *blueprinting,* helps readers know exactly what to expect as they read on. It also helps you, the writer, control the shape of your essay.

ESL

If you come from a culture that prefers an indirect approach in writing, you may feel that asserting a thesis early in an essay sounds unrefined or even rude. In Canada, however, a direct approach is usually appreciated; when you state your point as directly as possible, you show that you value your reader's time.

ON THE WEB

For electronic exercises on thesis statements and introductions, go to **www.dianahacker.com/writersref**

and click on ▶ **Electronic Writing Exercises**
▶ **E-ex C2–1 and C2–2**

C2-b Draft the body.

While drafting the body of an essay, think carefully about your thesis statement. What does the thesis promise readers? Try to keep this focus in mind.

It's a good idea to have a plan in mind as well. If you have sketched out a preliminary plan, try to block out your paragraphs accordingly. If you do not have a plan, you would be wise to pause a moment and sketch one (see C1-d). Of course it is also possible to begin without a plan—assuming you are prepared to treat your first attempt as a "discovery draft" that will almost certainly be tossed (or radically rewritten) once you discover what you really want to say.

For more advice about paragraphs and paragraphing, see C4.

C2-c Draft a conclusion.

The conclusion should echo your main idea, without dully repeating it. Often the concluding paragraph can be relatively short.

In addition to echoing your main idea, a conclusion might summarize your main point, pose a question for future study, offer advice, or propose a course of action. To end an essay detailing the social skills required of a bartender, one writer concludes with some advice:

> If someone were to approach me one day looking for the secret to running a good bar, I suppose I would offer the following advice: Get your customers to pour out their ideas at a greater rate than you pour out the liquor. You will both win in the end.
> —Kathleen Lewis, student

To make the conclusion memorable, consider including a detail, example, or image from the introduction to bring readers full circle; a quotation or bit of dialogue; an anecdote; or a humorous, witty, or ironic comment.

Whatever concluding strategy you choose, avoid introducing new ideas at the end of an essay. Also avoid apologies and other limp, indeterminate endings. You should end crisply, preferably on a positive note.

C3

Revising

For the experienced writer, revising is rarely a one-step process. Global matters generally receive attention first — the focus, organization, paragraphing, content, and point of view. Improvements in sentence structure, word choice, grammar, punctuation, and mechanics come later. (See pp. 18 and 19 for examples.)

C3-a Make global revisions.

Global revisions address the larger elements of writing. Usually they affect chunks of text longer than a sentence, and frequently they can be quite dramatic. Whole paragraphs might be dropped, others added. Material once stretched over two or three paragraphs might be condensed into one. Entire sections might be rearranged. Even the content may change dramatically, for the process of revising stimulates thought.

EXAMPLE OF GLOBAL REVISIONS

Sports on TV--A Win or a Loss?

Team sports are as much a part of Canadian life as snow and maple syrup, and they have a good tendency to bring people together. They encourage team members to cooperate with one another, they also create shared enthusiasm among fans. Thanks to television, this togetherness now seems available to nearly all of us at the flick of a switch. We do not have to buy tickets, and travel to a stadium, to see the World Series or the Grey Cup, these games are on television. We can enjoy the game in the comfort of our own living room. ~~After Thanksgiving or Christmas dinner, the whole family may gather around the TV set to watch football together.~~ It would appear that television has done us a great service. But is this really the case?

Although television does make sports more accessible, it also creates a distance between the sport and the fans and between athletes and the teams they play for.

The advantage of television is that it provides sports fans with greater convenience.

[insert]

We can see more games than if we had to attend each one in person, and we can follow greater varieties of sports.

Many of us resist global revisions because we find it difficult to distance ourselves from a draft. We tend to review our work from our own, not from our audience's, perspective.

To distance yourself from a draft, put it aside for a while, preferably overnight or even longer. When you return to it, try to play the role of your audience as you read. If possible, enlist the help of reviewers—persons willing to play the role of audience for you. Ask your reviewers to focus on the larger issues of writing, not on the fine points. The checklist for global revision on page 20 may help them get started.

EXAMPLE OF SENTENCE-LEVEL REVISIONS

> *Televised*
> Sports ~~on TV~~-- A Win or a Loss?

Team sports~~,~~ ~~are~~ as much a part of Canadian life as snow and maple

tend *us*

syrup, ~~and they have a good tendency~~ to bring ^people together. They

and

encourage team members to cooperate with one another,^ they ~~also~~ create

Because of

shared enthusiasm among fans. ~~Thanks to~~ television, this togetherness now

seems available ~~to nearly all of us~~^ at the flick of a switch. ~~It would appear~~

~~that television has done us a great service.~~ But is this really the case?

makes

Although television ~~does make~~ sports more accessible, it also creates a

their

distance between the sport and the fans and between athletes and ~~the~~

teams~~. they play for.~~^

The advantage of television is that it provides sports fans with greater

convenience. We do not have to buy tickets/ and travel to a stadium/ to see

but

the World Series or the Grey Cup/^ ~~these games are on television. We~~ can

any *rooms.*

enjoy ^~~the~~ game in the comfort of our own living ~~room.~~^ We can see more

games than if we had to attend each one in person, and we can follow

a *variety*

^greater ~~varieties~~^ of sports.

NOTE: When working on a computer, print out a hard copy so that you can read the draft as a whole rather than screen by screen. A computer screen focuses your attention on small chunks of text rather than the whole; a printout allows you to look at the entire paper when thinking about what global revisions to make.

Checklist for global revision

PURPOSE AND AUDIENCE

— Does the draft accomplish its purpose—to inform readers, to per-suade them, to entertain them, to call them to action (or some combination of these)?

— Is the draft appropriate for its audience? Does it take into consid-eration the audience's knowledge of the subject, level of interest in the subject, and possible attitudes toward the subject?

FOCUS

— Do the introduction and conclusion focus clearly on the main point? Is the thesis clear enough and is it placed where readers will notice it? (If there is no thesis, is there a good reason for omit-ting one?)

— Are any ideas obviously off the point?

ORGANIZATION AND PARAGRAPHING

— Are there enough organizational cues for readers (such as topic sentences or headings)?

— Are ideas ordered effectively?

— Does the paragraphing make sense?

— Are any paragraphs too long or too short for easy reading?

CONTENT

— Is the supporting material persuasive?

— Which ideas need further development?

— Are the parts proportioned sensibly? Do major ideas receive enough attention?

— Where might material be deleted?

POINT OF VIEW

— Is the draft free of distracting shifts in point of view (from *I* to *you,* for example, or from *it* to *they*)?

— Is the dominant point of view—first person (*I* or *we*), second per-son (*you*), or third person (*he, she, it, one,* or *they*)—appropriate, given the paper's purpose and audience? (See S4-a.)

ON THE WEB

For an electronic exercise on point of view, go to
www.dianahacker.com/writersref

and click on ▶ **Electronic Writing Exercises**
▶ **E-ex C3–2**

C3-b Revise and edit sentences.

Much of the rest of this book offers advice on revising sentences for
style and clarity and on editing them for grammar, punctuation,
and mechanics. The process of revising and editing sentences
should ordinarily occur right on the pages of a draft.

> Finally ~~we decided~~ *deciding* that perhaps our dream needed ~~some~~ prompting,
>
> ~~and~~ we visited a fertility doctor and began the expensive, time‑consuming
>
> round of procedures that held out ~~the~~ *some* promise of ~~fulfilling our dream.~~ *our dream's fulfillment.*
>
> *Our efforts, however, were*
> ~~All this was~~ to no avail~~. and as~~ *As* we approached the sixth year of our
>
> *could no longer*
> marriage, we ~~had reached the point where we couldn't~~ even discuss our
>
> childlessness without becoming very depressed. We questioned why this
>
> *such a*
> had happened to us~~.~~ Why had we been singled out for ~~this~~ major
>
> disappointment?

The original paragraph was flawed by wordiness and an excessive reliance on structures connected with *and*. Such problems can
be addressed through any number of acceptable revisions. The first
sentence, for example, could have been changed like this:

> Finally we decided that perhaps our dream needed ~~some~~ prompting~~.~~
>
> *After visiting*   *we*
> ~~and we visited~~ a fertility doctor, ~~and~~ began the expensive, time‑consuming
>
> *promised hope*
> round of procedures that ~~held out the promise~~ of fulfilling our dream.

Though some writers might argue about the effectiveness of these improvements compared with the previous revision, most would agree that both revisions are better than the original.

Some of the paragraph's improvements involve less choice and are less open to debate. For example, the hyphen in *time-consuming* is necessary, and the question mark in the next to last sentence must be changed to a period.

As it details the various rules for revising and editing sentences, *A Canadian Writer's Reference* suggests when an improvement is simply one among several possibilities and when it is more strictly a matter of right and wrong.

GRAMMAR CHECKERS on your computer can help with some but by no means all of the sentence-level problems in a typical draft. Because so many problems — such as faulty parallelism, mixed constructions, and misplaced modifiers — lack mathematical precision, they slip right past the grammar checker. Even when the grammar checker has the capability of flagging a potential problem, such as the passive voice, you must still decide whether your sentence is effective.

C3-c Proofread the final manuscript.

After revising and editing, you are ready to prepare the final manuscript. (See D2.) At this point, make sure to allow yourself enough time for proofreading — the final and most important step in manuscript preparation.

Proofreading is a special kind of reading: a slow and methodical search for misspellings, typographical mistakes, and omitted words or word endings. Such errors can be difficult to spot in your own work because you may read what you intended to write, not what is actually on the page. To fight this tendency, try proofreading out loud, articulating each word as it is actually written.

Although proofreading may be dull, it is crucial. Errors strewn throughout an essay are distracting and annoying. If the writer doesn't care about this piece of writing, thinks the reader, why should I? A carefully proofread essay, on the other hand, sends a positive message: It shows that you value your writing and respect your readers.

SPELL CHECKERS are more reliable than grammar checkers, but they too must be used with caution. Many typographical errors (such as *quiet* for *quite*) and misused words (such as *effect* for *affect*) slip past the spell checker because the checker flags only words not found in its dictionary.

ON THE WEB

To see a sample paper, along with its rough draft, go to
www.dianahacker.com/writersref

and click on   ▶ **Model Papers**
　　　　　　　 ▶ **Paper-in-progress: Watson**

C4

Writing paragraphs

Except for special-purpose paragraphs, such as introductions and conclusions (see C2-a and C2-c), paragraphs are clusters of information supporting an essay's main point (or advancing a story's action). Aim for paragraphs that are clearly focused, well developed, organized, coherent, and neither too long nor too short for easy reading.

C4-a   Focus on a main point.

A paragraph should be unified around a main point. The point should be clear to readers, and all sentences in the paragraph must relate to it.

Stating the main point in a topic sentence

As a rule, state the main point of a paragraph in a topic sentence — a one-sentence summary that tells readers what to expect as they read on. Usually the topic sentence comes first:

> *Nearly all living creatures manage some form of communica-*
> *tion.* The dance patterns of bees in their hive help to point the
> way to distant flower fields or announce successful foraging. Male
> stickleback fish regularly swim upside-down to indicate outrage in
> a courtship contest. Male deer and lemurs mark territorial owner-
> ship by rubbing their own body secretions on boundary stones or
> trees. Everyone has seen a frightened dog put his tail between his
> legs and run in panic. We, too, use gestures, expressions, postures,
> and movement to give our words point.
> — Olivia Vlahos, *Human Beginnings*

Although the topic sentence usually comes first, sometimes it
follows a transitional sentence linking the paragraph to earlier material, and occasionally it is withheld until the end of the paragraph. And at times a topic sentence is not needed: if a paragraph
continues developing an idea clearly introduced in an earlier paragraph, if the details of the paragraph unmistakably suggest its
main point, or if the paragraph appears in a narrative of events
where generalizations might interrupt the flow of the story.

Sticking to the point

Sentences that do not support the topic sentence destroy the unity
of a paragraph. If the paragraph is otherwise well focused, such of-
fending sentences can simply be deleted or perhaps moved elsewhere. In the following paragraph describing the inadequate facili-
ties in a high school, the information about the word processing
instructor (in italics) is clearly off the point.

> As the result of tax cuts, the educational facilities of Cedar-
> brae Collegiate have reached an all-time low. Some of the books
> date back to 1990 and have long since shed their covers. The lack
> of lab equipment makes it necessary for four to five students to
> work at one table, with most watching rather than performing ex-
> periments. The few computers in working order must share one
> printer. *Also, the word processing instructor left to have a baby at*
> *the beginning of the semester, and most of the students don't like*
> *the substitute.* As for the furniture, many of the upright chairs
> have become recliners, and the desk legs are so unbalanced that
> they play seesaw on the floor.

Sometimes the cure for a disunified paragraph is not as simple
as deleting or moving material. Writers often wander into un-
charted territory because they cannot think of enough evidence to
support a topic sentence. Feeling that it is too soon to break into a

new paragraph, they move on to new ideas for which they have not prepared the reader. When this happens, the writer is faced with a decision: Find more evidence to support the topic sentence or drop the paragraph and develop a new plan of attack.

ON THE WEB

For an electronic exercise on topic sentences, go to
www.dianahacker.com/writersref

and click on ▶ **Electronic Writing Exercises**
　　　　　　　▶ **E-ex C4–1**

C4-b　Develop the main point.

Though an occasional short paragraph is fine, particularly if it functions as a transition or emphasizes a point, a series of brief paragraphs usually suggests inadequate development. How much development is enough? That varies, depending on the writer's purpose and audience.

For example, when she wrote a paragraph attempting to convince readers that it is impossible to lose fat quickly, health columnist Jane Brody knew that she would have to present a great deal of evidence because many dieters want to believe the opposite. She did *not* write:

> When you think about it, it's impossible to lose — as many diets suggest — 10 pounds of *fat* in ten days, even on a total fast. Even a moderately active person cannot lose so much weight so fast. A less active person hasn't a prayer.

This three-sentence paragraph is too skimpy to be convincing. But the paragraph that Brody in fact wrote contains enough evidence to convince even skeptical readers.

> When you think about it, it's impossible to lose — as many diets suggest — 10 pounds of *fat* in ten days, even on a total fast. A pound of body fat represents 3,500 calories. To lose 1 pound of fat, you must expend 3,500 more calories than you consume. Let's say you weigh 170 pounds and, as a moderately active person, you burn 2,500 calories a day. If your diet contains only 1,500 calories, you'd have an energy deficit of 1,000 calories a day. In a week's time that would add up to a 7,000-calorie deficit, or 2 pounds of

real fat. In ten days, the accumulated deficit would represent nearly 3 pounds of lost body fat. Even if you ate nothing at all for ten days and maintained your usual level of activity, your caloric deficit would add up to 25,000 calories. . . . At 3,500 calories per pound of fat, that's still only 7 pounds of lost fat.

—Jane Brody, *Jane Brody's Nutrition Book*

C4-c Choose a suitable pattern of organization.

Although paragraphs may be patterned in an almost infinite number of ways, certain patterns of organization occur frequently, either alone or in combination: examples and illustrations, narration, description, process, comparison and contrast, analogy, cause and effect, classification and division, and definition. There is nothing particularly magical about these patterns (sometimes called *methods of development*). They simply reflect some of the ways in which we think.

Examples and illustrations

Examples, perhaps the most common pattern of organization, are appropriate whenever the reader might be tempted to ask, "For example?"

> Normally my parents abided scrupulously by "The Budget," but several times a year Dad would dip into his battered, black strongbox and splurge on some irrational, totally satisfying luxury. Once he bought over a hundred comic books at a flea market, doled out to us thereafter at the tantalizing rate of two a week. He always got a whole flat of pansies, Mom's favorite flower, for us to give her on Mother's Day. One day a boy stopped at our house selling fifty-cent raffle tickets on a sailboat and Dad bought every ticket the boy had left—three books' worth.
>
> —Connie Hailey, student

Illustrations are extended examples, frequently presented in story form.

> Part of Harriet Tubman's strategy of conducting was, as in all battle-field operations, the knowledge of how and when to retreat. Numerous allusions have been made to her moves when she suspected that she was in danger. When she feared the party was closely pursued, she would take it for a time on a train southward bound. No one seeing Negroes going in this direction would for an instant suppose them to be fugitives. Once on her return she was at a railway station. She saw some men reading a poster and she

heard one of them reading it aloud. It was a description of her, offering a reward for her capture. She took a southbound train to avert suspicion. At another time when Harriet heard men talking about her, she pretended to read a book which she carried. One man remarked, "This cannot be the woman. The one we want can't read or write." Harriet devoutly hoped the book was right side up.
—Earl Conrad, *Harriet Tubman*

Narration

A paragraph of narration tells a story or part of a story. The following paragraph recounts one of the author's experiences in the African wild.

One evening when I was wading in the shallows of the lake to pass a rocky outcrop, I suddenly stopped dead as I saw the sinuous black body of a snake in the water. It was all of six feet long, and from the slight hood and the dark stripes at the back of the neck I knew it to be a Storm's water cobra—a deadly reptile for the bite of which there was, at that time, no serum. As I stared at it an incoming wave gently deposited part of its body on one of my feet. I remained motionless, not even breathing, until the wave rolled back into the lake, drawing the snake with it. Then I leaped out of the water as fast as I could, my heart hammering.
— Jane Goodall, *In the Shadow of Man*

Description

A descriptive paragraph sketches a portrait of a person, place, or thing by using concrete and specific details that appeal to one or more senses—sight, sound, smell, taste, and touch. Consider, for example, the following description of the grasshopper invasions that devastated the midwestern United States in the late 1860s.

They came like dive bombers out of the west. They came by the millions with the rustle of their wings roaring overhead. They came in waves, like the rolls of the sea, descending with a terrifying speed, breaking now and again like a mighty surf. They came with the force of a williwaw and they formed a huge, ominous, dark brown cloud that eclipsed the sun. They dipped and touched earth, hitting objects and people like hailstones. But they were not hail. These were live demons. They popped, snapped, crackled, and roared. They were dark brown, an inch or longer in length, plump in the middle and tapered at the ends. They had transparent wings, slender legs, and two black eyes that flashed with a fierce intelligence.   —Eugene Boe, "Pioneers to Eternity"

Process

A process paragraph is structured in chronological order. A writer may choose this pattern either to describe how something is made or done or to explain to readers, step by step, how to do something. The following paragraph explains how to perform a "roll cast," a popular fly fishing technique.

> Begin by taking up a suitable stance, with one foot slightly in front of the other and the rod pointing down the line. Then begin a smooth, steady draw, raising your rod hand to just above shoulder height and lifting the rod to the 10:30 or 11:00 position. This steady draw allows a loop of line to form between the rod top and the water. While the line is still moving, raise the rod slightly, then punch it rapidly forward and down. The rod is now flexed and under maximum compression, and the line follows its path, belly-ing out slightly behind you and coming off the water close to your feet. As you power the rod down through the 3:00 position, the belly of the line will roll forward. Follow through smoothly so that the line unfolds and straightens above the water.
>
> —*The Dorling Kindersley Encyclopedia of Fishing*

Comparison and contrast

To compare is to draw attention to similarities, although the word *compare* also has a broader meaning that includes a consideration of differences. To contrast is to focus only on differences.

Whether a paragraph stresses similarities or differences, it is often patterned in one of two ways. The two subjects may be presented one at a time, as in the following paragraph of contrast.

> So Grant and Lee were in complete contrast, representing two diametrically opposed elements in American life. Grant was the modern man emerging; beyond him, ready to come on the stage, was the great age of steel and machinery, of crowded cities and a restless burgeoning vitality. Lee might have ridden down from the old age of chivalry, lance in hand, silken banner fluttering over his head. Each man was the perfect champion of his cause, drawing both his strengths and weaknesses from the people he led.
>
> —Bruce Catton, "Grant and Lee: A Study in Contrasts"

Or a paragraph may proceed point by point, treating two subjects together, one aspect at a time. The following paragraph uses the point-by-point method to contrast the writer's experiences in an American high school and an Irish convent.

Strangely enough, instead of being academically inferior to my American high school, the Irish convent was superior. In my class at home, *Love Story* was considered pretty heavy reading, so imagine my surprise at finding Irish students who could recite passages from *War and Peace.* In high school we complained about having to study *Romeo and Juliet* in one semester, whereas in Ireland we simultaneously studied *Macbeth* and Dickens's *Hard Times,* in addition to writing a composition a day in English class. In high school, I didn't even begin algebra until the ninth grade, while at the convent seventh graders (or their Irish equivalent) were doing calculus and trigonometry.

—Margaret Stack, student

Analogy

Analogies draw comparisons between items that appear to have little in common. In the following paragraph, physician Lewis Thomas draws an analogy between the behaviour of ants and that of humans.

Ants are so much like human beings as to be an embarrassment. They farm fungi, raise aphids as livestock, launch armies into wars, use chemical sprays to alarm and confuse enemies, capture slaves. The families of weaver ants engage in child labor, holding their larvae like shuttles to spin out the thread that sews the leaves together for their fungus gardens. They exchange information ceaselessly. They do everything but watch television.

—Lewis Thomas, "On Societies as Organisms"

Cause and effect

A paragraph may move from cause to effects or from an effect to its causes. The topic sentence in the following paragraph mentions an effect; the rest of the paragraph lists several causes.

The fantastic water clarity of the Mount Gambier sinkholes results from several factors. The holes are fed from aquifers holding rainwater that fell decades — even centuries — ago, and that has been filtered through miles of limestone. The high level of calcium that limestone adds causes the silty detritus from dead plants and animals to cling together and settle quickly to the bottom. Abundant bottom vegetation in the shallow sinkholes also helps bind the silt. And the rapid turnover of water prohibits stagnation.

—Hillary Hauser, "Exploring a Sunken Realm in Australia"

Classification and division

Classification is the grouping of items into categories according to some consistent principle. The following paragraph classifies species of electric fish.

> Scientists sort electric fishes into three categories. The first comprises the strongly electric species like the marine electric rays or the freshwater African electric catfish and South American electric eel. Known since the dawn of history, these deliver a punch strong enough to stun a human. In recent years, biologists have focused on a second category: weakly electric fish in the South American and African rivers that use tiny voltages for communication and navigation. The third group contains sharks, nonelectric rays, and catfish, which do not emit a field but possess sensors that enable them to detect the minute amounts of electricity that leak out of other organisms.
> —Anne Rudloe and Jack Rudloe, "Electric Warfare: The Fish That Kill with Thunderbolts"

Division takes one item and divides it into parts. As with classification, division should be made according to some consistent principle. The following paragraph describes the components that make up a baseball.

> Like the game itself, a baseball is composed of many layers. One of the delicious joys of childhood is to take apart a baseball and examine the wonders within. You begin by removing the red cotton thread and peeling off the leather cover—which comes from the hide of a Holstein cow and has been tanned, cut, printed, and punched with holes. Beneath the cover is a thin layer of cotton string, followed by several hundred yards of woolen yarn, which make up the bulk of the ball. Slice into the rubber and you'll find the ball's heart—a cork core. The cork is from Portugal, the rubber from southeast Asia, the covers are American, and the balls are assembled in Costa Rica.   —Dan Gutman, *The Way Baseball Works*

Definition

A definition puts a word or concept into a general class and then provides enough details to distinguish it from other members in the same class. In the following paragraph, the writer defines envy as a special kind of desire.

> Envy is so integral and so painful a part of what animates human behavior in market societies that many people have forgotten the full meaning of the word, simplifying it into one of the

synonyms of desire. It is that, which may be why it flourishes in market societies: democracies of desire, they might be called, with money for ballots, stuffing permitted. But envy is more or less than desire. It begins with the almost frantic sense of emptiness inside oneself, as if the pump of one's heart were sucking on air. One has to be blind to perceive the emptiness, of course, but that's just what envy is, a selective blindness. *Invidia,* Latin for envy, translates as "nonsight," and Dante had the envious plodding along under cloaks of lead, their eyes sewn shut with leaden wire. What they are blind to is what they have, God-given and humanly nurtured, in themselves.   —Nelson W. Aldrich Jr., *Old Money*

C4-d Make paragraphs coherent.

When sentences and paragraphs flow from one to another without discernible bumps, gaps, or shifts, they are said to be coherent. Coherence can be improved by strengthening the various ties between old information and new. A number of techniques for strengthening those ties are detailed in this section.

Linking ideas clearly

Readers expect to learn a paragraph's main point in a topic sentence early in the paragraph. Then, as they move into the body of the paragraph, they expect to encounter specific facts, details, or examples that support the topic sentence—either directly or indirectly. Consider the following paragraph, in which all of the sentences following the topic sentence directly support it.

> A passenger list of the early years of the Orient Express would read like a *Who's Who of the World,* from art to politics. Sarah Bernhardt and her Italian counterpart Eleonora Duse used the train to thrill the stages of Europe. For musicians there were Toscanini and Mahler. Dancers Nijinsky and Pavlova were there, while lesser performers like Harry Houdini and the girls of the Ziegfeld Follies also rode the rails. Violinists were allowed to practice on the train, and occasionally one might see trapeze artists hanging like bats from the baggage racks.
> —Barnaby Conrad III, "Train of Kings"

If a sentence does not support the topic sentence directly, readers expect it to support another sentence in the paragraph. The following paragraph begins with a topic sentence. The italicized sentences are direct supports, and the rest of the sentences are indirect supports.

Though the open-space classroom works for many children, it is not practical for my son, David. *First, David is hyperactive.* When he was placed in an open-space classroom, he became distracted and confused. He was tempted to watch the movement going on around him instead of concentrating on his own work. *Second, David has a tendency to transpose letters and numbers, a tendency that can be overcome only by individual attention from the instructor.* In the open classroom he was moved from teacher to teacher, with each one responsible for a different subject. No single teacher worked with David long enough to diagnose the problem, let alone help him with it. *Finally, David is not a highly motivated learner.* In the open classroom, he was graded "at his own level," not by criteria for a certain grade. He could receive a B in reading and still be a grade level behind, because he was doing satisfactory work "at his own level."

—Margaret Smith, student

Repeating key words

Repetition of key words is an important technique for gaining coherence. To prevent repetitions from becoming dull, you can use variations of the key word (*hike, hiker, hiking*), pronouns referring to the word (*gamblers . . . they*), and synonyms (*run, spring, race, dash*). In the following paragraph describing plots among indentured servants in the seventeenth century, historian Richard Hofstadter binds sentences together by repeating the key word *plots* and echoing it with variations (italicized).

Plots hatched by several servants to run away together occurred mostly in the plantation colonies, and the few recorded servant *uprisings* were entirely limited to those colonies. Virginia had been forced from its very earliest years to take stringent steps against *mutinous plots,* and severe punishments for *such behavior* were recorded. Most servant *plots* occurred in the seventeenth century: a contemplated *uprising* was nipped in the bud in York County in 1661; apparently led by some left-wing offshoots of the *Great Rebellion,* servants *plotted* an *insurrection* in Gloucester County in 1663, and four leaders were condemned and executed; some discontented servants apparently joined *Bacon's Rebellion* in the 1670's. In the 1680's, the planters became newly apprehensive of discontent among the servants "owing to their great necessities and want of clothes," and it was feared that they would *rise up* and *plunder* the storehouses and ships; in 1682 there were plant-cutting *riots* in which servants and laborers, as well as some planters, took part.

—Richard Hofstadter, *America at 1750*

Using parallel structures

Parallel structures are frequently used within sentences to underscore the similarity of ideas (see S1). They may also be used to bind together a series of sentences expressing similar information. In the following passage describing folk beliefs, anthropologist Margaret Mead presents similar information in parallel grammatical form.

> Actually, almost every day, even in the most sophisticated home, something is likely to happen that evokes the memory of some old folk belief. The salt spills. A knife falls to the floor. Your nose tickles. Then perhaps, with a slightly embarrassed smile, the person who spilled the salt tosses a pinch over his left shoulder. Or someone recites the old rhyme "Knife falls, gentleman calls." Or as you rub your nose you think, That means a letter. I wonder who's writing?
>
> — Margaret Mead, "New Superstitions for Old"

Maintaining consistency

Coherence suffers whenever a draft shifts confusingly from one point of view to another (for example, from *I* to *you* or from *anyone* to *they*). Coherence also suffers when a draft shifts without reason from one verb tense to another (for example, from *swam* to *swims*). For advice on avoiding shifts, see S4.

Providing transitions

Transitions are bridges between what has been read and what is about to be read. Transitions help readers move from sentence to sentence; they also alert readers to more global connections of ideas — those between paragraphs or even larger blocks of text.

SENTENCE-LEVEL TRANSITIONS   Certain words and phrases signal connections between (or within) sentences. Frequently used transitions are included in the chart on page 35.

Skilled writers use transitional expressions with care, making sure, for example, not to use a *consequently* when an *also* would be more precise. They are also careful to select transitions with an appropriate tone, perhaps preferring *so* to *thus* in an informal piece, *in summary* to *in short* for a scholarly essay.

In the following paragraph, taken from an argument that dinosaurs had the "'right-sized' brains for reptiles of their body size," biologist Stephen Jay Gould uses transitions (italicized) with skill:

I don't wish to deny that the flattened, minuscule head of the large bodied "Stegosaurus" houses little brain from our subjective, top-heavy perspective, *but* I do wish to assert that we should not expect more of the beast. *First of all,* large animals have relatively smaller brains than related, small animals. The correlation of brain size with body size among kindred animals (all reptiles, all mammals, *for example*) is remarkably regular. *As* we move from small to large animals, from mice to elephants *or* small lizards to Komodo dragons, brain size increases, *but* not so fast as body size. *In other words,* bodies grow faster than brains, *and* large animals have low ratios of brain weight to body weight. *In fact,* brains grow only about two-thirds as fast as bodies. *Since* we have no reason to believe that large animals are consistently stupider than their smaller relatives, we must conclude that large animals require relatively less brain to do as well as smaller animals. *If* we do not recognize this relationship, we are likely to underestimate the mental power of very large animals, dinosaurs in particular.

—Stephen Jay Gould,
"Were Dinosaurs Dumb?"

ON THE WEB

For an electronic exercise on transitions, go to
www.dianahacker.com/writersref

and click on   ▶ **Electronic Writing Exercises**
                ▶ **E-ex C4–2**

PARAGRAPH-LEVEL TRANSITIONS   Transitions between paragraphs usually link the *first* sentence of a new paragraph with the *first* sentence of the previous paragraph. In other words, the topic sentences signal global connections.

Look for opportunities to allude to the subject of a previous paragraph (as summed up in its topic sentence) in the topic sentence of the next paragraph. In his essay "Little Green Lies," Jonathan H. Alder uses this strategy in the following topic sentences, which appear in a passage describing the benefits of plastic packaging.

Consider aseptic packaging, the synthetic packaging for the "juice boxes" so many children bring to school with their lunch. [*Rest of paragraph omitted.*]

What is true for juice boxes is also true for other forms of synthetic packaging. [*Rest of paragraph omitted.*]

Common transitions

TO SHOW ADDITION and, also, besides, further, furthermore, in addition, moreover, next, too, first, second

TO GIVE EXAMPLES for example, for instance, to illustrate, in fact, specifically

TO COMPARE also, in the same manner, similarly, likewise

TO CONTRAST but, however, on the other hand, in contrast, nevertheless, still, even though, on the contrary, yet, although

TO SUMMARIZE OR CONCLUDE in other words, in short, in summary, in conclusion, to sum up, that is, therefore

TO SHOW TIME after, as, before, next, during, later, finally, meanwhile, then, when, while, immediately

TO SHOW PLACE OR DIRECTION above, below, beyond, farther on, nearby, opposite, close, to the left

TO INDICATE LOGICAL RELATIONSHIP if, so, therefore, consequently, thus, as a result, for this reason, since

---

TRANSITIONS BETWEEN BLOCKS OF TEXT In long essays, you may need to alert readers to connections between large blocks of text. You can do this by inserting transitional paragraphs at key points in the essay. Here, for example, is a transitional paragraph from a student research paper. It announces that the first part of her paper has come to a close and the second part is about to begin.

> Although the great apes have demonstrated significant language skills, one central question remains: Can they be taught to use that uniquely human language tool we call grammar, to learn the difference, for instance, between "ape bite human" and "human bite ape"? In other words, can an ape create a sentence?

C4-e If necessary, adjust paragraph length.

Most readers feel comfortable reading paragraphs that range between one hundred and two hundred words. Shorter paragraphs force too much starting and stopping, and longer ones strain the reader's attention span. There are exceptions to this guideline, however. Paragraphs longer than two hundred words frequently appear in scholarly writing, where they suggest seriousness and depth. Paragraphs shorter than one hundred words occur in newspapers because of narrow columns; in informal essays to quicken the pace; in business letters, where readers routinely skim for main ideas; and in e-mail for ease of reading on the computer screen.

In an essay, the first and last paragraphs will ordinarily be the introduction and conclusion. These special-purpose paragraphs are likely to be shorter than the paragraphs in the body of the essay. Typically, the body paragraphs will follow the essay's outline: one paragraph per point in short essays, a group of paragraphs per point in longer ones. Some ideas require more development than others, however, so it is best to be flexible. If an idea stretches to a length unreasonable for a paragraph, you should divide the paragraph, even if you have presented comparable points in the essay in single paragraphs.

Paragraph breaks are not always made for strictly logical reasons. Writers use them for all of the following reasons.

REASONS FOR BEGINNING A NEW PARAGRAPH

— to mark off the introduction and the conclusion

— to signal a shift to a new idea

— to indicate an important shift in time or place

— to emphasize a point (by placing it at the beginning or the end, not in the middle, of a paragraph)

— to highlight a contrast

— to signal a change of speakers (in dialogue)

— to provide readers with a needed pause

— to break up text that looks too dense

Beware of using too many short, choppy paragraphs, however. Readers want to see how your ideas connect, and they become irritated when you break their momentum by forcing them to pause every few sentences. Here are some reasons you might have for combining some of the paragraphs in a rough draft.

REASONS FOR COMBINING PARAGRAPHS

— to clarify the essay's organization

— to connect closely related ideas

— to bind together text that looks too choppy

C5

Constructing reasonable arguments

In argumentative writing, you take a stand on a debatable issue. The issue being debated might be a matter of public policy:

— Should religious groups be allowed to meet on public school property?

— What is the least dangerous way to dispose of nuclear waste?

— Should a state enact laws rationing medical care?

On such questions, reasonable people may disagree.

Reasonable men and women also disagree about many scholarly issues. Psychologists debate the validity of behaviourism; citizens interpreted the presence of the Union Jack on the Canadian flag quite differently; biologists conduct genetic experiments to challenge the conclusions of other researchers.

When you construct a *reasonable* argument, your goal is not simply to win or to have the last word. Your aim is to reveal your current understanding of the truth about a subject or to propose the best solution available for solving a problem — without being needlessly combative. Writing teacher Richard Fulkerson describes such aims well:

> The purpose of argumentation within a free society or within a research field is to reach the best conclusion possible at the time.
> — *Teaching the Argument in Writing*

C5-a Examine your issue's social and intellectual contexts.

Arguments appear in social and intellectual contexts. Public policy debates obviously arise in social contexts: Grounded in specific times and places, such debates are conducted among groups with competing values and interests. For example, the debate over nuclear power plants has been renewed in the United States in light of energy concerns and the September 11, 2001, attacks — with environmentalists, the nuclear industry, consumers, and concerned citizens all weighing in on the argument. Most public policy debates have intellectual dimensions that address scientific or theoretical concerns as well. In the case of the nuclear power issue, physicists, biologists, and economists all contribute their expertise.

Scholarly debates clearly play themselves out in intellectual contexts, but they have a social dimension too. Scholars and researchers rarely work in a vacuum: They respond to the contributions of other specialists in the field, often building on others' views and refining them, but at times challenging them. Social bonds develop among scholars who hold similar views, and bad feelings have been known to arise among those belonging to competing schools of thought.

Because many of your readers will be aware of the social and intellectual contexts in which your issue is grounded, you will be at a serious disadvantage if you are not informed. That's why it is a good idea to conduct some research before preparing your argument; consulting even a few sources can help. For example, the student whose paper appears on pages 44–46 became more knowledgeable about his issue — educating the children of illegal immigrants — after consulting just two brief print sources and one Web site. This student documented his sources using MLA style (see MLA-4).

C5-b View your audience as a panel of jurors.

Do not assume that your audience already agrees with you; instead, envision skeptical readers who, like a panel of jurors, will make up their minds after listening to all sides of the argument. If you are arguing a public policy issue, aim your paper at fellow citizens who represent a variety of opinions. In the case of the debate over nuclear power, for example, imagine a jury representative of those who have a stake in the matter: environmentalists, the nuclear industry, consumers, and citizens worried about public safety.

At times, of course, you can deliberately narrow your audience. If you are working within a word limit, for example, you might not have the space in which to address the concerns of all parties to the nuclear energy debate. Or you might be primarily interested in reaching one segment of a general audience, such as consumers. In such instances, you can still view your audience as a panel of jurors; the jury will simply be a less diverse group.

In the case of scholarly debates, you will be addressing readers who share your interest in an academic discipline such as literature or psychology. Such readers belong to what some have called a *discourse community,* a group with an agreed-upon way of investigating and talking about issues. Though they generally agree about procedures, scholars in an academic discipline often disagree about particular issues. Once you see how they disagree about your issue, it will be easy to imagine a jury that reflects the variety of opinions they hold.

C5-c In your introduction, establish credibility and state your thesis.

In argumentative writing, your introduction should ordinarily end with a thesis sentence that states your position on the issue you have chosen to debate (see also C2-a). In the sentences leading up to the thesis, establish your credibility with readers by showing that you are knowledgeable and fair-minded. If possible, build common ground with readers who may not be in initial agreement with your views.

In the following introduction, student Kevin Smith presents himself as someone worth listening to. His opening sentence shows that he is familiar with the legal issues surrounding school prayer. His next sentence reveals him to be fair-minded, and it builds common ground by showing that he, like many readers, believes in the value of prayer. Even Smith's thesis builds common ground: "Prayer is too important to be trusted to our public schools."

> Although the Supreme Court has ruled against prayer in public schools on First Amendment grounds, many people still feel that prayers should be allowed. These people, most of whom hold strong religious beliefs, are well intentioned. What they fail to realize is that the Supreme Court decision, although it was made on legal grounds, makes good sense on religious grounds as well. Prayer is too important to be trusted to our public schools.
>
> —Kevin Smith, student

Because Smith takes into consideration the values of those who disagree with him, readers are likely to approach his essay with an open mind.

C5-d Back up your thesis with persuasive lines of argument.

Arguments of any complexity contain lines of argument that, when taken together, might reasonably persuade readers that the thesis has merit. Here, for example, are the main lines of argument used by a student who opposes regulating use of cell phones while driving:

Thesis: We should not restrict the use of cell phones in moving vehicles.

— The risks of using a cell phone while driving have not been proved scientifically.

— Any risks must be weighed against the benefits of using a phone while driving.

— Instead of restricting use of the phones, we can educate the public on using them responsibly and enforce laws on negligent and reckless driving.

If you sum up your main lines of argument, as in the example just given, you will have a rough outline of your essay. The outline will consist of your central claim—the thesis—and any subordinate claims that back it up. In your paper, you will provide evidence for each of these claims.

C5-e Support your claims with specific evidence.

You will of course need to support your central claim and any subordinate claims with evidence: facts, statistics, examples and illustrations, expert opinion, and so on. Depending on the issue you have chosen to write about, you may or may not need to do some reading to gather evidence.

If any of your evidence is based on reading, you must document your sources. Documentation gives credit to the authors and shows readers how to locate a source in case they want to assess its credibility or explore the issue further (see R4).

Using facts and statistics

A fact is something that is known with certainty because it has been objectively verified: The capital of Wyoming is Cheyenne. Carbon has an atomic weight of 12. Lester Bowles Pearson won the Nobel Peace Prize in 1957. Statistics are collections of numerical facts: Alcohol abuse is a factor in nearly 40 percent of traffic fatalities. Nearly one out of four Canadian households currently owns a DVD player. As of 1999, North America held 8.4 percent of proven oil reserves; together, Iraq, Kuwait, and Saudi Arabia held 46 percent.

Most arguments are supported at least to some extent by facts and statistics. For example, in the following passage, the writer uses statistics to show that college students are granted unreasonably high credit limits:

According to Nellie Mae statistics, in 1998 undergraduates were granted an average credit limit of $3,683; for graduate students the figure jumped to $15,721. Nearly 10% of the students in the Nellie Mae study carried balances near or exceeding these credit limits (Blair).

Writers and politicians often use statistics in selective ways to bolster their partisan views. If you suspect that a writer's handling of statistics is not quite fair, read authors with opposing views, who may give you a fuller understanding of the numbers.

Using examples and illustrations

Examples and illustrations (extended examples, often in story form) rarely prove a point by themselves, but when used in combination with other forms of evidence they flesh out an argument and bring it to life. Because they often have an emotional dimension, they can reach readers in ways that statistics cannot.

In a paper arguing in favour of restricting the use of cell phones while driving, student Angela Daly gives examples of four people who were killed in just one month because drivers were distracted by their phones (see p. 371). Daly supplements this emotionally powerful anecdotal evidence with an analysis of scientific investigations on the dangers of using cell phones while driving.

Citing expert opinion

Although they are no substitute for careful reasoning of your own, the views of an expert can contribute to the force of your argument. For example, in a paragraph describing the dangers of using a cell phone while driving, Angela Daly relies on an expert:

> Frances Bents, an expert on the relation between cell phones and accidents, estimates that 450 to 1,000 crashes a year have some connection to cell phone use (Layton C9).

When you rely on expert opinion, make sure that your source is an authority in the field you are writing about. In some cases you may need to provide credentials showing why your source is worth listening to. When including expert testimony in your paper, you can summarize or paraphrase the expert's opinion or you can quote the expert's exact words. You will of course need to document the source, as in the example just given (see R4).

C5-f Anticipate objections; counter opposing arguments.

Readers who already agree with you need no convincing, although a well-argued case for their point of view is always welcome. But indifferent and skeptical readers may resist your arguments because they have minds of their own. To give up a position that seems reasonable, a reader has to see that there is an even more reasonable one. In addition to presenting your own case, therefore, you should review the opposing arguments and attempt to counter them.

There is no best place in an essay to deal with opposing views. Often it is useful to summarize the opposing position early in your essay. After stating your thesis but before developing your own arguments, you might have a paragraph beginning *Critics of this view argue that....* But sometimes a better plan is to anticipate objections as you develop your case paragraph by paragraph. Wherever you decide to deal with opposing arguments, do your best to counter them. Show that those who oppose you are not as persuasive as they claim because their arguments are flawed or because your arguments to the contrary have greater weight.

NOTE: Readers will judge the way you handle opposing views, so do your best to explain the arguments of others accurately and fairly (see C6-c).

C5-g Build common ground.

As you counter opposing arguments, try to build common ground with readers who do not initially agree with your views. If you can show that you share your readers' values, they may be able to switch to your position without giving up what they feel is important. For example, to persuade people opposed to shooting deer, a provincial wildlife agency would have to show that it too cares about preserving deer and does not want them to die needlessly. Having established these values in common, the agency might be able to persuade critics that a carefully controlled hunting season is good for the deer population because it prevents starvation caused by overpopulation.

People believe that intelligence and decency support their side of an argument. To change sides, they must continue to feel intelligent and decent. Otherwise they will persist in their opposition.

SAMPLE ARGUMENT PAPER

In the following paper, student Andrew Knutson argues that Americans should continue to educate the children of illegal immigrants. Notice that Knutson is careful to establish common ground with readers who may hold a different view. Notice too that he attempts to counter opposing arguments.

In writing the paper, Knutson consulted two written sources and one Internet source. When he quotes from or uses statistics from a source, he cites the source with an MLA (Modern Language Association) in-text citation. Citations in the paper refer readers to the list of works cited at the end of the paper. (See MLA-4.)

ON THE WEB

To read two student papers arguing different sides of the same issue, go to **www.dianahacker.com/writersref**

and click on ▶ **Model Papers**
       ▶ **MLA papers: Daly and Levi**

Andrew Knutson

Dr. Karr

English 102

8 March 2000

Why Educate the Children of Illegal Immigrants?

Opening sentences establish credibility by showing that the writer is informed.

Immigration laws have been a subject of debate throughout American history, especially in states such as California and Texas, where immigrant populations are high. Recently, some citizens have been questioning whether we should continue to educate the children of illegal immigrants. While this issue is steeped in emotional controversy, we must not allow divisive "us against them" rhetoric to cloud our thinking. Yes, educating undocumented immigrants costs us, but not educating them would cost us much more.

Thesis, at end of introductory paragraph, states the main point.

Writer addresses concerns of those who hold opposing views.

Those who propose barring the children of illegal immigrants from our schools have understandable worries. They worry that their state taxes will rise as undocumented children crowd their school systems. They worry about the crowding itself, given the loss of quality education that comes with large class sizes. They worry that school resources will be deflected from their children because of the linguistic and social problems that many of the newcomers face. And finally, they worry that even more illegal immigrants will cross our borders because of the lure of free education.

Writer counters opposing arguments.

This last worry is probably unfounded. It is unlikely that many parents are crossing the borders solely to educate their children. More likely, they are in desperate need of work, economic opportunity, and possibly political asylum. As Charles Wheeler of the National Immigration Law Center asserts, "There is no evidence that access to federal programs acts as a magnet to foreigners or that further restrictions would discourage illegal immigrants" (qtd. in "Exploiting").

Quotation is cited using MLA style.

Reasonable tone keeps argument from sounding biased.

The other concerns are more legitimate, but they can be addressed by less drastic measures than barring children from schools. Currently the responsibility of educating about 75% of undocumented children is borne by just a few states--California, New York, Texas, and Florida (Edmondson 1). One way to help these and other states is to have the federal government pick up the cost of educating undocumented children, with enough funds to alleviate the overcrowded classrooms that cause parents such concern. Such

Statistic is cited using MLA style.

Knutson 2

cost shifting could have a significant benefit, for if the federal government had to pay, it might work harder to stem the tide of illegal immigrants.

So far, attempts to bar undocumented children from public schools have failed. In the 1982 case of Plyler v. Doe, the Supreme Court ruled on the issue. In a 5-4 decision, it overturned a Texas law that allowed schools to deny education to illegal immigrants. Martha McCarthy reports that Texas had justified its law as a means of "preserving financial resources, protecting the state from an influx of illegal immigrants, and maintaining high quality education for resident children" (128). The Court considered these issues but concluded that in the long run the costs of educating immigrant children would pale in comparison to the costs--both to the children and to society-- of not educating them.

It isn't hard to figure out what the costs of not educating these children would be. The costs to innocent children are obvious: loss of the opportunity to learn English, to understand American culture and history, to socialize with other children in a structured environment, and to grow up to be successful, responsible adults.

The costs to society as a whole are fairly obvious as well. That is why we work so hard to promote literacy and prevent students from dropping out of school. An uneducated populace is dangerous to the fabric of society, contributing to social problems such as vandalism and crime, an underground economy, gang warfare, teenage pregnancy, substance abuse, and infectious and transmissible diseases. The health issue alone makes it worth our while to educate the children of undocumented immigrants, for when children are in school, we can make sure they are inoculated properly, and we can teach them the facts about health and disease.

Do we really want thousands of uneducated children growing up on the streets, where we have little control over them? Surely not. The lure of the streets is powerful enough already. Only by inviting all children into safe and nurturing and intellectually engaging schools can we combat that power. Our efforts will be well worth the cost.

Writer uses evidence to support his thesis.

Quotation is cited using MLA style.

Transitional topic sentence leads readers to next part of paper.

Writer builds common ground with readers.

Conclusion restates benefits of educating children of illegal immigrants.

NEW PAGE

Works cited page is formatted according to MLA style.

Knutson 3

Works Cited

Edmondson, Brad. "Life without Illegal Immigrants." American Demo-
graphics May 1996: 1.

"Exploiting Fears." Admissions Decisions: Should Immigration Be Restricted? 7 Oct. 1996. Public Agenda. 10 Feb. 2000
<http://www.vote-smart.org/issues/Immigration/chap2/
imm2itx.html>.

McCarthy, Martha M. "Immigrants in Public Schools: Legal Issues."
Educational Horizons 71 (1993): 128-30.

C6

Evaluating arguments

In your reading and in your own writing, evaluate all arguments
for logic and fairness. Many arguments can stand up to critical
scrutiny. Often, however, a line of argument that at first seems reasonable turns out to be fallacious, unfair, or both.

ON THE WEB

For links to resources that will help you evaluate arguments, go to
www.dianahacker.com/writersref

and click on   ▶ **Links Library**
               ▶ **Argument**

C6-a   Distinguish between reasonable and fallacious argumentative tactics.

A number of unreasonable argumentative tactics are known as *logical fallacies*. Most of the fallacies—such as hasty generalizations

and false analogies—are misguided or dishonest uses of legitimate argumentative strategies. The examples in this section suggest when such strategies are reasonable and when they are not.

Generalizing (inductive reasoning)

Writers and thinkers generalize all the time. We look at a sample of data and conclude that data we have not observed will most likely conform to what we have seen before. From a spoonful of soup, we conclude just how salty the whole bowl will be. After numerous bad experiences with an airline, we decide to book future flights with one of its competitors instead.

When we draw a conclusion from an array of facts, we are engaged in inductive reasoning. Such reasoning deals in probability, not certainty. For a conclusion to be highly probable, it must be based on evidence that is sufficient, representative, and relevant. (See the chart on p. 49.)

The fallacy known as a *hasty generalization* is a conclusion based on insufficient or unrepresentative evidence.

HASTY GENERALIZATION

Deaths from drug overdoses in Vancouver have doubled in the past three years. Therefore, more Canadians than ever are dying from drug abuse.

Data from one city do not justify a conclusion about all of Canada.

A *stereotype* is a hasty generalization about a group. Here are a few examples.

STEREOTYPES

Women are bad bosses.

Politicians are corrupt.

Asian students are exceptionally intelligent.

Stereotyping is common because of our human tendency to perceive selectively. We tend to see what we want to see; that is, we notice evidence confirming our already formed opinions and fail to notice evidence to the contrary. For example, if you have concluded that politicians are corrupt, your stereotype will be confirmed by news reports of members of Parliament being charged with crimes— even though every day the media describe conscientious officials serving the public honestly and well.

NOTE: Many hasty generalizations contain words like *all, every, always,* and *never,* when qualifiers such as *most, many, usually,* and *seldom* would be more accurate.

Drawing analogies

An analogy points out a similarity between two things that are otherwise different. Analogies can be an effective means of arguing a point. In fact, our system of case law, which relies heavily on precedents, makes extensive use of reasoning by analogy. A prosecutor may argue, for example, that X is guilty because his actions resemble those of Y and Z, who were judged guilty in previous rulings. In response, the defence may maintain that the actions of X bear only a superficial resemblance to those of Y and Z and that in legally relevant respects they are in fact quite different.

It is not always easy to draw the line between a reasonable and an unreasonable analogy. At times, however, an analogy is clearly off-base, in which case it is called a *false analogy.*

> **FALSE ANALOGY**
> If we can put humans on the moon, we should be able to find a cure for the common cold.

The writer has falsely assumed that because two things are alike in one respect, they must be alike in others. Putting human beings on the moon and finding a cure for the common cold are both scientific challenges, but the technical problems confronting medical researchers are quite different from those solved by space scientists.

Tracing causes and effects

Demonstrating a connection between causes and effects is rarely a simple matter. For example, to explain why a chemistry course has a high failure rate, you would begin by listing possible causes: inadequate preparation of students, poor teaching, large class size, lack of qualified tutors, and so on. Next you would investigate each possible cause. To see whether inadequate preparation contributes to the high failure rate, for instance, you might compare the math and science backgrounds of successful and failing students. To see whether large class size is a contributing factor, you might run a pilot program of small classes and compare grades in the small classes with those in the larger ones. Only after investigating the possible causes would you be able to weigh the relative impact of each cause and suggest appropriate remedies.

Testing inductive reasoning

Though inductive reasoning leads to probable and not absolute truth, you can assess a conclusion's likely probability by asking three questions. This chart shows how to apply those questions to a sample conclusion based on a survey.

CONCLUSION   The majority of students on our campus would likely subscribe to high-speed Internet access if it were available.

EVIDENCE   In a recent survey, 923 of 1515 students questioned say they would subscribe to high-speed Internet access.

1. Is the evidence sufficient?
   That depends. On a small campus (say, 3000 students), the pool of students surveyed would be sufficient for market research, but on a large campus (say, 30 000), 1515 students are only 5 percent of the population. If that 5 percent were known to be truly representative of the other 95 percent, however, even such a small sample would be sufficient (see question 2).

2. Is the evidence representative?
   The evidence is representative if those responding to the survey reflect the characteristics of the entire student population: age, sex, level of technical expertise, amount of disposable income, and so on. If most of those surveyed are majoring in technical fields, for example, the researchers would be wise to question the survey's conclusion.

3. Is the evidence relevant?
   The answer is yes. The results of the survey are directly linked to the conclusion. Evidence about the number of hours spent on the Internet, by contrast, would not be relevant, because it would not be about *subscribing to high-speed Internet access*.

Because cause-and-effect reasoning is so complex, it is not surprising that writers frequently oversimplify it. In particular, writers sometimes assume that because one event follows another, the first is the cause of the second. This common fallacy is known as *post hoc,* from the Latin *post hoc, ergo propter hoc,* meaning "after this, therefore because of this."

POST HOC FALLACY

Since Premier Smith took office, unemployment of visible minorities in the province has decreased by 7 percent. Premier Smith should be applauded for reducing unemployment among visible minorities.

The writer must show that Premier Smith's policies are responsible for the decrease in unemployment; it is not enough to show that the decrease followed the premier's taking office.

Weighing options

Especially when reasoning about problems and solutions, writers must weigh options. To be fair, a writer should mention the full range of options, showing why one is superior to the others or might work well in combination with others.

It is unfair to suggest that there are only two alternatives when in fact there are more. Writers who set up a false choice between their preferred option and one that is clearly unsatisfactory are guilty of the *either . . . or* fallacy.

> **EITHER . . . OR FALLACY**
>
> Our current war against drugs has not worked. Either we should legalize drugs or we should turn the drug war over to our armed forces and let them fight it.

Clearly there are other options, such as increased funding for drug prevention and treatment.

Making assumptions

An assumption is a claim that is taken to be true—without the need of proof. Most arguments are based to some extent on assumptions, since writers rarely have the time and space to prove all of the conceivable claims on which the argument is based. For example, someone arguing about the best means of limiting population growth in developing countries might well assume that the goal of limiting population growth is worthwhile. For most audiences, there would be no need to articulate this assumption or to defend it.

There is a danger, however, in failing to spell out and prove a claim that is clearly controversial. Consider the following short argument, in which a key claim is missing.

> **ARGUMENT WITH MISSING CLAIM**
>
> Violent crime is increasing.
> Therefore, we should reintroduce the death penalty.

The writer seems to be assuming that the death penalty will deter violent criminals—and that most audiences will agree. Obviously, neither is a safe assumption.

When a missing claim is an assertion that few would agree with, we say that a writer is guilty of a *non sequitur* (Latin for "does not follow").

NON SEQUITUR
Mariko loves good food; therefore she will be an excellent chef.

Few people would agree with the missing claim—that lovers of good food always make excellent chefs.

Deducing conclusions (deductive reasoning)

When we deduce a conclusion, we—like Sherlock Holmes—put things together. We establish that a general principle is true, that a specific case is an example of that principle, and that therefore a particular conclusion is a certainty. In real life, such absolute reasoning rarely happens. Approximations of it, however, sometimes occur.

Deductive reasoning can often be structured in a three-step argument called a *syllogism*. The three steps are the major premise, the minor premise, and the conclusion.

1. Anything that increases radiation in the environment is dangerous to public health. (Major premise)
2. Nuclear reactors increase radiation in the environment. (Minor premise)
3. Therefore, nuclear reactors are dangerous to public health. (Conclusion)

The major premise is a generalization. The minor premise is a specific case. The conclusion follows from applying the generalization to the specific case.

Deductive arguments break down if one of the premises is not true or if the conclusion does not logically follow from the premises. In the following short argument, the major premise is very likely untrue.

ARGUMENT WITH A QUESTIONABLE PREMISE
The police do not give speeding tickets to people driving less than eight kilometres per hour over the limit. Sam is driving ninety-five kilometres per hour in a ninety-kilometre-per-hour zone. Therefore, the police will not give Sam a speeding ticket.

The conclusion is true only if the premises are true. If the police sometimes give tickets for less than eight-kilometre-per-hour violations, Sam cannot safely conclude that he will avoid a ticket.

In the following argument, both premises might be true, but the conclusion does not follow logically from them.

CONCLUSION DOES NOT FOLLOW

All members of our club ran in this year's Royal Victoria Marathon. Jay ran in this year's Royal Victoria Marathon. Therefore, Jay is a member of our club.

The fact that Jay ran the marathon is no guarantee that he is a member of the club. Presumably, many runners are nonmembers.

Assuming that both premises are true, the following argument holds up.

CONCLUSION FOLLOWS

All members of our club ran in this year's Royal Victoria Marathon. Jay is a member of our club. Therefore, Jay ran in this year's Royal Victoria Marathon.

C6-b Distinguish between legitimate and unfair emotional appeals.

There is nothing wrong with appealing to readers' emotions. After all, many issues worth arguing about have an emotional as well as a logical dimension. For example, in a newspaper article, writers George McGovern and Robert Dole have a good reason for tugging at readers' emotions: Their subject is hungry schoolchildren. In their introduction, McGovern and Dole appeal to readers' emotions by describing a scene from a documentary.

LEGITIMATE EMOTIONAL APPEAL

The most moving scene was filmed in a school where all students — even those who were too poor to pay for a meal — were required to go to the cafeteria at lunchtime. One 9- or 10-year-old boy was asked how he felt standing at the rear of the room watching his better-off classmates eat. Lowering his head, the boy confessed softly, "I'm ashamed."

As we all know, however, emotional appeals are frequently misused. Many of the arguments we see in the media, for instance, strive to win our sympathy rather than our intelligent agreement. A TV commercial suggesting that you will be thin and sexy if you drink a certain diet beverage is making a pitch to emotions. So is a political speech that recommends electing John D'Eau because he is a devoted husband and father who set up a soup kitchen in his town.

The following passage illustrates several types of unfair emotional appeals.

UNFAIR EMOTIONAL APPEALS

This progressive proposal to build a ski resort in the provincial park has been carefully researched by Western Trust, the largest bank in the province; furthermore, it is favoured by a majority of the local merchants. The only opposition comes from narrow-minded, do-gooder environmentalists who care more about trees than they do about people; one of their leaders was actually arrested for disturbing the peace several years ago.

Words with strong positive or negative connotations, such as *progressive* and *do-gooder,* are examples of *biased language.* Attacking the persons who hold a belief (environmentalists) rather than refuting their argument is called *ad hominem,* a Latin term meaning "to the man." Associating a prestigious name (Western Trust) with the writer's side is called *transfer.* Claiming that an idea should be accepted because a large number of people are in favour (the majority of merchants) is called the *bandwagon appeal.* Bringing in irrelevant issues (the arrest) is a *red herring,* named after a trick used in fox hunts to mislead the dogs by dragging a smelly fish across the trail.

C6-c　Judge how fairly a writer handles opposing views.

The way in which a writer deals with opposing views is telling. Some writers address the arguments of the opposition fairly, conceding points when necessary and countering others, all in a civil spirit. Other writers will do almost anything to win an argument: either ignoring opposing views altogether or misrepresenting such views and attacking their proponents.

In your own writing, you build credibility by addressing opposing arguments fairly. (See also C5-f.) In your reading, you can assess the credibility of your sources by looking at how they deal with views not in agreement with their own.

Describing the views of others

Writers and politicians often deliberately misrepresent the views of others. One way they do this is by setting up a "straw man," a character so weak that he is easily knocked down. The *straw man* fallacy consists of an oversimplification or outright distortion of opposing views. For example, in a California debate over attempts to control the mountain lion population, pro-lion groups characterized their opponents as trophy hunters bent on shooting harmless lions and sticking them on the walls of their dens. In truth, such hunters were only one faction of those who saw a need to control the lion population.

In response to the District of Columbia's request for voting representation, some politicians have set up a straw man, as shown in the following example.

STRAW MAN FALLACY

Washington, D.C., residents are lobbying for statehood. Giving a city such as the District of Columbia the status of a state would be unfair.

The straw man wants statehood. In fact, most District citizens are lobbying for voting representation in any form, not necessarily through statehood.

Quoting opposing views

Writers often quote the words of writers who hold opposing views. In general, this is a good idea, for it ensures some level of fairness and accuracy. At times, though, both the fairness and accuracy are an illusion.

A source may be misrepresented when it is quoted out of context. All quotations are to some extent taken out of context, but a fair writer will explain that context to readers. To select a provocative sentence from a source and to ignore the more moderate sentences surrounding it is both unfair and misleading. Sometimes a source is deliberately distorted through the device of ellipsis dots. Ellipsis dots tell readers that words have been omitted from the original source (see P7-g). When those words are crucial to an author's meaning, omitting them is obviously unfair.

ORIGINAL SOURCE

Paulson's *Among Friends* is riddled with foolish dialogue and astonishing in its blatantly juvenile portrayal of parent-child relations.   —B. Riche, reviewer

MISLEADING QUOTATION

According to B. Riche, Paulson's *Among Friends* is "astonishing in its . . . portrayal of parent-child relations."

D

Document
Design

Document Design

The term *document* is broad enough to describe anything you might write in an English class, in other classes across the curriculum, in the business world, and in everyday life. How a document is designed can affect how it is received.

Instructors have certain expectations about how a college paper should look (see D2). Employers too expect documents such as business letters and memos to be formatted in standard ways (see D3). And those who read your e-mail and consult your Web pages will appreciate an effective document design (see D4).

ON THE WEB

For links to resources with advice about designing documents, go to **www.dianahacker.com/writersref**

and click on ▶ **Links Library**
　　　　　　　 ▶ **Document Design**

D1

Principles of document design

Good document design promotes readability, but what this means depends on your purpose and audience and perhaps on other elements of your writing situation, such as your subject and any length restrictions. (See the checklist on p. 4.) All of your design choices—word processing options and use of headings, displayed lists, and other visuals—should be made in light of your specific writing situation.

D1-a Select appropriate format options.

Word processing programs present you with abundant format options. Before you print a final draft, you should make sure that your margins, line spacing, and justification are set appropriately. If a number of fonts (typeface styles and sizes) are available, you should also determine which is most appropriate for your purposes.

Margins and line spacing

For documents printed on letter-sized paper, you should leave a margin of between one and one and a half inches (2.5 and 3.5 cm) on all sides of the page. These margins prevent the text from looking too crowded, and they allow room for annotations, such as an instructor's comments or an editor's suggestions.

Most manuscripts in progress are double-spaced to allow room for editing. Final copy is often double-spaced as well, since single-spacing is less inviting to read. But at times the advantages of double-spacing are offset by other considerations. In a business memo, for example, you may single-space to fit the memo on one easily scanned page. And in a technical report, you might single-space to save paper, for both ecological and financial reasons.

Justification (alignment)

Word processing programs give you a choice between left-justified or fully justified text. Left-justified text lines up against the left margin but has a ragged right margin. When text is fully justified, all of the words line up against both the left and the right margins, as they do on a typeset page like the one you are now reading.

Unfortunately, text that has been fully justified on a computer can be hard to read. The problem is that extra space is added between words in some lines, creating "rivers" of white that can be distracting. In addition, fully justified text may create the need for excessive hyphenation at the ends of lines. Unless your computer can create the real look of a typeset page, you will do readers a favour by turning off the full justification feature.

Fonts

If you have a choice of fonts, you should select a normal size (10 to 12 points) and a style that is not too offbeat. Although unusual styles of type, such as those that look handwritten, may seem attractive, they slow readers down. We all read more efficiently when a text meets our usual expectations.

CAUTION: Never write a college or university essay or any other document in all capital letters. Research shows that readers experience much frustration when they are forced to read more than a few words in a row printed in all capital letters.

D1-b Consider using headings.

There is little need for headings in short essays, especially if the writer uses paragraphing and clear topic sentences to guide readers. In more complex documents, however, such as research papers, grant proposals, business reports, and long Web documents, headings can be a useful visual cue for readers.

Headings help readers see at a glance the organization of a document. If more than one level of heading is used, the headings also indicate the hierarchy of ideas — as they do in this book.

Headings serve a number of functions, depending on the needs of different readers. When readers are simply looking up information, headings will help them find it quickly. When readers are scanning, hoping to pick up the gist of things, headings will guide them. Even when readers are committed enough to read every word, headings can help. Efficient readers preview a document before they begin reading; when previewing and while reading, they are guided by any visual cues the writer provides.

CAUTION: Avoid using more headings (or more levels of headings) than you really need. Excessive use of headings can make a text choppy.

Phrasing headings

Headings should be as brief and as informative as possible. Certain styles of headings — the most common being *-ing* phrases, noun phrases, and questions — work better for some purposes, audiences, and subjects than others.

Whatever style you choose, use it consistently for headings on the same level. In other words, headings on the same level of organization should be written in parallel structure (see S1), as in the following examples. The first set of headings appeared in a report written for an environmental think tank, the second in a history textbook, and the third in a mutual fund brochure.

-ING HEADINGS

Safeguarding the earth's atmosphere
Charting the path to sustainable energy
Conserving global forests
Triggering the technological revolution
Strengthening international institutions

NOUN PHRASE HEADINGS

The economics of slavery
The sociology of slavery
Psychological effects of slavery

QUESTIONS AS HEADINGS

How do I buy shares?
How do I redeem shares?
What is the history of the fund's performance?
What are the tax consequences of investing in the fund?

Placing and highlighting headings

Headings on the same level of organization should be placed and highlighted in a consistent way. For example, you might centre your first-level headings and print them in boldface; then you might place the second-level headings flush left (against the left margin) and underline them, like this:

First-level heading

<u>Second-level heading</u>

Most college papers should have only one level of heading, usually centred, as in the sample paper on pages 408–17. In business and technical writing, headings are usually placed flush left above flush-left text—without paragraph indents—to create strong alignment among elements on a page (see the memo on p. 72 for an example).

To highlight headings, consider using boldface, italics, underlining, all capital letters, colour, larger or smaller typeface than the text, a different font, or some combination of these:

boldface	colour
italics	larger typeface
<u>underlining</u>	smaller typeface
ALL CAPITAL LETTERS	different font

On the whole, it is best to use restraint. Excessive highlighting results in a page that looks too busy, and it defeats its own purpose, since readers need to see which headings are more important than others.

Important headings can be highlighted by using a fair amount of white space around them. Less important headings can be downplayed by using less white space or even by running them in with the text.

D1-c Consider using displayed lists.

Lists are easy to read or scan when they are displayed rather than run into your text. You might reasonably choose to display the following kinds of lists:

— steps in a process

— materials needed for a project

— parts of an object

— advice or recommendations

— items to be discussed

— criteria for evaluation (as in checklists)

Displayed lists should usually be introduced with an independent clause followed by a colon (see P4-a and the preceding list). Periods are not used after items in a list unless the items are sentences.

Lists are most readable when they are presented in parallel grammatical form (see S1). In the sample list, for instance, the items are all noun phrases. As with headings, some kinds of lists might be more appropriately presented as *-ing* phrases, as questions, or in some other grammatical form.

To draw the reader's eye to a list, consider using bullets (circles or squares) or dashes. If there is some reason to number the items, use an arabic number followed by a period for each item.

CAUTION: Although displayed lists can be a useful visual cue, they should not be overdone. Too many of them will give a document a choppy, cluttered look. And lists that are very long (sometimes called "laundry lists") should be avoided as well. Readers can hold only so many ideas in their short-term memory, so if a list grows too long, you should find some way of making it more concise or clustering similar items.

D1-d Consider adding visuals.

Visuals such as charts, graphs, tables, diagrams, maps, and photographs convey information concisely and vividly. In a student essay not intended for publication, you can use another person's visuals as long as you credit the borrowing (see R4). And with access to computer graphics, you can create your own visuals to enhance an essay or a report.

This section suggests when charts, graphs, tables, and diagrams might be appropriate for your purposes. It also discusses where you might place such visuals.

Using charts, graphs, tables, and diagrams

In documents that help readers follow a process or make a decision, flow charts can be useful; for an example, see page 203 of this book. Pie charts are appropriate for indicating ratios or apportionment, as in the following example.

PIE CHART

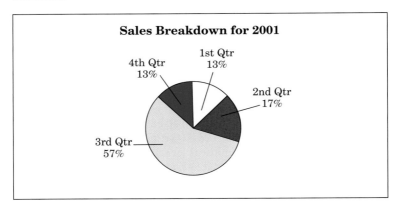

Line graphs and bar graphs illustrate disparities in numerical data. Line graphs are appropriate when you want to illuminate trends over a period of time, such as trends in sales, in unemployment, or in population growth. Bar graphs can be used for the same purpose. In addition, bar graphs are useful for highlighting comparisons, such as vote totals for rival political candidates or the number of refugees entering Canada during different time periods.

LINE GRAPH

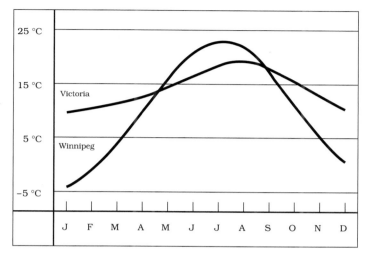

**MONTHLY MEAN TEMPERATURE IN
VICTORIA AND WINNIPEG**

BAR GRAPH

SALES BREAKDOWN BY REGION, 2001

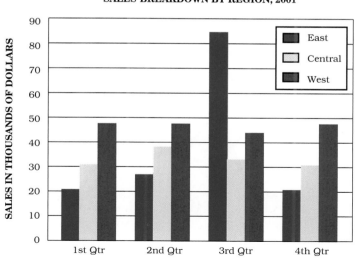

Tables are not as visually interesting as line graphs or charts, but they allow for inclusion of specific numerical data, such as exact percentages. The following table presents the responses of students and faculty to one question on a campus-wide questionnaire.

TABLE

Is North American education based too much on European history and values?

| | PERCENT | | |
	NO	UNDECIDED	YES
Canadian students	21	25	54
International students	55	29	16
Canadian faculty	16	19	65
International faculty	57	27	16

Diagrams are useful — and sometimes indispensable — in scientific and technical writing. It is more concise, for example, to use the following diagram than to explain the chemical formula in words.

DIAGRAM

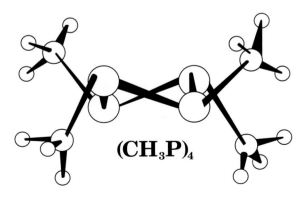

$(CH_3P)_4$

Placing visuals

A visual may be placed in the text of a document, near a discussion to which it relates, or it can be put in an appendix, labelled, and referred to in the text.

Placing visuals in the text of a document can be tricky. Usually you will want the visual to appear close to the sentences that relate to it, but page breaks won't always allow this placement. At times you may need to insert the visual at a later point and tell readers where it can be found or, with the help of software, you may be able to make the text flow around the visual.

In newsletters and in business and technical documents, page layout is both an art and a science. The best way to learn how to lay out pages is to work with colleagues who have had experience solving the many problems that can arise.

NOTE: Guidelines for using visuals vary by academic discipline. In English and humanities classes, follow the MLA (Modern Language Association) guidelines in MLA-5a. In social science classes, follow the APA (American Psychological Association) guidelines in APA-5a. For CMS (*Chicago Manual of Style*) guidelines, see CMS-5a.

D2

Academic manuscript formats

If your instructor provides formal guidelines for formatting an essay—or a more specialized document such as a lab report, a case study, or a research paper—you should of course follow them. Otherwise, use the manuscript format that is standard for the discipline in which you are writing.

In most English and humanities classes, you will be asked to use the MLA (Modern Language Association) format. For MLA manuscript guidelines and a sample paper, see MLA-5. If you have been asked to use APA (American Psychological Association) or CMS (*Chicago Manual of Style*) manuscript guidelines, see APA-5 or CMS-5.

D3

Business documents

This section provides guidelines for preparing business letters, résumés, and memos. For a more detailed discussion of these and other business documents—proposals, reports, executive summaries, and so on—consult a business writing textbook or take a look at examples currently being written at the organization for which you are writing.

ON THE WEB

For links to resources that will help you format a résumé and other business documents, go to
www.dianahacker.com/writersref

and click on ▶ **Links Library**
▶ **Document Design**

D3-a Business letters

In writing a business letter, be direct, clear, and courteous, but do not hesitate to be firm if necessary. State your purpose or request at the beginning of the letter and include only pertinent information in the body. By being as direct and concise as possible, you show that you value your reader's time.

A sample business letter appears on the following page. This letter is typed in what is called *full block* style. All elements of the letter are lined up against the left margin, making for a clean, businesslike look. Paragraphs are not indented and an extra line of space is added between paragraphs.

Below the signature, the abbreviation *Enc.* indicates that something is enclosed with the letter. You can also use the abbreviation *cc* followed by a colon and the name of someone who is receiving a copy of the letter.

BUSINESS LETTER IN FULL BLOCK FORM

121 Knox Road, #6
Toronto, ON M4K 3J7
March 4, 2002

— Return address

Linda Hennessee, Managing Editor
World Discovery
900 Bay Street
Toronto, ON M7A 1L2

— Inside address

Dear Ms. Hennessee: ⊐— Salutation

Please accept my application for the summer editorial internship listed with
the Career Development Centre at Ryerson University. Currently I am in
my third year at Ryerson University, with a double major in English and
journalism.

Over the past three years I have gained considerable experience in newspaper and magazine journalism, as you will see on my enclosed résumé. I am
familiar with the basic procedures of editing texts and photographs in both
traditional and digital media, but my primary interests lie in feature writing
and landscape photography. My professional goal is to work as a photojournalist with an international focus, preferably for a major magazine. I
cannot imagine a better introduction to that career than a summer at *World
Discovery.*

— Body

I am available for an interview almost any time and can be reached at
416-555-2651. My e-mail address is jrichard@ryerson.edu.

I look forward to hearing from you.

Sincerely, ——————— Close

Jeffrey Richardson

— Signature

Jeffrey Richardson

Enc.

D3-b Résumés

An effective résumé gives relevant information in a clear and concise form. The trick is to present yourself in the best possible light without going on at length and wasting your reader's time. When you send out your résumé, you should include a letter that tells what position you seek and where you learned about it (see p. 67). The letter should also summarize your education and past experience, relating them to the job you are applying for. End the letter with a suggestion for a meeting, and tell your prospective employer when you will be available.

You may be asked to produce a traditional résumé, a scannable résumé, or a Web résumé. Brief guidelines for each type of résumé appear in this section.

Traditional résumés

Traditional résumés are printed on paper, and they are screened by people, not by computers. Because screening committees may face stacks of applications, they often spend very little time looking at each résumé. Therefore you will need to make your résumé as reader-friendly as possible. Here are a few guidelines to follow:

— Limit your résumé to one page if possible, two pages at the most.

— Organize your information into clear categories — Education, Experience, and so on.

— Present your educational and work experience in reverse chronological order to highlight your most recent accomplishments.

— Use bullets to draw the reader's eye to listed information.

— Use strong, active verbs to emphasize your accomplishments. (Use present-tense verbs, such as *manage,* for current activities and past-tense verbs, such as *managed,* for past activities.)

A sample traditional résumé appears on the following page.

TRADITIONAL RÉSUMÉ

Jeffrey Richardson
121 Knox Road, #6
Toronto, ON M4K 3J7
416-555-2651
jrichard@ryerson.edu

OBJECTIVE   To obtain an editorial internship with a magazine

EDUCATION
Fall 1999–   Ryerson University
present   • B.A. expected in May 2003
                         • Double major: English and journalism
                         • GPA: 3.7 (on a 4-point scale)

EXPERIENCE
Fall 2000–   Photo editor, *The Eyeopener*, student newspaper
present   • Shoot, edit, and print photographs (film and digital)
                         • Select and lay out photographs and other visuals

Summer   Intern, *The Globe,* Ajax, Ontario
2001   • Wrote stories about local issues and personalities
                         • Interviewed political candidates
                         • Edited and proofread copy
                         • Contributed photographs
                         • Coedited "The Landscapes of Northern Canada:
                           A Photoessay"

Summers   Tutor, Ajax ESL Program
2000, 2001   • Tutored Latino students in English as a second language
                         • Trained new tutors

ACTIVITIES   Photographers' Workshop, French Club

REFERENCES   Available upon request

Scannable résumés

Scannable résumés are submitted on paper or via e-mail. The prospective employer puts the résumé through a scanner that enters the information from it into a database; the database matches keywords in a job description with keywords in the résumé. If a résumé survives the initial scan, it will later be reviewed by human beings.

A scannable résumé must be very simply formatted so that the scanner can accurately pick up its content. In general, follow these guidelines when preparing a scannable résumé:

— Include a Keywords section that gives characteristics of your experience that match the job description. Use nouns such as *manager,* not verbs such as *manage* or *managed.*

— Use standard résumé headings (for example, Education, Work Experience, References).

— Do not use graphic devices such as boldface or italics. To indicate italics, use an underscore before and after italicized words.

— Do not use word processor formatting, such as tabbed indents, columns, or bullets. Do not insert visuals.

— Use white, letter-sized paper and a laser or an ink-jet printer. Avoid folding or stapling the document.

Web résumés

A Web résumé makes it easy to provide prospective employers with recent information about your employment goals and accomplishments. It also allows you to present a number of details about yourself without overwhelming your readers. You can keep your opening screen simple and provide hyperlinks to take readers farther down the page. Readers can follow up on links as they choose.

Although Web résumés can vary considerably in scope and depth, you should generally adhere to the following guidelines:

— Put identifying information—your name, address, phone number, and e-mail address—at the top. Include a link to your e-mail address.

—Include a Keywords section. Keywords allow potential employers to find your résumé using a database.

—Be as concise as possible on the opening screen.

—Place links to sections such as Education and Experience high enough on the screen that readers won't need to scroll to see them.

—Keep your résumé current, and list the date on which you last updated it.

—Present traditional résumé information (key contact information and credentials) on a single, printable home page. Only supplementary materials, such as writing or design samples, should appear on linked internal pages.

D3-c Memos

Business memos (short for *memorandums*) are a form of communication used within a company or organization. Usually brief and to the point, a memo reports information, makes a request, or recommends an action. The format of a memo, which varies from company to company, is designed for easy distribution, quick reading, and efficient filing.

Most memos display the date, the name of the recipient, the name of the sender, and the subject on separate lines at the top of the page. Many companies have preprinted forms for memos, and some word processing programs allow you to call up a memo template that prints standard memo lines — "To," "cc" (for others receiving a copy of the memo), "From," and "Subject" — at the top of the page.

Because readers of memos are busy people, you cannot assume that they will read your memo word-for-word. Therefore the subject line should describe the subject as clearly and concisely as possible, and the introductory paragraph should get right to the point. In addition, the body of the memo should be well organized and easy to scan. To promote scanning, use headings where possible and display any items that deserve special attention by setting them off from the text. A sample memo with headings and a displayed list appears on page 72.

BUSINESS MEMO

Commonwealth Press

MEMORANDUM

February 5, 2002

To: Production, promotion, and editorial assistants

cc: Stephen Chapman

From: Helen Brown

Subject: New computers for staff

We will receive the new personal computers next week for the assistants in production, promotion, and editorial. In preparation, I would like you to take part in a training program and to rearrange your work areas to accommodate the new equipment.

Training Program

A computer consultant will teach in-house workshops on how to use our spreadsheet program. If you have already tried the program, be prepared to discuss any problems you have encountered.

Workshops for our three departments will be held in the training room at the following times:

- Production: Monday, March 4, 10:00 a.m. to 2:00 p.m.
- Promotion: Wednesday, March 6, 10:00 a.m. to 2:00 p.m.
- Editorial: Friday, March 8, 10:00 a.m. to 2:00 p.m.

Lunch will be provided in the cafeteria. If you cannot attend, please let me know by March 1.

Allocation and Setup

To give everyone access to a computer, we will set up the new computers as follows: two in the assistants' workspace in production; two in the area outside the conference room for the promotion assistants; and two in the library for the editorial assistants.

Assistants in all three departments should see me before the end of the week to discuss preparation of the spaces for the new equipment.

D4

Create effective electronic documents.

ON THE WEB

For links to advice on using and distributing electronic documents, including avoiding spam (unsolicited e-mail), participating in on-line discussion groups, and designing user-friendly Web pages, go to **www.dianahacker.com/writersref**

and click on ▶ **Links Library**
▶ **Document Design**

D4-a Follow the conventions of e-mail.

E-mail is fast replacing snail mail in the business world and in most people's personal lives. E-mail is also being used in the academic world for communication between professors and their students and among students in a class.

Especially in business and academic contexts, you will want to show readers that you value their time. Your message may be just one of many that your reader has to wade through. Here are some strategies for making an e-mail reader-friendly:

— Fill in the subject line with a meaningful, concise subject to help the reader sort through messages and set priorities.

— Put the most important part of your message where it will be seen on the first screen.

— For long, detailed messages, consider providing a summary at the beginning.

— Write concisely, and keep paragraphs fairly short, especially if your audience is likely to read your message on the screen. (In e-mails meant to be printed out, paragraphs can be somewhat longer.)

— Avoid writing in all capital letters or all lowercase letters, a practice that is easy on the writer but hard on the reader.

— Keep in mind that a recipient's e-mail system may not accept attachments. When possible, include the text of an attachment in the body of the e-mail.

— Proofread for typos and obvious errors that are likely to slow down or annoy the reader.

D4-b   Create effective Web sites.

Web sites in the academic and business worlds are usually aimed at audiences looking for ideas and information, not entertainment. You may have noticed that the most effective informational Web sites give you quick and easy access to what you're looking for.

A Web site consists of a home page and internal pages linked to the home page. Deciding what to put on the home page and how to organize internal pages can present a challenge. When making such decisions, consider your readers' needs and expectations:

— Why are they visiting your site?

— What are they expecting to find?

— What is their level of interest?

— Do they plan to read on-screen or to print hard copy?

The design of your site will depend on the answers to such questions.

The home page

A home page consists of text and visuals on an opening screen and any other material that can be reached by scrolling. Because many Web users will resist scrolling — at least initially — you will need to take advantage of the opening screen.

The opening screen of your home page should introduce visitors to the site, give them an overview of its contents, and show them that you have their needs (not your own agenda) in mind. It should also include navigational links, words or visual images that, at the click of the mouse, will send them to other locations or pages within the site. Usually these links are clustered together — often along the top of the screen or on one side — leaving room in the centre for the name of the author or sponsor, the title, a relevant visual or two, and an indication of the purpose of the site. The following example illustrates a well-designed opening screen; the site sponsors community service and teaching internships for students.

SAMPLE HOME PAGE

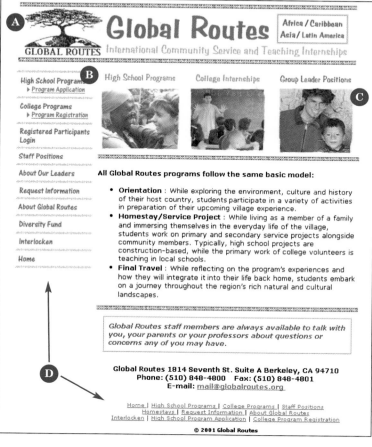

Global Routes Africa / Caribbean Asia / Latin America

GLOBAL ROUTES International Community Service and Teaching Internships

High School Programs
▸ Program Application

College Programs
▸ Program Registration

Registered Participants
Login

Staff Positions

About Our Leaders

Request Information

About Global Routes

Diversity Fund

Interlocken

Home

High School Programs   College Internships   Group Leader Positions

All Global Routes programs follow the same basic model:

- **Orientation** : While exploring the environment, culture and history of their host country, students participate in a variety of activities in preparation of their upcoming village experience.
- **Homestay/Service Project** : While living as a member of a family and immersing themselves in the everyday life of the village, students work on primary and secondary service projects alongside community members. Typically, high school projects are construction-based, while the primary work of college volunteers is teaching in local schools.
- **Final Travel** : While reflecting on the program's experiences and how they will integrate it into their life back home, students embark on a journey throughout the region's rich natural and cultural landscapes.

Global Routes staff members are always available to talk with you, your parents or your professors about questions or concerns any of you may have.

Global Routes 1814 Seventh St. Suite A Berkeley, CA 94710
Phone: (510) 848-4800   Fax: (510) 848-4801
E-mail: mail@globalroutes.org

Home | High School Programs | College Programs | Staff Positions
Homestays | Request Information | About Global Routes
Interlocken | High School Program Application | College Program Registration

© 2001 Global Routes

Ⓐ The sponsoring organization and purpose of the site are clearly defined at the top of the page.

Ⓑ By highlighting the main audiences for the site, this home page allows readers to skip information that is not relevant to their search.

Ⓒ Appealing visual images emphasize the site's three main audiences.

Ⓓ Links to internal pages are consistently placed on the left side of the screen and in the footer to help readers navigate the site.

Structure and navigation

Web sites often have hierarchical structures: General pages link to more specific pages, which in turn may link to even more specific pages. At the bottom of this page is an example of a Web site structure for a chain of fitness centres.

How shallow or how deep should your hierarchy be? In other words, how many levels make sense? The answer depends on the complexity of your material and your audience's needs, but two cautions are in order. A structure is too shallow if your readers must deal with long "laundry lists" of choices (unless they can be arranged alphabetically or by date). A structure is too deep if readers are needlessly forced to drill down through several layers of your hierarchy to reach what they need.

Visitors to your site will navigate it in different ways, depending on their interests. They will choose some links and ignore others, landing on internal pages in an order that you can't predict. Indeed, some visitors may arrive at one of your internal pages without having gone through your home page. Because of this unpredictability, provide as much context as possible for each internal page:

— Put key information on each internal page: a title, a link to the home page, and perhaps a list of links to other pages (such lists create context by outlining the site).

— Provide a brief overview that puts the internal page in context; make sure the content of the page can be understood on its own.

SAMPLE WEB SITE STRUCTURE

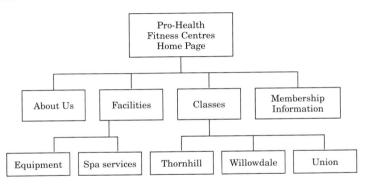

—Repeat design elements so that visitors will feel at home: Place navigational aids consistently, and use consistent background colours, fonts, visual motifs, and formatting.

In addition to providing links within your site, you may want to link to other sites. When you decide that an external link enhances the message of your site, create some context for it so that visitors will understand why it is worthwhile and what to expect if they follow it. Because a link to another site is an implicit endorsement of that site, you should evaluate potential sites before linking to them. Also check your links to external sites periodically to make sure the sites are still functioning.

Page layout and writing style

Don't expect Web site visitors to read in the traditional way. Most will scan your site, looking for information of interest and ignoring the rest. To keep the attention of a Web audience, make your page layout and writing style as user-friendly as possible.

EXCEPTION: If content on your site is scholarly work meant to be printed out, you can assume that your audience is motivated to read, not just to scan. Even so, visitors will appreciate a reader-friendly page layout and writing style.

PAGE LAYOUT   To promote easy scanning, break up your text with headings and displayed lists and, when appropriate, display information with graphics such as clip art, photos, and charts. (See D1-b, D1-c, and D1-d.)

Some common design practices make a site needlessly hard to read. If you are an experienced Web user, you no doubt could have written the following advice:

—Don't stretch lines of text across the full width of the screen. The reader's eye gets lost as it swoops from line to line.

—Limit page width so readers do not need to scroll sideways.

—Avoid ALL CAPS or *all italic* text. It slows readers down.

—Steer clear of busy backgrounds that make the print illegible.

—Avoid nonstop animations. They are distracting.

Graphics and other media, such as films and sound clips, can enhance a Web site, but they should be used thoughtfully—to support your message. If you've used a lot of graphics, provide a printable version of your text minus the graphics; graphics can be slow to print and may be irrelevant for your readers' purposes.

WRITING STYLE   As a rule, visitors to your Web site want concise, factual information that they can understand right away. For example, they expect to learn the key idea of a paragraph in its first sentence; if it's not there, they may well move on. They also prefer sentences that waste no words; a verbose, pseudointellectual style will send them elsewhere.

Web users are also sensitive to tone. There is so much promotional hype on the Web that many users have a keen ear for it. The tone of your site will vary, of course, depending on your purpose and audience, but in general aim for an objective—not a promotional—tone.

PROMOTIONAL

Our site tells you everything you want to know about hang gliding! Check out our awesome video clips and click on links to the coolest sites on the Web.

OBJECTIVE

Whether you're a beginning hang glider or a seasoned flier, this site will show you how and where to glide. Visit our Video Window for an animated bird's-eye view.

An objective tone enhances your credibility and makes it likely that readers will trust you enough to stay with you.

S

Sentence
Style

S

Sentence Style

S1

Parallelism

If two or more ideas are parallel, they are easier to grasp when expressed in parallel grammatical form. Single words should be balanced with single words, phrases with phrases, clauses with clauses.

A kiss can be a comma, a question mark, or an exclamation point.
— Mistinguett

This novel is not to be tossed lightly aside, but to be hurled with great force.
— Dorothy Parker

In matters of principle, stand like a rock; in matters of taste, swim with the current.
— Thomas Jefferson

GRAMMAR CHECKERS do not flag faulty parallelism. Because computer programs have no way of assessing whether two or more ideas are parallel in meaning, they fail to catch the faulty parallelism in sentences such as this: *In my high school, boys were either jocks, preppies, or studied constantly.*

S1-a Balance parallel ideas in a series.

Readers expect items in a series to appear in parallel grammatical form. When one or more of the items violate readers' expectations, a sentence will be needlessly awkward.

▶ Abused children commonly exhibit one or more of the following symptoms: withdrawal, rebelliousness, restlessness, and *depression.*
~~they are depressed.~~

The revision presents all of the items as nouns.

▶ Hooked on romance novels, I learned that nothing is more
important than being rich, looking good, and ~~to have~~ a good
                                                having

time.

The revision uses *-ing* forms for all items in the series.

▶ After assuring us that he was sober, Sam drove down the middle
                               went through
of the road, ran one red light, and two stop signs.

The revision adds a verb to make the three items parallel: *drove . . . ,*
ran . . . , went through. . . .

NOTE: For parallelism in headings and lists, see D1-b and D1-c.

S1-b Balance parallel ideas presented as pairs.

When pairing ideas, underscore their connection by expressing
them in similar grammatical form. Paired ideas are usually connected in one of these ways:

   —with a coordinating conjunction such as *and, but,* or *or*

   —with a pair of correlative conjunctions such as *either. . . or*
     or *not only . . . but also*

   —with a word introducing a comparison, usually *than* or *as*

Parallel ideas linked with coordinating conjunctions

Coordinating conjunctions (*and, but, or, nor, for, so,* and *yet*) link
ideas of equal importance. When those ideas are closely parallel in
content, they should be expressed in parallel grammatical form.

▶ At Laurier Collegiate, vandalism can result in suspension
                   expulsion
or even ~~being expelled~~ from school.

The revision balances the nouns *suspension* and *expulsion.*

▶ Many states are reducing property taxes for home owners and
           extending
~~extend~~ financial aid in the form of tax credits to renters.

The revision balances the *-ing* verb forms *reducing* and *extending.*

Parallel ideas linked with correlative conjunctions

Correlative conjunctions come in pairs: *either. . . or, neither. . . nor, not only. . . but also, both . . . and, whether. . . or.* Make sure that the grammatical structure following the second half of the pair is the same as that following the first half.

▶ Alexander Graham Bell was not only a prolific inventor but also

~~was~~ a devoted educator.

A prolific inventor follows *not only,* so *a devoted educator* should follow *but also.* Repeating *was* creates an unbalanced effect.

▶ I was advised either to change my flight or ^to^ take the train.

To change my flight, which follows *either,* should be balanced with *to take the train,* which follows *or.*

Comparisons linked with *than* or as

In comparisons linked with *than* or *as,* the elements being compared should be expressed in parallel grammatical structure.

▶ It is easier to speak in abstractions than ^to ground^ ~~grounding~~ one's thoughts

in reality.

▶ Mother could not persuade me that giving is as much a joy as receiving.
~~to receive.~~

To speak in abstractions is balanced with *to ground one's thoughts in reality. Giving* is balanced with *receiving.*

NOTE: Comparisons should also be logical and complete. See S2-c.

S1-c Repeat function words to clarify parallels.

Function words such as prepositions (*by, to*) and subordinating conjunctions (*that, because*) signal the grammatical nature of the word groups to follow. Although they can sometimes be omitted, include them whenever they signal parallel structures that might otherwise be missed by readers.

▶ Many hooked smokers try switching to a brand
to
they find distasteful or⌃a low tar and nicotine

cigarette.

In the original sentence the prepositional phrase was too complex for easy reading. The repetition of the preposition *to* prevents readers from losing their way.

ON THE WEB

For electronic exercises on parallelism, go to
www.dianahacker.com/writersref

and click on ▶ **Electronic Grammar Exercises**
　　　　　　▶ **Sentence Style**
　　　　　　　▶ **E-ex S1–1 through S1–3**

S2

Needed words

Do not omit words necessary for grammatical or logical completeness. Readers need to see at a glance how the parts of a sentence are connected.

Languages sometimes differ in the need for certain words. In particular, be alert for missing articles, verbs, subjects, or expletives. See T1, T2-e, and T3-a.

GRAMMAR CHECKERS do not flag the vast majority of missing words. They can, however, catch some missing verbs (see G2-e). Although they can flag some missing articles (*a*, *an*, and *the*), they often suggest that an article is missing when in fact it is not. (See also T1.)

S2-a Add words needed to complete compound structures.

In compound structures, words are often omitted for economy: *Tom is a man who means what he says and [who] says what he means.* Such omissions are perfectly acceptable as long as the omitted word is common to both parts of the compound structure.

If the shorter version defies grammar or idiom because an omitted word is not common to both parts of the compound structure, the word must be put back in.

▶ Some of the regulars are acquaintances whom we see at work or *who*

 live in our community.

 The word *who* must be included because *whom live in our community* is not grammatically correct.

▶ Mayor Davis never has and never will *accepted* accept a bribe.

 Has . . . accept is not grammatically correct.

▶ Many South Pacific tribes still believe *in* and live by ancient

 laws.

 Believe . . . by is not idiomatic English.

S2-b Add the word *that* if there is any danger of misreading without it.

If there is no danger of misreading, the word *that* may sometimes be omitted when it introduces a subordinate clause: *The value of a principle is the number of things [that] it will explain.* Occasionally, however, a sentence might be misread without *that*.

▶ From the family room Sarah saw *that* her favourite tree, which she had

 climbed so often as a child, was gone.

 Sarah didn't see the tree; she saw that the tree was gone.

S2-c   Add words needed to make comparisons logical and complete.

Comparisons should be made between like items. To compare unlike items is illogical and distracting.

▶ The forests of North America are much more extensive than
those of
Europe.
  ^

Forests must be compared with forests.

                                Our   *graduate at a higher rate*
▶ ~~The graduation rate of our~~ student athletes ~~is higher~~ than the
                           ^   ^

rest of the student population.

A rate cannot be logically compared with a population. The writer could revise the sentence by inserting *that of* after *than,* but the preceding revision is more concise.

▶ Some say that Ella Fitzgerald's renditions of Cole Porter's songs
                         singer's.
are better than any other ~~singer.~~
                          ^

Ella Fitzgerald's renditions cannot be logically compared with a singer. The revision uses the possessive form *singer's,* with the word *renditions* being implied.

Sometimes the word *other* must be inserted to make a comparison logical.

                     other
▶ Jupiter is larger than any planet in our solar system.
                          ^

Jupiter cannot be larger than itself.

Sometimes the word *as* must be inserted to make a comparison grammatically correct.

                               as
▶ The city of Fredericton is as old, if not older than, the neighbouring
                                  ^

city of Moncton.

The construction *as old* is not complete without a second *as: as old as . . . the neighbouring city of Moncton.*

Comparisons should be complete enough so that readers will understand what is being compared.

INCOMPLETE   Brand X is less salty.

COMPLETE   Brand X is less salty than Brand Y.

Also, you should leave no ambiguity about meaning. In the following sentence, two interpretations are possible.

AMBIGUOUS   Mr. Kelly helped me more than Sam.

CLEAR   Mr. Kelly helped me more than he helped Sam.

CLEAR   Mr. Kelly helped me more than Sam did.

S2-d Add the articles *a, an,* and *the* where necessary for grammatical completeness.

Articles are sometimes omitted in recipes and other instructions that are meant to be followed while they are being read. Such omissions are inappropriate, however, in nearly all other forms of writing, whether formal or informal.

▶ Blood can be drawn only by *a* doctor or by *an* authorized person who has been trained in *the* procedure.

It is not always necessary to repeat articles with paired items: *We bought a computer and printer.* However, if one of the items requires *a* and the other requires *an,* both articles must be included.

▶ We bought a computer and *an* ink-jet printer.

ON THE WEB

For electronic exercises on adding needed words, go to
www.dianahacker.com/writersref

and click on ▶ **Electronic Grammar Exercises**
        ▶ **Sentence Style**
           ▶ **E-ex S2–1 and S2–2**

S3

Problems with modifiers

Modifiers, whether they are single words, phrases, or clauses, should point clearly to the words they modify. As a rule, related words should be kept together.

GRAMMAR CHECKERS can flag split infinitives, such as *to carefully and thoroughly sift* (S3-d). However, they don't alert you to other problems with modifiers, including danglers like this one: *When a young man, my mother enrolled me in tap dance classes, hoping I would become the next Gregory Hines.*

S3-a Put limiting modifiers in front of the words they modify.

Limiting modifiers such as *only, even, almost, nearly,* and *just* should appear in front of a verb only if they modify the verb: *At first I couldn't even touch my toes.* If they limit the meaning of some other word in the sentence, they should be placed in front of that word.

> ▶ Lasers ~~only~~ destroy ^{*only*} the target, leaving the surrounding healthy
>
> tissue intact.

> ▶ The turtle ~~only~~ makes progress ^{*only*} when it sticks its neck out.

The limiting modifier *not* is frequently misplaced, suggesting a meaning the writer did not intend.

> ▶ In the United States in 1860, ^{*not*} all black southerners were ~~not~~
>
> slaves.
>
> The original sentence says that no black southerners were slaves. The revision makes the writer's real meaning clear: Some (but not all) black southerners were slaves.

S3-b   Place phrases and clauses so that readers can see at a glance what they modify.

Although phrases and clauses can appear at some distance from the words they modify, make sure that your meaning is clear. When phrases or clauses are oddly placed, absurd misreadings can result.

MISPLACED   The child returned to the clinic where he had undergone heart surgery in a limousine sent by an anonymous benefactor.

REVISED   Traveling in a limousine sent by an anonymous benefactor, the child returned to the clinic where he had undergone heart surgery.

The king did not undergo heart surgery in a limousine. The revision corrects this false impression.

▶   *On the walls*
     ~~There~~ are many pictures of comedians who have performed at
         ^
     Gavin's. ~~on the walls.~~
             ^

The comedians weren't performing on the walls; the pictures were on the walls.

▶   *70-kg,*
     The robber was described as a 180-cm-tall man with a mustache.
                                      ^   ^
     ~~weighing 70 kg.~~

The robber, not the mustache, weighed 70 kg.

Occasionally the placement of a modifier leads to an ambiguity, in which case two revisions will be possible, depending on the writer's intended meaning.

AMBIGUOUS   The exchange students we met for coffee occasionally questioned us about our latest slang.

CLEAR   The exchange students we occasionally met for coffee questioned us about our latest slang.

CLEAR   The exchange students we met for coffee questioned us occasionally about our latest slang.

In the original version, it was not clear whether the meeting or the questioning happened occasionally. The revisions eliminate the ambiguity.

S3-c Move awkwardly placed modifiers.

As a rule, a sentence should flow from subject to verb to object, without lengthy detours along the way. When a long adverbial element separates a subject from its verb, a verb from its object, or a helping verb from its main verb, the result is usually awkward.

> ▶ ~~Hong Kong,~~ after more than 150 years of British rule, was
>   *Hong Kong*
>
>   transferred back to Chinese control in 1997.

There is no reason to separate the subject *Hong Kong* from the verb *was transferred* with a long adverb phrase.

EXCEPTION: Occasionally a writer may choose to delay a verb or an object to create suspense. In the following passage, for example, Robert Mueller inserts the *after* phrase between the subject *women* and the verb *walk* to heighten the dramatic effect.

> I asked a Burmese why women, after centuries of following their men, now walk ahead. He said there were many unexploded land mines since the war. —Robert Mueller

S3-d Avoid split infinitives when they are awkward.

An infinitive consists of *to* plus a verb: *to think, to breathe, to dance.* When a modifier appears between its two parts, an infinitive is said to be "split": *to carefully balance.*

When a long word or a phrase appears between the parts of the infinitive, the result is usually awkward.

> *If possible, patients*
> ▶ ~~Patients~~ should try to ~~if possible~~ avoid going up and down stairs.

Attempts to avoid split infinitives can result in equally awkward sentences. When alternative phrasing sounds unnatural, most experts allow—and even encourage—splitting the infinitive.

> AWKWARD   We decided actually to enforce the law.
>
> BETTER   We decided to actually enforce the law.

At times, neither the split infinitive nor its alternative sounds particularly awkward. In such situations, you may want to unsplit the infinitive, especially in formal writing.

▶ The candidate decided to ~~formally~~ launch her campaign⟋ *formally.*

ON THE WEB

The rules on avoiding split infinitives have sparked debates. If you're interested in learning why, go to
www.dianahacker.com/writersref

and click on ▶ **Language Debates**
　　　　　　　 ▶ **Split infinitives**

S3-e Repair dangling modifiers.

A dangling modifier fails to refer logically to any word in the sentence. Dangling modifiers are easy to repair, but they can be hard to recognize, especially in your own writing.

Recognizing dangling modifiers

Dangling modifiers are usually word groups (such as verbal phrases) that suggest but do not name an actor. When a sentence opens with such a modifier, readers expect the subject of the next clause to name the actor. If it doesn't, the modifier dangles.

▶ *When the driver opened*
　~~Opening~~ the window to let out a huge bumblebee, the car

accidentally swerved into an oncoming car.

The car didn't open the window; the driver did.

▶ After completing seminary training, ~~women's~~ access to the pulpit⟋ *women have often been denied*

~~has often been denied.~~

The women (not their access to the pulpit) complete the training.

The following sentences illustrate four common kinds of dangling modifiers.

DANGLING　*Deciding to join the navy,* the recruiter enthusiastically pumped Joe's hand. [Participial phrase]

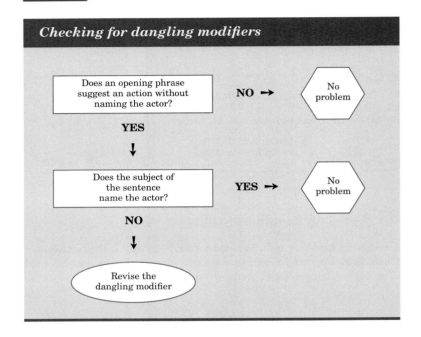

Checking for dangling modifiers

Does an opening phrase suggest an action without naming the actor? — **NO →** No problem

YES
↓

Does the subject of the sentence name the actor? — **YES →** No problem

NO
↓

Revise the dangling modifier

DANGLING *Upon entering the doctor's office,* a skeleton caught my attention. [Preposition followed by a gerund phrase]

DANGLING *To please the children,* some fireworks were set off a day early. [Infinitive phrase]

DANGLING *Though only sixteen,* UCLA accepted Martha's application. [Elliptical clause with an understood subject and verb]

These dangling modifiers falsely suggest that the recruiter decided to join the navy, that the skeleton entered the doctor's office, that the fireworks intended to please the children, and that UCLA is sixteen years old.

Although most readers will understand the writer's intended meaning in such sentences, the inadvertent humour can be distracting, and it can make the writer appear somewhat foolish.

ON THE WEB

The rules on avoiding dangling modifiers have sparked debates. If you're interested in learning why, go to
www.dianahacker.com/writersref

and click on ▶ **Language Debates**
▶ **Dangling modifiers**

Repairing dangling modifiers

To repair a dangling modifier, you can revise the sentence in one of two ways:

1. Name the actor in the subject of the sentence or
2. name the actor in the modifier.

Depending on your sentence, one of these revision strategies may be more appropriate than the other.

ACTOR NAMED IN SUBJECT

> Upon entering the doctor's office, a skeleton *I noticed*, ~~caught my attention.~~
>   ^   ^

> To please the children, *we set off* some fireworks ~~were set off~~ a day early.
>   ^

ACTOR NAMED IN MODIFIER

> *When Joe decided* ~~Deciding~~ to join the navy, the recruiter enthusiastically pumped
> ^*his*
> ~~Joe's~~ hand.
> ^

> Though only sixteen years old, *Martha was* UCLA accepted *her* ~~Martha's~~
>   ^   ^
> application.

NOTE: You cannot repair a dangling modifier just by moving it. Consider, for example, the sentence about the skeleton. If you put the modifier at the end of the sentence (*A skeleton caught my attention upon entering the doctor's office*), you are still suggesting — absurdly, of course — that the skeleton entered the office. The only way to avoid the problem is to put the word *I* in the sentence, either as the subject or in the modifier. (See p. 94 for examples.)

I noticed
▶ Upon entering the doctor's office, a skeleton. ~~caught my attention.~~
                                          ^   ^

As I entered
▶ ~~Upon entering~~ the doctor's office, a skeleton caught my attention.
  ^

ON THE WEB

For electronic exercises on misplaced and dangling modifiers, go to
www.dianahacker.com/writersref

and click on ▶ **Electronic Grammar Exercises**
                ▶ **Sentence Style**
                  ▶ **E-ex S3–1 through S3–4**

S4

Shifts

 GRAMMAR CHECKERS do not flag the shifts discussed in this section. Even the most obvious errors such as this one will slip right past most grammar checkers: *My three-year-old fell into the pool and to my surprise she swims to the shallow end.*

S4-a Make the point of view consistent.

The point of view of a piece of writing is the perspective from which it is written: first person (*I* or *we*), second person (*you*), or third person (*he / she / it / one* or *they*). The *I* (or *we*) point of view, which emphasizes the writer, is a good choice for informal letters and writing based primarily on personal experience. The *you* point of view, which emphasizes the reader, works well for giving advice or explaining how to do something. The third-person point of view, which emphasizes the subject, is appropriate in formal academic and professional writing.

Writers who are having difficulty settling on an appropriate point of view sometimes shift confusingly from one to another. The solution is to choose a suitable perspective and then stay with it.

> One week our class met in a junkyard to practise rescuing a
>
> victim trapped in a wrecked car. We learned to dismantle the car
>
> ~~You~~ were graded on ~~your~~ speed and ~~your~~
> with the essential tools. *We*   *our*   *our*
>
> skill in extricating the victim.

The writer should have stayed with the *we* point of view. *You* is inappropriate because the writer is not addressing the reader directly. (See also G3-b.)

> *You*
> ~~Everyone~~ should purchase a lift ticket unless you plan to spend
>
> most of your time walking or crawling up a steep hill.

Here *You* is an appropriate choice, since the writer is giving advice directly to readers.

Shifts from the third-person singular to the third-person plural are especially common.

> *Police officers are*
> ~~A police officer is~~ often criticized for always being there when
>
> they aren't needed and never being there when they are.

The writer shifted from the third-person singular (*police officer*) to the third-person plural (*they*). (See also G3-a.)

S4-b Maintain consistent verb tenses.

Consistent verb tenses clearly establish the time of the actions being described. When a passage begins in one tense and then shifts without warning and for no reason to another, readers are distracted and confused.

> There was no way I could fight the current. Just as I was losing
>
> *jumped*   *swam*
> hope, a stranger ~~jumps~~ off a passing boat and ~~swims~~ toward me.

Writers often shift verb tenses when writing about literature. The literary convention is to describe fictional events consistently in the present tense. (See also G2-f.)

► The scarlet letter is a punishment sternly placed on Hester's

  breast by the community, and yet it ~~was~~ an extremely fanciful and
  ^{is}

  imaginative product of Hester's own needlework.

S4-c Make verbs consistent in mood and voice.

Unnecessary shifts in the mood of a verb can be as distracting as needless shifts in tense. There are three moods in English: the indicative, used for facts, opinions, and questions; the imperative, used for orders or advice; and the subjunctive, used for wishes or conditions contrary to fact. (See G2-g.)

The following passage shifts confusingly from the indicative to the imperative mood.

► The officers advised against allowing access to our homes

  without proper identification. ~~Also,~~ alert neighbours to
  They also suggested that we

  vacation schedules.

  Since the writer's purpose was to report the officers' advice, the revision puts both sentences in the indicative.

The voice of a verb may be either active (with the subject doing the action) or passive (with the subject receiving the action). (See W3-a.) If a writer shifts without warning from one to the other, readers may be left wondering why.

► When the tickets are ready, the travel agent notifies the client/,

  ~~Each~~ ticket ~~is then listed~~ on a daily register form, and a copy of
  lists each   *files*

  the itinerary. ~~is filed.~~

  The original version began in the active voice (*agent notifies*) and then switched to the passive (*ticket is listed . . . copy is filed*). Because the active voice is clearer and more direct, the writer put all the verbs in the active voice.

S4-d Avoid sudden shifts from indirect to direct questions or quotations.

An indirect question reports a question without asking it: *We asked whether we could take a swim.* A direct question asks directly: *Can we take a swim?* Sudden shifts from indirect to direct questions are awkward.

► I wonder whether the sister knew about the theft and, if so,
    whether she reported
    ~~did she report~~ it to the police.
    ^

The revision poses both questions indirectly. The writer could also ask both questions directly: *Did the sister know about the theft and, if so, did she report it to the police?*

An indirect quotation reports someone's words without quoting word-for-word: *Anna said that she is a teacher.* A direct quotation presents someone's exact words, set off with quotation marks: *Anna said, "I am a teacher."* Unannounced shifts from indirect to direct quotations are distracting and confusing.

► Mother said that she would be an hour late for dinner and
    asked me not to   *came*
    ~~please do not~~ leave for choir practice until Dad ~~comes~~
    ^   ^

home from work.

The revision reports all of the mother's words. The writer could also quote the mother's words directly: *Mother said, "I will be an hour late for dinner. Please do not leave for choir practice until Dad comes home from work."*

ON THE WEB

For electronic exercises on distracting shifts, go to
www.dianahacker.com/writersref

and click on ► **Electronic Grammar Exercises**
               ► **Sentence Style**
                    ► **E-ex S4–1 through S4–4**

S5

Mixed constructions

A mixed construction contains elements that do not sensibly fit together. The mismatch may be a matter of grammar or of logic.

 GRAMMAR CHECKERS can flag *is when, is where,* and *reason . . . is because* constructions (S5-c), but they fail to identify nearly all other mixed constructions, including sentences as tangled as this one: *Depending on the number and strength of drinks, the amount of time that has passed, and one's body weight determines the concentration of alcohol in the blood.*

S5-a Untangle the grammatical structure.

Once you head into a sentence, your choices are limited by the range of grammatical patterns in English. (See B2 and B3.) You cannot begin with one grammatical plan and switch without warning to another.

> **MIXED** For most drivers who have a blood alcohol level of 0.05 percent double their risk of causing an accident.

> **REVISED** For most drivers who have a blood alcohol level of 0.05 percent, the risk of causing an accident is doubled.

> **REVISED** Most drivers who have a blood alcohol level of 0.05 percent double their risk of causing an accident.

The writer began with a long prepositional phrase that was destined to be a modifier but then tried to press it into service as the subject of the sentence. This cannot be done. If the sentence is to begin with the prepositional phrase, the writer must finish the sentence with a subject and verb (*risk . . . is doubled*). The writer who wishes to stay with the original verb (*double*) must head into the sentence another way (*Most drivers . . .*).

>   *Being*
> ▶ ~~When an employee is~~ promoted without warning can be alarming.
>   ^

The adverb clause *When an employee is promoted without warning* cannot serve as the subject of the sentence. The revision replaces the adverb clause with a gerund phrase, a word group that can function as the subject. (See B3-b and B3-e.)

▶ **Although Canada is one of the wealthiest nations in the world,**

~~but~~ **almost 17 percent of our children live in poverty.**

The *Although* clause is subordinate, so it cannot be linked to an independent clause with the coordinating conjunction *but*. (If you speak English as a second language, see also T3-d.)

Occasionally a mixed construction is so tangled that it defies grammatical analysis. When this happens, back away from the sentence, rethink what you want to say, and then say it again as clearly as you can.

> MIXED   In the whole-word method children learn to recognize entire words rather than by the phonics method in which they learn to sound out letters and groups of letters.
>
> REVISED   The whole-word method teaches children to recognize entire words; the phonics method teaches them to sound out letters and groups of letters.

ESL

English does not allow double subjects, nor does it allow an object or adverb to be repeated in an adjective clause. See T3-b and T3-c.

S5-b Straighten out the logical connections.

The subject and the predicate should make sense together. When they don't, the error is known as *faulty predication*.

▶ **Reluctantly we decided that** ~~Tiffany's welfare~~ **would not be safe**
                                                  Tiffany

living with her mother.

Tiffany, not her welfare, would not be safe.

► Under the revised plan, seniors, ~~who now receive a double~~ *the double personal exemption for*
^

~~personal exemption,~~ will be abolished.

The exemption, not the seniors, will be abolished.

An appositive and the noun to which it refers should be logically equivalent. When they are not, the error is known as *faulty apposition.*

► ~~The tax accountant,~~ a very lucrative field, requires intelligence, *Tax accounting,*
^

patience, and attention to detail.

The tax accountant is a person, not a field.

S5-c Avoid *is when, is where,* and *reason . . . is because* constructions.

In formal English many readers object to *is when, is where,* and *reason . . . is because* constructions on either logical or grammatical grounds.

► Anorexia nervosa is ~~where people,~~ believing they are too fat, diet *a disorder suffered by people who,*
^

to the point of starvation.

Anorexia nervosa is a disorder, not a place.

► ~~The reason~~ I was late ~~is~~ because my motorcycle broke down.

The writer might have replaced the word *because* with *that,* but the preceding revision is more concise.

ON THE WEB

For electronic exercises on mixed constructions, go to
www.dianahacker.com/writersref

and click on ► **Electronic Grammar Exercises**
► **Sentence Style**
► **E-ex S5–1 and S5–2**

S6

Sentence emphasis

Within each sentence, emphasize your point by expressing it in the subject and verb of an independent clause, the words that receive the most attention from readers (see S6-a to S6-e).

Within longer stretches of prose, you can draw attention to ideas deserving special emphasis by using a variety of techniques, often involving an unusual twist or some element of surprise (see S6-f).

S6-a Coordinate equal ideas; subordinate minor ideas.

When combining two or more ideas in one sentence, you have two choices: coordination or subordination. Choose coordination to indicate that the ideas are equal or nearly equal in importance. Choose subordination to indicate that one idea is less important than another.

Coordination

Coordination draws equal attention to two or more ideas. To coordinate words or phrases, join them with a coordinating conjunction (*and, but, or, nor, for, so, yet*). To coordinate independent clauses (word groups that can stand alone as sentences), join them with a comma and a coordinating conjunction or with a semicolon. The semicolon is often accompanied by a conjunctive adverb such as *therefore, moreover,* or *however.*

> Grandmother lost her sight, but her hearing sharpened.
>
> Grandmother lost her sight; however, her hearing sharpened.

Subordination

To give unequal emphasis to two or more ideas, express the major idea in an independent clause and place any minor ideas in subordinate clauses or phrases. (See B3.) Subordinate clauses, which cannot stand alone, typically begin with one of the following subordinating conjunctions or relative pronouns.

after	if	until	while
although	since	when	who
as	that	where	whom
because	though	whether	whose
before	unless	which	

Deciding which idea to emphasize is not simply a matter of right and wrong. Consider the two ideas about Grandmother's sight and hearing.

Grandmother lost her sight. Her hearing sharpened.

If your purpose is to stress your grandmother's acute hearing rather than her vision loss, subordinate the idea concerning her vision loss.

As Grandmother lost her sight, her hearing sharpened.

To focus on your grandmother's vision loss, subordinate the idea concerning her hearing.

Though her hearing sharpened, Grandmother gradually lost her sight.

S6-b Combine choppy sentences.

Short sentences demand attention, so they should be used primarily for emphasis. Too many short sentences, one after the other, create a choppy style.

If an idea is not important enough to deserve its own sentence, try combining it with a sentence close by. Put any minor ideas in subordinate structures such as phrases or subordinate clauses.

▶ We keep our use of insecticides, herbicides, and fungicides
to a minimum./~~We~~ *because we* are concerned about their effect on the
environment.

A minor idea is now expressed in a subordinate clause beginning with *because.*

▶ The St. Lawrence Seaway,~~is~~ a 3700-km waterway/, ~~It~~ links the
Great Lakes region to global markets.

A minor idea is now expressed in an appositive phrase (*a 3700-km waterway*). (See B3-c.)

▶ ~~Sister Consilio was~~ $\overset{E}{e}$nveloped in a black robe with only her face
  $\overset{Sister\ Consilio}{\text{and hands visible}/,\ \text{~~She~~}}$ was an imposing figure.

A minor idea is now expressed in a participial phrase beginning with *Enveloped*. (See B3-b.)

▶ My sister owes much of her recovery to a bodybuilding program/
  $\overset{that\ she}{\text{~~She~~}}$ began ~~the program~~ three years ago.

A minor idea is now expressed in an adjective clause beginning with *that*. (See B3-e.)

Although subordination is ordinarily the most effective technique for combining short, choppy sentences, coordination is appropriate when the ideas are equal in importance.

▶ The hospital decides when patients will sleep and wake/, ~~It~~ dictates
  $\overset{and}{\text{what and when they will eat}/,\ \text{~~It~~}}$ tells them when they may be with

  family and friends.

Three sentences have become one, with equivalent ideas expressed in a coordinate series.

ESL

> When combining sentences, do not repeat the subject of the sentence; also do not repeat an object or adverb in an adjective clause. See T3-b and T3-c.

ON THE WEB

For electronic exercises on combining choppy sentences, go to
www.dianahacker.com/writersref

and click on ▶ **Electronic Grammar Exercises**
  ▶ **Sentence Style**
    ▶ **E-ex S6–1 and S6–2**

S6-c Avoid ineffective coordination.

Coordinate structures are appropriate only when you intend to draw the reader's attention equally to two or more ideas: *Gregory praises loudly, and he criticizes softly.* If one idea is more important than another — or if a coordinating conjunction does not clearly signal the relation between the ideas — you should subordinate the lesser idea.

▶ *After four hours,*
~~Four hours went by, and~~ a rescue truck finally arrived, but by

that time the injured swimmer had been evacuated in a helicopter.

Three independent clauses were excessive. The least important idea has become a prepositional phrase. (See B3-a.)

S6-d Do not subordinate major ideas.

If a sentence buries its major idea in a subordinate construction, readers are not likely to give it enough attention. Express the major idea in an independent clause and subordinate any minor ideas.

▶ *had polio as a child,*
Lanie, who now walks with the help of braces/. ~~had polio as a~~

~~child.~~

The writer wanted to focus on Lanie's ability to walk, but the original sentence buried this idea in an adjective clause. The revision puts the major idea in an independent clause and tucks the less important idea into an adjective clause (*who had polio as a child*). (See B3-e.)

▶ *When*
Jason walked over to his new Miata, ~~and~~ he saw that its

windshield had been smashed.

The minor idea has become a subordinate clause beginning with *When.*

▶ *noticing*
My uncle, ~~noticed~~ my frightened look, ~~and~~ told me that the

dentures in the glass were not real teeth.

The less important idea has become a participial phrase modifying the noun *uncle.*

▶ As
  ⌃I was driving home from my new job, heading down Yonge Street,

  ~~when~~ my car suddenly overheated.

The revision puts the major idea—that the car overheated—in the independent clause and subordinates the other information. (See B3-e.)

ON THE WEB

For an electronic exercise on subordination, go to
www.dianahacker.com/writersref

and click on ▶ **Electronic Grammar Exercises**
                ▶ **Sentence Style**
                  ▶ **E-ex S6–3**

S6-e Do not subordinate excessively.

In attempting to avoid short, choppy sentences, writers sometimes move to the opposite extreme, putting more subordinate ideas into a sentence than its structure can bear. If a sentence collapses of its own weight, occasionally it can be restructured. More often, however, such sentences must be divided.

▶ Our job is to stay between the stacker and the tie machine
                                      If they do,
  watching to see if the newspapers jam/. ~~in which case~~ we pull the
                                  ⌃
  bundles off and stack them on a skid, because otherwise they

  would back up in the stacker.

S6-f Experiment with techniques for gaining special emphasis.

By experimenting with certain techniques, usually involving some element of surprise, you can draw attention to ideas that deserve special emphasis. Use such techniques sparingly, however, or they will lose their punch. The writer who tries to emphasize everything ends up emphasizing nothing.

Using sentence endings for emphasis

You can highlight an idea simply by withholding it until the end of a sentence. The technique works something like a punch line. In the following example, the sentence's meaning is not revealed until its very last word.

> The only completely consistent people are the dead.
> —Aldous Huxley

Using parallel structure for emphasis

Parallel grammatical structure draws special attention to paired ideas or to items in a series. (See S1.) When parallel ideas are paired, the emphasis falls on words that underscore comparisons or contrasts, especially when they occur at the end of a phrase or clause.

> We must *stop talking* about the *American dream* and *start listening* to the *dreams of Americans.*
> —Reubin Askew

In a parallel series, the emphasis falls at the end, so it is generally best to end with the most dramatic or climactic item in the series.

> Sister Charity enjoyed passing out writing punishments: translate the Ten Commandments into Latin, type a thousand-word essay on good manners, copy the New Testament with a quill pen.
> —Marie Visosky, student

Using an occasional short sentence for emphasis

Too many short sentences in a row will fast become monotonous (see S6-b), but an occasional short sentence, when played off against longer sentences in the same passage, will draw attention to an idea.

> The great secret, known to internists and learned early in marriage by internists' wives [or husbands], but still hidden from the general public, is that most things get better by themselves. Most things, in fact, are better by morning.
> —Lewis Thomas

S7

Sentence variety

When a rough draft is filled with too many same-sounding sentences, try to inject some variety—as long as you can do so without sacrificing clarity or ease of reading.

 GRAMMAR CHECKERS are of little help with sentence variety. It takes a human ear to know when and why sentence variety is needed.

Some programs tell you when you have used the same word to open several sentences, but sometimes it is a good idea to do so—if you are trying to highlight parallel ideas, for example (see p. 33).

S7-a Use a variety of sentence structures.

A writer should not rely too heavily on simple sentences and compound sentences, for the effect tends to be both monotonous and choppy. (See S6-a and S6-b.) Too many complex sentences, however, can be equally monotonous. If your style tends to one or the other extreme, try to achieve a better mix of sentence types.

For a discussion of sentence types, see B4-a.

S7-b Use a variety of sentence openings.

Most sentences in English begin with the subject, move to the verb, and continue to an object, with modifiers tucked in along the way or put at the end. For the most part, such sentences are fine. Put too many of them in a row, however, and they become monotonous.

Adverbial modifiers, being easily movable, can often be inserted ahead of the subject. Such modifiers might be single words, phrases, or clauses.

► *Eventually a*
A few drops of sap ~~eventually~~ began to trickle into the pail.

▶ *Just as the sun was coming up, a*
A̬ pair of black ducks flew over the lake. ~~just as the sun was~~
~~coming up.~~

Participial phrases can frequently be moved to the beginning of a sentence without loss of clarity. (See B3-b.)

▶ *Tired of the struggle in Vietnam, many Americans*
~~Many Americans, tired of the struggle in Vietnam,~~ began to
sympathize with antiwar protesters.

▶   *José and I*
~~José and I,~~ anticipating a peaceful evening, sat down at the
campfire to brew a cup of coffee.

CAUTION: When beginning a sentence with a participial phrase, make sure that the subject of the sentence names the person or thing described in the introductory phrase. If it doesn't, the phrase will dangle. (See S3-e.)

S7-c Try inverting sentences occasionally.

A sentence is inverted if it does not follow the normal subject-verb-object pattern. Many inversions sound artificial and should be avoided except in the most formal contexts. But if an inversion sounds natural, it can provide a welcome touch of variety.

▶ *Opposite the produce section is a*
A̬ refrigerated case of mouth-watering cheeses. ~~is opposite the~~
~~produce section.~~

▶ *Set at the top two corners of the stage were huge*
~~Huge~~ lavender hearts outlined in bright white lights. ~~were set at~~
~~the top two corners of the stage.~~

W

Word Choice

Word Choice

W1

Glossary of usage

This glossary includes words commonly confused (such as *accept* and *except*), words commonly misused (such as *aggravate*), and words that are nonstandard (such as *hisself*). It also lists colloquialisms and jargon. Colloquialisms are expressions that may be appropriate in informal speech but are inappropriate in formal writing. Jargon is needlessly technical or pretentious language that is inappropriate in most contexts. If an item is not listed here, consult the index. For irregular verbs (such as *sing, sang, sung*), see G2-a. For idiomatic use of prepositions, see W5-d.

 GRAMMAR CHECKERS can point out commonly confused words and suggest that you check your usage. It is up to you, however, to determine the correct word for your intended meaning.

ON THE WEB

Some matters of usage included in this glossary have sparked debates. If you are interested in learning why, go to
www.dianahacker.com/writersref

and click on ▶ **Language Debates**
bad versus *badly*
however at the beginning of a sentence
lie versus *lay*
myself
that versus *which*
Absolute concepts such as *unique*
who versus *which* or *that*
who versus *whom*
you

---

a, an   Use *an* before a vowel sound, *a* before a consonant sound: *an apple, a peach.* Problems sometimes arise with words beginning with *h.* If the *h* is silent, the word begins with a vowel sound, so use *an: an hour, an heir, an honest senator, an honourable deed.* If the *h* is pronounced, the word begins with a consonant sound, so use *a: a hospital, a hymn, a* *historian, a hotel.* When an abbreviation or acronym begins with a vowel sound, use *an: an EKG, an MRI, an AIDS patient.*

accept, except   *Accept* is a verb meaning "to receive." *Except* is usually a preposition meaning "excluding." *I will accept all the packages except that one. Except* is also a verb meaning "to exclude." *Please except that item from the list.*

adapt, adopt   *Adapt* means "to adjust or become accustomed"; it is usually followed by *to. Adopt* means "to take as one's own." *Our family adopted a Vietnamese orphan, who quickly adapted to his new life.*

adverse, averse   *Adverse* means "unfavourable." *Averse* means "opposed" or "reluctant"; it is usually followed by *to. I am averse to your proposal because it could have an adverse impact on the economy.*

advice, advise   *Advice* is a noun, *advise* a verb. *We advise you to follow John's advice.*

affect, effect   *Affect* is usually a verb meaning "to influence." *Effect* is usually a noun meaning "result." *The drug did not affect the disease, and it had adverse side effects. Effect* can also be a verb meaning "to bring about." *Only the president can effect such a dramatic change.*

aggravate   *Aggravate* means "to make worse or more troublesome." *Overgrazing aggravated the soil erosion.* In formal writing, avoid the colloquial use of *aggravate* meaning "to annoy or irritate." *Her babbling annoyed* (not *aggravated*) *me.*

ain't   *Ain't* is nonstandard. Use *am not, are not* (*aren't*), or *is not* (*isn't*). *I am not* (not *ain't*) *going home for the holidays.*

all ready, already   *All ready* means "completely prepared." *Already* means "previously." *Susan was all ready for the concert, but her friends had already left.*

all right   *All right* is written as two words. *Alright* is nonstandard.

all together, altogether   *All together* means "everyone gathered." *Altogether* means "entirely." *We were not altogether certain that we could bring the family all together for the reunion.*

allude   To *allude* to something is to make an indirect reference to it. Do not use *allude* to mean "to refer directly." *In his lecture the professor referred* (not *alluded*) *to several pre-Socratic philosophers.*

allusion, illusion   An *allusion* is an indirect reference. An *illusion* is a misconception or false impression. *Did you catch my allusion to Shakespeare? Mirrors give the room an illusion of depth.*

a lot   *A lot* is two words. Do not write *alot. Sam lost a lot of weight.*

among, between   See *between, among.*

amongst   In Canadian English, *among* is preferred.

amoral, immoral   *Amoral* means "neither moral nor immoral"; it also means "not caring about moral judgments." *Immoral* means "morally wrong." *Until recently, most business courses were taught from an amoral perspective. Murder is immoral.*

amount, number   Use *amount* with quantities that cannot be counted; use *number* with those that can. *This recipe calls for a large amount of sugar. We have a large number of toads in our garden.*

an   See *a, an.*

and etc.   *Et cetera (etc.)* means "and so forth," so *and etc.* is redundant.

and/or   Avoid the awkward construction *and/or* except in technical or legal documents.

ante-, anti-   The prefix *ante-* means "earlier" or "in front of"; the prefix *anti-* means "against" or "opposed to." *William Lloyd Garrison was one of the leaders of the antislavery movement during the antebellum period.*

anybody, anyone   Both words are singular. (See G1-e and G3-a.)

anymore   Reserve the adverb *anymore* for negative contexts, where it means "any longer." *Moviegoers are rarely shocked anymore by profanity.* Do not use *anymore* in positive contexts. Use *now* or *nowadays* instead. *Interest rates are so low nowadays* (not *anymore*) *that more people can afford to buy homes.*

anyone   See *anybody, anyone.*

anyone, any one   *Anyone,* an indefinite pronoun, means "any person at all." *Any one,* the pronoun *one* preceded by the adjective *any,* refers to a particular person or thing in a group. *Anyone from Halifax may choose any one of the games on display.*

anyplace   In formal writing, use *anywhere.*

anyways, anywheres   Both words are nonstandard. Use *anyway* and *anywhere.*

as   *As* is sometimes used to mean "because." But do not use it if there is any chance of ambiguity. *We cancelled the picnic because* (not *as*) *it began raining. As* here could mean "because" or "when."

as, like   See *like, as.*

as to   *As to* is jargon for *about. He inquired about* (not *as to*) *the job.*

averse   See *adverse, averse.*

awful   The adjective *awful* and the adverb *awfully* are too colloquial for formal writing. *I was very* (not *awfully*) *upset last night. Susan had a terrible* (not *an awful*) *time calming her nerves.*

awhile, a while   *Awhile* is an adverb; it can modify a verb, but it cannot be the object of a preposition such as *for.* The two-word form *a while* is a noun preceded by an article and therefore can be the object of a preposition. *Stay awhile. Stay for a while.*

back up, backup   *Back up* is a verb phrase. *Be sure to back up your hard drive.* A *backup* is a duplicate of electronically stored data. *Keep your backup in a safe place.*

bad, badly   *Bad* is an adjective, *badly* an adverb. (See G4-a and G4-b.) *They felt bad about being early and ruining the surprise. Her arm hurt badly after she slid headfirst into second base.*

being as, being that   *Being as* and *being that* are nonstandard expressions. Write *because* or *since* instead. *Because* (not *Being as*) *I slept late, I had to skip breakfast.*

beside, besides   *Beside* is a preposition meaning "at the side of" or "next to." *Annie Oakley slept with her gun beside her bed. Besides* is a preposition meaning "except" or "in addition to." *No one besides Terrie can have that ice cream. Besides* is also an adverb meaning "in addition." *I'm not hungry; besides, I don't like ice cream.*

between, among   Ordinarily, use *among* with three or more entities, *between* with two. *The prize was divided among several contestants. You have a choice between carrots and beans.* This is not a hard-and-fast rule, however. *Between* may be correctly used to indicate one-to-one relations involving more than two entities: *We were fascinated by an online chat between five experts on terrorism.*

bring, take   Use *bring* when an object is being transported toward you, *take* when it is being moved away. *Please bring me a glass of water. Please take these flowers to Mr. Scott.*

burst, bursted; bust, busted   *Burst* is an irregular verb meaning "to come open or fly apart suddenly or violently." Its principal parts are *burst, burst, burst. Bursted, bust,* and *busted* are nonstandard.

can, may   The distinction between *can* and *may* is fading, but some writers still observe it. *Can* is traditionally reserved for ability, *may* for permission. *Can you speak French? May I help you?*

capital, capitol   *Capital* refers to a city, *capitol* to a building where lawmakers meet. *Capital* also refers to wealth or resources. *The capitol has undergone extensive renovations. The residents of the provincial capital protested the development plans.*

censor, censure   *Censor* means "to remove or suppress material considered objectionable." *Censure* means "to criticize severely." *The school's policy of censoring books has been censured by the media.*

cite, site   *Cite* means "to quote as an authority or example." *Site* is usually a noun meaning "a particular place." *He cited the zoning law in his argument against the proposed site of the gas station.* Locations on the Web are referred to as *sites*.

climactic, climatic   *Climactic* is derived from *climax,* the point of greatest intensity in a series or progression of events. *Climatic* is derived from *climate* and refers to meteorological conditions. *The climactic period in the dinosaurs' reign was reached just before severe climatic conditions brought on an ice age.*

coarse, course   *Coarse* means "crude" or "rough in texture." *The coarse weave of the wall hanging gave it a three-dimensional quality.* Course usually refers to a path, a playing field, or a unit of study; the expression *of course* means "certainly." *I plan to take a course in car repair this summer. Of course, you are welcome to join me.*

compare to, compare with   *Compare to* means "to represent as similar." *She compared him to a wild stallion. Compare with* means "to examine the ways in which two things are similar." *The study compared the language ability of apes with that of dolphins.*

complement, compliment   *Complement* is a verb meaning "to go with or complete" or a noun meaning "something that completes." *Compliment* as a verb means "to flatter"; as a noun it means "flattering remark." *Her skill at rushing the net complements his skill at volleying. Mother's flower arrangements receive many compliments.*

conscience, conscious   *Conscience* is a noun meaning "moral principles." *Conscious* is an adjective meaning "aware or alert." *Let your conscience be your guide. Were you conscious of his love for you?*

continual, continuous   *Continual* means "repeated regularly and frequently." *She grew weary of the continual telephone calls. Continuous* means "extended or prolonged without interruption." *The broken siren made a continuous wail.*

could care less   *Could care less* is a nonstandard expression. Write *couldn't care less* instead. *He couldn't* (not *could*) *care less about his psychology final.*

could of   Write *could have. We could have* (not *could of*) *taken the train.*

council, counsel   A *council* is a deliberative body, and a *councillor* is a member of such a body. *Counsel* usually means "advice" and can also mean "lawyer"; *counsellor* is one who gives advice or guidance. *The councillors met to draft the council's position paper. The pastor offered wise counsel to the troubled teenager.*

criteria   *Criteria* is the plural of *criterion,* which means "a standard or rule or test on which a judgment or decision can be based." *The only criterion for the scholarship is ability.*

data   Although technically plural, *data* is now accepted as a singular noun. *The new data suggest* (or *suggests*) *that our theory is correct.* (The singular *datum* is rarely used.)

different from, different than Ordinarily, write *different from*. *Your sense of style is different from Jim's.* However, *different than* is acceptable to avoid an awkward construction. *Please let me know if your plans are different than* (to avoid *from what*) *they were six weeks ago.*

differ from, differ with *Differ from* means "to be unlike"; *differ with* means "to disagree." *She differed with me about the wording of the agreement. My approach to the problem differed from hers.*

disinterested, uninterested *Disinterested* means "impartial, objective"; *uninterested* means "not interested." *We sought the advice of a disinterested counsellor to help us solve our problem. He was uninterested in anyone's opinion but his own.*

due to *Due to* is an adjective phrase and should not be used as a preposition meaning "because of." *The trip was cancelled because of* (not *due to*) *lack of interest. Due to* is acceptable as a subject complement and usually follows a form of the verb *be. His success was due to hard work.*

each *Each* is singular. (See G1-e and G3-a.)

effect, affect See *affect, effect.*

either *Either* is singular. (See G1-e and G3-a.) For *either . . . or* constructions, see G1-d and G3-a.

elicit, illicit *Elicit* is a verb meaning "to bring out" or "to evoke." *Illicit* is an adjective meaning "unlawful." *The reporter was unable to elicit any information from the police about illicit drug traffic.*

emigrate from, immigrate to *Emigrate* means "to leave one country or region to settle in another." *In 1900, my grandfather emigrated from Russia to escape the religious pogroms. Immigrate* means "to enter another country and reside there." *Many Filipinos immigrate to Canada to find work.*

eminent, imminent *Eminent* means "outstanding" or "distinguished." *We met an eminent professor of Greek history. Imminent* means "about to happen." *The announcement is imminent.*

enthused Many people object to the use of *enthused* as an adjective. Use *enthusiastic* instead. *The children were enthusiastic* (not *enthused*) *about going to the circus.*

etc. Avoid ending a list with *etc.* It is more emphatic to end with an example, and in most contexts readers will understand that the list is not exhaustive. When you don't wish to end with an example, *and so on* is more graceful than *etc.*

eventually, ultimately Often used interchangeably, *eventually* is the better choice to mean "at an unspecified time in the future" and *ultimately* is better to mean "the furthest possible extent or greatest extreme." *He knew that eventually he would complete his degree. The existentialist considered suicide the ultimately rational act.*

everybody, everyone Both words are singular. (See G1-e and G3-a.)

everyone, every one *Everyone* is an indefinite pronoun. *Every one,* the pronoun *one* preceded by the adjective *every,* means "each individual or thing in a particular group." *Every one* is usually followed by *of. Everyone wanted to go. Every one of the missing books was found.*

except, accept See *accept, except.*

expect Avoid the colloquial use of *expect* meaning "to believe, think, or suppose." *I think* (not *expect*) *it will rain tonight.*

explicit, implicit *Explicit* means "expressed directly" or "clearly defined"; *implicit* means "implied, unstated." *I gave him explicit instructions not to go swimming. My mother's silence indicated her implicit approval.*

farther, further *Farther* usually describes distances. *Further* usually suggests quantity or degree. *Altona is farther from Kenora than I thought. You extended the curfew further than you should have.*

fewer, less *Fewer* refers to items that can be counted; *less* refers to general amounts. *Fewer people are living in the city. Please put less sugar in my tea.*

finalize *Finalize* is jargon meaning "to make final or complete." Use ordinary English instead. *The architect prepared final drawings* (not *finalized the drawings*).

firstly *Firstly* sounds pretentious, and it leads to the ungainly series *firstly, secondly, thirdly,* and so on. Write *first, second, third* instead.

further See *farther, further.*

get In formal writing, avoid using *get* to mean "to evoke an emotional response" (*That music always gets to me*) or "to annoy" (*After a while his sulking got to me*).

good, well *Good* is an adjective, *well* an adverb. (See G4.) *He hasn't felt good about his game since he sprained his wrist last season. She performed well on the uneven parallel bars.*

graduate Both of the following uses of *graduate* are standard: *My sister was graduated from UCLA last year. My sister graduated from UCLA last year.* It is nonstandard, however, to drop the word *from: My sister graduated UCLA last year.* Though this usage is common in informal English, many readers object to it.

grow Phrases such as *to grow the economy* and *to grow a business* are jargon. Usually the verb *grow* is intransitive (it does not take a direct object). *Our business has grown very quickly.* When *grow* is used in a transitive sense, with a direct object, it means "to cultivate" or "to allow to grow." *We plan to grow tomatoes this year. John is growing a beard.*

hanged, hung *Hanged* means "to execute." *The prisoner was hanged at dawn. Hung* means "to fasten or suspend." *The stockings were hung by the chimney with care.*

has got, have got *Got* is unnecessary and awkward with *has* or *have. We have* (not *have got*) *three days to prepare for the opening.*

he At one time *he* was commonly used to mean "he or she." Today such usage is inappropriate. (See W4-e and G3-a.)

he/she, his/her In formal writing, use *he or she* or *his or her.* For alternatives to these wordy constructions, see W4-e and G3-a.

hisself *Hisself* is nonstandard. Use *himself.*

hopefully *Hopefully* means "in a hopeful manner." *We looked hopefully to the future.* Some usage experts object to the use of *hopefully* as a sentence adverb, apparently on grounds of clarity. To be safe, avoid using *hopefully* in sentences such as the following: *Hopefully, your son will recover soon.* At least some educated readers will want you to indicate who is doing the hoping: *I hope that your son will recover soon.*

however In the past, some writers objected to *however* at the beginning of a sentence, but current experts advise you to place the word according to your meaning and desired emphasis. Any of the following sentences is correct, depending on the intended contrast. *Pam decided, however, to attend Harvard. However, Pam decided to attend Harvard.* (She had been considering other schools.) *Pam, however, decided to attend Harvard.* (Unlike someone else, Pam opted for Harvard.)

hung See *hanged, hung.*

if, whether Use *if* to express a condition and *whether* to express alternatives. *If you go on a trip, whether it be to Charlottetown or Regina, remember to bring traveller's cheques.*

illusion See *allusion, illusion.*

immigrate See *emigrate from, immigrate to.*

imminent See *eminent, imminent.*

immoral See *amoral, immoral.*

implement *Implement* is a pretentious way of saying "do," "carry out," or "accomplish." Use ordinary language instead. *We carried out* (not *implemented*) *the director's orders with some reluctance.*

imply, infer *Imply* means "to suggest or state indirectly"; *infer* means "to draw a conclusion." *Jin implied that he knew all about computers, but the interviewer inferred that Jin was inexperienced.*

ingenious, ingenuous   *Ingenious* means "clever." *Sarah's solution to the problem was ingenious. Ingenuous* means "naive" or "frank." *For a successful manager, Ed is surprisingly ingenuous.*

in, into   *In* indicates location or condition; *into* indicates movement or a change in condition. *They found the lost letters in a box after moving into the house.*

in regards to   *In regards to* confuses two different phrases: *in regard to* and *as regards.* Use one or the other. *In regard to* (or *As regards*) *the contract, ignore the first clause.*

irregardless   *Irregardless* is nonstandard. Use *regardless.*

is when, is where   These mixed constructions are often incorrectly used in definitions. *A run-off election is a second election held to break a tie* (not *is when a second election breaks a tie*). (See S5-c.)

its, it's   *Its* is a possessive pronoun; *it's* is a contraction for *it is.* (See P5-c and P5-e.) *The dog licked its wound whenever its owner walked into the room. It's a perfect day to walk the thirty-kilometre trail.*

kind(s)   *Kind* is singular and should be treated as such. Don't write *These kind of chairs are rare.* Write instead *This kind of chair is rare. Kinds* is plural and should be used only when you mean more than one kind. *These kinds of chairs are rare.*

kind of, sort of   Avoid using *kind of* or *sort of* to mean "somewhat." *The movie was somewhat* (not *kind of*) *boring.* Do not put *a* after either phrase. *That kind of* (not *kind of a*) *salesclerk annoys me.*

lay   See *lie, lay.*

lead, led   *Lead* is a noun referring to a metal. *Led* is the past tense of the verb *lead. He led me to the treasure.*

learn, teach   *Learn* means "to gain knowledge"; *teach* means "to impart knowledge." *I must teach* (not *learn*) *my sister to read.*

leave, let   *Leave* means "to exit." Avoid using it with the nonstandard meaning "to permit." *Let* (not *Leave*) *me help you with the dishes.*

less   See *fewer, less.*

let   See *leave, let.*

liable   *Liable* means "obligated" or "responsible." Do not use it to mean "likely." *You're likely* (not *liable*) *to trip if you don't tie your shoelaces.*

lie, lay   *Lie* is an intransitive verb meaning "to recline or rest on a surface." Its principal parts are *lie, lay, lain. Lay* is a transitive verb meaning "to put or place." Its principal parts are *lay, laid, laid.* (See G2-b.)

like, as *Like* is a preposition; it can be followed only by a noun or a noun phrase. *As* is a subordinating conjunction that introduces a subordinate clause. In casual speech you may say *She looks like she hasn't slept* or *You don't know her like I do.* But in formal writing, use *as. She looks as if she hasn't slept. You don't know her as I do.* (See also B1-f and B1-g.)

loose, lose *Loose* is an adjective meaning "not securely fastened." *Lose* is a verb meaning "to misplace" or "to not win." *Did you lose your only loose pair of work pants?*

lots, lots of *Lots* and *lots of* are colloquial substitutes for *many, much,* or *a lot.* Avoid using them in formal writing.

mankind Avoid *mankind* whenever possible. It offends many readers because it excludes women. (See W4-e.)

may See *can, may.*

maybe, may be *Maybe* is an adverb meaning "possibly." *May be* is a verb phrase. *Maybe we will win. Tomorrow may be our lucky day.*

may of, might of *May of* and *might of* are nonstandard for *may have* and *might have. We may have* (not *may of*) *had too many cookies.*

media, medium *Media* is the plural of *medium. Of all the media that cover the Olympics, television is the medium that best captures the spectacle of the events.*

must of See *may of, might of.*

myself *Myself* is a reflexive or intensive pronoun. Reflexive: *I cut myself.* Intensive: *I will drive you myself.* Do not use *myself* in place of *I* or *me. He gave the flowers to Melinda and me* (not *myself*). (See also G3-c.)

neither *Neither* is singular. (See G1-e and G3-a.) For *neither . . . nor* constructions, see G1-d and G3-a.

none *None* may be singular or plural. (See G1-e.)

nowheres *Nowheres* is nonstandard for *nowhere.*

number See *amount, number.*

off of *Off* is sufficient. Omit *of. The ball rolled off* (not *off of*) *the table.*

OK, O.K., okay All three spellings are acceptable, but in formal speech and writing avoid these colloquial expressions.

parameters *Parameter,* a mathematical term, has become jargon for "boundary" or "guideline." Use plain English instead. *The task force was asked to work within certain guidelines* (not *parameters*).

passed, past *Passed* is the past tense of the verb *pass. Mother passed me another slice of cake. Past* usually means "belonging to a former time" or "beyond a time or place." *Our past president spoke until past midnight. The hotel is just past the next intersection.*

percent, per cent, percentage   *Percent* (also spelled *per cent*) is always used with a specific number. *Percentage* is used with a descriptive term such as *large* or *small,* not with a specific number. *The candidate won 80 percent of the primary vote. Only a small percentage of registered voters turned out for the election.*

phenomena   *Phenomena* is the plural of *phenomenon,* which means "an observable occurrence or fact." *Strange phenomena occur at all hours of the night in that house, but last night's phenomenon was the strangest of all.*

plus   *Plus* should not be used to join independent clauses. *This raincoat is dirty; moreover* (not *plus*), *it has a hole in it.*

precede, proceed   *Precede* means "to come before." *Proceed* means "to go forward." *As we proceeded up the mountain path, we noticed fresh tracks in the mud, evidence that a group of hikers had preceded us.*

principal, principle   *Principal* is a noun meaning "the head of a school or an organization" or "a sum of money." It is also an adjective meaning "most important." *Principle* is a noun meaning "a basic truth or law." *The principal expelled her for three principal reasons. We believe in the principle of equal justice for all.*

proceed   See *precede, proceed.*

quote, quotation   *Quote* is a verb; *quotation* is a noun. Avoid using *quote* as a shortened form of *quotation. Her quotations* (not *quotes*) *from Shakespeare intrigued us.*

raise, rise   *Raise* is a transitive verb meaning "to move or cause to move upward." It takes a direct object. *I raised the shades. Rise* is an intransitive verb meaning "to go up." *Heat rises.*

real, really   *Real* is an adjective; *really* is an adverb. *Real* is sometimes used informally as an adverb, but avoid this use in formal writing. *She was really* (not *real*) *angry.* (See G4-a.)

reason . . . is because   Use *that* instead of *because. The reason I'm late is that* (not *because*) *my car broke down.* (See S5-c.)

reason why   The expression *reason why* is redundant. *The reason* (not *The reason why*) *Jones lost the election is clear.*

relation, relationship   *Relation* describes a connection between things. *Relationship* describes a connection between people. *There is a relation between poverty and infant mortality. Our business relationship has cooled over the years.*

respectfully, respectively *Respectfully* means "showing or marked by respect." *Respectively* means "each in the order given." *He respectfully submitted his opinion to the judge. John, Tom, and Larry were a butcher, a baker, and a lawyer, respectively.*

sensual, sensuous *Sensual* means "gratifying the physical senses," especially those associated with sexual pleasure. *Sensuous* means "pleasing to the senses," especially those involved in the experience of art, music, and nature. *The sensuous music and balmy air led the dancers to more sensual movements.*

set, sit *Set* is a transitive verb meaning "to put" or "to place." Its principal parts are *set, set, set. Sit* is an intransitive verb meaning "to be seated." Its principal parts are *sit, sat, sat. She set the dough in a warm corner of the kitchen. The cat sat in the warmest part of the room.*

shall, will The word *shall* occurs primarily in polite questions. (*Shall I find you a pillow?*) and in legalistic sentences suggesting duty or obligation (*The applicant shall file form 1080 by December 31*). In other situations, use *will.*

should of Write *should have. They should have* (not *should of*) *been home an hour ago.*

since Do not use *since* to mean "because" if there is any chance of ambiguity. *Because* (not *Since*) *we won the game, we have been celebrating with a pitcher of beer. Since* here could mean "because" or "from the time that."

sit See *set, sit.*

site See *cite, site.*

somebody, someone Both words are singular. (See G1-e and G3-a.)

something *Something* is singular. (See G1-e.)

sometime, some time, sometimes *Sometime* is an adverb meaning "at an indefinite or unstated time." *Some time* is the adjective *some* modifying the noun *time* and is spelled as two words to mean "a period of time." *Sometimes* is an adverb meaning "at times, now and then." *I'll see you sometime soon. I haven't lived there for some time. Sometimes I run into him at the library.*

suppose to Write *supposed to.*

sure and Write *sure to. We were all taught to be sure to* (not *and*) *look both ways before crossing a street.*

take See *bring, take.*

than, then *Than* is a conjunction used in comparisons; *then* is an adverb denoting time. *That pizza is more than I can eat. Tom laughed, and then we recognized him.*

that See *who, which, that.*

that, which Many writers reserve *that* for restrictive clauses, *which* for nonrestrictive clauses. (See P1-e.)

theirselves *Theirselves* is nonstandard for *themselves. The crash victims pushed the car out of the way themselves* (not *theirselves*).

them The use of *them* in place of *those* is nonstandard. *Please send those* (not *them*) *flowers to the patient in room 220.*

then See *than, then.*

there, their, they're *There* is an adverb specifying place; it is also an expletive. Adverb: *Sylvia is lying there unconscious.* Expletive: *There are two plums left. Their* is a possessive pronoun. *Fred and Céline finally washed their car. They're* is a contraction of *they are. They're later than usual today.*

they The use of *they* to indicate possession is nonstandard. Use *their* instead. *Sabine and Sam decided to sell their* (not *they*) *1975 Corvette.*

this kind See *kind(s).*

to, too, two *To* is a preposition; *too* is an adverb; *two* is a number. *Too many of your shots slice to the left, but the last two were just right.*

toward, towards *Toward* and *towards* are generally interchangeable, although *toward* is preferred in Canadian English.

try and *Try and* is nonstandard for *try to. The teacher asked us all to try to* (not *and*) *write an original haiku.*

ultimately, eventually See *eventually, ultimately.*

unique Avoid expressions such as *most unique, more straight, less perfect, very round.* Either something is unique or it isn't. It is illogical to suggest degrees of uniqueness. (See G4-c.)

usage The noun *usage* should not be substituted for *use* when the meaning is "employment of." The *use* (not *usage*) *of computers dramatically increased the company's profits.*

use to Write *used to.*

utilize *Utilize* means "to make use of." It often sounds pretentious; in most cases, *use* is sufficient. *I used* (not *utilized*) *the laser printer.*

wait for, wait on *Wait for* means "to be in readiness for" or "await." *Wait on* means "to serve." *We're only waiting for* (not *waiting on*) *Ruth to take us to the game.*

ways *Ways* is colloquial when used to mean "distance." *The city is a long way* (not *ways*) *from here.*

weather, whether   The noun *weather* refers to the state of the atmosphere. *Whether* is a conjunction referring to a choice between alternatives. *We wondered whether the weather would clear up.*

well   See *good, well.*

where   Do not use *where* in place of *that. I heard that* (not *where*) *the crime rate is increasing.*

which   See *that, which* and *who, which, that.*

while   Avoid using *while* to mean "although" or "whereas" if there is any chance of ambiguity. *Although* (not *While*) *Gloria lost money in the slot machine, Tom won it at roulette.* Here *While* could mean either "although" or "at the same time that."

who, which, that   Do not use *which* to refer to persons. Use *who* instead. *That,* though generally used to refer to things, may be used to refer to a group or class of people. *Fans wondered how an old man who* (not *that* or *which*) *walked with a limp could play football. The team that scores the most points in this game will win the tournament.*

who, whom   *Who* is used for subjects and subject complements; *whom* is used for objects. (See G3-d.)

who's, whose   *Who's* is a contraction of *who is; whose* is a possessive pronoun. *Who's ready for more popcorn? Whose coat is this?* (See P5-c and P5-e.)

will   See *shall, will.*

would of   *Would of* is nonstandard for *would have. She would have* (not *would of*) *had a chance to play if she had arrived on time.*

you   In formal writing, avoid *you* in an indefinite sentence meaning "anyone." (See G3-b.) *Any spectator* (not *You*) *could tell by the way John caught the ball that his throw would be too late.*

your, you're   *Your* is a possessive pronoun; *you're* is a contraction of *you are. Is that your new motorcycle? You're on the list of finalists.* (See P5-c and P5-e.)

W2

Wordy sentences

Long sentences are not necessarily wordy, nor are short sentences always concise. A sentence is wordy if its meaning can be conveyed in fewer words.

GRAMMAR CHECKERS can flag some, but not all, wordy constructions. Most programs alert you to common redundancies, such as *true fact,* and empty or inflated phrases, such as *in my opinion* or *in order that.* In addition, they alert you to wordiness caused by passive verbs, such as *is determined* (see also W3). They are less helpful in identifying sentences with needlessly complex structures.

W2-a Eliminate redundancies.

Redundancies such as *cooperate together, close proximity, basic essentials,* and *true fact* are a common source of wordiness. There is no need to say the same thing twice.

▶ Black slaves were ~~portrayed or~~ stereotyped as lazy even though

they were the main labour force of the American South.

▶ Daniel is now employed at a private rehabilitation centre ~~working~~
works

as a registered physical therapist.

Although modifiers ordinarily add meaning to the words they modify, occasionally they are redundant.

▶ Sylvia ~~very hurriedly~~ scribbled her name, address, and phone

number on the back of a greasy napkin.

▶ Joel was determined ~~in his mind~~ to lose weight.

W2-b Avoid unnecessary repetition of words.

Although words may be repeated deliberately, for effect, repetitions will seem awkward if they are clearly unnecessary. When a more concise version is possible, choose it.

▶ The candidate from Cornwall is ~~an~~ experienced. ~~candidate.~~

▶ The best teachers help each student to ~~become a better student~~
grow

both academically and emotionally.

W2-c   Cut empty or inflated phrases.

An empty phrase can be cut with little or no loss of meaning. Common examples are introductory word groups that apologize or hedge: *in my opinion, I think that, it seems that, one must admit that,* and so on.

▶ ~~In my opinion,~~ O̸ur current immigration policy is misguided on

several counts.

Inflated phrases can be reduced to a word or two without loss of meaning.

INFLATED	CONCISE
along the lines of	like
as a matter of fact	in fact
at all times	always
at the present time	now, currently
at this point in time	now, currently
because of the fact that	because
by means of	by
due to the fact that	because
for the purpose of	for
for the reason that	because
have the ability to	can, be able to
in order to	to
in spite of the fact that	although, though
in the event that	if
in the final analysis	finally
in the nature of	like
in the neighbourhood of	about
until such time as	until

▶ We will file the appropriate papers ~~in the event that~~ *if* we are

unable to meet the deadline.

W2-d   Simplify the structure.

If the structure of a sentence is needlessly indirect, try simplifying it. Look for opportunities to strengthen the verb.

▶ The CEO claimed that because of volatile market conditions she

could not ~~make an~~ estimate ~~of~~ the company's future profits.

The verb *estimate* is more vigorous and more concise than *make an estimate of.*

The colourless verbs *is, are, was,* and *were* frequently generate excess words. (See also W3-b.)

▶ The administrative secretary *monitors and balances* ~~is responsible for monitoring~~

~~and balancing~~ the budgets for travel and personnel.

The expletive constructions *there is* and *there are* (or *there was* and *there were*) can also generate excess words. The same is true of expletive constructions beginning with *it.*

▶ ~~There is~~ *A* nother videotape ~~that~~ tells the story of Charles Darwin

and introduces the theory of evolution.

▶ ~~It is important that~~ *H*ikers *must* remain inside the park boundaries.

Finally, verbs in the passive voice may be needlessly indirect. When the active voice expresses your meaning as well, use it. (See also W3-a.)

▶ All too often, athletes with marginal academic skills *our coaches have recruited* ~~have been~~

~~recruited by our coaches.~~

W2-e Reduce clauses to phrases, phrases to single words.

Word groups functioning as modifiers can often be made more compact. Look for any opportunities to reduce clauses to phrases or phrases to single words.

▶ We visited Kitchener, ~~which was~~ the birthplace of William Lyon

Mackenzie King.

▶ Susan's stylish *leather* pants, ~~made of leather,~~ were too warm for summer.

ON THE WEB

For electronic exercises on wordy sentences, go to
www.dianahacker.com/writersref

and click on ▶ **Electronic Grammar Exercises**
  ▶ **Word Choice**
    ▶ **E-ex W2–1 through W2–3**

W3

Active verbs

Active verbs express meaning more emphatically and vigorously than their weaker counterparts—forms of the verb *be* or verbs in the passive voice. Verbs in the passive voice lack strength because their subjects receive the action instead of doing it (see also B2-b). Forms of the verb *be* (*be, am, is, are, was, were, being, been*) lack vigour because they convey no action.

Although passive verbs and forms of *be* have legitimate uses, if an active verb can carry your meaning, use it.

PASSIVE   The coolant pumps *were destroyed* by a power surge.

BE VERB   A power surge *was* responsible for the destruction of the coolant pumps.

ACTIVE   A power surge *destroyed* the coolant pumps.

Even among active verbs, some are more active—and therefore more vigorous and colourful—than others. Carefully selected verbs can energize a piece of writing.

▶ The goalie crouched low, ~~reached~~ *swept* out his stick, and ~~sent~~ *hooked* the
 rebound away from the mouth of the net.

Some speakers of English as a second language avoid the passive voice even when it is appropriate. For advice on transforming an active-voice sentence to the passive, see B2-b.

ESL

GRAMMAR CHECKERS are fairly good at flagging passive verbs, such as *were given*. However, because passive verbs are sometimes appropriate, you—not the computer program—must decide whether to make a passive verb active.

W3-a   Use the active voice unless you have a good reason for choosing the passive.

In the active voice, the subject of the sentence does the action; in the passive voice, the subject receives the action. (See also B2-b.)

ACTIVE   Hernando *caught* the fly ball.

PASSIVE   The fly ball *was caught* by Hernando.

In passive sentences, the actor (in this case *Hernando*) frequently disappears from the sentence: *The fly ball was caught.*

In most cases, you will want to emphasize the actor, so you should use the active voice. To replace a passive verb with an active alternative, make the actor the subject of the sentence.

▶ Lightning struck the transformer,
   ~~The transformer was struck by lightning,~~ plunging us into
   ^
   darkness.

The active verb (*struck*) makes the point more forcefully than the passive verb (*was struck*).

The passive voice is appropriate if you wish to emphasize the receiver of the action or to minimize the importance of the actor.

APPROPRIATE   Many native Hawaiians *are forced* to leave their
PASSIVE   beautiful beaches to make room for hotels and
                        condominiums.

APPROPRIATE   As the time for harvest approaches, the tobacco
PASSIVE   plants *are sprayed* with a chemical to retard the
                        growth of suckers.

The writer of the first sentence wished to emphasize the receivers of the action, Hawaiians. The writer of the second sentence wished to focus on the tobacco plants, not on the people spraying them.

In much scientific writing, the passive voice properly puts the emphasis on the experiment or process being described, not on the researcher.

APPROPRIATE The solution *was heated* to the boiling point, and
PASSIVE then it was reduced in volume by 50 percent.

ON THE WEB

Rules on avoiding the passive voice have sparked debates. If you're interested in learning why, go to
www.dianahacker.com/writersref

and click on ▶ **Language Debates**
　　　　　　▶ **Passive voice**

W3-b Replace *be* verbs that result in dull or wordy sentences.

Not every *be* verb needs replacing. The forms of *be* (*be, am, is, are, was, were, being, been*) work well when you want to link a subject to a noun that clearly renames it or to an adjective that describes it: *History is a bucket of ashes. Scoundrels are always sociable.* (See B2-b.) And when used as helping verbs before present participles (*is flying, are disappearing*) to express ongoing action, *be* verbs are fine: *Derrick was plowing the field when his wife went into labour.* (See G2-f.)

If using a *be* verb makes a sentence needlessly dull or wordy, however, consider replacing it. Often a phrase following the verb will contain a word (such as *violation*) that suggests a more vigorous, active alternative (*violate*).

▶ Burying nuclear waste in Antarctica would ~~be in violation of~~ *violate*

an international treaty.

Violate is less wordy and more vigorous than *be in violation of.*

▶ When Rosa Parks ~~was resistant to~~ *resisted* giving up her seat on the bus,

she became a civil rights hero.

Resisted is stronger than *was resistant to.*

ON THE WEB

For electronic exercises on using active verbs, go to
www.dianahacker.com/writersref

and click on ▶ **Electronic Grammar Exercises**
▶ **Word Choice**
▶ **E-ex W3–1 through W3–3**

W4

Appropriate language

Language is appropriate when it suits your subject, conforms to the needs of your audience, and blends naturally with your own voice.

W4-a Stay away from jargon.

Jargon is specialized language used among members of a trade, profession, or group. Use jargon only when readers will be familiar with it; even then, use it only when plain English will not do as well.

JARGON   For years the indigenous body politic of South Africa attempted to negotiate legal enfranchisement without result.

REVISED   For years the indigenous people of South Africa negotiated in vain for the right to vote.

Broadly defined, jargon includes puffed-up language designed more to impress readers than to inform them. Common examples in business, government, higher education, and the military are given in the following list, with plain English translations in parentheses.

ameliorate (improve)   impact on (affect)
commence (begin)   indicator (sign)
components (parts)   optimal (best, most favourable)
endeavour (try)   parameters (boundaries, limits)
exit (leave)   peruse (read, look over)
facilitate (help)   prior to (before)
factor (consideration, cause) utilize (use)
finalize (finish)   viable (workable)

Sentences filled with jargon are hard to read, and they are often wordy as well.

▶ All ~~employees functioning in the capacity of~~ work-study students

must prove that they are currently enrolled.
~~are required to give evidence of current enrollment.~~
                    ^

                    begin   *improving*
▶ Mayor Summers will ~~commence~~ his term of office by ~~ameliorating~~
                        ^   ^
                    poor neighbourhoods.
living conditions in ~~economically deprived zones.~~
                        ^

W4-b Avoid pretentious language, most euphemisms, and "doublespeak."

Hoping to sound profound or poetic, some writers embroider their thoughts with large words and flowery phrases, language that in fact sounds pretentious. Pretentious language is so ornate and often so wordy that it obscures the thought that lies beneath.

            parents become old,
▶ When our ~~progenitors reach their silver-haired and golden years,~~
            ^
                bury   *old-age*
we frequently ~~ensepulcher~~ them in homes ~~for senescent beings~~ as
                ^   ^
                    dead.
if they were already ~~among the deceased.~~
                        ^

Euphemisms, nice-sounding words or phrases substituted for words thought to sound harsh or ugly, are sometimes appropriate. It is customary, for example, to say that a couple is "sleeping together" or that someone has "passed away." Most euphemisms, however, are needlessly evasive or even deceitful. Like pretentious language, they obscure the intended meaning.

EUPHEMISM	PLAIN ENGLISH
adult entertainment	pornography
preowned automobile	used car
economically deprived	poor
selected out	fired
negative savings	debts
strategic withdrawal	retreat or defeat
revenue enhancers	taxes
chemical dependency	drug addiction
incendiary device	bomb
correctional facility	prison

The term *doublespeak,* coined by George Orwell in the novel *1984,* applies to any deliberately evasive or deceptive language, including euphemisms. Doublespeak is especially common in politics, where missiles are named "Peacekeepers," airplane crashes are termed "uncontrolled contact with the ground," and a military retreat is described as "tactical redeployment." Business also gives us its share of doublespeak. When the manufacturer of a pacemaker writes that its product "may result in adverse health consequences in pacemaker-dependent patients as a result of sudden 'no output' failure," it takes an alert reader to grasp the message: The pacemakers might suddenly stop functioning and cause a heart attack or even death.

GRAMMAR CHECKERS can be helpful in identifying jargon and pretentious language. For example, they commonly advise against using words such as *utilize, finalize, facilitate,* and *effectuate.* You may find, however, that a program advises you to "simplify" language that is appropriate in academic writing.

ON THE WEB

For an electronic exercise on eliminating jargon, go to
www.dianahacker.com/writersref

and click on   ▶ **Electronic Grammar Exercises**
                      ▶ **Word Choice**
                            ▶ **E-ex W4–1**

W4-c   In most contexts, avoid slang, regional expressions, and nonstandard English.

Slang is an informal and sometimes private vocabulary that expresses the solidarity of a group such as teenagers, rock musicians, or football fans; it is subject to more rapid change than standard English. For example, the slang teenagers use to express approval changes every few years; *cool, groovy, neat, wicked, awesome, phat,* and *money* have replaced one another within the last three decades. Sometimes slang becomes so widespread that it is accepted as standard vocabulary. *Jazz,* for example, started as slang but is now generally accepted to describe a style of music.

Although slang has a certain vitality, it is a code that not everyone understands, and it is very informal. Therefore, it is inappropriate in most written work.

▶ If we don't begin studying for the final, a whole semester's work ~~is~~
   will be wasted.
   ~~going down the tubes.~~
    ^

                                                        disgust you.
▶ The government's "filth" guidelines for food will ~~gross you out.~~
                                                         ^

Regional expressions are common to a group in a geographical area. *Let's talk with the bark off* (for *Let's speak frankly*) is an expression in the southern United States, for example. Regional expressions have the same limitations as slang and are therefore inappropriate in most writing.

▶ With her map in hand and her camera around her neck, Annalie
                        tourist
   resembled a ~~gorby.~~
                ^

▶ I'm not ~~for~~ sure, but I think the dance has been postponed.

Standard English is the language used in all academic, business, and professional fields. Nonstandard English is spoken by people with a common regional or social heritage. Although nonstandard English may be appropriate when spoken within a close group, it is out of place in most formal and informal writing.

          has
▶ The counselor ~~have~~ so many problems in her own life that she
   doesn't   ^
   ~~don't~~ know how to advise anyone else.
    ^

If you speak a nonstandard dialect, try to identify the ways in which your dialect differs from standard English. Look especially for the following features of nonstandard English, which commonly cause problems in writing:

Misuse of verb forms such as *began* and *begun* (See G2-a.)

Omission of *-s* endings on verbs (See G1-a and G2-c.)

Omission of *-ed* endings on verbs (See G2-d.)

Omission of necessary verbs (See G2-e.)

Double negatives (See G4-d.)

You might also scan the Glossary of Usage (W1), which alerts you to nonstandard words and expressions such as *ain't, could of, hisself, theirselves, them* (meaning "those"), *they* (meaning "their"), and so on.

W4-d Choose an appropriate level of formality.

In deciding on a level of formality, consider both your subject and your audience. Does the subject demand a dignified treatment, or is a relaxed tone more suitable? Will the audience be put off if you assume too close a relationship with them, or might you alienate them by seeming too distant?

For most postsecondary and professional writing, some degree of formality is appropriate. In a letter applying for a job, for example, it is a mistake to sound too breezy and informal.

TOO INFORMAL	I'd like to get that receptionist's job you've got in the paper.
MORE FORMAL	I would like to apply for the receptionist's position listed in the *Peterborough Examiner.*

Informal writing is appropriate for private letters, business correspondence between close associates, articles in popular magazines, and personal narratives. In such writing, formal language can seem out of place.

▶ Once a pitcher for the Blue Jays, Rich shared with me the
  began
  secrets of his trade. His lesson ~~commenced~~ with his famous curve
  which he threw   ^
  ball, ~~implemented~~ by tucking the little finger behind the ball
  ^
  revealed
  instead of holding it straight out. Next he ~~elucidated~~ the mysteries
  ^
  of the sucker pitch, a slow ball coming behind a fast windup.

GRAMMAR CHECKERS can flag slang and some informal language. Be aware, though, that they tend to be conservative on the matter of using contractions. If your ear tells you that a contraction such as *isn't* or *doesn't* strikes the right tone, stay with it.

W4-e　Avoid sexist language.

Sexist language is language that stereotypes or demeans men or women, usually women. Using nonsexist language is a matter of courtesy — of respect for and sensitivity to the feelings of others.

ON THE WEB

The rules on avoiding sexist language have sparked debates. If you're interested in learning why, go to
www.dianahacker.com/writersref

and click on　▶ **Language Debates**
　　　　　　　　▶ **Sexist language**

Recognizing sexist language

Some sexist language is easy to recognize because it reflects genuine contempt for women: referring to a woman as a "broad," for example, or calling a lawyer a "lady lawyer," or saying in an advertisement, "If our new sports car were a lady, it would get its bottom pinched."

Other forms of sexist language are less blatant. The following practices, while they may not result from conscious sexism, reflect stereotypical thinking: referring to nurses as women and doctors as men, using different conventions when naming or identifying women and men, or assuming that all of one's readers are men.

STEREOTYPICAL LANGUAGE

After the nursing student graduates, *she* must face a difficult provincial board examination. [Not all nursing students are women.]

Running for city council are Jake Stein, an attorney, and *Mrs.* Cynthia Jones, a professor of English *and mother of three*. [The title *Mrs.* and the phrase *and mother of three* are irrelevant.]

Wives of senior government officials are required to report any gifts they receive that are valued at more than $100. [Not all senior government officials are men.]

Still other forms of sexist language result from outmoded traditions. The pronouns *he, him,* and *his,* for instance, were traditionally used to refer generically to persons of either sex.

GENERIC *HE* OR *HIS*

When a physician prescribes medication, *he* can do so electronically or on paper.

A journalist is stimulated by *his* deadline.

Today, however, such usage is widely viewed as sexist because it excludes women and encourages sex-role stereotyping—the view that men are somehow more suited than women to be doctors, journalists, and so on.

Like the pronouns *he, him,* and *his,* the nouns *man* and *men* were once used indefinitely to refer to persons of either sex. Current usage demands gender-neutral terms instead.

INAPPROPRIATE	APPROPRIATE
anchorman	anchor
businessman	business executive, businessperson
chairman	chairperson, moderator, chair, head
clergyman	member of the clergy, minister, pastor
congressman	member of Congress, representative, legislator
fireman	firefighter
forefathers	ancestors
foreman	supervisor
mailman	mail carrier, postal worker, letter carrier
mankind	people, humans
manpower	personnel
policeman	police officer
salesman	sales associate, sales representative
to man	to operate, to staff
weatherman	weather forecaster, meteorologist
workman	worker, labourer

GRAMMAR CHECKERS are good at flagging sexist words, such as *mankind,* but they may also flag words, such as *girl* and *woman,* when they aren't being used in a sexist manner. It's sexist to call a woman a girl or a doctor a woman doctor, but you don't need to avoid the words *girl* and *woman* entirely and replace them with needlessly abstract terms like *female* and *individual.* All in all, just use your common sense. It's usually easy to tell when a word is offensive— and when it is not.

Revising sexist language

When revising sexist language, be sparing in your use of the wordy constructions *he or she* and *his or her.* Although these constructions are fine in small doses, they become awkward when repeated throughout an essay. A better revision strategy, many writers have discovered, is to write in the plural; yet another strategy is to recast the sentence so that the problem does not arise.

SEXIST

When a physician prescribes medication, *he* can do so electronically or on paper.

A journalist is stimulated by *his* deadline.

ACCEPTABLE BUT WORDY

When a physician prescribes medication, *he or she* can do so electronically or on paper.

A journalist is stimulated by *his or her* deadline.

BETTER: USING THE PLURAL

When *physicians* prescribe medication, *they* can do so electronically or on paper.

Journalists are stimulated by *their* deadlines.

BETTER: RECASTING THE SENTENCE

When prescribing medication, *a physician* can do so electronically or on paper.

A journalist is stimulated by *a* deadline.

For more examples of these revision strategies, see G3-a.

ON THE WEB

For an electronic exercise on avoiding sexist language, go to
www.dianahacker.com/writersref

and click on ▶ **Electronic Grammar Exercises**
　　　　　　　　▶ **Word Choice**
　　　　　　　　　　▶ **E-ex W4–2**

W4-f   Revise language that may offend groups of people.

Obviously it is impolite to use offensive terms such as *Polack* or *redneck,* but offensive language can take more subtle forms. Because language evolves over time, names once thought acceptable may become offensive. When describing groups of people, choose names that the groups currently use to describe themselves.

　　　　　　　　　　　　　　　　Inuit
▶ Nunavut takes its name from the ~~Eskimo~~ word meaning
　　　　　　　　　　　　　　　　　^

　"our land."

▶ Many ~~Oriental~~ immigrants have recently settled in our small

    Asian (above "Oriental")

West Coast town.

Negative stereotypes (such as "drives like a teenager" or "haggard as an old crone") are of course offensive. But you should avoid stereotyping a person or a group even if you believe your generalization to be positive.

▶ It was no surprise that Greer, ~~a Chinese American,~~ was selected

    an excellent math and science student,

for the honours chemistry program.

W5

Exact language

Two reference works will help you find words to express your meaning exactly: a good dictionary and a book of synonyms and antonyms such as *Roget's International Thesaurus.* (See W6.)

W5-a Select words with appropriate connotations.

In addition to their strict dictionary meanings (or *denotations*), words have *connotations,* emotional colourings that affect how readers respond to them. The word *steel* denotes "made of or resembling commercial iron that contains carbon," but it also calls up a cluster of images associated with steel, such as the sensation of touching it. These associations give the word its connotations — cold, smooth, unbending.

If the connotation of a word does not seem appropriate for your purpose, your audience, or your subject matter, you should change the word. When a more appropriate word does not come quickly to mind, consult a dictionary or a thesaurus. (See W6.)

▶ The model was ~~skinny~~ and fashionable.

    slender (above "skinny")

The connotation of the word *skinny* is too negative.

▶ As I covered the boats with marsh grass, the ~~perspiration~~ *sweat* I had

worked up evaporated in the wind, making the cold morning air

even colder.

The term *perspiration* is too dainty for the context, which suggests vigorous exercise.

W5-b Prefer specific, concrete nouns.

Unlike general nouns, which refer to broad classes of things, specific nouns point to definite and particular items. *Film,* for example, names a general class, *science fiction film* names a narrower class, and *Jurassic Park* is more specific still.

Unlike abstract nouns, which refer to qualities and ideas (*justice, beauty, realism, dignity*), concrete nouns point to immediate, often sensate experience and to physical objects (*steeple, asphalt, lilac, stone, garlic*).

Specific, concrete nouns express meaning more vividly than general or abstract ones. Although general and abstract language is sometimes necessary to convey your meaning, ordinarily prefer specific, concrete alternatives.

▶ The lieutenant-governor spoke about the challenges of the future:
problems ~~concerning the environment and world peace.~~ *of famine, pollution, dwindling resources, and terrorism.*

Nouns such as *thing, area, factor,* and *individual* are especially dull and imprecise.

▶ A career in transportation management offers many ~~things.~~ *challenges.*

▶ Try pairing a trainee with an ~~individual with technical experience.~~ *experienced technician.*

W5-c Do not misuse words.

If a word is not in your active vocabulary, you may find yourself misusing it, sometimes with embarrassing consequences. When in doubt, check the dictionary.

▶ The fans were ~~migrating~~ *climbing* up the bleachers in search of good seats.

▶ Drugs have so ~~diffused~~ our culture that they touch all segments of
  ^*permeated*^
  our society.

Be especially alert for misused word forms — using a noun such
as *absence, significance,* or *persistence,* for example, when your
meaning requires the adjective *absent, significant,* or *persistent.*

▶ Most dieters are not ~~persistence~~ enough to make a permanent
                        ^*persistent*^
  change in their eating habits.

ON THE WEB

For an electronic exercise on misused words, go to
www.dianahacker.com/writersref

and click on ▶ **Electronic Grammar Exercises**
              ▶ **Word Choice**
                ▶ **E-ex W5–1**

W5-d Use standard idioms.

Idioms are speech forms that follow no easily specified rules. The
British say "Maria went *to hospital,*" an idiom strange to North
American ears, which are accustomed to hearing *the* in front of
hospital. Native speakers of a language seldom have problems with
idioms, but prepositions sometimes cause trouble, especially when
they follow certain verbs and adjectives. When in doubt, consult a
good desk dictionary: Look up the word preceding the troublesome
preposition.

UNIDIOMATIC	IDIOMATIC
abide with (a decision)	abide by (a decision)
according with	according to
agree to (an idea)	agree with (an idea)
angry at (a person)	angry with (a person)
capable to	capable of
comply to	comply with
desirous to	desirous of
different than (a person or thing)	different from (a person or thing)
intend on doing	intend to do

UNIDIOMATIC	IDIOMATIC
off of	off
plan on doing	plan to do
preferable than	preferable to
prior than	prior to
superior than	superior to
sure and	sure to
try and	try to
type of a	type of

ESL

Because idioms follow no particular rules, you must learn them individually. You may find it helpful to keep a list of idioms that you frequently encounter in conversation and in reading.

GRAMMAR CHECKERS can flag some nonstandard idioms, such as *comply to.* However, to choose some idioms, such as *angry at* or *angry with,* you need to consider context.

ON THE WEB

For an electronic exercise on standard idioms, go to
www.dianahacker.com/writersref

and click on   ▶ **Electronic Grammar Exercises**
              ▶ **Word Choice**
                ▶ **E-ex W5-2**

W5-e Do not rely heavily on clichés.

The pioneer who first announced that he had "slept like a log" no doubt amused his companions with a fresh and unlikely comparison. Today, however, that comparison is a cliché, a saying that has lost its dazzle from overuse. No longer can it surprise.

To see just how predictable clichés are, put your hand over the right-hand column below and then finish the phrases given on the left.

cool as a	cucumber
beat around	the bush
blind as a	bat
busy as a	bee, beaver

crystal	clear
dead as a	doornail
out of the frying pan and	into the fire
light as a	feather
like a bull	in a china shop
playing with	fire
nutty as a	fruitcake
selling like	hotcakes
starting out at the bottom	of the ladder
water under the	bridge
white as a	sheet, ghost
avoid clichés like the	plague

The cure for clichés is frequently simple: Just delete them. When this won't work, try adding some element of surprise. One student, for example, who had written that she had butterflies in her stomach, revised her cliché like this:

> If all of the action in my stomach is caused by butterflies, there must be a horde of them, with horseshoes on.

The image of butterflies wearing horseshoes is fresh and unlikely, not dully predictable like the original cliché.

 GRAMMAR CHECKERS are fairly good at flagging clichés such as *leave no stone unturned* or *selling like hotcakes,* but they tend not to suggest alternative expressions.

ON THE WEB

The rules on avoiding clichés have sparked debates. If you're interested in learning why, go to
www.dianahacker.com/writersref

and click on ▶ **Language Debates**
▶ **Clichés**

W5-f Use figures of speech with care.

A figure of speech is an expression that uses words imaginatively (rather than literally) to make abstract ideas concrete. Most often, figures of speech compare two seemingly unlike things to reveal surprising similarities.

In a *simile,* the writer makes the comparison explicitly, usually by introducing it with *like* or *as:* "By the time cotton had to be picked, grandfather's neck was as red as the clay he plowed." In a *metaphor,* the *like* or *as* is omitted, and the comparison is implied. For example, in the Old Testament Song of Solomon, a young woman compares the man she loves to a fruit tree: "With great delight I sat in his shadow, and his fruit was sweet to my taste."

Writers sometimes use figures of speech without thinking carefully about the images they evoke. This can result in a *mixed metaphor,* the combination of two or more images that don't make sense together.

▶ Crossing the Prairies in his new Corvette, my father flew
at jet speed.
~~under a full head of steam.~~
  ^

▶ Our office had decided to put all controversial issues on a back

burner.~~in a holding pattern.~~
      ^

ON THE WEB

For an electronic exercise on clichés and mixed metaphors, go to
www.dianahacker.com/writersref

and click on ▶ **Electronic Grammar Exercises**
              ▶ **Word Choice**
                ▶ **E-ex W5–3**

W6

The dictionary and thesaurus

W6-a   The dictionary

A good desk dictionary—such as *The American Heritage Dictionary of the English Language, The Canadian Oxford Dictionary, The Gage Canadian Dictionary,* the *Oxford English Dictionary,* or the *Nelson Canadian Dictionary of the English Language*—is an indispensable writer's aid.

The following word entry is taken from *The American Heritage Dictionary*. Labels show where various kinds of information about a word can be found in that dictionary.

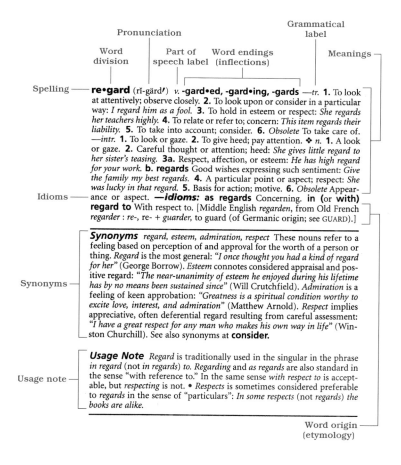

Pronunciation

Grammatical label

Word division

Part of speech label

Word endings (inflections)

Meanings

Spelling — **re•gard** (rĭ-gärd′) *v.* **-gard•ed, -gard•ing, -gards** —*tr.* **1.** To look at attentively; observe closely. **2.** To look upon or consider in a particular way: *I regard him as a fool.* **3.** To hold in esteem or respect: *She regards her teachers highly.* **4.** To relate or refer to; concern: *This item regards their liability.* **5.** To take into account; consider. **6.** *Obsolete* To take care of. —*intr.* **1.** To look or gaze. **2.** To give heed; pay attention. ❖ *n.* **1.** A look or gaze. **2.** Careful thought or attention; heed: *She gives little regard to her sister's teasing.* **3a.** Respect, affection, or esteem: *He has high regard for your work.* **b.** **regards** Good wishes expressing such sentiment: *Give the family my best regards.* **4.** A particular point or aspect; respect: *She was lucky in that regard.* **5.** Basis for action; motive. **6.** *Obsolete* Appearance or aspect. —*idioms:* **as regards** Concerning. **in** (or **with**) **regard to** With respect to. [Middle English *regarden,* from Old French *regarder* : *re-,* re- + *guarder,* to guard (of Germanic origin; see GUARD).]

Idioms

Synonyms *regard, esteem, admiration, respect* These nouns refer to a feeling based on perception of and approval for the worth of a person or thing. *Regard* is the most general: *"I once thought you had a kind of regard for her"* (George Borrow). *Esteem* connotes considered appraisal and positive regard: *"The near-unanimity of esteem he enjoyed during his lifetime has by no means been sustained since"* (Will Crutchfield). *Admiration* is a feeling of keen approbation: *"Greatness is a spiritual condition worthy to excite love, interest, and admiration"* (Matthew Arnold). *Respect* implies appreciative, often deferential regard resulting from careful assessment: *"I have a great respect for any man who makes his own way in life"* (Winston Churchill). See also synonyms at **consider.**

Synonyms

Usage Note *Regard* is traditionally used in the singular in the phrase *in regard* (not *in regards*) *to. Regarding* and *as regards* are also standard in the sense "with reference to." In the same sense *with respect to* is acceptable, but *respecting* is not. • *Respects* is sometimes considered preferable to *regards* in the sense of "particulars": *In some respects* (not *regards*) *the books are alike.*

Usage note

Word origin (etymology)

Spelling, word division, pronunciation

The main entry (*re·gard* in the sample entry) shows the correct spelling of the word. When there are two correct spellings of a word (as in *collectible, collectable,* for example), both are given, with the preferred spelling usually appearing first.

The main entry also shows how the word is divided into syllables. The dot between *re* and *gard* separates the word's two syllables. When a word is compound, the main entry shows how to write it: as one word (*crossroad*), as a hyphenated word (*cross-stitch*), or as two words (*cross section*).

The word's pronunciation is given just after the main entry. The accents indicate which syllables are stressed; the other marks are explained in the dictionary's pronunciation key.

Word endings and grammatical labels

When a word takes endings to indicate grammatical functions (called *inflections*), the endings are listed in boldface, as with *-garded, -garding,* and *-gards* in the sample entry.

Labels for the parts of speech and for other grammatical terms are abbreviated. The most commonly used abbreviations are these:

n.	noun	adj.	adjective
pl.	plural	adv.	adverb
sing.	singular	pron.	pronoun
v.	verb	prep.	preposition
tr.	transitive verb	conj.	conjunction
int.	intransitive verb	interj.	interjection

Meanings, word origin, synonyms, and antonyms

Each meaning for the word is given a number. Occasionally a word's use is illustrated in a quoted sentence.

Sometimes a word can be used as more than one part of speech (*regard,* for instance, can be used as either a verb or a noun). In such a case, all the meanings for one part of speech are given before all the meanings for another, as in the sample entry. The entry also gives idiomatic uses of the word.

The origin of the word, called its *etymology,* appears in brackets after all the meanings (in some dictionaries it appears before the meanings).

Synonyms, words similar in meaning to the main entry, are frequently listed. In the sample entry, the dictionary draws distinctions in meaning among the various synonyms. Antonyms, which do not appear in the sample entry, are words having a meaning opposite from that of the main entry.

Usage

Usage labels indicate when, where, or under what conditions a particular meaning for a word is appropriately used. Common labels are *informal* (or *colloquial*), *slang, nonstandard, dialect, obsolete, archaic, poetic,* and *British.* In the sample entry, two meanings of *regard* are labelled *obsolete* because they are no longer in use.

Dictionaries sometimes include usage notes as well. In the sample entry, the dictionary offers advice on several uses of *regard* not specifically covered by the meanings. Such advice is based on the opinions of many experts and on actual usage in current magazines, newspapers, and books.

W6-b The thesaurus

When you are looking for just the right word, you may want to consult a book of synonyms and antonyms such as *Roget's International Thesaurus* (or its software equivalent). Look up (or click on) the adjective *still,* for example, and you will find synonyms such as *tranquil, quiet, quiescent, reposeful, calm, pacific, halcyon, placid,* and *unruffled.* Unless your vocabulary is better than average, the list will contain words you've never heard of or with which you are only vaguely familiar. Whenever you are tempted to use one of these words, look it up in the dictionary first to avoid misusing it.

On discovering the thesaurus, many writers use it for the wrong reasons, so a word of caution is in order. Do not turn to a thesaurus in search of exotic, fancy words—such as *halcyon*—with which to embellish your essays. Look instead for words that express your meaning exactly. Most of the time these words will be familiar to both you and your readers. The first synonym on the list—*tranquil*—was probably the word you were looking for all along.

G

Grammatical Sentences

G

Grammatical Sentences

G1

Subject-verb agreement

Native speakers of standard English know by ear that *he talks, she has,* and *it doesn't* (not *he talk, she have,* and *it don't*) are standard subject-verb combinations. For such speakers, problems with subject-verb agreement arise only in certain tricky situations, which are detailed in G1-b to G1-k.

If you don't trust your ear — perhaps because you speak English as a second language, perhaps because you speak or hear nonstandard English in your community — you will need to learn the standard forms explained in G1-a. Even if you do trust your ear, take a quick look at G1-a to see what "subject-verb agreement" means.

> **GRAMMAR CHECKERS** attempt to flag faulty subject-verb agreement, but they have mixed success. They fail to flag many problems; in addition, they flag a number of correct sentences, usually because they have misidentified the subject, the verb — or both. For example, one program flagged the following correct sentence: *Nearly everyone on the panel favours the health care reform proposal.* The program identified the subject as *care* and the verb as *reform;* in fact, the subject is *everyone* and the verb is *favours.*

G1-a Consult this section for standard subject-verb combinations.

In the present tense, verbs agree with their subjects in number (singular or plural) and in person (first, second, or third). The present-tense ending -*s* (or -*es*) is used on a verb if its subject is third-person singular; otherwise the verb takes no ending. Consider, for example, the present-tense forms of the verb *love,* given at the beginning of the chart on page 152.

The verb *be* varies from this pattern; unlike any other verb, it has special forms in *both* the present and the past tense. These forms appear at the end of the chart on page 152.

If you aren't confident that you know the standard forms, use the charts on pages 152 and 153 as you proofread for subject-verb agreement. You may also want to take a look at G2-c, which discusses the matter of -*s* endings in some detail.

Subject-verb agreement at a glance

PRESENT-TENSE FORMS OF *LOVE*
(A TYPICAL VERB)

	SINGULAR		PLURAL	
FIRST PERSON	I	love	we	love
SECOND PERSON	you	love	you	love
THIRD PERSON	he/she/it	loves	they	love

PRESENT-TENSE FORMS OF *HAVE*

	SINGULAR		PLURAL	
FIRST PERSON	I	have	we	have
SECOND PERSON	you	have	you	have
THIRD PERSON	he/she/it	has	they	have

PRESENT-TENSE FORMS OF *DO*

	SINGULAR		PLURAL	
FIRST PERSON	I	do/don't	we	do/don't
SECOND PERSON	you	do/don't	you	do/don't
THIRD PERSON	he/she/it	does/doesn't	they	do/don't

PRESENT-TENSE AND PAST-TENSE
FORMS OF *BE*

	SINGULAR		PLURAL	
FIRST PERSON	I	am/was	we	are/were
SECOND PERSON	you	are/were	you	are/were
THIRD PERSON	he/she/it	is/was	they	are/were

G1-b Make the verb agree with its subject, not with a word that comes between.

Word groups often come between the subject and the verb. Such word groups, usually modifying the subject, may contain a noun that at first appears to be the subject. By mentally stripping away such modifiers, you can isolate the noun that is in fact the subject.

The *samples* on the tray in the lab *need* testing.

▶ High levels of air pollution causes̶ damage to the respiratory tract.

When to use the -s (or -es) form of a present-tense verb

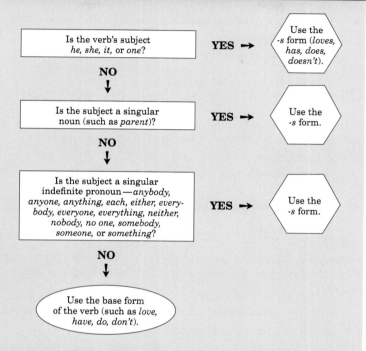

EXCEPTION: Choosing the correct present-tense form of *be* (*am, is,* or *are*) is not quite so simple. See the chart on the previous page for both present- and past-tense forms of *be*.

ESL CAUTION: Do not use the *-s* form of a verb that follows a helping verb such as *can, must,* or *should*. (See T2-a.)

The subject is *levels*, not *pollution*. Strip away the phrase *of air pollution* to hear the correct verb: *levels cause*.

► The slaughter of pandas for their pelts ~~have~~ *has* caused the panda

population to decline drastically.

The subject is *slaughter*, not *pandas* or *pelts*.

NOTE: Phrases beginning with the prepositions *as well as, in addition to, accompanied by, together with,* and *along with* do not make a singular subject plural.

▶ The pilot, as well as the attendant, ~~were~~ calm during the crisis.
   was
   ^

To emphasize that two people were calm, the writer could use *and* instead: *The pilot and the attendant were calm during the crisis.*

G1-c Treat most subjects joined with *and* as plural.

A subject with two or more parts is said to be compound. If the parts are connected by *and,* the subject is nearly always plural.

Leon and Jan often *jog* together.

▶ Jill's natural ability and her desire to help others ~~has~~ led to a
   have
   ^

career in the ministry.

EXCEPTIONS: When the parts of the subject form a single unit or when they refer to the same person or thing, treat the subject as singular.

Strawberries and cream was a last-minute addition to the menu.

Sue's friend and adviser was surprised by her decision.

When a compound subject is preceded by *each* or *every,* treat the subject as singular.

Each tree, shrub, and vine needs to be sprayed.

G1-d With subjects connected by *or* or *nor* (or by *either . . . or* or *neither . . . nor*), make the verb agree with the part of the subject nearer to the verb.

A driver's *licence* or credit *card is* required.

A driver's *licence* or two credit *cards are* required.

▶ If a relative or neighbour ~~are~~ abusing a child, notify the police.
   is
   ^

► Neither the professor nor his assistants ~~was~~ *were* able to solve the

   mystery of the eerie glow in the laboratory.

G1-e Treat most indefinite pronouns as singular.

Indefinite pronouns refer to nonspecific persons or things. Even though the following indefinite pronouns may seem to have plural meanings, treat them as singular in formal English: *anybody, anyone, anything, each, either, everybody, everyone, everything, neither, nobody, no one, somebody, someone, something.*

   Everyone on the team *supports* the coach.

► Each of the furrows ~~have~~ *has* been seeded.

► Everybody who signed up for the ski trip ~~were~~ *was* taking lessons.

   A few indefinite pronouns (*all, any, none, some*) may be singular or plural depending on the noun or pronoun they refer to.

   Some of our *luggage was* lost. *None* of his *advice makes* sense.

   Some of the *rocks are* slippery. *None* of the *eggs were* broken.

NOTE: When the meaning of *none* is emphatically "not one," *none* may be treated as singular: *None* [meaning "Not one"] *of the eggs was broken.* However, some experts advise using *not one* instead: *Not one of the eggs was broken.*

ON THE WEB

The rules on whether to treat *none* as singular or plural have sparked debates. If you're interested in learning why, go to
www.dianahacker.com/writersref

and click on ► **Language Debates**
            ► *none*

G1-f Treat collective nouns as singular unless the meaning is clearly plural.

Collective nouns such as *jury, committee, audience, crowd, class, troop, family,* and *couple* name a class or a group. In Canadian English, collective nouns are usually treated as singular: They emphasize the group as a unit. Occasionally, when there is some reason to draw attention to the individual members of the group, a collective noun may be treated as plural. (See also G3-a.)

SINGULAR   The *class respects* the teacher.

PLURAL   The *class are* debating among themselves.

To underscore the notion of individuality in the second sentence, many writers would add a clearly plural noun such as *members: The members of the class are debating among themselves.*

▶ The board of trustees ~~meet~~ *meets* in Saskatoon on the first Tuesday of

each month.

The board as a whole meets; there is no reason to draw attention to its individual members.

▶ A young couple ~~was~~ *were* arguing about politics while holding hands.

The meaning is clearly plural. Only individuals can argue and hold hands.

NOTE: The phrase *the number* is treated as singular, *a number* as plural.

SINGULAR   *The number* of school-age children *is* declining.

PLURAL   *A number* of children *are* attending the wedding.

NOTE: When units of measurement are used collectively, treat them as singular; when they refer to individual persons or things, treat them as plural.

SINGULAR   *Three-fourths* of the pie *has* been eaten.

PLURAL   *One-fourth* of the drivers *were* driving at least fifteen kilometres per hour over the speed limit.

G1-g Make the verb agree with its subject even when the subject follows the verb.

Verbs ordinarily follow subjects. When this normal order is reversed, it is easy to become confused. Sentences beginning with *There is* or *There are* (or *There was* or *There were*) are inverted; the subject follows the verb.

There *are* surprisingly few *children* in our neighbourhood.

Occasionally you may decide to invert a sentence for variety or effect. When you do so, check to make sure that your subject and verb agree.

▶ In the bay window ~~is~~ *are* a large ficus tree and several hanging ferns.

The subject *tree and ferns* is plural, so the verb must be *are*.

G1-h Make the verb agree with its subject, not with a subject complement.

One sentence pattern in English consists of a subject, a linking verb, and a subject complement: *Jack is an attorney.* (See B2-b.) Because the subject complement names or describes the subject, it is sometimes mistaken for the subject.

▶ A tent and a sleeping bag ~~is~~ *are* the required equipment.

Tent and bag is the subject, not *equipment*.

▶ A major force in today's economy ~~are~~ *is* women—as earners,

consumers, and investors.

Force is the subject, not *women*. If the correct sentence seems awkward, you can make *women* the subject: *Women are a major force in today's economy. . . .*

G1-i *Who, which,* and *that* take verbs that agree with their antecedents.

Like most pronouns, the relative pronouns *who, which,* and *that* have antecedents, nouns or pronouns to which they refer. Relative pronouns used as subjects of subordinate clauses take verbs that agree with their antecedents. (See B3-e.)

Take a *suit that travels* well.

Constructions such as *one of the students who* [or *one of the things that*] cause problems for writers. Do not assume that the antecedent must be *one.* Instead, you should consider the logic of the sentence.

▶ Our ability to use language is one of the things that sets us apart from animals.

The antecedent of *that* is *things,* not *one.* Several things set us apart from animals.

When the word *only* comes before *one,* you are safe in assuming that *one* is the antecedent of the relative pronoun.

▶ Dr. Barker knew that Frank was the only one of his sons who
  was
  ~~were~~ responsible enough to direct the family's charitable
  ^
  foundation.

The antecedent of *who* is *one,* not *sons.* Only one son was responsible enough.

ON THE WEB

The rules on *one of those who* constructions have sparked debates. If you're interested in learning why, go to
www.dianahacker.com/writersref

and click on ▶ Language Debates
              ▶ *one of those who* (or *that*)

G1-j Words such as *athletics, economics, mathematics, physics, statistics, measles,* and *news* are usually singular, despite their plural form.

> ▸ Statistics ~~are~~ among the most difficult courses in our program.
>   *is*

EXCEPTION: When they describe separate items rather than a collective body of knowledge, words such as *athletics, mathematics, physics,* and *statistics* are plural: *The statistics on school retention rates are impressive.*

G1-k Titles of works, company names, words mentioned as words, and gerund phrases are singular.

> ▸ *Lost Cities* ~~describe~~ the discoveries of many ancient civilizations.
>   *describes*

> ▸ Delmonico Brothers ~~specialize~~ in organic produce and
>   *specializes*
>
>   additive-free meats.

> ▸ *Controlled substances* ~~are~~ a euphemism for illegal drugs.
>   *is*

A gerund phrase consists of an *-ing* verb form followed by any objects, complements, or modifiers (see B3-b). Treat gerund phrases as singular.

> ▸ Encountering busy signals ~~are~~ troublesome to our clients,
>   *is*
>
>   so we have hired two new switchboard operators.

ON THE WEB

For electronic exercises on subject-verb agreement, go to
www.dianahacker.com/writersref

and click on ▸ **Electronic Grammar Exercises**
              ▸ **Grammatical Sentences**
                ▸ **E-ex G1–1 through G1–3**

G2

Other problems with verbs

The verb is the heart of the sentence, so it is important to get it right. Section G1 deals with the problem of subject-verb agreement, and section W3 offers advice on use of active and passive verbs. This section describes a number of other potential problems with verbs:

a. irregular verb forms (such as *drive, drove, driven*)
b. *lie* and *lay*
c. *-s* (or *-es*) endings on verbs
d. *-ed* endings on verbs
e. omitted verbs
f. tense
g. subjunctive mood

ESL

If English is not your native language, see also T2, Special Problems with Verbs.

G2-a   Choose standard English forms of irregular verbs.

Except for the verb *be,* all verbs in English have five forms. The following list gives the five forms and provides a sample sentence in which each might appear.

BASE FORM	Usually I (*walk, ride*).
PAST TENSE	Yesterday I (*walked, rode*).
PAST PARTICIPLE	I have (*walked, ridden*) many times before.
PRESENT PARTICIPLE	I am (*walking, riding*) right now.
-S FORM	He/she/it usually (*walks, rides*).

For regular verbs, such as *walk,* the past-tense and past-participle forms are the same (ending in *-ed* or *-d*), so there is no danger of confusion. This is not true, however, for irregular verbs such as *ride.* Writers sometimes confuse the past-tense and past-participle forms of irregular verbs, producing nonstandard sentences.

NONSTANDARD	Have you rode on the new subway?
STANDARD	Have you ridden on the new subway?

 GRAMMAR CHECKERS can flag some misused irregular verbs, such as *had drove* or *Lucia swum,* but they miss about twice as many errors as they find.

Choosing standard English forms

The past-tense form, which expresses action that occurred entirely in the past, never has a helping verb. (For a complete list of helping verbs, see B1-c.) The past participle is used with a helping verb — either with *has, have,* or *had* to form one of the perfect tenses or with *be, am, is, are, was, were, being,* or *been* to form the passive voice.

PAST TENSE	Last July, we *went* to Paris.
PAST PARTICIPLE	We have *gone* to Paris twice.

When you aren't sure which verb form to choose (*went* or *gone, began* or *begun,* and so on), consult the list of common irregular verbs that starts on page 162. Choose the past-tense form if the verb in your sentence doesn't have a helping verb; use the past-participle form if it does.

▶ Yesterday we ~~seen~~ *saw* an unidentified flying object.

▶ The reality of the situation ~~sunk~~ *sank* in.

The past-tense forms *saw* and *sank* are required.

▶ The truck was apparently ~~stole~~ *stolen* while the driver ate lunch.

▶ By the end of the day, the stock market had ~~fell~~ *fallen* two hundred points.

Because of the helping verbs, the past-participle forms are required: *was stolen, had fallen.*

Common irregular verbs

When in doubt about the standard English forms of irregular verbs, consult the following list or look up the base form of the verb in the dictionary, which also lists any irregular forms. (If no additional forms are listed in the dictionary, the verb is regular, not irregular.)

BASE FORM	PAST TENSE	PAST PARTICIPLE
arise	arose	arisen
awake	awoke, awaked	awaked, awoke
be	was, were	been
beat	beat	beaten, beat
become	became	become
begin	began	begun
bend	bent	bent
bite	bit	bitten, bit
blow	blew	blown
break	broke	broken
bring	brought	brought
build	built	built
burst	burst	burst
buy	bought	bought
catch	caught	caught
choose	chose	chosen
cling	clung	clung
come	came	come
cost	cost	cost
deal	dealt	dealt
dig	dug	dug
dive	dived, dove	dived
do	did	done
drag	dragged	dragged
draw	drew	drawn
dream	dreamed, dreamt	dreamed, dreamt
drink	drank	drunk
drive	drove	driven
eat	ate	eaten
fall	fell	fallen
fight	fought	fought
find	found	found
fly	flew	flown
forget	forgot	forgotten, forgot
freeze	froze	frozen
get	got	gotten, got
give	gave	given
go	went	gone
grow	grew	grown

BASE FORM	PAST TENSE	PAST PARTICIPLE
hang (suspend)	hung	hung
hang (execute)	hanged	hanged
have	had	had
hear	heard	heard
hide	hid	hidden
hurt	hurt	hurt
keep	kept	kept
know	knew	known
lay (put)	laid	laid
lead	led	led
lend	lent	lent
let (allow)	let	let
lie (recline)	lay	lain
lose	lost	lost
make	made	made
prove	proved	proved, proven
read	read	read
ride	rode	ridden
ring	rang	rung
rise (get up)	rose	risen
run	ran	run
say	said	said
see	saw	seen
send	sent	sent
set (place)	set	set
shake	shook	shaken
shoot	shot	shot
shrink	shrank	shrunk, shrunken
sing	sang	sung
sink	sank	sunk
sit (be seated)	sat	sat
slay	slew	slain
sleep	slept	slept
speak	spoke	spoken
spin	spun	spun
spring	sprang	sprung
stand	stood	stood
steal	stole	stolen
sting	stung	stung
strike	struck	struck, stricken
swear	swore	sworn
swim	swam	swum
swing	swung	swung
take	took	taken
teach	taught	taught
throw	threw	thrown

BASE FORM	PAST TENSE	PAST PARTICIPLE
wake	woke, waked	waked, woken
wear	wore	worn
wring	wrung	wrung
write	wrote	written

ON THE WEB

For an electronic exercise on irregular verbs, go to
www.dianahacker.com/writersref

and click on   ▶ **Electronic Grammar Exercises**
▶ **Grammatical Sentences**
▶ **E-ex G2–1**

G2-b Distinguish among the forms of *lie* and *lay*.

Writers and speakers frequently confuse the various forms of *lie* (meaning "to recline or rest on a surface") and *lay* (meaning "to put or place something"). *Lie* is an intransitive verb; it does not take a direct object: *The tax forms lie on the table.* The verb *lay* is transitive; it takes a direct object: *Please lay the tax forms on the table.* (See B2-b.)

In addition to confusing the meaning of *lie* and *lay*, writers and speakers are often unfamiliar with the standard English forms of these verbs.

BASE FORM	PAST TENSE	PAST PARTICIPLE	PRESENT PARTICIPLE
lie	lay	lain	lying
lay	laid	laid	laying

▶ Nandini was so exhausted that ~~she~~ laid down for a nap.
lay

The past-tense form of *lie* ("to recline") is *lay*.

▶ The patient had ~~laid~~ in an uncomfortable position all night.
lain

The past-participle form of *lie* ("to recline") is *lain*. If the correct English seems too stilted, recast the sentence: *The patient had been lying in an uncomfortable position all night.*

▶ The prosecutor ~~lay~~ the pistol on a table close to the jurors.
laid

The past-tense form of *lay* ("to place") is *laid*.

▶ Letters dating from the War of 1812 were ~~laying~~ *lying* in the corner of

the chest.

The present participle of *lie* ("to rest on a surface") is *lying.*

ON THE WEB

The rules on using *lie* and *lay* have sparked debates. If you're
interested in learning why, go to
www.dianahacker.com/writersref

and click on   ▶ **Language Debates**
                ▶ *lie* **versus** *lay*

G2-c Use -*s* (or -*es*) endings on present-tense verbs that have third-person singular subjects.

When the subject of a sentence is third-person singular, its verb
takes an -*s* or -*es* ending in the present tense. (See also G1-a and
the charts on pp. 152–53.)

	SINGULAR		**PLURAL**	
FIRST PERSON	I	know	we	know
SECOND PERSON	you	know	you	know
THIRD PERSON	he/she/it	knows	they	know
	child	knows	parents	know
	everyone	knows		

All singular nouns (such as *child*) and the pronouns *he, she,* and *it*
are third-person singular; indefinite pronouns (such as *everyone*)
are also third-person singular.

In nonstandard speech, the -*s* ending required by standard
English is sometimes omitted.

▶ Sulphur dioxide ~~turn~~ *turns* leaves yellow, ~~dissolve~~ *dissolves* marble, and ~~eat~~ *eats* away

iron and steel.

The subject *sulphur dioxide* is third-person singular, so the verbs must
end in -*s.*

CAUTION: Do not add the -*s* ending to the verb if the subject is not
third-person singular.

▶ I prepared program specifications and logic diagrams.

▶ The dirt floors required continual sweeping.

The subject *I* is first-person singular. The subject *floors* is third-person plural.

In nonstandard speech, the *-s* verb form *has, does,* or *doesn't* is sometimes replaced with *have, do,* or *don't.* In standard English, use *has, does,* or *doesn't* with a third-person singular subject. (See also G1-a.)

▶ This respected musician always ~~have~~ _{has} a message in his work.

▶ ~~Do~~ _{Does} she know the correct procedure for the experiment?

▶ My uncle ~~don't~~ _{doesn't} want to change jobs right now.

GRAMMAR CHECKERS can catch some problems with *-s* endings on verbs. Unfortunately, they flag quite a few correct sentences, so you need to know how to interpret what the programs tell you. (See the grammar checker advice on p. 151 for more detailed information.)

G2-d Do not omit *-ed* endings on verbs.

Speakers who do not fully pronounce *-ed* endings sometimes omit them unintentionally in writing. Failure to pronounce *-ed* endings is common in many dialects and in informal speech even in standard English. In the following frequently used words and phrases, for example, the *-ed* ending is not always fully pronounced.

advised	developed	prejudiced	stereotyped
asked	fixed	pronounced	used to
concerned	frightened	supposed to	

When a verb is regular, both the past tense and the past participle are formed by adding *-ed* to the base form of the verb.

Past tense

Use an *-ed* or *-d* ending to express the past tense of regular verbs. The past tense is used when the action occurred entirely in the past.

> *fixed*
> ► Over the weekend, Ed ~~fix~~ his brother's skateboard and tuned up
>
> his mother's 1955 Thunderbird.

> *advised*
> ► Last summer my counselor ~~advise~~ me to ask my family for help.

Past participles

Past participles are used in three ways: (1) following *have, has,* or *had* to form one of the perfect tenses; (2) following *be, am, is, are, was, were, being,* or *been* to form the passive voice; and (3) as adjectives modifying nouns or pronouns. The perfect tenses are listed on page 169, and the passive voice is discussed in W3-a. For a discussion of participles functioning as adjectives, see B3-b.

> *asked*
> ► Robin has ~~ask~~ me to go to California with her.

Has asked is present perfect tense (*have* or *has* followed by a past participle).

> *publicized*
> ► Though it is not a new phenomenon, domestic violence is ~~publicize~~
>
> more frequently than before.

Is publicized is in the passive voice (a form of *be* followed by a past participle).

> *tightened*
> ► All aerobics classes end in a cool-down period to stretch ~~tighten~~
>
> muscles.

Tightened is a participle used as an adjective to modify the noun *muscles.*

GRAMMAR CHECKERS can catch some missing *-ed* endings, but they tend to slip past as many as they catch. For example, although programs flagged *was accustom,* they ignored *has change* and *was pass.*

G2-e Do not omit needed verbs.

Although standard English allows some linking verbs and helping verbs to be contracted, at least in informal contexts, it does not allow them to be omitted.

Linking verbs, used to link subjects to subject complements, are frequently a form of *be: be, am, is, are, was, were, being, been.* (See B2-b.) Some of these forms may be contracted (*I'm, she's, we're*), but they should not be omitted altogether.

▶ Aaron $\overset{is}{\underset{\wedge}{}}$ a man who can defend himself.

Helping verbs, used with main verbs, include forms of *be, do,* and *have* or the words *can, will, shall, could, would, should, may, might,* and *must.* (See B1-c.) Some helping verbs may be contracted (*he's leaving, we'll celebrate, they've been told*), but they should not be omitted altogether.

▶ Do you know someone who $\overset{would}{\underset{\wedge}{}}$ be good for the job?

ESL

Speakers of English as a second language sometimes have problems with omitted verbs and correct use of helping verbs. See T2-e and T2-a.

ON THE WEB

For an electronic exercise on verb forms, go to
www.dianahacker.com/writersref

and click on ▶ **Electronic Grammar Exercises**
                ▶ **Grammatical Sentences**
                    ▶ **E-ex G2–2**

G2-f Choose the appropriate verb tense.

Tenses indicate the time of an action in relation to the time of the speaking or writing about that action.

The most common problem with tenses—shifting from one tense to another—is discussed in S4-b. Other problems with tenses are detailed in this section, after the following survey of tenses.

Survey of tenses

Tenses are classified as present, past, and future, with simple, perfect, and progressive forms for each.

The simple tenses indicate relatively simple time relations. The simple present tense is used primarily for actions occurring at the time of the speaking or for actions occurring regularly. The simple past tense is used for actions completed in the past. The simple future tense is used for actions that will occur in the future. In the following table, the simple tenses are given for the regular verb *walk,* the irregular verb *ride,* and the highly irregular verb *be.*

SIMPLE PRESENT

SINGULAR		PLURAL	
I	walk, ride, am	we	walk, ride, are
you	walk, ride, are	you	walk, ride, are
he/she/it	walks, rides, is	they	walk, ride, are

SIMPLE PAST

SINGULAR		PLURAL	
I	walked, rode, was	we	walked, rode, were
you	walked, rode, were	you	walked, rode, were
he/she/it	walked, rode, was	they	walked, rode, were

SIMPLE FUTURE

I, you, he/she/it, we, they	will walk, ride, be

More complex time relations are indicated by the perfect tenses. A verb in one of the perfect tenses (a form of *have* plus the past participle) expresses an action that was or will be completed at the time of another action.

PRESENT PERFECT

I, you, we, they	have walked, ridden, been
he/she/it	has walked, ridden, been

PAST PERFECT

I, you, he/she/it, we, they	had walked, ridden, been

FUTURE PERFECT

I, you, he/she/it, we, they	will have walked, ridden, been

The simple and perfect tenses just discussed have progressive forms that describe actions in progress. A progressive verb consists of a form of *be* followed by a present participle.

PRESENT PROGRESSIVE

I	am walking, riding, being
he/she/it	is walking, riding, being
you, we, they	are walking, riding, being

PAST PROGRESSIVE

I, he/she/it	was walking, riding, being
you, we, they	were walking, riding, being

FUTURE PROGRESSIVE

I, you, he/she/it, we, they	will be walking, riding, being

PRESENT PERFECT PROGRESSIVE

I, you, we, they	have been walking, riding, being
he/she/it	has been walking, riding, being

PAST PERFECT PROGRESSIVE

I, you, he/she/it, we, they	had been walking, riding, being

FUTURE PERFECT PROGRESSIVE

I, you, he/she/it, we, they	will have been walking, riding, being

ESL

The progressive forms are not normally used with mental activity verbs such as *believe*. See T2-a.

Special uses of the present tense

Use the present tense when expressing general truths, when writing about literature, and when quoting, summarizing, or paraphrasing an author's views.

General truths or scientific principles should appear in the present tense, unless such principles have been disproved.

▶ Galileo taught that the earth ~~revolved~~ around the sun.
                                   revolves

Since Galileo's teaching has not been discredited, the verb should be in the present tense. The following sentence, however, is acceptable: *Ptolemy taught that the sun revolved around the earth.*

When writing about a work of literature, you may be tempted to use the past tense. The convention, however, is to describe fictional events in the present tense.

▶ In Masuji Ibuse's *Black Rain,* a child ~~reached~~ *reaches* for a pomegranate in his mother's garden, and a moment later he ~~was~~ *is* dead, killed by the blast of the atomic bomb.

When you are quoting, summarizing, or paraphrasing the author of a nonliterary work, use present-tense verbs such as *writes, reports, asserts,* and so on. This convention is usually followed even when the author is dead (unless a date or the context specifies the time of writing).

▶ Baron Bowan of Colwood ~~wrote~~ *writes* that a metaphysician is "one who goes into a dark cellar at midnight without a light, looking for a black cat that is not there."

EXCEPTION: When you are documenting a paper with the APA (American Psychological Association) style of in-text citations, which include a date after the author's name, use past tense verbs such as *reported* or *demonstrated* or present perfect verbs such as *has reported* or *has demonstrated.*

> E. Wilson (1994) reported that positive reinforcement alone was a less effective teaching technique than a mixture of positive reinforcement and constructive criticism.

The past perfect tense

The past perfect tense consists of a past participle preceded by *had* (*had worked, had gone*). This tense is used for an action already completed by the time of another past action or for an action already completed at some specific past time.

> Everyone *had spoken* by the time I arrived.

> Everyone *had spoken* by 10:00 A.M.

Writers sometimes use the simple past tense when they should use the past perfect.

▶ We built our cabin high on a pine knoll, twelve metres above an
abandoned quarry that ~~was~~ flooded in 1920 to create a lake.
had been inserted above "was"

The building of the cabin and the flooding of the quarry both occurred
in the past, but the flooding was completed before the time of building.

▶ By the time we arrived at the party, the guest of honour left.
had inserted before "left"

The past perfect tense is needed because the action of leaving was completed at a specific past time (by the time we arrived).

Some writers tend to overuse the past perfect tense. Do not use
the past perfect if two past actions occurred at the same time.

▶ When we arrived in Paris, Pauline ~~had~~ met us at the train

station.

Sequence of tenses with infinitives and participles

An infinitive is the base form of a verb preceded by *to*. (See B3-b.)
Use the present infinitive to show action at the same time as or
later than the action of the verb in the sentence.

▶ The club had hoped to ~~have raised~~ a thousand dollars by April 1.
raise inserted above "have raised"

The action expressed in the infinitive (*to raise*) occurred later than the
action of the sentence's verb (*had hoped*).

Use the perfect form of an infinitive (*to have* followed by the
past participle) for an action occurring earlier than that of the verb
in the sentence.

▶ Dan would like to ~~join~~ the navy, but he did not pass the physical.
have joined inserted above "join"

The liking occurs in the present; the joining would have occurred in the
past.

Like the tense of an infinitive, the tense of a participle is also
governed by the tense of the sentence's verb. Use the present participle (ending in *-ing*) for an action occurring at the same time as
that of the sentence's verb.

Hiking the Trans Canada Trail in early summer, we spotted many
wildflowers.

Use the past participle (such as *given* or *helped*) or the present perfect participle (*having* plus the past participle) for an action occurring before that of the verb.

> *Discovered* off the coast of Newfoundland, the ship yielded many treasures.

> *Having worked* her way through college, Lee graduated debt-free.

G2-g Use the subjunctive mood in the few contexts that require it.

There are three moods in English: the *indicative,* used for facts, opinions, and questions; the *imperative,* used for orders or advice; and the *subjunctive,* used in certain contexts to express wishes, requests, or conditions contrary to fact. Of these moods, the subjunctive is most likely to cause problems for writers.

Forms of the subjunctive

In the subjunctive mood, present-tense verbs do not change form to indicate the number and person of the subject (see G1-a). Instead, the subjunctive uses the base form of the verb (*be, drive, employ*) with all subjects.

> It is important that you *be* [not *are*] prepared for the interview.

> We asked that she *drive* [not *drives*] more slowly.

Also, in the subjunctive mood, there is only one past-tense form of *be: were* (never *was*).

> If I *were* [not *was*] you, I'd proceed more cautiously.

Uses of the subjunctive

The subjunctive mood appears in only a few contexts: in contrary-to-fact clauses beginning with *if* or expressing a wish; in *that* clauses following verbs such as *ask, insist, recommend, request,* and *suggest;* and in certain set expressions.

IN CONTRARY-TO-FACT CLAUSES BEGINNING WITH *IF* When a subordinate clause beginning with *if* expresses a condition contrary to fact, use the subjunctive mood.

▶ If I ~~was~~ *were* a member of Parliament, I would vote for that bill.

▶ We could be less cautious if Jake ~~was~~ *were* more trustworthy.

The verbs in these sentences express conditions that do not exist: The writer is not a member of Parliament, and Jake is not trustworthy.

Do not use the subjunctive mood in *if* clauses expressing conditions that exist or may exist.

If Marjorie *wins* the contest, she will leave for Barcelona in June.

IN CONTRARY-TO-FACT CLAUSES EXPRESSING A WISH   In formal English the subjunctive is used in clauses expressing a wish or desire; in informal speech, however, the indicative is more commonly used.

FORMAL   I wish that Dr. Kurtinitis *were* my professor.

INFORMAL   I wish that Dr. Kurtinitis *was* my professor.

IN *THAT* CLAUSES FOLLOWING VERBS SUCH AS *ASK, INSIST, RECOMMEND, REQUEST,* AND *SUGGEST*   Because requests have not yet become reality, they are expressed in the subjunctive mood.

▶ Professor Moore insists that her students ~~are~~ *be* on time.

▶ We recommend that Lambert ~~files~~ *file* form T-1 General soon.

IN CERTAIN SET EXPRESSIONS   The subjunctive mood, once more widely used in English, remains in certain set expressions: *be that as it may, as it were, come rain or shine, far be it from me,* and so on.

ON THE WEB

For an electronic exercise on verb tense and mood, go to
www.dianahacker.com/writersref

and click on   ▶ **Electronic Grammar Exercises**
                      ▶ **Grammatical Sentences**
                            ▶ **E-ex G2–3**

GRAMMAR CHECKERS rarely flag problems with the subjunctive mood. They may at times question your correct use of the subjunctive, since your correct use will seem to violate the rules of subject-verb agreement (see G1). For example, one program suggested using *was* instead of *were* in the following correct sentence: *This isn't my dog; if it were, I would feed it.* Because the sentence describes a condition contrary to fact, the subjunctive form *were* is correct.

G3

Problems with pronouns

Pronouns are words that substitute for nouns (see B1-b). Four frequently encountered problems with pronouns are discussed in this section:

a. pronoun-antecedent agreement (singular vs. plural)
b. pronoun reference (clarity)
c. pronoun case (personal pronouns such as *I* vs. *me, she* vs. *her*)
d. pronoun case (*who* vs. *whom*)

For other problems with pronouns, consult the Glossary of Usage (W1).

G3-a Make pronouns and antecedents agree.

The antecedent of a pronoun is the word the pronoun refers to. A pronoun and its antecedent agree when they are both singular or both plural.

SINGULAR The *doctor* finished *her* rounds.

PLURAL The *doctors* finished *their* rounds.

ESL

The pronouns *he, his, she, her, it,* and *its* must agree in gender (masculine, feminine, or neuter) with their antecedents, not with the words they modify.

Jane visited *her* [not *his*] brother in St. John's.

GRAMMAR CHECKERS do not flag problems with pronoun-antecedent agreement. It takes a human eye to see that a singular noun, such as *logger,* does not agree with a plural pronoun, such as *their,* in a sentence like this: *The logger in the Northwest Territories relies on the old forest growth for their living.*

Indefinite pronouns

Indefinite pronouns refer to nonspecific persons or things. Even though the following indefinite pronouns may seem to have plural meanings, treat them as singular in formal English: *anybody, anyone, anything, each, either, everybody, everyone, everything, neither, nobody, no one, somebody, someone, something.*

In this class *everyone* performs at *his or her* [not *their*] fitness level.

When a plural pronoun refers mistakenly to a singular indefinite pronoun, you can usually choose one of three options for revision.

1. Replace the plural pronoun with *he or she* (or *his or her*).
2. Make the antecedent plural.
3. Rewrite the sentence so that no problem of agreement arises.

▶ When someone has been drinking, ~~they are~~ *he or she is* more likely to speed.

▶ When ~~someone has~~ *drivers have* been drinking, they are more likely to speed.

▶ ~~When someone~~ *Someone who* has been drinking/ ~~they are~~ *is* more likely to speed.

Because the *he or she* construction is wordy, often the second or third revision strategy is more effective.

NOTE: The traditional use of *he* (or *his*) to refer to persons of either sex is now widely considered sexist (see W4-e).

Generic nouns

A generic noun represents a typical member of a group, such as a typical student, or any member of a group, such as any lawyer. Although generic nouns may seem to have plural meanings, they are singular.

Every *runner* must train vigorously if *he or she* wants [not *they* want] to excel.

When a plural noun refers mistakenly to a generic noun, you will usually have the same three revision options as just mentioned for indefinite pronouns.

▶ A medical student must study hard if ~~they want~~ *he or she wants* to succeed.

▶ *Medical students*
~~A medical student~~ must study hard if they want to succeed.

▶ A medical student must study hard ~~if they want~~ to succeed.

Collective nouns

Collective nouns such as *jury, committee, audience, crowd, class, troop, family, team,* and *couple* name a class or group. If the group functions as a unit, treat the noun as singular; if the members of the group function individually, treat the noun as plural.

AS A UNIT   The planning *committee* granted *its* permission to build.

AS INDIVIDUALS   The *committee* put *their* signatures on the document.

When treating a collective noun as plural, many writers prefer to add a clearly plural antecedent such as *members* to the sentence: *The members of the committee put their signatures on the document.*

To some extent, you can choose whether to treat a collective noun as singular or plural depending on your meaning. Make sure, however, that you are consistent.

▶ The jury has reached ~~their~~ decision.
$\overset{its}{\underset{\wedge}{}}$

The writer selected the verb *has* to match the singular noun *jury* (see G1-a), so for consistency the pronoun must be *its*.

Compound antecedents

Treat compound antecedents joined by *and* as plural.

Joanne and John moved to the mountains, where *they* built a log cabin.

With compound antecedents joined by *or* or *nor,* make the pronoun agree with the nearer antecedent.

Either *Bruce* or *James* should receive first prize for *his* sculpture.

Neither the *mouse* nor the *rats* could find *their* way through the maze.

NOTE: If one of the antecedents is singular and the other plural, as in the second example, put the plural one last to avoid awkwardness.

EXCEPTION: If one antecedent is male and the other female, do not follow the traditional rule. The sentence *Either Bruce or Anita should receive the blue ribbon for her sculpture* makes no sense. The best solution is to recast the sentence: *The blue ribbon for best sculpture should go to Bruce or Anita.*

ON THE WEB

The rules on pronoun-antecedent agreement have sparked debates. If you're interested in learning why, go to
www.dianahacker.com/writersref

and click on   ▶ **Language Debates**
                      ▶ **Pronoun-antecedent agreement**

ON THE WEB

For electronic exercises on pronoun-antecedent agreement, go to
www.dianahacker.com/writersref

and click on ▶ **Electronic Grammar Exercises**
▶ **Grammatical Sentences**
▶ **E-ex G3–1 through G3–3**

G3-b   Make pronoun references clear.

Pronouns substitute for nouns; they are a kind of shorthand. In a sentence like *After Andrew intercepted the ball, he kicked it as hard as he could,* the pronouns *he* and *it* substitute for the nouns *Andrew* and *ball.* The word a pronoun refers to is called its *antecedent.*

A pronoun should refer clearly to its antecedent. A pronoun's reference will be unclear if it is ambiguous, implied, vague, or indefinite.

GRAMMAR CHECKERS do not flag problems with pronoun reference. Although a computer program can identify pronouns, it has no way of knowing which words, if any, they refer to. For example, grammar checkers miss the fact that the pronoun *it* has an ambiguous reference in the following sentence: *The thief stole the woman's purse and her car and then destroyed it.* Did the thief destroy the purse or the car? It takes human judgment to realize that readers might be confused.

Ambiguous reference

Ambiguous reference occurs when the pronoun could refer to two possible antecedents.

▶ When Gloria set ~~the pitcher~~ *it* on the glass-topped table, ~~it~~ *the pitcher* broke.

▶ Tom told James, ~~that he had~~ *"You have"* won the lottery.

What broke—the table or the pitcher? Who won the lottery—Tom or James? The revisions eliminate the ambiguity.

Implied reference

A pronoun must refer to a specific antecedent, not to a word that is implied but not present in the sentence.

▶ After braiding Ann's hair, Sue decorated ~~them~~ with ribbons.

    the braids

The pronoun *them* referred to Ann's braids (implied by the term *braiding*), but the word *braids* did not appear in the sentence.

Modifiers, such as possessives, cannot serve as antecedents. A modifier may strongly imply the noun that the pronoun might logically refer to, but it is not itself that noun.

    Euripides

▶ In ~~Euripides'~~ *Medea,* he describes the revenge of a woman rejected

by her husband.

The pronoun *he* cannot refer logically to the possessive modifier *Euripides'*.

Broad reference of this, that, which, *and* it

For clarity, the pronouns *this, that, which,* and *it* should ordinarily refer to specific antecedents rather than to whole ideas or sentences. When a pronoun's reference is needlessly broad, either replace the pronoun with a noun or supply an antecedent to which the pronoun clearly refers.

▶ More and more often, we are finding ourselves victims of serious

    our fate

crimes. We learn to accept ~~this~~ with minor complaints.

▶ Romeo and Juliet were both too young to have acquired much

    a fact

wisdom, which accounts for their rash actions.

Indefinite reference of they, it, *or* you

The pronoun *they* should refer to a specific antecedent. Do not use *they* to refer indefinitely to persons who have not been specifically mentioned.

    Parliament

▶ ~~They~~ shut down all government agencies for more than a month

until the budget crisis was finally resolved.

The word *it* should not be used indefinitely in constructions such as "In the article it says that. . . ."

▶   *The*
 ~~In the~~ encyclopedia ~~it~~ states that male moths can smell female
       ^

moths from several kilometres away.

The pronoun *you* is appropriate when the writer is addressing the reader directly: *Once you have kneaded the dough, let it rise in a warm place.* Except in very informal contexts, however, the indefinite *you* (meaning "anyone in general") is inappropriate.

                                            a guest
▶   Ms. Pickersgill's *Guide to Etiquette* stipulates that ~~you~~ should not
                                             ^

arrive at a party too early or leave too late.

The writer could have replaced *you* with *one,* but in Canadian English the pronoun *one* can seem stilted.

ON THE WEB

The rule on avoiding the indefinite *you* has sparked debates. If you're interested in learning why, go to
www.dianahacker.com/writersref

and click on   ▶ **Language Debates**
                ▶ ***you***

ON THE WEB

For electronic exercises on pronoun reference, go to
www.dianahacker.com/writersref

and click on   ▶ **Electronic Grammar Exercises**
                ▶ **Grammatical Sentences**
                 ▶ **E-ex G3–4 through G3–6**

G3-c   Distinguish between pronouns such as *I* and *me*.

The personal pronouns in the following chart change what is known as case form according to their grammatical function in a sentence. Pronouns functioning as subjects or subject complements appear in the *subjective* case; those functioning as objects appear in the *objective* case; and those functioning as possessives appear in the *possessive* case.

SUBJECTIVE CASE	OBJECTIVE CASE	POSSESSIVE CASE
I	me	my
we	us	our
you	you	your
he/she/it	him/her/it	his/her/its
they	them	their

This section explains the difference between the subjective and objective cases; then it alerts you to certain structures that may tempt you to choose the wrong pronoun. Finally, it describes a special use of possessive-case pronouns.

GRAMMAR CHECKERS can flag some incorrect pronouns and explain the rules for using *I* or *me, he* or *him, she* or *her, we* or *us,* and *they* or *them.* You should not assume, however, that a computer program will catch all incorrect pronouns. For example, grammar checkers did not flag *more than I* in this sentence, where the writer's meaning requires *me: I get a little jealous that our dog likes my neighbour more than I.*

Subjective case

When a pronoun functions as a subject or a subject complement, it must be in the subjective case (*I, we, you, he/she/it, they*).

SUBJECT	Sylvia and *he* shared the award.
SUBJECT COMPLEMENT	Greg announced that the winners were Sylvia and *he.*

Subject complements — words following linking verbs that complete the meaning of the subject — frequently cause problems for writers, since we rarely hear the correct form in casual speech. (See B2-b.)

▶ **During the sensational trial, Paul Bernardo repeatedly denied**

        he.
that the killer was ~~him.~~
        ^

If *killer was he* seems too stilted, rewrite the sentence: *During the sensational trial, Paul Bernardo repeatedly denied that he was the killer.*

Objective case

When a pronoun functions as a direct object, an indirect object, or the object of a preposition, it must be in the objective case (*me, us, you, him/her/it, them*).

DIRECT OBJECT	Bruce found Tony and brought *him* home.
INDIRECT OBJECT	Alice gave *me* a surprise party.
OBJECT OF A PREPOSITION	Katya wondered if the call was for *her.*

Compound word groups

When a subject or an object appears as part of a compound structure, you may occasionally become confused. To test for the correct pronoun, mentally strip away all of the compound word group except the pronoun in question.

▶ Joel ran away from home because his stepfather and ~~him~~ ^{he} had

quarrelled.

> *His stepfather and he* is the subject of the verb *had quarrelled.* If we strip away the words *his stepfather and,* the correct pronoun becomes clear: *he had quarrelled* (not *him had quarrelled*).

▶ The most traumatic experience for her father and ~~I~~ ^{me} occurred long

after her operation.

> *Me* is the object of the preposition *for.* We would not say *the most traumatic experience for I.*

When in doubt about the correct pronoun, some writers try to evade the choice by using a reflexive pronoun such as *myself.* Such evasions are nonstandard, even though they are used by some educated persons.

▶ The Egyptian cab driver gave my husband and ~~myself~~ ^{me} some good

tips on travelling in North Africa.

> *My husband and me* is the indirect object of the verb *gave.* For correct uses of *myself,* see the Glossary of Usage (W1).

ON THE WEB

The rule on avoiding *myself* as a substitute for *I* or *me* has sparked debates. If you're interested in learning why, go to
www.dianahacker.com/writersref

and click on   ▶ **Language Debates**
                              ▶ ***myself***

Appositives

Appositives are noun phrases that rename nouns or pronouns. A pronoun used as an appositive has the same function as the noun or pronoun it renames.

▶ The chief strategists, Dr. Bell and ~~me~~ *I,* could not agree on a plan.

The appositive *Dr. Bell and I* renames the subject, *strategists.* Test: *I could not agree* (not *me could not agree*).

▶ The reporter interviewed only two witnesses, the shopkeeper and ~~I.~~ *me.*

The appositive *the shopkeeper and me* renames the direct object *witnesses.*

We *or* us *before a noun*

When deciding whether *we* or *us* should precede a noun, choose the pronoun that would be appropriate if the noun were omitted.

▶ ~~Us~~ *We* tenants would rather fight than move.

▶ Management is shortchanging ~~we~~ *us* tenants.

No one would say *Us would rather fight than move* or *Management is shortchanging we.*

Comparisons with *than or* as

Sentence parts, usually verbs, are often omitted in comparisons beginning with *than* or *as.* To test for the correct pronoun, mentally complete the sentence.

▶ Even though he is sometimes ridiculed by the other boys,

           they.
Norman is much better off than ~~them.~~
                             ^

They is the subject of the verb *are,* which is understood: *Norman is much better off than they* [are]. If the correct English seems too formal, you can always add the verb.

▶ The members of the board respected no other candidate as much

   her.
as ~~she.~~
   ^

Her is the direct object of an understood verb: *The members of the board respected no other candidate as much as* [they respected] *her.*

Subjects and objects of infinitives

An infinitive is the word *to* followed by the base form of a verb. (See B3-b.) Subjects of infinitives are an exception to the rule that subjects must be in the subjective case. Whenever an infinitive has a subject, it must be in the objective case. Objects of infinitives also are in the objective case.

                         me   *her*
▶ Ms. Wilson asked John and ~~I~~ to drive the mayor and ~~she~~ to
                             ^   ^

the airport.

John and me is the subject of the infinitive *to drive; mayor and her* is the direct object of the infinitive.

Possessive case to modify a gerund

If a pronoun modifies a gerund or a gerund phrase, it should appear in the possessive case (*my, our, your, his/her/its, their*). A gerund is a verb form ending in *-ing* that functions as a noun. (See B3-b.)

                    your
▶ The chances against ~~you~~ being hit by lightning are about two
                     ^

million to one.

Your modifies the gerund phrase *being hit by lightning.*

    Nouns as well as pronouns may modify gerunds. To form the possessive case of a noun, use an apostrophe and an *-s* (*a victim's suffering*) or just an apostrophe (*victims' suffering*). See P5-a.

► The old order in France paid a high price for the ~~aristocracy~~ ^{aristocracy's}
^

exploiting the lower classes.

The possessive noun *aristocracy's* modifies the gerund phrase *exploiting the lower classes*.

ON THE WEB

The rule on using a possessive before a gerund has sparked debates. If you're interested in learning why, go to
www.dianahacker.com/writersref

and click on ► **Language Debates**
► **Possessive before a gerund**

ON THE WEB

For electronic exercises on pronoun case, go to
www.dianahacker.com/writersref

and click on ► **Electronic Grammar Exercises**
► **Grammatical Sentences**
► **E-ex G3–7 and G3–8**

G3-d Distinguish between *who* and *whom*.

The choice between *who* and *whom* (or *whoever* and *whomever*) occurs primarily in subordinate clauses and in questions. *Who* and *whoever,* subjective-case pronouns, are used for subjects and subject complements. *Whom* and *whomever,* objective-case pronouns, are used for objects.

An exception to this general rule occurs when the pronoun functions as the subject of an infinitive. See page 188.

In subordinate clauses

The case of a relative pronoun in a subordinate clause is determined by its function *within the subordinate clause.*

GRAMMAR CHECKERS can flag some sentences with a misused *who* or *whom* and explain the nature of the error. However, at times the programs skip past a misused *who* or *whom,* as they did with this sentence: *Now that you have studied with both musicians, whom in your opinion is the better teacher?* The programs could not tell that the objective-case pronoun *whom* functions, incorrectly, as the subject of the verb *is.*

>   *who*
> ▶ The prize goes to the runner ~~whom~~ collects the most points.
>   ^

The subordinate clause is *who collects the most points.* The verb of the clause is *collects,* and its subject is *who.*

When it functions as an object in a subordinate clause, *whom* appears out of order, before both the subject and the verb. To choose the correct pronoun, you can mentally restructure the clause.

>   *whom*
> ▶ You will work with our senior engineers, ~~who~~ you will meet later.
>   ^

Whom is the direct object of the verb of the subordinate clause, *will meet.* This becomes clear if you mentally restructure the clause: *you will meet whom.* (See also B3-e.)

>   *whom*
> ▶ The tutor ~~who~~ I was assigned to was very supportive.
>   ^

Whom is the object of the preposition *to.* If the correct English seems too formal, drop *whom: The tutor I was assigned to. . . .*

NOTE: Ignore inserted expressions such as *they know* or *I think* when determining the case of a relative pronoun.

>   *who*
> ▶ All of the school bullies want to take on a big guy ~~whom~~ they
>   ^
>
> know will not hurt them.

Who is the subject of *will hurt,* not the object of *know.*

In questions

The case of an interrogative pronoun is determined by its function within the question.

▶ *Who*
   ~~Whom~~ is responsible for creating that computer virus?
   ^

Who is the subject of the verb *is*.

When *whom* appears as an object in a question, it appears out of order, before both the subject and the verb. To choose the correct pronoun, you can mentally restructure the question.

▶ *Whom*
   ~~Who~~ did the New Democratic Party nominate in 1976?
   ^

Whom is the direct object of the verb *did nominate*. This becomes clear if you restructure the question: *The New Democratic Party did nominate whom in 1976?*

For subjects or objects of infinitives

An infinitive is the word *to* followed by the base form of a verb. (See B3-b.) Subjects of infinitives are an exception to the rule that subjects must be in the subjective case. Whenever an infinitive has a subject, it must be in the objective case. Objects of infinitives also are in the objective case.

▶ On the subject of health care, I don't know ~~who~~ to believe.
                                              ^ *whom*

ON THE WEB

The rules on using *who* and *whom* have sparked debates. If you're interested in learning why, go to
www.dianahacker.com/writersref

and click on ▶ **Language Debates**
             ▶ *who* **versus** *whom*

ON THE WEB

For electronic exercises on using *who* and *whom*, go to
www.dianahacker.com/writersref

and click on ▶ **Electronic Grammar Exercises**
             ▶ **Grammatical Sentences**
             ▶ **E-ex G3–9 and G3–10**

G4

Adjectives and adverbs

Adjectives modify nouns or pronouns; adverbs modify verbs, adjectives, or other adverbs. (See B1-d and B1-e.)

Many adverbs are formed by adding *-ly* to adjectives (*formal, formally*). But don't assume that all words ending in *-ly* are adverbs or that all adverbs end in *-ly*. Some adjectives end in *-ly* (*lovely, friendly*) and some adverbs don't (*always, here, there*). When in doubt, consult a dictionary.

ESL

In English, adjectives are not pluralized to agree with the words they modify: *The red* [not *reds*] *roses were a wonderful surprise.*

GRAMMAR CHECKERS can flag a number of problems with adjectives and adverbs: some misuses of *bad* or *badly* and *good* or *well;* some double comparisons, such as *more meaner;* some absolute comparisons, such as *most unique;* and some double negatives, such as *can't hardly.* However, the programs slip past more problems than they find. Programs ignored errors like these: *could have been handled more professional* and *hadn't been bathed regular.*

G4-a Use adverbs, not adjectives, to modify verbs, adjectives, and adverbs.

When adverbs modify verbs (or verbals), they usually answer one of these questions: When? Where? How? Why? Under what conditions? How often? To what degree?

The incorrect use of adjectives in place of adverbs to modify verbs occurs primarily in casual or nonstandard speech.

▶ The manager must see that the office runs ~~smooth~~ and ~~efficient.~~
                                               smoothly   *efficiently.*

The incorrect use of the adjective *good* in place of the adverb *well* is especially common in casual and nonstandard speech.

> We were glad that Nemo had done ~~good~~ on the CPA exam.
>   well

NOTE: The word *well* is an adjective when it means "healthy," "satisfactory," or "fortunate": *I am very well, thank you. All is well. It is just as well.*

Adjectives are sometimes used incorrectly to modify adjectives or other adverbs.

> In the early 1970s, chances for survival of the bald eagle looked
>   really
>   ~~real~~ slim.

ESL

Placement of adjectives and adverbs can be a tricky matter for second-language speakers. See T3-e.

G4-b Use adjectives, not adverbs, as subject complements.

Adjectives ordinarily precede nouns, but they can also function as subject complements following linking verbs (see B2-b). When an adjective functions as a subject complement, it describes the subject.

> Justice is *blind.*

Problems can arise with verbs such as *smell, taste, look,* and *feel,* which may or may not be linking. If the word following one of these verbs describes the subject, use an adjective; if it modifies the verb, use an adverb.

> **ADJECTIVE**   The detective looked *cautious.*
>
> **ADVERB**   The detective looked *cautiously* for the fingerprints.

Linking verbs suggest states of being, not actions. For example, to look cautious suggests the state of being cautious, whereas to look cautiously is to perform an action in a cautious way.

▶ The lilacs in our backyard smell especially ~~sweetly~~ this year.
      sweet

▶ Lori looked ~~well~~ in her new raincoat.
      good

▶ We felt ~~badly~~ upon hearing of your grandmother's death.
      bad

The verbs *smell, looked,* and *felt* suggest states of being, not actions. Therefore, they should be followed by adjectives, not adverbs.

ON THE WEB

The rules on using *bad* and *badly* have sparked debates. If you're interested in learning why, go to
www.dianahacker.com/writersref

and click on ▶ Language Debates
             ▶ *bad* versus *badly*

G4-c Use comparatives and superlatives with care.

Most adjectives and adverbs have three forms: the positive, the comparative, and the superlative.

POSITIVE	COMPARATIVE	SUPERLATIVE
soft	softer	softest
fast	faster	fastest
careful	more careful	most careful
bad	worse	worst
good	better	best

Comparative versus superlative

Use the comparative to compare two things, the superlative to compare three or more.

▶ Which of these two brands of toothpaste is ~~best?~~
                                            better?

▶ Though Shaw and Jackson are impressive, Hobbs is the ~~more~~
                                                      most

qualified of the three candidates running for mayor.

Form of comparatives and superlatives

To form comparatives and superlatives of most one- and two-syllable adjectives, use the endings *-er* and *-est: smooth, smoother, smoothest; easy, easier, easiest.* With longer adjectives, use *more* and *most: exciting, more exciting, most exciting.*

Some one-syllable adverbs take the endings *-er* and *-est* (*fast, faster, fastest*), but longer adverbs and all of those ending in *-ly* form the comparative and superlative with *more* and *most.*

The comparative and superlative forms of the following adjectives and adverbs are irregular: *good, better, best; bad, worse, worst; badly, worse, worst.*

>   *most talented*
> ▶ The Kirov was the ~~talentedest~~ ballet company we had ever seen.

>   *worse*
> ▶ Lloyd's luck couldn't have been ~~worser~~ than David's.

Double comparatives or superlatives

Do not use a double comparative (an *-er* ending and the word *more*) or a double superlative (an *-est* ending and the word *most*).

>   *likely*
> ▶ All the polls indicated that Chrétien was more ~~likelier~~ to win
>
>   than Campbell.

> ▶ Of all her family, Jamila is the ~~most~~ happiest about the move
>
>   to Calgary.

Absolute concepts

Do not use comparatives or superlatives with absolute concepts such as *unique* or *perfect.* Either something is unique or it isn't. It is illogical to suggest that absolute concepts come in degrees.

>   *unusual*
> ▶ That is the most ~~unique~~ wedding gown I have ever seen.

>   *valuable*
> ▶ The painting would have been even more ~~priceless~~ had it been
>
>   signed.

ON THE WEB

The rule on avoiding absolute concepts in comparisons has sparked debates. If you're interested in learning why, go to
www.dianahacker.com/writersref

and click on ▶ **Language Debates**
                      ▶ **Absolute concepts such as *unique***

G4-d Avoid double negatives.

Standard English allows two negatives only if a positive meaning is intended: *The orchestra was not unhappy with its performance.* Double negatives used to emphasize negation are nonstandard.

Negative modifiers such as *never, no,* and *not* should not be paired with other negative modifiers or with negative words such as *neither, none, no one, nobody,* and *nothing.*

▶   Management is not doing ~~nothing~~ to see that the trash is

picked up.

The modifiers *hardly, barely,* and *scarcely* are considered negatives in standard English, so they should not be used with other negatives such as *not, no one,* and *never.*

▶   Maxine is so weak from her surgery she ~~can't~~ hardly

climb stairs.

ON THE WEB

For electronic exercises on using adjectives and adverbs, go to
www.dianahacker.com/writersref

and click on ▶ **Electronic Grammar Exercises**
                      ▶ **Grammatical Sentences**
                              ▶ **E-ex G4–1 and G4–2**

G5

Sentence fragments

A sentence fragment is a word group that pretends to be a sentence. Sentence fragments are easy to recognize when they appear out of context, like these:

> On the old wooden stool in the corner of my grandmother's kitchen.

> And immediately popped their flares and life vests.

When fragments appear next to related sentences, however, they are harder to spot.

> On that morning I sat in my usual spot. On the old wooden stool in the corner of my grandmother's kitchen.

> The pilots ejected from the burning plane, landing in the water not far from the ship. And immediately popped their flares and life vests.

GRAMMAR CHECKERS can flag as many as half of the sentence fragments in a sample; but that means, of course, that they miss half or more of them. If fragments are a serious problem for you, you will still need to proofread for them.

Sometimes you will get "false positives," sentences that have been flagged but are not fragments. For example, one program flagged this complete sentence as a possible fragment: *I bent down to crawl into the bunker.* When a program spots a possible fragment, you should check to see if it is really a fragment. You can do this by using the flow chart on page 195.

ESL

Unlike some languages, English does not allow omission of subjects (except in imperative sentences); nor does it allow omission of verbs. See T3-a and T2-e.

Test for sentence completeness

Is there a verb?*	**NO** →	It is a fragment.

YES ↓

Is there a subject?**	**NO** →	It is a fragment.

YES ↓

Is the word group merely a subordinate clause or phrase?***	**YES** →	It is a fragment.

NO ↓

It is a sentence.

*Do not mistake verbals for verbs. (See B3-b).
**The subject of a sentence may be *you,* understood. (See B2-a.)
***A sentence may open with a subordinate clause or phrase, but the sentence must also include an independent clause. (See B3.)

If you find any fragments, try one of these methods of revision:

1. Attach the fragment to a nearby sentence.
2. Turn the fragment into a sentence.

Recognizing sentence fragments

To be a sentence, a word group must consist of at least one full independent clause. An independent clause has a subject and a verb, and it either stands alone or could stand alone.

To test a word group for sentence completeness, use the flow chart on page 195. For example, by using the flow chart, you can see exactly why *On the old wooden stool in the corner of my grand-mother's kitchen* is a fragment: It lacks both a subject and a verb. *And immediately popped their flares and life vests* is a fragment because it lacks a subject.

Repairing sentence fragments

You can repair most fragments in one of two ways: Either pull the fragment into a nearby sentence or turn the fragment into a sentence.

▶   On that morning I sat in my usual spot⸝ ~~On~~ the old wooden
                                   ^*on*

stool in the corner of my grandmother's kitchen.

▶   The pilots ejected from the burning plane, landing in the water
                                           They
not far from the ship. ~~And~~ immediately popped their flares and
                       ^

life vests.

G5-a   Attach fragmented subordinate clauses or turn them into sentences.

A subordinate clause is patterned like a sentence, with both a subject and a verb, but it begins with a word that tells readers it cannot stand alone — a word such as *after, although, because, before, if, though, unless, until, when, where, who, which,* or *that.* (See B3-e.)

Most fragmented subordinate clauses beg to be pulled into a sentence nearby.

                                                    because
▶   Normally the bride-price consists of cattle and sheep⸝ ~~Because~~
                                                     ^

money has little value to these isolated people.

If a fragmented clause cannot be attached to a nearby sentence or if you feel that attaching it would be awkward, try turning it into a sentence. The simplest way to turn a subordinate clause into a sentence is to delete the opening word or words that mark it as subordinate.

▶ Population increases and uncontrolled development are taking a

deadly toll on the environment. ~~So that in~~ *In* many parts of the world,

fragile ecosystems are collapsing.

G5-b　Attach fragmented phrases or turn them into sentences.

Like subordinate clauses, phrases function within sentences as adjectives, as adverbs, or as nouns. They cannot stand alone. Fragmented phrases are often prepositional or verbal phrases; sometimes they are appositives, words or word groups that rename nouns or pronouns. (See B3-a, B3-b, and B3-c.)

Many fragmented phrases may simply be pulled into nearby sentences.

▶ The archaeologists worked slowly/, ~~Examining~~ *examining* and labelling

every pottery shard they uncovered.

The word group beginning with *Examining* is a verbal phrase.

▶ Mary is suffering from agoraphobia/, ~~A~~ *a* fear of the outside

world.

A fear of the outside world is an appositive renaming the noun *agoraphobia*.

If a fragmented phrase cannot be pulled into a nearby sentence effectively, turn the phrase into a sentence. You may need to add a subject, a verb, or both.

▶ In the computer training session, Eugene explained how to install

our new software. ~~Also~~ *He also taught us* how to organize our files, connect to the

Internet, and back up our hard drives.

The word group beginning *Also how to organize* is a fragmented verbal phrase. The revision turns the fragment into a sentence by adding a subject and a verb.

G5-c   Attach other fragmented word groups or turn them into sentences.

Other word groups that are commonly fragmented include parts of compound predicates, lists, and examples introduced by *such as, for example,* or similar expressions.

Parts of compound predicates

A predicate consists of a verb and its objects, complements, and modifiers (see p. 454). A compound predicate includes two or more predicates joined by a coordinating conjunction such as *and, but,* or *or.* Because the parts of a compound predicate share the same subject, they should appear in the same sentence.

▶ The woodpecker finch of the Galápagos Islands carefully selects a

                                 and

    twig of a certain size and shape. ~~And~~ then uses this tool to pry out

    grubs from trees.

    The word group beginning with *and* is part of a compound predicate. Notice that no comma appears between the parts of a compound predicate. (See P2-a.)

Lists

When a list is mistakenly fragmented, it can often be attached to a nearby sentence with a colon or a dash. (See P4-a and P7-d.)

▶ It has been said that there are only three indigenous American art

               j

    forms. : ~~J~~azz, musical comedy, and soap opera.

Examples introduced by such as, for example, *or similar expressions*

Expressions that introduce examples (or explanations) can lead to unintentional fragments. Although you may begin a sentence with some of the following words or phrases, make sure that what you have written is a sentence, not a fragment.

also	especially	in addition	namely	that is
and	for example	like	or	
but	for instance	mainly	such as	

Sometimes fragmented examples can be attached to the preceding sentence.

▶ Canada has produced some of the most distinguished twentieth-century writers~~,~~ ^such^ ~~Such~~ as Margaret Atwood, June Callwood, Michael Ondaatje, Alice Munro, Robertson Davies, and Alistair Macleod.

At times, however, it may be necessary to turn the fragment into a sentence.

▶ If Dushan doesn't get his way, he goes into a fit of rage. For example, ^he lies^ ~~lying~~ on the floor screaming or ^opens^ ~~opening~~ the cabinet doors and then ^slams^ ~~slamming~~ them shut.

The writer corrected this fragment by adding a subject — *he* — and substituting verbs — *lies, opens,* and *slams* — for the verbals *lying, opening,* and *slamming.*

G5-d Exception: Fragments may be used for special purposes.

Skilled writers occasionally use sentence fragments for the following special purposes.

FOR EMPHASIS	Following the dramatic Americanization of their children, even my parents grew more publicly confident. *Especially my mother.* — Richard Rodriguez
TO ANSWER A QUESTION	Are these new drug tests 100 percent reliable? *Not in the opinion of most experts.*
AS A TRANSITION	*And now the opposing arguments.*
EXCLAMATIONS	*Not again!*
IN ADVERTISING	*Fewer calories. Improved taste.*

Although fragments are sometimes appropriate, writers and readers do not always agree on when they are appropriate. Therefore you will find it safer to write in complete sentences.

ON THE WEB

For electronic exercises on sentence fragments, go to
www.dianahacker.com/writersref

and click on ▶ **Electronic Grammar Exercises**
　　　　　　　▶ **Grammatical Sentences**
　　　　　　　　　▶ **E-ex G5–1 through G5–3**

G6

Run-on sentences

Run-on sentences are independent clauses that have not been joined correctly. An independent clause is a word group that can stand alone as a sentence. (See B4.) When two independent clauses appear in one sentence, they must be joined in one of these ways:

—with a comma and a coordinating conjunction (*and, but, or, nor, for, so, yet*)

—with a semicolon (or occasionally a colon or a dash)

Recognizing run-on sentences

There are two types of run-on sentences. When a writer puts no mark of punctuation and no coordinating conjunction between independent clauses, the result is called a *fused sentence.*

　　　　　　┌─────────── INDEPENDENT CLAUSE ───────────┐
FUSED　　Gestures are a means of communication for everyone

　　　　　　┌────────── INDEPENDENT CLAUSE ──────────┐
　　　　　　they are essential for the hearing-impaired.

A far more common type of run-on sentence is the *comma splice*—two or more independent clauses joined by a comma without a coordinating conjunction. In some comma splices, the comma appears alone.

COMMA　　Gestures are a means of communication for everyone,
SPLICE　　they are essential for the hearing-impaired.

In other comma splices, the comma is accompanied by a joining word that is *not* a coordinating conjunction. There are only seven coordinating conjunctions in English: *and, but, or, nor, for, so, yet.* Notice that all of these words are short — only two or three letters long. (See also G6-a.)

COMMA   Gestures are a means of communication for everyone,
SPLICE   however, they are essential for the hearing-impaired.

To review your writing for possible run-on sentences, use the chart on page 203.

ON THE WEB

The rules on avoiding comma splices have sparked debates. If you're interested in learning why, go to
www.dianahacker.com/writersref

and click on   ▶ **Language Debates**
                ▶ **Comma splices**

GRAMMAR CHECKERS can flag only about 20 to 50 percent of the run-on sentences in a sample. The programs tend to be cautious, telling you that you "may have" a run-on sentence; you will almost certainly get a number of "false positives," sentences that have been flagged but are not run-ons. For example, a grammar checker flagged the following acceptable sentence as a possible run-on: *They believe that requiring gun owners to purchase a licence is sufficient.*

If you have a problem with run-ons, you will need to proofread for them even after using a grammar checker. Also, if your program spots a "possible" run-on, you will need to check to see if it is in fact a run-on. You can do this by using the flow chart on page 203.

Revising run-on sentences

To revise a run-on sentence, you have four choices:

1. Use a comma and a coordinating conjunction (*and, but, or, nor, for, so, yet*).

▶ Gestures are a means of communication for everyone, *but* they are

   essential for the hearing-impaired.

2. Use a semicolon (or, if appropriate, a colon or a dash). A semicolon may be used alone; it can also be accompanied by a transitional expression (see also G6-b and P3-b).

▶ Gestures are a means of communication for everyone/; they are essential for the hearing-impaired.

▶ Gestures are a means of communication for everyone/ *; however,* they are essential for the hearing-impaired.

3. Make the clauses into separate sentences.

▶ Gestures are a means of communication for everyone/. *T*hey are essential for the hearing-impaired.

4. Restructure the sentence, perhaps by subordinating one of the clauses.

▶ *Although gestures* ~~Gestures~~ are a means of communication for everyone, they are essential for the hearing-impaired.

One of these revision techniques will often work better than the others for a particular sentence. The fourth technique, the one requiring the most extensive revision, is frequently the most effective.

G6-a Consider separating the clauses with a comma and a coordinating conjunction.

There are seven coordinating conjunctions in English: *and, but, or, nor, for, so,* and *yet.* When a coordinating conjunction joins independent clauses, it must be preceded by a comma. (See P1-a.)

▶ The paramedic asked where I was hurt, *and* as soon as I motioned toward my pain, he cut up the leg of my favorite pair of designer jeans.

Recognizing run-on sentences

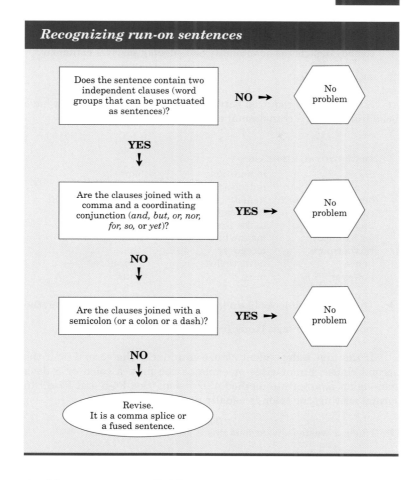

Does the sentence contain two independent clauses (word groups that can be punctuated as sentences)?

NO → No problem

YES
↓

Are the clauses joined with a comma and a coordinating conjunction (*and, but, or, nor, for, so,* or *yet*)?

YES → No problem

NO
↓

Are the clauses joined with a semicolon (or a colon or a dash)?

YES → No problem

NO
↓

Revise.
It is a comma splice or a fused sentence.

▶ Many government officials privately admit that the polygraph is
    yet
unreliable, ~~however,~~ they continue to use it as a security measure.
    ^

G6-b Consider separating the clauses with a semicolon (or, if appropriate, with a colon or a dash).

When the independent clauses are closely related and their relation is clear without a coordinating conjunction, a semicolon is an acceptable method of revision. (See P3-a.)

▶ Tragedy depicts the individual confronted with the fact of death, ; comedy depicts the adaptability and ongoing survival of human society.

A semicolon is required between independent clauses that have been linked with a transitional expression (see also P3-b).

TRANSITIONAL EXPRESSIONS

also	in addition	now
as a result	indeed	of course
besides	in fact	on the other hand
consequently	in other words	otherwise
finally	in the first place	similarly
for example	meanwhile	still
furthermore	moreover	then
hence	nevertheless	therefore
however	next	thus

▶ The timber wolf looks like a large German shepherd, ; however, the wolf has longer legs, larger feet, and a wider head.

If the first independent clause introduces the second or if the second clause summarizes or explains the first, a colon or a dash may be an appropriate method of revision. (See P4-b and P7-d.) In formal writing, the colon is usually preferred to the dash.

▶ Nuclear waste is hazardous ~~this~~ : This is an indisputable fact.

▶ The female black widow spider is often a widow of her own making, -- she has been known to eat her partner after mating.

If the first independent clause introduces a quoted sentence, a colon is an appropriate method of revision.

▶ Carolyn Heilbrun has this to say about the future, : "Today's shocks are tomorrow's conventions."

G6-c Consider making the clauses into separate sentences.

▶ Why should we spend money on expensive space exploration/?
  We
  ~~we~~ have enough underfunded programs here on earth.
  ^

Since one independent clause is a question and the other is a statement, they should be separate sentences.

                                                          Then
▶ I gave the necessary papers to the police officer/.~~then~~ he said I
                                                       ^
  would have to accompany him to the police station, where a

  counsellor would talk with me and call my parents.

Because the second independent clause is quite long, a sensible revision is to use separate sentences.

NOTE: When two quoted independent clauses are divided by explanatory words, make each clause its own sentence.

▶ "It's always smart to learn from your mistakes," quipped my boss/.
  "It's
  "~~it's~~ even smarter to learn from the mistakes of others."
  ^

G6-d Consider restructuring the sentence, perhaps by subordinating one of the clauses.

If one of the independent clauses is less important than the other, try turning it into a subordinate clause or phrase. (See S6-a.)

  Although many
▶ ~~Many~~ scholars dismiss the abominable snowman of the Himalayas
  ^
  as a myth, others claim it may be a kind of ape.

▶ The most famous geyser in Yellowstone National Park is
                        which
  Old Faithful, ~~it~~ can reach forty-five metres in height.
              ^

▶ Mary McLeod Bethune,~~was~~ the child of former slaves, ~~she~~
                     ^
  founded the U.S. National Council of Negro Women in 1935.

T

ESL Trouble
Spots

T

ESL Trouble Spots

This section of *A Canadian Writer's Reference* has a special audience: speakers of English as a second language (ESL) who have learned English but continue to have difficulty with a few trouble spots.

T1

Articles

Except for occasional difficulty in choosing between *a* and *an,* native speakers of English encounter few problems with articles. To speakers whose native language is not English, however, articles can prove troublesome, for the rules governing their use are surprisingly complex. This section summarizes those rules.

ON THE WEB

For an electronic exercise on articles, go to
www.dianahacker.com/writersref

and click on   ▶ **Electronic Grammar Exercises**
              ▶ **ESL Trouble Spots**
              ▶ **E-ex T1–1**

The articles a, an, *and* the

The indefinite articles *a* and *an* and the definite article *the* signal that a noun is about to appear. The noun may follow the article immediately, or modifiers may intervene (see B1-a and B1-d).

ART   N   ART   N
a sunset   an incredible sunset

ART   N   ART   N
the table   the round pine table

Other noun markers

Articles are not the only words used to mark nouns. Noun markers (sometimes called *determiners*) also include words such as the following, which identify or quantify nouns.

—possessive nouns, such as *Elena's*

—*my, your, his, her, its, our*

—*this, that, these, those*

—*all, any, each, either, every, few, many, more, most, much, neither, several, some*

—numbers: *one, two,* and so on

Usually an article is not used with another noun marker. Common exceptions include expressions such as *a few, the most,* and *all the.*

GRAMMAR CHECKERS can flag some missing or misused articles, pointing out, for example, that an article usually precedes a word such as *paintbrush* or *vehicle* or that the articles *a* and *an* are not usually used before a noncount noun such as *sugar* or *advice.*

However, the programs fail to flag many missing or misused articles. For example, in two paragraphs with eleven missing or misused articles, grammar checkers caught only two of the problems.

T1-a Use *a* (or *an*) with singular count nouns whose specific identity is not known to the reader.

Count nouns refer to persons, places, or things that can be counted: *one girl, two girls; one city, three cities; one apple, four apples.* Noncount nouns refer to entities or abstractions that cannot be counted: *water, silver, air, furniture, patience, knowledge.* To see what nouns English categorizes as noncount nouns, refer to the chart on page 212 or consult an ESL dictionary such as the *Longman Dictionary of American English.*

If the specific identity of a singular count noun is not known to the reader—perhaps because it is being mentioned for the first time, perhaps because its specific identity is unknown even to the writer—the noun should be preceded by *a* or *an* unless it has been preceded by another noun marker. *A* (or *an*) usually means "one among many" but can also mean "any one."

▶ Mary Beth arrived in ^a^ limousine.

▶ We are looking for ^an^ apartment close to the lake.

NOTE: *A* is used before a consonant sound: *a banana, a tree, a picture, a hand, a happy child. An* is used before a vowel sound: *an eggplant, an occasion, an uncle, an hour, an honourable person.* Notice that words beginning with *h* can have either a consonant sound (*hand, happy*) or a vowel sound (*hour, honourable*). (See also W1.)

T1-b Do not use *a* (or *an*) with noncount nouns.

A (or *an*) is not used to mark noncount nouns. A noncount noun refers to an entity or an abstract concept that cannot be counted: *sugar, gold, honesty, jewellery.* For a list of commonly used noncount nouns, see the chart on page 212.

▶ Claudia asked her mother for ~~an~~ advice.

If you want to express an approximate amount, you can often use one of the following quantifiers with a noncount noun.

QUANTIFIER	NONCOUNT NOUN
a great deal of	candy, courage
a little	salt, rain
any	sugar, homework
enough	bread, wood, money
less	meat, violence
little (*or* a little)	knowledge, time
more	coffee, information
much (*or* a lot of)	snow, pollution
plenty of	paper, lumber
some	tea, news, work

To express a more specific amount, you can often precede a noncount noun with a unit word that is typically associated with it. Here are some common combinations.

A OR *AN* + UNIT + *OF*	NONCOUNT NOUNS
a bottle of	water, vinegar
a carton of	ice cream, milk, yogurt
a head of	cabbage, lettuce
an ounce of	courage
a piece of	meat, furniture, advice
a kilogram of	sugar
a litre of	milk, ice cream
a slice of	bread, bacon

Commonly used noncount nouns

FOOD AND DRINK
bacon, beef, bread, broccoli, butter, cabbage, candy, cauliflower, celery, cereal, cheese, chicken, chocolate, coffee, corn, cream, fish, flour, fruit, ice cream, lettuce, meat, milk, oil, pasta, rice, salt, spinach, sugar, tea, water, wine, yogurt

NONFOOD SUBSTANCES
air, cement, coal, dirt, gasoline, gold, paper, petroleum, plastic, rain, silver, snow, soap, steel, wood, wool

ABSTRACT NOUNS
advice, anger, beauty, confidence, courage, employment, fun, happiness, health, honesty, information, intelligence, knowledge, love, poverty, satisfaction, truth, wealth

OTHER
biology (and other areas of study), clothing, equipment, furniture, homework, jewellery, luggage, lumber, machinery, mail, money, news, poetry, pollution, research, scenery, traffic, transportation, violence, weather, work

NOTE: A few noncount nouns may also be used as count nouns, especially in informal English: *Bill loves chocolate; Bill offered me a chocolate. I'll have coffee; I'll have a coffee.*

CAUTION: Noncount nouns do not have plural forms, and they should not be used with numbers or words suggesting plurality (such as *several, many, a few, a couple of, a number of*).

▶ We need some information*s̸* about rain forests.

       much
▶ Do you have ~~many~~ money with you?
         ^

T1-c Use *the* with most nouns whose specific identity is known to the reader.

The definite article *the* is used with most nouns whose identity is known to the reader. (For exceptions, see T1-d.) Usually the identity will be clear to the reader for one of the following reasons:

— The noun has been previously mentioned.

— A phrase or clause following the noun restricts its identity.

— A superlative such as *best* or *most intelligent* makes the noun's identity specific.

— The noun describes a unique person, place, or thing.

— The context or situation makes the noun's identity clear.

▶ A truck loaded with dynamite cut in front of our van. When ^{the} truck skidded a few seconds later, we almost plowed into it.

The noun *truck* is preceded by *A* when it is first mentioned. When the noun is mentioned again, it is preceded by *the* since readers now know the specific truck being discussed.

▶ Bob warned me that ^{the} gun on the top shelf of the cupboard was loaded.

The phrase *on the top shelf of the cupboard* identifies the specific gun.

▶ Our petite daughter dated ^{the} tallest boy in her class.

The superlative *tallest* restricts the identity of the noun *boy*.

▶ During an eclipse, one should not look directly at ^{the} sun.

There is only one sun in our solar system, so its identity is clear.

▶ Please don't slam ^{the} door when you leave.

Both the speaker and the listener know which door is meant.

T1-d Do not use *the* with plural or noncount nouns meaning "all" or "in general"; do not use *the* with most singular proper nouns.

When a plural or a noncount noun means "all" or "in general," it is not marked with *the*.

▶ ~~The~~ ^Ffountains are an expensive element of landscape design.

▶ In some parts of the world, ~~the~~ rice is preferred to all other grains.

the *with geographical names*

WHEN TO OMIT *THE*

streets, squares, parks	Sherbrooke Street, Union Square, Fundy National Park
cities, provinces, counties	Windsor, Stathcona County, Yukon
most countries	Italy, Nigeria, China
continents	South America, Africa
bays, single lakes	Hudson Bay, Lake Ontario
single mountains, islands	Mount Everest, Crete

WHEN TO USE *THE*

united countries	the United States, the Republic of China
large regions, deserts	the East Coast, the Sahara
peninsulas	the Iberian Peninsula
oceans, seas, gulfs	the Pacific, the Dead Sea, the Persian Gulf
canals and rivers	the Panama Canal, the Amazon
mountain ranges	the Rocky Mountains, the Alps
groups of islands	the Solomon Islands

Proper nouns — which name specific people, places, or things — are capitalized. Although there are many exceptions, *the* is not used with most singular proper nouns, such as *Judge Ito, Bloor Street,* and *Lake Huron.* However, *the* is used with plural proper nouns, such as *the United Nations, the Bahamas,* and *the Maritimes.*

Geographical names create problems because there are so many exceptions to the rules. When in doubt, consult the chart on this page or ask a native speaker.

T2

Special problems with verbs

Both native and nonnative speakers of English encounter the following problems with verbs, which are treated elsewhere in this book:

problems with subject-verb agreement (G1)

misuse of verb forms (G2-a to G2-d)

problems with tense and mood (G2-f, G2-g)

problems with active and passive voice (W3-a)

This section focuses on features of the English verb system that cause special difficulties for second-language speakers.

ON THE WEB

For electronic exercises on ESL problems with verbs, go to
www.dianahacker.com/writersref

and click on ▶ **Electronic Grammar Exercises**
　　　　　　　 ▶ **ESL Trouble Spots**
　　　　　　　　　 ▶ **E-ex T2–1 through T2–3**

T2-a Match helping verbs and main verbs appropriately.

Only certain combinations of helping verbs and main verbs make sense in English. The correct combinations are discussed in this section, after the following review of helping verbs and main verbs.

Review of helping verbs and main verbs

Helping verbs always appear before main verbs. (See B1-c.)

　　　　 HV　MV　　　　　　　　　　　　 HV　　 MV
We *will leave* for the picnic at noon. *Do* you *want* a ride?

Some helping verbs—*have, do,* and *be*—change form to indicate tense; others, known as modals, do not.

FORMS OF *HAVE, DO,* AND *BE*

have, has, had
do, does, did
be, am, is, are, was, were, being, been

MODALS

can, could, may, might, must, shall, should, will, would
(*also* ought to)

Every main verb has five forms (except *be,* which has eight forms). The following list shows these forms for the regular verb *help* and the irregular verb *give.* (See G2-a for a list of common irregular verbs.)

BASE FORM	help, give
PAST TENSE	helped, gave
PAST PARTICIPLE	helped, given
PRESENT PARTICIPLE	helping, giving
-S FORM	helps, gives

Modal + base form

After the modals *can, could, may, might, must, shall, should, will,* and *would,* use the base form of the verb.

▶ My cousin will send̸ us photographs from her wedding.

          speak
▶ We could ~~spoke~~ Spanish when we were young.
         ^

CAUTION: Do not use *to* in front of a main verb that follows a modal. (*Ought to* is an exception.)

▶ Gina can ~~to~~ drive us home from the party if we miss the last

    subway train.

Do, does, *or* did + *base form*

After helping verbs that are a form of *do,* use the base form of the verb. The helping verbs *do, does,* and *did* are used in three ways: (1) to express a negative meaning with the adverb *not* or *never,* (2) to ask a question, and (3) to emphasize a main verb used in a positive sense.

▶ Mariko does not want̸ any more dessert.

         buy
▶ Did Janice ~~bought~~ the gift for Katherine?
        ^

       hope
▶ We do ~~hoping~~ that you will come to Hernando's graduation party
     ^

    next Saturday night.

Have, has, *or* **had** + *past participle (perfect tenses)*

After the helping verb *have, has,* or *had,* use the past participle to form one of the perfect tenses. (See G2-f.) Past participles usually end in *-ed, -d, -en, -n,* or *-t.* (See G2-a.)

> On cold nights many churches in the city have ~~offer~~ shelter to the
>   *offered*
> homeless.

> *spoken*
> An-Mei has not ~~speaking~~ Chinese since she was a child.

The helping verb *have* is sometimes preceded by a modal such as *will: By nightfall, we will have driven eight hundred kilometres.* (See also perfect tenses, G2-f.)

Form of **be** + *present participle (progressive forms)*

After the helping verb *be, am, is, are, was, were,* or *been,* use the present participle (the *-ing* form of the verb) to express a continuing action. (See G2-f.)

> *building*
> Carlos is ~~build~~ his house on a cliff overlooking the ocean.

> *driving*
> Uncle Roy was ~~driven~~ a brand-new red Corvette.

The helping verb *be* must be preceded by a modal (*can, could, may, might, must, shall, should, will,* or *would*): *Edith will be going to Germany soon.* The helping verb *been* must be preceded by *have, has,* or *had: Andy has been studying English for five years.* (See also progressive forms, G2-f.)

CAUTION: Certain verbs are not normally used in the progressive sense in English. In general, these verbs express a state of being or mental activity, not a dynamic action. Common examples are *appear, believe, belong, contain, have, hear, know, like, need, see, seem, taste, think, understand,* and *want.*

> *want*
> I ~~am wanting~~ to see August Wilson's *Fences* at Arena Stage.

Some of these verbs, however, have special uses in which progressive forms are normal (*We are thinking about going to the Bahamas*). You will need to make a note of exceptions as you encounter them.

Form of *be* + *past participle (passive voice)*

When a sentence is written in the passive voice, the subject receives the action instead of doing it (*Melissa was given a special award*).

To form the passive voice, use *am, is, are, was, were, being, be,* or *been* followed by a past participle (usually ending in *-ed, -d, -en, -n,* or *-t*). (See also W3-a.)

> *written*
> ▶ *Bleak House* was ~~wrote~~ by Charles Dickens.
>   ^

> *honoured*
> ▶ The scientists were ~~honour~~ for their work with endangered
>   ^
> species.

When the helping verb is *be, being,* or *been,* it must be preceded by another helping verb. *Be* must be preceded by a modal such as *will: Counciller Doucet will be nominated. Being* must be preceded by *am, is, are, was,* or *were: The child was being teased. Been* must be preceded by *have, has,* or *had: I have been invited to a party.*

CAUTION: Although they may seem to have passive meanings, verbs such as *occur, happen, sleep, die,* and *fall* may not be used to form the passive voice because they are intransitive. Only transitive verbs, those that take direct objects, may be used to form the passive voice. (See transitive and intransitive verbs, B2-b.)

> ▶ The earthquake ~~was~~ occurred last Wednesday.

GRAMMAR CHECKERS can catch some mismatches of helping and main verbs. They can tell you, for example, that the base form of the verb should be used after certain helping verbs, such as *did* and *could,* in incorrect sentences like these: *Did you understood my question? Could Alan comes with us?*

Programs can also catch some, but not all, problems with main verbs following forms of *have* or *be.* For example, grammar checkers flagged *have spend,* explaining that the past participle *spent* is required, and they flagged *are expose,* suggesting that either *exposed* or *exposing* is required. However, programs failed to flag problems in many other sentences, such as these: *Angelina has change her major three times. The provisions of the legal contract were broke by both parties.*

T2-b   In conditional sentences, choose verbs with care.

Conditional sentences state that one set of circumstances depends on whether another set of circumstances exists. Choosing verbs in such sentences can be tricky, partly because two clauses are involved: usually an *if* or a *when* or an *unless* clause and an independent clause.

Three kinds of conditional sentences are discussed in this section: factual, predictive, and speculative.

Factual

Factual conditional sentences express factual relationships. When such sentences express scientific truths, use the present tense in both clauses.

> If water *cools* to 0 °C, it *freezes.*

When such sentences describe conditions that are habitually true, use the same tense in both clauses.

> When Sue *bicycles* along the canal, her dog *runs* ahead of her.

> Whenever the coach *asked* for help, I *volunteered.*

Predictive

Predictive conditional sentences are used to predict the future or to express future plans or possibilities. In such a sentence, an *if* or *unless* clause contains a present-tense verb; the verb in the independent clause usually consists of the modal *will, can, may, should,* or *might* followed by the base form of the verb.

> If you *practise* regularly, your tennis game *will improve.*

> We *will lose* our remaining wetlands unless we *act* now.

Speculative

Speculative conditional sentences are used for three purposes: (1) to speculate about unlikely possibilities in the present or future, (2) to speculate about events that did not happen in the past, and (3) to speculate about conditions that are contrary to fact. Each of these purposes requires its own combination of verbs.

UNLIKELY POSSIBILITIES Somewhat confusingly, English uses the past tense in an *if* clause to speculate about a possible but unlikely condition in the present or future. The verb in the independent clause consists of *would, could,* or *might* plus the base form of the verb.

> If I *had* the time, I *would travel* to Senegal.

> If Katya *studied* harder, she *could master* calculus.

In the *if* clause, the past-tense form *were* is used with subjects that would normally take *was: Even if I were* [not *was*] *invited, I wouldn't go to the picnic.* (See also G2-g.)

EVENTS THAT DID NOT HAPPEN English uses the past perfect tense in an *if* clause to speculate about an event that did not happen in the past or to speculate about a state of being that was unreal in the past. (See past perfect tense, G2-f.) The verb in the independent clause consists of *would have, could have,* or *might have* plus the past participle.

> If I *had saved* enough money, I *would have traveled* to Senegal last year.

> If Aunt Grace *had been* alive for your graduation, she *would have been* very proud.

CONDITIONS CONTRARY TO FACT To speculate about conditions that are currently unreal or contrary to fact, English usually uses the past-tense verb *were* (never *was*) in an *if* clause. (See G2-g.) The verb in the independent clause consists of *would, could,* or *might* plus the base form of the verb.

> If Aunt Grace *were* alive today, she *would be* very proud of you.

> I *would assign* only one paper if I *were* the teacher.

T2-c Become familiar with verbs that may be followed by gerunds or infinitives.

A gerund is a verb form that ends in *-ing* and is used as a noun: *sleeping, dreaming.* (See B3-b.) An infinitive is the base form of the verb preceded by the word *to: to sleep, to dream.* The word *to* is not a preposition in this use but an infinitive marker.

A few verbs may be followed by either a gerund or an infinitive; others may be followed by a gerund but not by an infinitive; still others may be followed by an infinitive (either directly or with a noun or pronoun intervening) but not by a gerund.

Verb + gerund or infinitive

The following commonly used verbs may be followed by a gerund or an infinitive, with little or no difference in meaning:

begin	continue	like	start
can't stand	hate	love	

I love *skiing.* I love *to ski.*

With a few verbs, however, the choice of a gerund or an infinitive changes the meaning dramatically:

forget	remember	stop	try

She stopped *speaking* to Lucia. [She no longer spoke to Lucia.]

She stopped *to speak* to Lucia. [She paused so that she could speak to Lucia.]

Verb + gerund

These verbs may be followed by a gerund but not by an infinitive:

admit	discuss	imagine	put off	risk
appreciate	enjoy	miss	quit	suggest
avoid	escape	postpone	recall	tolerate
deny	finish	practise	resist	

Bill enjoys *playing* [not *to play*] the piano.

Verb + infinitive

These verbs may be followed by an infinitive but not by a gerund:

agree	decide	manage	plan	wait
ask	expect	mean	pretend	want
beg	have	need	promise	wish
claim	hope	offer	refuse	

Jill has offered *to water* [not *watering*] the plants while we are away.

Verb + *noun or pronoun* + *infinitive*

With certain verbs in the active voice, a noun or pronoun must come between the verb and the infinitive that follows it. The noun or pronoun usually names a person who is affected by the action.

advise	encourage	remind
allow	have	require
cause	instruct	tell
command	order	urge
convince	persuade	warn

The class encouraged *Luis to tell* the story of his escape.

A few verbs may be followed either by an infinitive directly or by an infinitive preceded by a noun or pronoun.

ask	expect	need	promise	want	would like

We asked *to speak* to the congregation.

We asked *Rabbi Abrams to speak* to our congregation.

Verb + *noun or pronoun* + *unmarked infinitive*

An unmarked infinitive is an infinitive without *to*. A few verbs may be followed by a noun or pronoun and an unmarked (but not a marked) infinitive.

have ("cause")	let ("allow")	make ("force")

Please let *me pay* [not *to pay*] for the tickets.

T2-d Use two-word verbs correctly.

Many verbs in English consist of a verb followed by a preposition or an adverb known as a *particle* (see B1-c). A two-word verb (also known as a *phrasal verb*) often expresses an idiomatic meaning that cannot be understood literally. Consider the verbs in the following sentences, for example.

We *ran across* Dr. Neff on the way to the bookstore.

Calvin *dropped in* on his adviser this morning.

Regina told me to *look* her *up* when I got to Edmonton.

As you probably know, *ran across* means "encountered," *dropped in* means "paid an unexpected visit," and *look up* means "visit." When you were first learning English, however, these two-word verbs must have suggested strange meanings. When in doubt about the meaning of a two-word verb, consult the dictionary.

Some two-word verbs are intransitive; they do not take direct objects. (See B2-b.)

> This morning I *got up* at dawn.

Transitive two-word verbs (those that take direct objects) have particles that are either separable or inseparable. Separable particles may be separated from the verb by the direct object.

> Lucinda *called* the wedding *off*.

When the direct object is a noun, a separable particle may also follow the verb immediately.

> At the last minute, Lucinda *called off* the wedding.

When the direct object is a pronoun, however, the particle must be separated from the verb.

> Why was there no wedding? Lucinda *called* it *off* [not *called off* it].

Inseparable particles must follow the verb immediately. A direct object cannot come between the verb and the particle.

> The police will *look into* the matter [not *look* the matter *into*].

T2-e Do not omit needed verbs.

Some languages allow the omission of the verb when the meaning is clear without it; English does not.

> ▶ Jim ^*is* exceptionally intelligent.

> ▶ Many streets in San Francisco ^*are* very steep.

T3

Sentence structure

ON THE WEB

For electronic exercises on ESL problems with sentence structure, go to **www.dianahacker.com/writersref**

and click on　▶ **Electronic Grammar Exercises**
　　　　　　　　▶ **ESL Trouble Spots**
　　　　　　　　▶ **E-ex T3–1 and T3–2**

T3-a　Do not omit subjects or the expletive *there* or *it*.

English requires a subject for all sentences except imperatives, in which the subject *you* is understood (*Give to the poor*). (See B2-a.) If your native language allows the omission of an explicit subject in other sentences or clauses, be especially alert to this requirement in English.

▶　*I have*
　　H̶a̶v̶e̶ a large collection of baseball cards.

▶　Your aunt is very energetic; *she* seems young for her age.

When the subject has been moved from its normal position before the verb, English sometimes requires an expletive (*there* or *it*) at the beginning of the sentence or clause. (See B2-a.) *There* is used at the beginning of a sentence or clause that draws the reader's (or listener's) attention to the location or existence of something.

▶　*There is*
　　I̶s̶ an apple in the refrigerator.

▶　As you know, *there* are many religious sects in India.

Notice that the verb agrees with the subject that follows it: *apple is, sects are.* (See G1-g.)

　　In one of its uses, the word *it* functions as an expletive, to call attention to a subject following the verb.

▶ *It is*
   I̶s̶ healthy to eat fruit and grains.
    ^

▶ *It is*
   I̶s̶ clear that we must change our approach.
    ^

The subjects of these sentences are *to eat fruit and grains* (an infinitive phrase) and *that we must change our approach* (a noun clause). (See B3-b and B3-e.)

As you probably know, the word *it* is also used as the subject of sentences describing the weather or temperature, stating the time, indicating distance, or suggesting an environmental fact.

> It is raining in the valley, and it is snowing in the mountains.

> In July, it is very hot in Hamilton.

> It is 9:15 A.M.

> It is three hundred kilometres to Ottawa.

> It gets noisy in our dorm on weekends.

GRAMMAR CHECKERS can flag some sentences with a missing expletive (*there* or *it*), but they often misdiagnose the problem, suggesting that if a sentence opens with a word such as *Is* or *Are,* it may need a question mark at the end. Consider this sentence, which grammar checkers flagged: *Are two grocery stores on Elm Street.* Clearly, the sentence doesn't need a question mark. What it needs is an expletive: *There are two grocery stores on Elm Street.*

T3-b   Do not repeat the subject of a sentence.

English does not allow a subject to be repeated in its own clause.

▶ The doctor s̶h̶e̶ advised me to cut down on salt.

    The pronoun *she* repeats the subject *doctor.*

The subject of a sentence should not be repeated even if a word group intervenes between the subject and the verb.

▶ The car that had been stolen i̶t̶ was found.

    The pronoun *it* repeats the subject *car.*

T3-c Do not repeat an object or an adverb in an adjective clause.

In some languages, an object or an adverb is repeated later in the adjective clause in which it appears; in English such repetitions are not allowed. Adjective clauses begin with relative pronouns (*who, whom, whose, which, that*) or relative adverbs (*when, where*), and these words always serve a grammatical function within the clauses they introduce. (See B3-e.) Another word in the clause cannot also serve that same grammatical function.

When a relative pronoun functions as the object of a verb or the object of a preposition, do not add another word with the same function later in the clause.

▶ The puppy ran after the car that we were riding in. ~~it.~~
    ^

> The relative pronoun *that* is the object of the preposition *in,* so the object *it* is not allowed.

Even when the relative pronoun has been omitted, do not add another word with its same function.

▶ The puppy ran after the car we were riding in. ~~it.~~
    ^

> The relative pronoun *that* is understood even though it is not present in the sentence.

Like a relative pronoun, a relative adverb should not be echoed later in its clause.

▶ The place where I work ~~there~~ is one hour from the city.

> The adverb *there* should not echo the relative adverb *where.*

GRAMMAR CHECKERS usually fail to flag sentences with repeated subjects or objects. One program flagged some sentences with repeated subjects, such as this one: *The roses that they brought home they cost three dollars each.* However, the program misdiagnosed the problem, calling the sentence a run-on. The sentence is not a run-on; the problem is that the second *they* repeats the subject *roses.*

T3-d Avoid mixed constructions beginning with *although* or *because.*

In English, using both *although* and *but* (or *however*) to link two word groups results in a mixed construction, which consists of sentence parts that don't go together (see S5-a). Using both *because* and *so* (or *therefore*) results in the same problem.

If you want to retain the subordinating conjunction *although* or *because,* drop the other linking word.

▶ Because finance laws are not always enforced, ~~therefore~~ investing

in the former Soviet Union can be very risky.

If you want to retain the coordinating conjunction (*but, so*) or the transitional expression (*however, therefore*), drop *although* or *because.*

▶ ~~Although~~ the sales figures look impressive, but the company is

losing money.

T3-e Place adjectives and adverbs with care.

Adjectives modify nouns or pronouns; adverbs modify verbs, adjectives, or other adverbs (see B1-d, B1-e). Both native and nonnative speakers encounter problems in the use of adjectives and adverbs (see G4). For nonnative speakers, the placement of adjectives and adverbs can also be troublesome.

Placement of adjectives

No doubt you have already learned that in English adjectives usually precede the nouns they modify and that they may also appear following linking verbs. (See B1-d and B2-b.)

Janine wore a *new* necklace. Janine's necklace was *new.*

When adjectives pile up in front of a noun, however, you may sometimes have difficulty arranging them. English is quite particular about the order of cumulative adjectives, those not separated by commas. (See P2-d.)

Usual order of cumulative adjectives

ARTICLE OR OTHER NOUN MARKER   a, an, the, her, Joe's, two, many, some

EVALUATIVE WORD   attractive, dedicated, delicious, ugly, disgusting

SIZE   large, enormous, small, little

LENGTH OR SHAPE   long, short, round, square

AGE   new, old, young, antique

COLOR   yellow, blue, crimson

NATIONALITY   French, Peruvian, Vietnamese

RELIGION   Catholic, Protestant, Jewish, Muslim

MATERIAL   silver, walnut, wool, marble

NOUN/ADJECTIVE   tree (as in *tree house*), kitchen (as in *kitchen table*)

THE NOUN MODIFIED   house, sweater, bicycle, bread, woman, priest

Janine was wearing *a beautiful antique silver* necklace [not *a silver antique beautiful* necklace].

The chart above shows the order in which cumulative adjectives ordinarily appear in front of the noun they modify. This list is only a guide; don't be surprised if you encounter exceptions.

Placement of adverbs

Adverbs modifying verbs appear in various positions: at the beginning or end of the sentence, before or after the verb, or between a helping verb and its main verb.

Slowly, we drove along the rain-slick road.

Mother wrapped the gift *carefully*.

Martin *always* wins our tennis matches.

Christina is *rarely* late for our lunch dates.

My daughter has *often* spoken of you.

An adverb may not, however, be placed between a verb and its direct object.

> *carefully*
> ► Mother wrapped ~~carefully~~ the gift.
>   ^

The adverb *carefully* may be placed at the beginning or at the end of this sentence or before the verb. It cannot appear after the verb because the verb is followed by the direct object *the gift.*

T4

Other trouble spots

ON THE WEB

For electronic exercises on ESL problems with participles and prepositions, go to **www.dianahacker.com/writersref**

and click on ► **Electronic Grammar Exercises**
                  ► **ESL Trouble Spots**
                      ► **E-ex T4–1 and T4–2**

T4-a Distinguish between present participles and past participles used as adjectives.

Both present and past participles may be used as adjectives. The present participle always ends in *-ing*. Past participles usually end in *-ed, -d, -en, -n,* or *-t.* (See G2-a.)

PRESENT PARTICIPLES   confusing, speaking

PAST PARTICIPLES   confused, spoken

Participles used as adjectives can precede the nouns they modify; they can also follow linking verbs, in which case they describe the subject of the sentence. (See B2-b.)

It was a *depressing* movie. Jim was a *depressed* young man.

The essay was *confusing*. The student was *confused*.

A present participle should describe a person or thing causing or stimulating an experience; a past participle should describe a person or thing undergoing an experience.

The lecturer was *boring* [not *bored*].

The audience was *bored* [not *boring*].

In the first example, the lecturer is causing boredom, not experiencing it. In the second example, the audience is experiencing boredom, not causing it.

The participles that cause the most trouble for nonnative speakers are those describing mental states:

annoying/annoyed	exhausting/exhausted
boring/bored	fascinating/fascinated
confusing/confused	frightening/frightened
depressing/depressed	satisfying/satisfied
exciting/excited	surprising/surprised

When you come across these words in your drafts, check to see that you have used them correctly.

GRAMMAR CHECKERS do not flag problems with present and past participles used as adjectives. Not surprisingly, the programs have no way of knowing the meaning a writer intends. For example, both of the following sentences could be correct, depending on the writer's meaning: *My roommate was annoying. My roommate was annoyed.*

T4-b Become familiar with common prepositions that show time and place.

The most frequently used prepositions in English are *at, by, for, from, in, of, on, to,* and *with.* Each of these prepositions has a variety of uses that must be learned gradually, in context.

Prepositions that indicate time and place can be difficult to master because the differences among them are subtle and idiomatic. The chart on the following page limits itself to four troublesome prepositions that show time and place: *at, on, in,* and *by.*

at, on, in, *and* by *to show time and place*

Showing time

AT   *at* a specific time: *at* 7:20, *at* dawn, *at* dinner

ON   *on* a specific day or date: *on* Tuesday, *on* June 4

IN   *in* a part of a 24-hour period: *in* the afternoon, *in* the daytime [but *at* night]

   in a year or month: *in* 1999, *in* July

   in a period of time: finished *in* three hours

BY   *by* a specific time or date: *by* 4:15, *by* Boxing Day

Showing place

AT   *at* a meeting place or location: *at* home, *at* the club

   at the edge of something: sitting *at* the desk

   at the corner of something: turning *at* the intersection

   at a target: throwing the snowball *at* Lucy

ON   *on* a surface: placed *on* the table, hanging *on* the wall

   on a street: the house *on* Spring Street

   on an electronic medium: *on* television, *on* the Internet

IN   *in* an enclosed space: *in* the garage, *in* the envelope

   in a geographic location: *in* New Brunswick

   in a print medium: *in* a book, *in* a magazine

BY   *by* a landmark: *by* the fence, *by* the flagpole

Not every possible use is listed in the chart, so don't be surprised when you encounter exceptions and idiomatic uses that you must learn one at a time. For example, in English we ride *in* a car but *on* a bus, train, or subway. And when we fly *on* (not *in*) a plane, we are not sitting on top of the plane.

P

Punctuation

P

Punctuation

P1

The comma

The comma was invented to help readers. Without it, sentence parts can collide into one another unexpectedly, causing misreadings.

CONFUSING   If you cook Elmer will do the dishes.

CONFUSING   While we were eating a rattlesnake approached our campsite.

Add commas in the logical places (after *cook* and *eating*), and suddenly all is clear. No longer is Elmer being cooked, the rattlesnake being eaten.

Various rules have evolved to prevent such misreadings and to speed readers along through complex grammatical structures. Those rules are detailed in this section.

 GRAMMAR CHECKERS have mixed success in flagging missing or misused commas. They can tell you that a comma is usually used before *which* but not before *that* (see P1-e), and they can flag some missing commas after an introductory word or word group or between items in a series. In general, however, the programs are unreliable. For example, in an essay with ten missing commas and five misused ones, a grammar checker spotted only one missing comma (after the word *therefore*).

P1-a Use a comma before a coordinating conjunction joining independent clauses.

When a coordinating conjunction connects two or more independent clauses—word groups that could stand alone as separate sentences—a comma must precede it. There are seven coordinating conjunctions in English: *and, but, or, nor, for, so,* and *yet.*

A comma tells readers that one independent clause has come to a close and that another is about to begin.

▶ Nearly everyone has heard of love at first sight‸but I fell in love at first dance.

EXCEPTION: If the two independent clauses are short and there is no danger of misreading, the comma may be omitted.

The plane took off and we were on our way.

CAUTION: As a rule, do *not* use a comma to separate compound elements that are not independent clauses. (See P2-a.)

▶ A good money manager controls expenses/and invests surplus dollars to meet future needs.

The word group following *and* is not an independent clause; it is the second half of a compound predicate.

P1-b Use a comma after an introductory word group.

The most common introductory word groups are clauses and phrases functioning as adverbs. Such word groups usually tell when, where, how, why, or under what conditions the main action of the sentence occurred. (See B3-a, B3-b, and B3-e.)

A comma tells readers that the introductory clause or phrase has come to a close and that the main part of the sentence is about to begin.

▶ When Irwin was ready to eat‸his cat jumped onto the table and started to purr.

▶ Near a small stream at the bottom of the canyon‸we discovered an abandoned shelter.

EXCEPTION: The comma may be omitted after a short adverb clause or phrase if there is no danger of misreading.

In no time we were at eight hundred metres.

Sentences also frequently begin with participial phrases describing the noun or pronoun immediately following them. The comma tells readers that they are about to learn the identity of the person or thing described; therefore, the comma is usually required even when the phrase is short. (See also B3-b.)

▶ **Thinking his motorcade drive through Dallas was routine,**

President Kennedy smiled and waved at the crowds.

▶ **Buried under layers of younger rocks, the earth's oldest rocks**

contain no fossils.

NOTE: Other introductory word groups include conjunctive adverbs, transitional expressions, and absolute phrases. (See P1-f.)

P1-c Use a comma between all items in a series.

Unless you are writing for a publication that follows another convention, separate all items in a series — including the last two — with commas.

▶ **Bubbles of air, leaves, ferns, bits of wood, and insects are often**

found trapped in amber.

Although some publications omit the comma between the last two items, be aware that its omission can result in ambiguity or misreading.

▶ **My uncle willed me all of his property, houses, and warehouses.**

Did the uncle will his property *and* houses *and* warehouses — or simply his property, consisting of houses and warehouses? If the first meaning is intended, a comma is necessary to prevent ambiguity.

▶ **The activities include a search for lost treasure, dubious**

financial dealings, much discussion of ancient heresies, and

midnight orgies.

Without the comma, the people seem to be discussing orgies, not participating in them. The comma makes it clear that *midnight orgies* is a separate item in the series.

ON THE WEB

The rules on using commas with items in a series have sparked debates. If you're interested in learning why, go to
www.dianahacker.com/writersref

and click on   ▶ **Language Debates**
                        ▶ **Commas with items in a series**

P1-d Use a comma between coordinate adjectives not joined by *and*. Do not use a comma between cumulative adjectives.

When two or more adjectives each modify a noun separately, they are *coordinate*.

> Roberto is a *warm, gentle, affectionate* father.

Adjectives are coordinate if they can be joined with *and* (warm *and* gentle *and* affectionate).

Two or more adjectives that do not modify the noun separately are cumulative.

> *Three large grey* shapes moved slowly toward us.

Beginning with the adjective closest to the noun *shapes,* these modifiers lean on one another, piggyback style, with each modifying a larger word group. *Grey* modifies *shapes, large* modifies *grey shapes,* and *three* modifies *large grey shapes.* We cannot insert the word *and* between cumulative adjectives (three *and* large *and* grey shapes).

COORDINATE ADJECTIVES

▶ Patients with severe‚irreversible brain damage should not be put
                                          ^

on life support systems.

CUMULATIVE ADJECTIVES

▶ Ira ordered a rich⁄chocolate⁄layer cake for his mother's

birthday dinner.

P1-e   Use commas to set off nonrestrictive elements. Do not use commas to set off restrictive elements.

Word groups describing nouns or pronouns (adjective clauses, adjective phrases, and appositives) can be restrictive or nonrestrictive. A *restrictive* element defines or limits the meaning of the word it modifies and is therefore essential to the meaning of the sentence. Because it contains essential information, a restrictive element is not set off with commas.

> **RESTRICTIVE**
> For camp the children needed clothes *that were washable.*

If you remove a restrictive element from a sentence, the meaning changes significantly, becoming more general than you intended. The writer of the example sentence does not mean that the children needed clothes in general. The intended meaning is more limited: The children needed *washable* clothes.

A *nonrestrictive* element describes a noun or pronoun whose meaning has already been clearly defined or limited. Because it contains nonessential or parenthetical information, a nonrestrictive element is set off with commas.

> **NONRESTRICTIVE**
> For camp the children needed sturdy shoes, *which were expensive.*

If you remove a nonrestrictive element from a sentence, the meaning does not change dramatically. Some meaning is lost, to be sure, but the defining characteristics of the person or thing described remain the same as before. The children needed *sturdy shoes,* and these happened to be expensive.

NOTE: Often it is difficult to tell whether a word group is restrictive or nonrestrictive without seeing it in context and considering the writer's meaning. Both of the following sentences are grammatically correct, but their meanings are slightly different.

> The dessert made with fresh raspberries was delicious.

> The dessert, made with fresh raspberries, was delicious.

In the example without commas, the phrase *made with fresh raspberries* tells readers which of two or more desserts the writer is referring to. In the example with commas, the phrase merely adds information about the particular dessert served with the meal.

Adjective clauses

Adjective clauses are patterned like sentences, containing subjects and verbs, but they function within sentences as modifiers of nouns or pronouns. Adjective clauses begin with a relative pronoun (*who, whom, whose, which, that*) or with a relative adverb (*where, when*).

Nonrestrictive adjective clauses are set off with commas; restrictive adjective clauses are not.

NONRESTRICTIVE CLAUSE

▶ Ed's country house⌃which is located on five hectares⌃was

completely furnished with bats in the rafters and mice in the

kitchen.

The clause *which is located on five hectares* does not restrict the meaning of *Ed's country house,* so the information is nonessential.

RESTRICTIVE CLAUSE

▶ An office manager for a corporation∕that had government

contracts∕asked her supervisor for permission to reprimand

her co-workers for smoking.

Because the adjective clause *that had government contracts* identifies the corporation, the information is essential.

NOTE: Use *that* only with restrictive clauses. Many writers prefer to use *which* only with nonrestrictive clauses, but usage varies.

ON THE WEB

The rules on using *that* versus *which* have sparked debates. If you're interested in learning why, go to
www.dianahacker.com/writersref

and click on ▶ **Language Debates**
              ▶ *that* **versus** *which*

Phrases functioning as adjectives

Prepositional or verbal phrases functioning as adjectives may be restrictive or nonrestrictive. Nonrestrictive phrases are set off with commas; restrictive phrases are not.

NONRESTRICTIVE PHRASE

▶ The helicopter, with its 100 000-candlepower spotlight

illuminating the area, circled above.

The *with* phrase is nonessential because its purpose is not to specify which of two or more helicopters is being discussed.

RESTRICTIVE PHRASE

▶ One corner of the attic was filled with newspapers/ dating from

the 1920s.

Dating from the 1920s restricts the meaning of *newspapers,* so the comma should be omitted.

Appositives

An appositive is a noun or noun phrase that renames a nearby noun. Nonrestrictive appositives are set off with commas; restrictive appositives are not.

NONRESTRICTIVE APPOSITIVE

▶ Darwin's most important book, *On the Origin of Species,* was the

result of many years of research.

The term *most important* restricts the meaning to one book, so the appositive *On the Origin of Species* is nonrestrictive.

RESTRICTIVE APPOSITIVE

▶ The song/ "Fire It Up/" was blasted out of amplifiers three

metres tall.

Once they've read *song,* readers still don't know precisely which song the writer means. The appositive following *song* restricts its meaning.

P1-f Use commas to set off transitional and parenthetical expressions, absolute phrases, and contrasted elements.

Transitional expressions

Transitional expressions serve as bridges between sentences or parts of sentences. They include conjunctive adverbs such as *however, therefore,* and *moreover* and transitional phrases such as *for example, as a matter of fact,* and *in other words.* (For a more complete list, see P3-b.)

When a transitional expression appears between independent clauses in a compound sentence, it is preceded by a semicolon and is usually followed by a comma.

▶ **Minh did not understand our language; moreover, he was**

   unfamiliar with our customs.

When a transitional expression appears at the beginning of a sentence or in the middle of an independent clause, it is usually set off with commas.

▶ **As a matter of fact, American football was established by fans**

   who wanted to play a more organized game of rugby.

▶ **Natural foods are not always salt free; celery, for example,**

   contains more sodium than most people would imagine.

EXCEPTION: If a transitional expression blends smoothly with the rest of the sentence, calling for little or no pause in reading, it does not need to be set off with commas. Expressions such as *also, at least, certainly, consequently, indeed, of course, no doubt, perhaps, then,* and *therefore* do not always call for a pause.

   Bill's bicycle is broken; *therefore* you will need to borrow Sue's.

   Bill's bicycle is broken; you will *therefore* need to borrow Sue's.

Parenthetical expressions

Expressions that are distinctly parenthetical should be set off with commas. Providing supplemental comments or information, they interrupt the flow of a sentence or appear as afterthoughts.

▶ Evolution, so far as we know, doesn't work this way.

▶ The bluefish weighed five kilograms, give or take a few grams.

Absolute phrases

Absolute phrases should be set off with commas. An absolute phrase, which modifies the whole sentence, usually consists of a noun followed by a participle or participial phrase. It may appear at the beginning or at the end of a sentence. (See B3-d.)

▶ Our grant having been approved, we were at last able to begin the archaeological dig.

▶ Elvis Presley made music industry history in the 1950s, his records having sold more than ten million copies.

CAUTION: Do not insert a comma between the noun and participle of an absolute construction.

▶ The next day/ being a school day, we turned down the invitation.

Contrasted elements

Sharp contrasts beginning with words such as *not* and *unlike* are set off with commas.

▶ The Epicurean philosophers sought mental, not bodily, pleasures.

▶ Unlike Robert, Celia loved dance contests.

P1-g Use commas to set off nouns of direct address, the words *yes* and *no*, interrogative tags, and mild interjections.

▶ Forgive us, Dr. Spock, for spanking Brian.

▶ Yes, the loan will probably be approved.

▶ The film was faithful to the book, wasn't it?
     ^

▶ Well, cases like these are difficult to decide.
    ^

P1-h Use commas with expressions such as *he said* to set off direct quotations. (See also P6-f.)

▶ Naturalist Arthur Cleveland Bent once remarked, "In
                                               ^
   part the peregrine declined unnoticed because it is not

   adorable."

▶ "Convictions are more dangerous foes of truth than lies," wrote
                                                         ^
   philosopher Friedrich Nietzsche.

P1-i Use commas with dates, addresses, titles, and numbers.

Dates

In dates, the year is set off from the rest of the sentence with a pair of commas.

▶ On December 12, 1890, orders were sent out for the arrest of
               ^   ^
   Sitting Bull.

EXCEPTIONS: Commas are not needed if the date is inverted or if only the month and year are given.

> Our downtown office's recycling plan went into effect on
> 15 April 2002.

> January 2001 was an extremely cold month.

Addresses

The elements of an address or place name are followed by commas. A zip code, however, is not preceded by a comma.

▶ John Lennon was born in Liverpool, England, in 1940.
                                  ^   ^

▶ Please send the package to Greg Tarvin at 708 Spring Street‸

Winnipeg‸Manitoba R3T 2N2.

Titles

If a title follows a name, separate it from the rest of the sentence with a pair of commas.

▶ Sandra Barnes‸M.D.‸performed the surgery.

Numbers

In numbers more than four digits long, use spaces to separate the numbers into groups of three, starting from the right. In numbers four digits long, a space is optional.

> 3 500 [*or* 3500]
> 100 000
> 5 000 000

EXCEPTIONS: Do not use spaces in street numbers, telephone numbers, or years.

P1-j Use a comma to prevent confusion.

In certain contexts, a comma is necessary to prevent confusion. If the writer has omitted a word or phrase, for example, a comma may be needed to signal the omission.

▶ To err is human; to forgive‸divine.

If two words in a row echo each other, a comma may be needed for ease of reading.

▶ All of the catastrophes that we had feared might happen‸

happened.

Sometimes a comma is needed to prevent readers from grouping words in ways that do not match the writer's intention.

▶ Patients who can‸walk up and down the halls several times a day.

ON THE WEB

For electronic exercises on using commas, go to
www.dianahacker.com/writersref

and click on   ▶ **Electronic Grammar Exercises**
              ▶ **Punctuation**
                ▶ **E-ex P1–1 through P1–3**

P2

Unnecessary commas

P2-a Do not use a comma between compound elements that are not independent clauses.

Although a comma is used before a coordinating conjunction joining independent clauses (see P1-a), this rule should not be extended to other compound word groups.

▶ Marie Curie discovered radium⁄ and later applied her work on

radioactivity to medicine.

And links two verbs in a compound predicate: *discovered* and *applied.*

▶ Jake still does not realize that his illness is serious⁄ and that he

will have to alter his diet to improve.

And connects two subordinate clauses, each beginning with *that.*

P2-b Do not use a comma to separate a verb from its subject or object.

A sentence should flow from subject to verb to object without unnecessary pauses. Commas may appear between these major sentence elements only when a specific rule calls for them.

▶ Zoos large enough to give the animals freedom to roam⁄ are

becoming more popular.

▶ Francesca explained to Mike⁄ that she was expecting an important

call from her brother in Milan.

The subject *Zoos* should not be separated from its verb, *are becoming.* In the second sentence, the comma should not separate the verb, *explained,* from its object, the subordinate clause *that she was expecting an important call.*

P2-c Do not use a comma before the first or after the last item in a series.

Though commas are required between items in a series (see P1-c), do not place them either before or after the series.

▶ Other causes of asthmatic attacks are⁄ stress, change in

temperature, humidity, and cold air.

▶ Ironically, this job that appears so glamorous, carefree, and easy⁄

carries a high degree of responsibility.

P2-d Do not use a comma between cumulative adjectives, between an adjective and a noun, or between an adverb and an adjective.

Though commas are required between coordinate adjectives (those that can be joined with *and*), they do not belong between cumulative adjectives (those that cannot be joined with *and*). (For a full discussion, see P1-d.)

▶ In the corner of the closet we found an old⁄ maroon hatbox

from Sears.

A comma should never be used to separate an adjective from the noun that follows it.

▶ It was a senseless, dangerous⁄ mission.

Nor should a comma be used to separate an adverb from an adjective that follows it.

▶ The Hurst Home is unsuitable as a rehab facility for severely͵

injured burn victims.

P2-e Do not use commas to set off restrictive or mildly parenthetical elements.

Restrictive elements are modifiers or appositives necessary for identifying the nouns they follow; therefore, they are essential to the meaning of the sentence and should not be set off with commas. (For a full discussion, see P1-e.)

▶ Drivers͵ who think they own the road͵ make cycling a dangerous

sport.

The *who* clause restricts the meaning of *Drivers* and is therefore essential to the meaning of the sentence. Putting commas around the *who* clause falsely suggests that all drivers think they own the road.

▶ Margaret Mead's book͵ *Coming of Age in Samoa͵* stirred up

considerable controversy when it was first published.

Since Margaret Mead wrote more than one book, the appositive contains information essential to the meaning of the sentence.

Although commas should be used with distinctly parenthetical expressions (see P1-f), do not use them to set off elements that are only mildly parenthetical.

▶ Charisse believes that the Internet is͵ essentially͵ a bastion of

advertising.

P2-f Do not use a comma to set off a concluding adverb clause that is essential to the meaning of the sentence.

When adverb clauses introduce a sentence, they are nearly always followed by a comma (see P1-b). When they conclude a sentence, however, they are not set off by commas if their content is essential to the meaning of the earlier part of the sentence. Adverb clauses beginning with *after, as soon as, before, because, if, since, unless, until,* and *when* are usually essential.

▶ **Don't visit Paris at the height of the tourist season,/ unless**

you have booked hotel reservations.

Without the concluding *unless* clause, the meaning of the sentence would be broader than the writer intended.

When a concluding adverb clause is nonessential, it should be preceded by a comma. Clauses beginning with *although, even though, though,* and *whereas* are usually nonessential.

▶ **The lecture seemed to last only a short time, although the clock**

said it had gone on for more than an hour.

P2-g Avoid other common misuses of the comma.

Do not use a comma in the following situations.

AFTER A COORDINATING CONJUNCTION (*AND, BUT, OR, NOR, FOR, SO, YET*)

▶ **Most soap operas are performed live, but/ some are taped.**

AFTER *SUCH AS* OR *LIKE*

▶ **Many shade-loving plants, such as/ begonias, impatiens, and coleus, can add colour to a shady garden.**

BEFORE *THAN*

▶ **Touring Crete was more thrilling for us/ than visiting the Greek islands frequented by rich Europeans.**

AFTER *ALTHOUGH*

▶ **Although/ the air was balmy, the water was too cold for swimming.**

BEFORE A PARENTHESIS

▶ At Bell Sylvia began at the bottom/ (with only three and a half

walls and a swivel chair), but within five years she had been

promoted to supervisor.

TO SET OFF AN INDIRECT (REPORTED) QUOTATION

▶ Samuel Goldwyn once said/ that a verbal contract isn't worth the

paper it's written on.

WITH A QUESTION MARK OR AN EXCLAMATION POINT

▶ "Why don't you try it?/" she coaxed.

ON THE WEB

For an electronic exercise on the use and misuse of commas, go to
www.dianahacker.com/writersref

and click on   ▶ **Electronic Grammar Exercises**
                          ▶ **Punctuation**
                                  ▶ **E-ex P2–1**

P3

The semicolon

The semicolon is used to separate major sentence elements of equal
grammatical rank.

GRAMMAR CHECKERS flag some, but not all, misused semicolons
(P3-d). In addition, they can alert you to some run-on sentences
(G6). However, they miss more run-on sentences than they identify,
and they sometimes flag correct sentences as possible run-ons. (See
also the grammar checker advice in G6.)

P3-a Use a semicolon between closely related independent clauses not joined with a coordinating conjunction.

When related independent clauses appear in one sentence, they are ordinarily connected with a comma and a coordinating conjunction (*and, but, or, nor, for, so, yet*). The conjunction expresses the relation between the clauses. If the relation is clear without the conjunction, a writer may choose to connect the clauses with a semicolon instead.

> Injustice is relatively easy to bear; what stings is justice.
> — H. L. Mencken

A semicolon must be used whenever a coordinating conjunction has been omitted between independent clauses. To use merely a comma creates a kind of run-on sentence known as a comma splice. (See G6.)

▶ In 1800, a traveler needed six weeks to get from New York City to

Chicago/; in 1860, the trip by railroad took two days.

CAUTION: Do not overuse the semicolon as a means of revising comma splices. For other revision strategies, see G6.

P3-b Use a semicolon between independent clauses linked with a transitional expression.

Transitional expressions include conjunctive adverbs and transitional phrases.

CONJUNCTIVE ADVERBS

accordingly	finally	likewise	similarly
also	furthermore	meanwhile	specifically
anyway	hence	moreover	still
besides	however	nevertheless	subsequently
certainly	incidentally	next	then
consequently	indeed	nonetheless	therefore
conversely	instead	otherwise	thus

TRANSITIONAL PHRASES

after all	even so	in fact
as a matter of fact	for example	in other words
as a result	for instance	in the first place
at any rate	in addition	on the contrary
at the same time	in conclusion	on the other hand

When a transitional expression appears between two independent clauses, it is preceded by a semicolon and often followed by a comma.

▶ Many corals grow very gradually/; in fact, the creation of a coral

reef can take centuries.

When a transitional expression appears in the middle or at the end of the second independent clause, the semicolon goes *between the clauses*.

Most singers gain fame through hard work and dedication; Evita, however, found other means.

Transitional expressions should not be confused with the coordinating conjunctions *and, but, or, nor, for, so,* and *yet,* which are preceded by a comma when they link independent clauses. (See P1-a and G6-a.)

P3-c Use a semicolon between items in a series containing internal punctuation.

▶ Classic science fiction sagas are *Star Trek,* with Mr. Spock

and his large pointed ears/; *Battlestar Galactica,* with its Cylon

Raiders/; and *Star Wars,* with Han Solo, Luke Skywalker, and

Darth Vader.

Without the semicolons the reader must sort out the major groupings, distinguishing between important and less important pauses according to the logic of the sentence. By inserting semicolons at the major breaks, the writer does this work for the reader.

P3-d Avoid common misuses of the semicolon.

Do not use a semicolon in the following situations.

BETWEEN A SUBORDINATE CLAUSE AND THE REST OF THE SENTENCE

▶ Unless you brush your teeth within ten or fifteen minutes after

eating; brushing does almost no good.

BETWEEN AN APPOSITIVE AND THE WORD IT REFERS TO

▶ The scientists were fascinated by the species *Argyroneta*

acquatica; a spider that lives underwater.

TO INTRODUCE A LIST

▶ Some of my favourite film stars have home pages on the Web;:

John Travolta, Susan Sarandon, and Leonardo DiCaprio.

BETWEEN INDEPENDENT CLAUSES JOINED BY *AND, BUT, OR, NOR, FOR, SO,* OR *YET*

▶ Five of the applicants had worked with spreadsheets; but only

one was familiar with database management.

EXCEPTIONS: If at least one of the independent clauses contains internal punctuation, you may use a semicolon even though the clauses are joined with a coordinating conjunction.

> As a vehicle [the model T] was hard-working, commonplace, and heroic; and it often seemed to transmit those qualities to the person who rode in it. —E. B. White

Although a comma would also be correct in this sentence, the semicolon is more effective, for it indicates the relative weights of the pauses.

Occasionally, a semicolon may be used to emphasize a sharp contrast or a firm distinction between clauses joined with a coordinating conjunction.

> We hate some persons because we do not know them; and we will not know them because we hate them. —Charles Caleb Colton

ON THE WEB

For electronic exercises on using semicolons, go to
www.dianahacker.com/writersref

and click on   ▶ **Electronic Grammar Exercises**
                   ▶ **Punctuation**
                       ▶ **E-ex P3–1 and P3–2**

P4

The colon

The colon is used primarily to call attention to the words that follow it. In addition, the colon has some conventional uses.

GRAMMAR CHECKERS do not flag missing or misused colons. For example, they failed to catch the misused colon in this sentence: *Uncle Carlos left behind: his watch, his glasses, and his favourite pen.* Occasionally grammar checkers flag misused semicolons in contexts where a colon is required.

P4-a   Use a colon after an independent clause to direct attention to a list, an appositive, or a quotation.

A LIST

A typical routine includes the following: twenty knee bends, fifty sit-ups, fifteen leg lifts, and five minutes of running in place.

AN APPOSITIVE

My roommate is guilty of two of the seven deadly sins: gluttony and sloth.

A QUOTATION

Consider the words of Saul Bellow: "The best argument is an undeniably good book."

For other ways of introducing quotations, see P6-f.

P4-b Use a colon between independent clauses if the second summarizes or explains the first.

Faith is like love: It cannot be forced.

NOTE: When an independent clause follows a colon, it may begin with a lowercase or a capital letter.

P4-c Use a colon after the salutation in a formal letter, to indicate hours and minutes, to show proportions, between a title and subtitle, and between city and publisher in bibliographic entries.

Dear Sir or Madam:

5:30 P.M. (or p.m.)

The ratio of women to men was 2:1.

The Glory of Hera: Greek Mythology and the Greek Family

Scarborough: Gage, 2002

NOTE: In biblical references, a colon is ordinarily used between chapter and verse (Luke 2:14). The Modern Language Association recommends a period instead (Luke 2.14).

P4-d Avoid common misuses of the colon.

A colon must be preceded by a full independent clause. Therefore, avoid using it in the following situations.

BETWEEN A VERB AND ITS OBJECT OR COMPLEMENT

▶ Some important vitamins and minerals in vegetables are:/

vitamin A, thiamine, niacin, iron, potassium, and vitamin C.

BETWEEN A PREPOSITION AND ITS OBJECT

▶ The heart's two pumps each consist of:/ an upper chamber, or

atrium, and a lower chamber, or ventricle.

AFTER *SUCH AS, INCLUDING,* OR *FOR EXAMPLE*

▶ The trees on our campus include many fine Japanese specimens

such as⁄ black pines, ginkgos, and weeping cherries.

ON THE WEB

For an electronic exercise on using colons, go to
www.dianahacker.com/writersref

and click on ▶ **Electronic Grammar Exercises**
  ▶ **Punctuation**
   ▶ **E-ex P4–1**

P5

The apostrophe

 GRAMMAR CHECKERS can flag some, but not all, missing or misused apostrophes. They can catch missing apostrophes in common contractions, such as *don't.* They can also flag some problems with possessives, although they miss others. The programs usually phrase their advice cautiously, telling you that you have a "possible possessive error" in a phrase such as *a days work* or *sled dogs feet.* Therefore, you—not the grammar checker—must decide whether to add an apostrophe and, if so, whether to put it before or after the *-s.*

P5-a Use an apostrophe to indicate that a noun is possessive.

Possessive nouns usually indicate ownership, as in *Tim's hat* or *the lawyer's desk.* Frequently, however, ownership is only loosely implied: *the tree's roots, a day's work.* If you are not sure whether a noun is possessive, try turning it into an *of* phrase: *the roots of the tree, the work of a day.*

When to add *-*'s

If the noun does not end in *-s,* add *-'s.*

> Roy managed to climb out on the driver's side.

> Thank you for refunding the children's money.

If the noun is singular and ends in *-s,* add *-'s.*

> Lois's sister spent last year in India.

EXCEPTION: If pronunciation would be awkward with the added *-'s,* some writers use only the apostrophe. Either use is acceptable.

> Sophocles' plays are among my favourites.

When to add only an apostrophe

If the noun is plural and ends in *-s,* add only an apostrophe.

> Both diplomats' briefcases were stolen.

Joint possession

To show joint possession, use *-'s* (or *-s'*) with the last noun only; to show individual possession, make all nouns possessive.

> Have you seen Joyce and Greg's new camper?

> Hernando's and Maria's expectations of marriage couldn't have been more different.

In the first sentence, Joyce and Greg jointly own one camper. In the second sentence, Hernando and Maria individually have different expectations.

Compound nouns

If a noun is compound, use *-'s* (or *-s'*) with the last element.

> Her father-in-law's sculpture won first place.

P5-b Use an apostrophe and -*s* to indicate that an indefinite pronoun is possessive.

Indefinite pronouns are pronouns that refer to no specific person or thing: *everyone, someone, no one, something.* (See B1-b.)

> Someone's raincoat has been left behind.

P5-c Use an apostrophe to mark contractions.

In contractions the apostrophe takes the place of missing letters. In the following sentence, *It's* stands for *It is* and *can't* stands for *cannot.*

> It's a shame that Frank can't go on the tour.

The apostrophe is also used to mark the omission of the first two digits of a year (the class of '99) or years (the '60s generation).

P5-d An apostrophe is often optional in plural numbers, abbreviations, letters, and words mentioned as words.

Traditionally, an apostrophe has been used to pluralize numbers, abbreviations, letters, and words mentioned as words. The trend, however, is toward omitting the apostrophe. Either use is correct, but be consistent.

PLURAL NUMBERS AND ABBREVIATIONS   To pluralize a number or an abbreviation, you may add -*s* or -*'s.*

> Peggy skated nearly perfect figure 8s (*or* 8's).

> We collected only four IOUs (*or* IOU's) out
> of forty.

NOTE: To pluralize decades, most current writers omit the apostrophe: 1920s (*not* 1920's).

PLURAL LETTERS   Italicize the letter and use roman type for the -s ending. Use of an apostrophe is usually optional; the Modern Language Association continues to recommend the apostrophe.

Two large *J*s (*or J*'s) were painted on the door.

PLURALS OF WORDS MENTIONED AS WORDS   Italicize the word and use roman type for the -s ending. Use of an apostrophe is optional.

We've heard enough *maybe*s (or *maybe*'s).

Words mentioned as words may also appear in quotation marks. When you choose this option, use the apostrophe: We've heard enough "maybe's."

P5-e Avoid common misuses of the apostrophe.

Do not use an apostrophe in the following situations.

WITH NOUNS THAT ARE NOT POSSESSIVE

▶ Some ~~outpatient's~~ ^outpatients^ are given special parking permits.

IN THE POSSESSIVE PRONOUNS *ITS, WHOSE, HIS, HERS, OURS, YOURS,* AND *THEIRS*

▶ Each area has ^its^ ~~it's~~ own conference room.

It's means "it is." The possessive pronoun *its* contains no apostrophe despite the fact that it is possessive.

ON THE WEB

For an electronic exercise on using apostrophes, go to
www.dianahacker.com/writersref

and click on ▶ **Electronic Grammar Exercises**
　　　　　　　▶ **Punctuation**
　　　　　　　　▶ **E-ex P5–1**

P6

Quotation marks

> **GRAMMAR CHECKERS** can tell you to put commas and periods inside quotation marks; they can also flag "unbalanced quotes," an opening quotation mark that is not paired with a closing quotation mark. The programs can't tell you, however, when you should or shouldn't use quotation marks.

P6-a   Use quotation marks to enclose direct quotations.

Direct quotations of a person's words, whether spoken or written, must be in quotation marks.

> "A foolish consistency is the hobgoblin of little minds," wrote Ralph Waldo Emerson.

CAUTION: Do not use quotation marks around indirect quotations. An indirect quotation reports someone's ideas without using that person's exact words.

> Ralph Waldo Emerson believed that consistency for its own sake is the mark of a small mind.

NOTE: In dialogue, begin a new paragraph to mark a change in speaker.

> "Mom, his name is Willie, not William. A thousand times I've told you, it's *Willie.*"
> "Willie is a derivative of William, Lester. Surely his birth certificate doesn't have Willie on it, and I like calling people by their proper names."
> "Yes, it does, ma'am. My mother named me Willie K. Mason."
> —Gloria Naylor

If a single speaker utters more than one paragraph, introduce each paragraph with quotation marks, but do not use closing quotation marks until the end of the speech.

P6-b Set off long quotations of prose or poetry by indenting.

MLA, APA, and CMS styles have slightly different guidelines for setting off long quotations (see MLA-2a, APA-2a, or CMS-2a). The guidelines given in this section are those of the Modern Language Association (MLA).

When a quotation of prose runs to more than four typed lines in your paper, set it off by indenting ten spaces from the left margin. Quotation marks are not required because the indented format tells readers that the quotation is taken word-for-word from a source. Long quotations are ordinarily introduced by a sentence ending with a colon.

> After studying the historical record, James Horan evaluates Billy the Kid like this:
>
> > The portrait that emerges of [the Kid] from the thousands of pages of affidavits, reports, trial transcripts, his letters, and his testimony is neither the mythical Robin Hood nor the stereotyped adenoidal moron and pathological killer. Rather Billy appears as a disturbed, lonely young man, honest, loyal to his friends, dedicated to his beliefs, and betrayed by our institutions and the corrupt, ambitious, and compromising politicians of his time. (158)

The number in parentheses is a citation handled according to the Modern Language Association style. (See MLA-4.)

NOTE: When you quote two or more paragraphs from the source, indent the first line of each paragraph an additional three spaces.

When quoting more than three lines of a poem, set the quoted lines off from the text by indenting ten spaces from the left margin. Use no quotation marks unless they appear in the poem itself. (To punctuate two or three lines of poetry, see P7-h.)

> Although many anthologizers "modernize" her punctuation, Emily Dickinson relied heavily on dashes, using them, perhaps, as a musical device. Here, for example, is the original version of the opening stanza from "The Snake":
>
> > A narrow Fellow in the Grass
> >
> > Occasionally rides--
> >
> > You may have met Him--did you not
> >
> > His notice sudden is--

P6-c Use single quotation marks to enclose a quotation within a quotation.

> According to Paul Eliott, Inuit hunters "chant an ancient magic song to the seal they are after: 'Beast of the sea! Come and place yourself before me in the early morning!'"

P6-d Use quotation marks around the titles of short works: newspaper and magazine articles, poems, short stories, songs, episodes of television and radio programs, and chapters or subdivisions of books.

> Katherine Mansfield's "The Garden Party" provoked a lively discussion in our short-story class last night.

NOTE: Titles of books, plays, Web sites, and films and names of magazines and newspapers are put in italics or underlined. (See M6-a.)

P6-e Quotation marks may be used to set off words used as words.

Although words used as words are ordinarily underlined or italicized (see M6-d), quotation marks are also acceptable.

> The words "accept" and "except" are frequently confused.

> The words *accept* and *except* are frequently confused.

P6-f Use punctuation with quotation marks according to convention.

This section describes the conventions used by most Canadian publishers in placing various marks of punctuation inside or outside quotation marks. It also explains how to punctuate when introducing quoted material.

Periods and commas

Always place periods and commas inside quotation marks.

"This is a stick-up," said the well-dressed young couple. "We want all your money."

This rule applies to single quotation marks as well as double quotation marks. (See P6-c.) It also applies to all uses of quotation marks: for quoted material, for titles of works, and for words used as words.

EXCEPTION: In the Modern Language Association's style of parenthetical in-text citations (see MLA-4), the period follows the citation in parentheses.

> James M. McPherson comments, approvingly, that the Whigs "were not averse to extending the blessings of American liberty, even to Mexicans and Indians" (48).

Colons and semicolons

Put colons and semicolons outside quotation marks.

> Harold wrote, "I regret that I am unable to attend the fundraiser for AIDS research"; his letter, however, contained a substantial contribution.

Question marks and exclamation points

Put question marks and exclamation points inside quotation marks unless they apply to the sentence as a whole.

> Contrary to tradition, bedtime at my house is marked by "Mommy, can I tell you a story now?"

> Have you heard the old proverb "Do not climb the hill until you reach it"?

In the first sentence, the question mark applies only to the quoted question. In the second sentence, the question mark applies to the whole sentence.

NOTE: MLA parenthetical citations create a special problem. According to MLA, the question mark or exclamation point should appear before the quotation mark, and a period should follow the parenthetical citation.

> Rosie Thomas asks, "Is nothing in life ever straight and clear, the way children see it?" (77).

Introducing quoted material

After a word group introducing a quotation, choose a colon, a comma, or no punctuation at all, whichever is appropriate in context.

FORMAL INTRODUCTION   If a quotation has been formally introduced, a colon is appropriate. A formal introduction is a full independent clause, not just an expression such as *he said* or *she remarked.*

> Morrow views personal ads in the classifieds as an art form: "The personal ad is like a haiku of self-celebration, a brief solo played on one's own horn."

EXPRESSION SUCH AS *HE SAID*   If a quotation is introduced with an expression such as *he said* or *she remarked* — or if it is followed by such an expression — a comma is needed.

> Stephen Leacock once said, "I am a great believer in luck, and I find the harder I work the more I have of it."

> "You can be a little ungrammatical if you come from the right part of the country," said Robert Frost.

BLENDED QUOTATION   When a quotation is blended into the writer's own sentence, either a comma or no punctuation is appropriate, depending on the way in which the quotation fits into the sentence structure.

> The future champion could, as he put it, "float like a butterfly and sting like a bee."

> Susan Munroe noted that "Paul Martin made his mark in the Chrétien government as finance minister."

BEGINNING OF SENTENCE   If a quotation appears at the beginning of a sentence, set it off with a comma unless the quotation ends with a question mark or an exclamation point.

> "We shot them like dogs," boasted Davy Crockett, who was among Jackson's troops.

> "What is it?" I asked, bracing myself.

interrupted quotation   If a quoted sentence is interrupted by explanatory words, use commas to set off the explanatory words.

> "A great many people think they are thinking," wrote William James, "when they are merely rearranging their prejudices."

If two successive quoted sentences from the same source are interrupted by explanatory words, use a comma before the explanatory words and a period after them.

> "I was a flop as a daily reporter," admitted E. B. White. "Every piece had to be a masterpiece—and before you knew it, Tuesday was Wednesday."

P6-g   Avoid common misuses of quotation marks.

Do not use quotation marks to draw attention to familiar slang, to disown trite expressions, or to justify an attempt at humour.

▶ Between Thanksgiving and Super Bowl Sunday, many American wives become ⁄"football widows."

Do not use quotation marks around indirect quotations. (See also P6-a.)

▶ After leaving the scene of the domestic quarrel, the officer said that ⁄"he was due for a coffee break."

Do not use quotation marks around the title of your own essay.

ON THE WEB

For an electronic exercise on using quotation marks, go to
www.dianahacker.com/writersref

and click on   ▶ **Electronic Grammar Exercises**
　　　　　　　　　▶ **Punctuation**
　　　　　　　　　　　▶ **E-ex P6–1**

P7

Other marks

 GRAMMAR CHECKERS are of little help with end punctuation and the other marks discussed in this section. Most notably, they neglect to tell you when your sentence is missing end punctuation.

P7-a The period

Use a period to end all sentences except direct questions or genuine exclamations. Also use periods in abbreviations according to convention.

To end sentences

Everyone knows that a period should be used to end most sentences. The only problems that arise concern the choice between a period and a question mark or between a period and an exclamation point.

If a sentence reports a question instead of asking it directly, it should end with a period, not a question mark.

▶ Celia asked whether the picnic would be cancelled?.

If a sentence is not a genuine exclamation, it should end with a period, not an exclamation point.

▶ After years of working her way through school, Pat finally

graduated with high honours!.

In abbreviations

A period is conventionally used in abbreviations such as these:

Mr.	B.A.	B.C.	i.e.	A.M. (or a.m.)
Mrs.	M.A.	B.C.E.	e.g.	P.M. (or p.m.)
Ms.	Ph.D.	A.D.	etc.	
Dr.	R.N.	C.E.		

A period is not used in Canada Post abbreviations for provinces and territories: NB, AB, PQ.

Ordinarily a period is not used in abbreviations of organization names:

NATO	UNESCO	TSSA	PUSH	IBM
TSX	CCRA	CWPE	NVBA	FTC
USA (*or* U.S.A.)	CSA	CAW	NDP	NHL

Usage varies, however. When in doubt, consult a dictionary, a style manual, or a publication by the agency in question. Even the yellow pages can help.

NOTE: If a sentence ends with a period marking an abbreviation, do not add a second period.

P7-b The question mark

Obviously a direct question should be followed by a question mark.

What is the horsepower of a 747 engine?

If a polite request is written in the form of a question, it may be followed by a period.

Would you please send me your catalogue of lilies.

CAUTION: Do not use a question mark after an indirect question (one that is reported rather than asked directly). Use a period instead.

▶ He asked me who was teaching the mythology course?.
                                                    ^

NOTE: Questions in a series may be followed by question marks even when they are not complete sentences.

We wondered where Calamity had hidden this time. Under the sink? Behind the furnace? On top of the bookcase?

P7-c The exclamation point

Use an exclamation point after a word group or sentence that expresses exceptional feeling or deserves special emphasis.

When Gloria entered the room, I switched on the lights and we all yelled "Surprise!"

CAUTION: Do not overuse the exclamation point.

▶ In the fisherman's memory the fish lives on, increasing in length

and weight with each passing year, until at last it is big enough to

shade a fishing boat~~!~~.
           ^

This sentence doesn't need to be pumped up with an exclamation point. It is emphatic enough without it.

▶ Whenever I see Venus lunging forward to put away an

overhead smash, it might as well be me~~!~~. She does it just the
                                         ^

way I would!

The first exclamation point should be deleted so that the second one will have more force.

P7-d The dash

When typing, use two hyphens to form a dash (--). Do not put spaces before or after the dash. (If your word processing program has what is known as an "em-dash," you may use it instead, with no space before or after it.) Dashes are used for the following purposes.

To set off parenthetical material that deserves emphasis

Everything that went wrong—from the peeping Tom at her window last night to my head-on collision today—was blamed on our move.

To set off appositives that contain commas

An appositive is a noun or noun phrase that renames a nearby noun. Ordinarily most appositives are set off with commas (see P1-e), but when the appositive contains commas, a pair of dashes helps readers see the relative importance of all the pauses.

In my hometown the basic needs of people—food, clothing, and shelter—are less costly than in Vancouver.

To prepare for a list, a restatement, an amplification, or a dramatic shift in tone or thought

> Along the wall are the bulk liquids — sesame seed oil, honey, safflower oil, maple syrup, and peanut butter.

> Consider the amount of sugar in the average person's diet — forty-seven kilograms per year, 90 percent more than that consumed by our ancestors.

> Everywhere we looked there were little kids — a box of Cracker Jacks in one hand and mommy's or daddy's sleeve in the other.

> Kiere took a few steps back, came running full speed, kicked a mighty kick — and missed the ball.

In the first two examples, the writer could also use a colon. (See P4-a.) The colon is more formal than the dash and not quite as dramatic.

CAUTION: Unless there is a specific reason for using the dash, avoid it. Unnecessary dashes create a choppy effect.

▶ **Insisting that our young people learn to use computers as**

   instructional tools ⫻ for information retrieval ⫻ makes good sense.

   Herding them ⫻ sheeplike ⫻ into computer technology does not.

P7-e Parentheses

Use parentheses to enclose supplemental material, minor digressions, and afterthoughts.

> After taking her temperature, pulse, and blood pressure (routine vital signs), the nurse made Becky as comfortable as possible.

> The weights Javid was first able to move (not lift, mind you) were measured in grams.

Use parentheses to enclose letters or numbers labelling items in a series.

> Regulations stipulated that only the following equipment could be used on the survival mission: (1) a knife, (2) ten metres of parachute line, (3) a book of matches, (4) two ponchos, (5) an *E* tool, and (6) a signal flare.

CAUTION: Do not overuse parentheses. Rough drafts are likely to contain more afterthoughts than necessary. As writers head into a sentence, they often think of additional details, occasionally working them in as best they can with parentheses. Usually such sentences should be revised so that the additional details no longer seem to be afterthoughts.

▶ Researchers have said that ~~ten million (estimates run as high as~~ *from ten million to fifty million*

~~fifty million)~~ Americans have hypoglycemia.

P7-f Brackets

Use brackets to enclose any words or phrases that you have inserted into an otherwise word-for-word quotation.

> *Audubon* reports that "if there are not enough young to balance deaths, the end of the species [California condor] is inevitable."

The *Audubon* article did not contain the words *California condor* in the sentence quoted, since the context made clear what species was meant. Out of context, however, the words *California condor* are needed.

The Latin word "sic" in brackets indicates that an error in a quoted sentence appears in the original source.

> According to the review, Darci Kistler's performance was brilliant, "exceding [sic] the expectations of even her most loyal fans."

Do not overuse "sic," however, since calling attention to others' mistakes can appear snobbish. The quotation above, for example, might have been handled like this instead: *According to the review, Darci Kistler's performance was so brilliant that it surpassed "the expectations of even her most loyal fans."*

P7-g The ellipsis mark

The ellipsis mark consists of three spaced periods. Use an ellipsis mark to indicate that you have deleted material from an otherwise word-for-word quotation.

> Reuben reports that "when the amount of cholesterol circulating in the blood rises over . . . 300 milligrams per 100, the chances of a heart attack increase dramatically."

If you delete a full sentence or more in the middle of a quoted passage, use a period before the three ellipsis dots.

> "Most of our efforts," writes Dave Erikson, "are directed toward saving the bald eagle's wintering habitat along the Mississippi River. . . . It's important that the wintering birds have a place to roost, where they can get out of the cold wind and be undisturbed by man."

CAUTION: Ordinarily, do not use the ellipsis mark at the beginning or at the end of a quotation. Readers will understand that the quoted material is taken from a longer passage. If you have cut some words from the end of the final sentence quoted, however, MLA requires an ellipsis mark, as in the second example on page 337.

In quoted poetry, use a full line of dots to indicate that you have dropped a line or more from the poem:

> Had we but world enough, and time,
> This coyness, lady, were no crime.
> . . . .
> But at my back I always hear
> Time's wingèd chariot hurrying near;
>
> —Andrew Marvell

The ellipsis mark may also be used to mark a hesitation or an interruption in speech or to suggest unfinished thoughts.

> "The apartment building next door . . . it's going up in flames!" yelled Marcia.

> Before falling into a coma, the victim whispered, "It was a man with a tattoo on his . . ."

P7-h The slash

Use the slash to separate two or three lines of poetry that have been run in to your text. Add a space both before and after the slash.

> In the opening lines of "Jordan," George Herbert pokes gentle fun at popular poems of his time: "Who says that fictions only and false hair / Become a verse? Is there in truth no beauty?"

More than three lines of poetry should be handled as a block quotation set off from the text. (See P6-b.)

The slash may occasionally be used to separate paired terms such as *pass/fail* and *producer/director.* Do not use a space before or after the slash.

> Roger Sommers, the team's manager/owner, announced a change in the lineup.

Be sparing, however, in this use of the slash. In particular, avoid the use of *and/or, he/she,* and *his/her.*

ON THE WEB

For an electronic exercise on using the dash, parentheses, brackets, the ellipsis mark, and the slash, go to
www.dianahacker.com/writersref

and click on   ▶ **Electronic Grammar Exercises**
                       ▶ **Punctuation**
                                 ▶ **E-ex P7–1**

M

Mechanics

Mechanics

M1

Spelling

You learned to spell from repeated experience with words in both reading and writing, but especially writing. Words have a look, a sound, and even a feel to them as the hand moves across the page. As you proofread, you can probably tell if a word doesn't look quite right. In such cases, the solution is obvious: Look up the word in the dictionary. (See W6-a.)

> **SPELL CHECKERS** are useful alternatives to a dictionary, but only to a point. A spell checker will not tell you how to spell words not listed in its dictionary; nor will it help you catch words commonly confused, such as *accept* and *except,* or some typographical errors, such as *own* for *won.* You will still need to proofread, and for some words you may need to turn to the dictionary.

M1-a Become familiar with the major spelling rules.

i *before* e *except after* c

Use *i* before *e* except after *c* or when sounded like *ay,* as in *neighbour* and *weigh.*

I BEFORE *E*	relieve, believe, sieve, niece, fierce, frieze
E BEFORE *I*	receive, deceive, sleigh, freight, eight
EXCEPTIONS	seize, either, weird, height, foreign, leisure

Suffixes

FINAL SILENT -*E* Generally, drop a final silent -*e* when adding a suffix that begins with a vowel. Keep the final -*e* if the suffix begins with a consonant.

combine, combination	achieve, achievement
desire, desiring	care, careful
prude, prudish	entire, entirety
remove, removable	gentle, gentleness

Words such as *changeable, judgment, argument,* and *truly* are exceptions.

FINAL -Y   When adding *-s* or *-d* to words ending in *-y,* ordinarily change *-y* to *-ie* when the *-y* is preceded by a consonant but not when it is preceded by a vowel.

comedy, comedies   monkey, monkeys
dry, dried   play, played

With proper names ending in *-y,* however, do not change the *-y* to *-ie* even if it is preceded by a consonant: *the Dougherty family, the Doughertys.*

FINAL CONSONANTS   If a final consonant is preceded by a single vowel *and* the consonant ends a one-syllable word or a stressed syllable, double the consonant when adding a suffix beginning with a vowel.

bet, betting   occur, occurrence
commit, committed

Plurals

-S OR -ES   Add *-s* to form the plural of most nouns; add *-es* to singular nouns ending in *-s, -sh, -ch,* and *-x.*

table, tables   church, churches
paper, papers   dish, dishes

Ordinarily add *-s* to nouns ending in *-o* when the *-o* is preceded by a vowel. Add *-es* when it is preceded by a consonant.

radio, radios   hero, heroes
video, videos   tomato, tomatoes

OTHER PLURALS   To form the plural of a hyphenated compound word, add the *-s* to the chief word even if it does not appear at the end.

mother-in-law, mothers-in-law

English words derived from other languages such as Latin or French sometimes form the plural as they would in their original language.

medium, media   chateau, chateaux
criterion, criteria

ESL

Spelling may vary slightly among English-speaking countries. This can prove particularly confusing for ESL students, who may have learned American or British English. Following is a list of some common words spelled differently in Canadian, American, and British English. Consult a dictionary for others.

CANADIAN	AMERICAN	BRITISH
cancelled	canceled	cancelled
colour	color	colour
judgment	judgment	judgement
cheque	check	cheque
realize	realize	realise
defence	defense	defence
anemia	anemia	anaemia
theatre	theater	theatre
fetus	fetus	foetus
mould	mold	mould
civilization	civilization	civilisation
connection	connection	connexion
licorice	licorice	liquorice

NOTE: For rules on pluralizing numbers, abbreviations, letters, and words mentioned as words, see P5-d.

M1-b Discriminate between words that sound alike but have different meanings.

Words that sound alike or nearly alike but have different meanings and spellings are easy to confuse. The following sets of words are so commonly confused that a good proofreader will double-check their every use.

affect (verb: "to exert an influence")
effect (verb: "to accomplish"; noun: "result")

its (possessive pronoun: "of or belonging to it")
it's (contraction for "it is")

loose (adjective: "free, not securely attached")
lose (verb: "to fail to keep, to be deprived of")

principal (adjective: "most important"; noun: "head of a school")
principle (noun: "a general or fundamental truth")

their (possessive pronoun: "belonging to them")
they're (contraction for "they are")
there (adverb: "that place or position")

who's (contraction for "who is")
whose (possessive form of "who")

your (possessive form of "you")
you're (contraction of "you are")

To check for correct use of these and other commonly confused words, consult the Glossary of Usage in this book (W1).

ON THE WEB

For links to online dictionaries and other resources that will help you with grammar, style, and punctuation, go to
www.dianahacker.com/writersref

and click on ▶ **Links Library**
▶ **Grammar, Style, and Punctuation**

M2

The hyphen

M2-a Consult the dictionary to determine how to treat a compound word.

The dictionary will tell you whether to treat a compound word as a hyphenated compound (*water-repellent*), one word (*waterproof*), or two words (*water table*). If the compound word is not in the dictionary, treat it as two words.

▶ The prosecutor chose not to cross⌃examine any witnesses.

▶ Grandma kept a small note͡book in her apron pocket.

▶ Alice walked through the looking⁄glass into a backward world.

M2-b Use a hyphen to connect two or more words functioning together as an adjective before a noun.

▶ Mrs. Douglas gave Mary a seashell and some newspaper␣-wrapped

fish to take home to her mother.

▶ Priscilla Hood is not yet a well␣-known candidate.

Newspaper-wrapped and *well-known* are adjectives used before the nouns *fish* and *candidate*.

Generally, do not use a hyphen when such compounds follow the noun.

▶ After our television campaign, Priscilla Hood will be well/known.

Do not use a hyphen to connect -*ly* adverbs to the words they modify.

▶ A slowly/moving truck tied up traffic.

NOTE: In a series, hyphens are suspended.

Do you prefer first-, second-, or third-class tickets?

M2-c Hyphenate the written form of fractions and of compound numbers from twenty-one to ninety-nine.

▶ One␣-fourth of my salary goes toward provincial and federal

income taxes.

M2-d Use a hyphen with the prefixes *all-*, *ex-*, and *self-* and with the suffix -*elect*.

▶ The charity is funnelling more money into self␣-help projects.

▶ Carmen is our club's president␣-elect.

M2-e A hyphen is used in some words to avoid ambiguity or to separate awkward double or triple letters.

Without the hyphen there would be no way to distinguish between words such as *re-creation* and *recreation*.

> Bicycling in the country is my favourite recreation.

> The film was praised for its astonishing re-creation of nineteenth-century London.

Hyphens are sometimes used to separate awkward double or triple letters in compound words (*anti-intellectual, cross-stitch*). Check a dictionary for the standard form of the word.

M2-f If a word must be divided at the end of a line, divide it correctly.

Divide words between syllables; never divide a one-syllable word.

▶ When I returned from my travels overseas, I didn't ~~reco-~~ *recog-*
nize
~~gnize~~ one face on the magazine covers.

▶ Grandfather didn't have the courage or the ~~stren-~~
strength
~~gth~~ to open the door.

Never divide a word so that a single letter stands alone at the end of a line or fewer than three letters begin a line.

▶ She'll bring her brother with her when she comes ~~a-~~
again.
~~gain.~~

▶ As audience to *The Mousetrap*, Hamlet is a ~~watch-~~
watcher
~~er~~ watching watchers.

When dividing a compound word at the end of a line, either make the break between the words that form the compound or put the whole word on the next line.

▶ My niece Monica is determined to become a long-~~dis-~~
distance
~~tance~~ runner when she grows up.
‸

To divide a long Internet address at the end of a line, do not use a hyphen. If the address is mentioned in the text of your paper, break it after a slash or after a period.

The *Berkeley Digital Library SunSITE* can be reached at <http://sunsite.berkeley.edu>.

If the address appears in a paper using MLA or APA style, follow the guidelines on page 357 or 407, respectively.

ON THE WEB

For an electronic exercise on using hyphens, go to
www.dianahacker.com/writersref

and click on   ▶ **Electronic Grammar Exercises**
  ▶ **Mechanics**
    ▶ **E-ex M2–1**

M3

Capitalization

In addition to the following rules, a good dictionary can often tell you when to use capital letters.

M3-a Capitalize proper nouns and words derived from them; do not capitalize common nouns.

Proper nouns are the names of specific persons, places, and things. All other nouns are common nouns. The following types of words are usually capitalized: names for the deity, religions, religious followers, sacred books; words of family relationship used as names; particular places; nationalities and their languages, races, tribes; educational institutions, departments, degrees, particular courses;

government departments, organizations, political parties; historical movements, periods, events, documents; specific electronic sources; and trade names.

PROPER NOUNS	COMMON NOUNS
God (used as a name)	a god
Book of Jeremiah	a book
Uncle Pedro	my uncle
Father (used as a name)	my father
Lake Superior	a picturesque lake
the Hummingbird Centre	a centre for the arts
the Prairies	a Canadian province
Japan, a Japanese garden	an ornamental garden
University of Manitoba	a good university
Geology 101	geology
Environmental Protection Agency	a federal agency
the New Democratic Party	a political party
the Enlightenment	the eighteenth century
Great Depression	a recession
the Charter of Rights and Freedoms	a treaty
the World Wide Web, the Web	a home page
the Internet, the Net	a computer network
Kleenex	a tissue

Months, holidays, and days of the week are treated as proper nouns; the seasons and numbers of the days of the month are not.

Our town fair begins in July, right after Canada Day.

My mother's birthday is in early spring, on the fifth of April.

Names of school subjects are capitalized only if they are names of languages. Names of particular courses are capitalized.

This semester Austin is taking math, geography, geology, French, and English.

Professor Anderson offers Modern American Fiction 501 to graduate students.

CAUTION: Do not capitalize common nouns to make them seem important. *Our company is currently hiring computer programmers* [not *Company, Computer Programmers*].

M3-b Capitalize titles of persons when used as part of a proper name but usually not when used alone.

> Prof. Margaret Barnes; Dr. Harold Stevens; John Scott Williams Jr.; Anne Tilton, LL.D.

> Attorney General Marshall appointed four provincial judges last year.

> The attorney general announced four appointments.

Usage varies when the title of an important public figure is used alone. *The prime minister* [or *Prime Minister*] *signed the bill.*

M3-c Capitalize the first, last, and all major words in titles and subtitles of works such as books, articles, songs, and online documents.

In both titles and subtitles, major words—nouns, verbs, adjectives, and adverbs—should be capitalized. Minor words—articles, prepositions, and coordinating conjunctions—are not capitalized unless they are the first or last word of a title or subtitle. Capitalize the second part of a hyphenated term in a title if it is a major word but not if it is a minor word.

> *The Impossible Theater: A Manifesto*
> *The F-Plan Diet*
> "Fire and Ice"
> "I Want to Hold Your Hand"
> *The Canadian Green Page*

Capitalize chapter titles and the titles of other major divisions of a work following the same guidelines used for titles of complete works.

> "Work and Play" in Santayana's *The Nature of Beauty*

> "Size Matters" on the Web site *Discovery Channel Online*

M3-d Capitalize the first word of a sentence.

Obviously the first word of a sentence should be capitalized.

> When lightning struck the house, the chimney collapsed.

When a sentence appears within parentheses, capitalize its first word unless the parentheses appear within another sentence.

> Early detection of breast cancer significantly increases survival rates. (See table 2.)

> Early detection of breast cancer significantly increases survival rates (see table 2).

M3-e Capitalize the first word of a quoted sentence but not a quoted phrase.

> In *Time* magazine Robert Hughes writes, "There are only about sixty Watteau paintings on whose authenticity all experts agree."

> Russell Baker has written that sports are "the opiate of the masses."

If a quoted sentence is interrupted by explanatory words, do not capitalize the first word after the interruption. (See also P6-f.)

> "If you wanted to go out," he said sharply, "you should have told me."

When quoting poetry, copy the poet's capitalization exactly. Many poets capitalize the first word of every line of poetry; a few contemporary poets dismiss capitalization altogether.

> When I consider everything that grows
> Holds in perfection but a little moment
> —Shakespeare

> it was the week   that
> i felt the city's narrow breezes rush about
> me
> —Don L. Lee

M3-f Do not capitalize the first word after a colon unless it begins an independent clause, in which case capitalization is optional.

> Most bar patrons can be divided into two groups: the occasional after-work socializers and the nothing-to-go-home-to regulars.

> This we are forced to conclude: The [*or* the] federal government is needed to protect the rights of minorities.

M3-g Capitalize abbreviations for departments and agencies of government, other organizations, and corporations; capitalize the call letters of radio and television stations.

CSA, CCRA, OPEC, IBM, WCTV, YTV

ON THE WEB

For an electronic exercise on capitalization, go to
www.dianahacker.com/writersref

and click on ▶ **Electronic Grammar Exercises**
　　　　　　　　▶ **Mechanics**
　　　　　　　　　　▶ **E-ex M3–1**

M4

Abbreviations

M4-a Use standard abbreviations for titles immediately before and after proper names.

TITLES BEFORE PROPER NAMES	TITLES AFTER PROPER NAMES
Mr. Raphael Zabala	William Albert Sr.
Ms. Nancy Linehan	Thomas Hines Jr.
Mrs. Edward Horn	Anita Lor, Ph.D.
Dr. Margaret Simmons	Robert Simkowski, M.D.
Rev. John Stone	William Lyons, M.A.
St. Joan of Arc	Margaret Chin, LL.D.
Prof. James Russo	Polly Stein, D.D.S.

Do not abbreviate a title if it is not used with a proper name.

　　　　　　　professor
▶ My history ~~prof.~~ was a specialist on America's use of the atomic
　　　　　　　　^
bomb in World War II.

Avoid redundant titles such as *Dr. Susan Hassel, M.D.* Choose one title or the other: *Dr. Susan Hassel* or *Susan Hassel, M.D.*

M4-b Use abbreviations only when you are sure your readers will understand them.

Familiar abbreviations, often written without periods, are acceptable.

> CIA, FBI, CUPE, RSVP, IBM, UPS, CBC, USA (*or* U.S.A.), IOU, CD-ROM, ESL

> The YMCA has opened a new gym close to my office.

NOTE: When using an unfamiliar abbreviation (such as EAC for the Editors' Association of Canada) throughout a document, write the full name followed by the abbreviation in parentheses at the first mention of the name. You may use the abbreviation alone from then on.

M4-c Use B.C., A.D., A.M., P.M., No., and $ only with specific dates, times, numbers, and amounts.

The abbreviation B.C. ("before Christ") follows a date, and A.D. ("*anno Domini*") precedes a date. Alternatives are B.C.E. ("before the common era") and C.E. ("common era"), which follow dates.

> 40 B.C. (or 40 B.C.E.)   4:00 A.M. (or a.m.)   No. 12 (or no. 12)
> A.D. 44 (or 44 C.E.)   6:00 P.M. (or p.m.) $150

Avoid using A.M., P.M., No., or $ when not accompanied by a figure.

> ▶ We set off for the lake early in the ~~A.M.~~ *morning.*

M4-d Be sparing in your use of Latin abbreviations.

Latin abbreviations are appropriate in bibliographic citations and in informal writing.

> cf. (Latin *confer,* "compare")
> e.g. (Latin *exempli gratia,* "for example")
> et al. (Latin *et alii,* "and others")
> etc. (Latin *et cetera,* "and so forth")
> i.e. (Latin *id est,* "that is")
> N.B. (Latin *nota bene,* "note well")
> P.S. (Latin *postscriptum,* "postscript")

Alfred Hitchcock directed many classic thrillers (e.g., *Psycho, Rear Window,* and *Vertigo*).

Harold Simms et al., *The Race for Space*

In formal writing use the appropriate English phrases.

▶ Many obsolete laws remain on the books, ~~e.g.,~~ a law in Vermont ^*for example,*^

forbidding an unmarried man and woman to sit less than six

inches apart on a park bench.

M4-e Avoid inappropriate abbreviations.

In formal writing, abbreviations for the following are not commonly accepted: personal names; units of measurement; days of the week; holidays; months; courses of study; divisions of written works; provinces, territories, states, and countries.

In company names, use abbreviated forms such as *Co., Inc.,* and *&* if they are part of the official name: *Temps & Co., Bogart Inc.* Do not abbreviate such forms if they are not part of the official name: *Dunn Photographic Associates* (not *Dunn Photo. Assoc.*). When in doubt about a company's official name, consult a business card, company letterhead, or the yellow pages.

PERSONAL NAME Charles (*not* Chas.)

UNITS OF MEASUREMENT kilogram (*not* kg)

DAYS OF THE WEEK Monday (*not* Mon.)

HOLIDAYS Christmas (*not* Xmas)

MONTHS March (*not* Mar.)

COURSES OF STUDY political science (*not* poli. sci.)

DIVISIONS OF WRITTEN WORKS chapter, page (*not* ch., p.)

PROVINCES, COUNTRIES Quebec (*not* PQ or Que.)

PARTS OF A BUSINESS NAME Adams Lighting Company (*not* Adams Lighting Co.); Kim and Brothers, Inc. (*not* Kim and Bros., Inc.)

▶ Eliza promised to buy me one ~~kg~~ of Godiva chocolate for my ^*kilogram*^

birthday, which was last ~~Fri.~~ ^*Friday.*^

┌───┐
│ **ON THE WEB**   │
│   │
│ For an electronic exercise on using abbreviations, go to │
│ **www.dianahacker.com/writersref**   │
│   │
│ and click on   ▶ **Electronic Grammar Exercises**   │
│   ▶ **Mechanics**   │
│   ▶ **E-ex M4–1**   │
└───┘

M5

Numbers

M5-a Spell out numbers of one or two words or those that begin a sentence. Use figures for numbers that require more than two words to spell out.

▶ Now, some ~~8~~ *eight* years later, Muffin is still with us.

▶ I counted ~~one hundred seventy-six~~ *176* CDs on the shelves next to the

fireplace.

If a sentence begins with a number, spell out the number or rewrite the sentence.

▶ *One hundred fifty* ~~150~~ children in our program need expensive dental treatment.

Rewriting the sentence may be less awkward if the number is long: *In our program 150 children need expensive dental treatment.*

EXCEPTIONS: In technical and some business writing, figures are preferred even when spellings would be brief, but usage varies.

When several numbers appear in the same passage, many writers choose consistency rather than strict adherence to the rule.

When one number immediately follows another, spell out one and use figures for the other: *three 100-m events, 60 four-poster beds.*

M5-b Generally, figures are acceptable for dates, addresses, percentages, fractions, decimals, scores, statistics and other numerical results, exact amounts of money, divisions of books and plays, pages, identification numbers, and the time.

DATES   July 4, 1776, 56 B.C., A.D. 30

ADDRESSES   77 Latches Lane, 519 West 42nd Street

PERCENTAGES   55 percent (or 55%)

FRACTIONS, DECIMALS   ½, 0.047

SCORES   7 to 3, 21–18

STATISTICS   average age 37, average weight 81 kg

SURVEYS   4 out of 5

EXACT AMOUNTS OF MONEY $105.37, $106 000, $0.05

DIVISIONS OF BOOKS   volume 3, chapter 4, page 189

DIVISIONS OF PLAYS   act III, scene iii (*or* act 3, scene 3)

IDENTIFICATION NUMBERS   serial number 10988675

TIME OF DAY   4:00 P.M., 1:30 A.M.

$255 000
▶ Several doctors put up ~~two hundred fifty-five thousand dollars~~ for
the construction of a golf course.

NOTE: When not using A.M. or P.M., write out the time in words (*four o'clock in the afternoon, twelve noon, seven in the morning*).

ON THE WEB

For an electronic exercise on using numbers, go to
www.dianahacker.com/writersref

and click on   ▶ **Electronic Grammar Exercises**
        ▶ **Mechanics**
            ▶ **E-ex M5–1**

M6

Italics (underlining)

Italics, a slanting typeface used in printed material, can be produced by word processing programs. In handwritten or typed papers, this typeface is indicated by underlining. Some instructors prefer underlining even if their students can produce italics.

NOTE: Some e-mail systems do not allow for italics or underlining. In e-mail, you can indicate italics by preceding and ending the term with underscore marks or asterisks. Punctuation should follow the coding.

CAUTION: In World Wide Web documents, underlining indicates a hot link. When creating a Web document, use italics, not underlining, for the conventions described in this section.

M6-a   Underline or italicize the titles of works according to convention.

Titles of the following kinds of works should be underlined or italicized:

TITLES OF BOOKS   *The Great Gatsby, A Distant Mirror*

MAGAZINES   *Time, Canadian Geographic*

NEWSPAPERS   the *St. Louis Post-Dispatch*

PAMPHLETS   *Common Sense, Facts about Marijuana*

LONG POEMS   *The Waste Land, Paradise Lost*

PLAYS   *King Lear, A Raisin in the Sun*

FILMS   *Casablanca, The Matrix*

TELEVISION PROGRAMS   *Survivor, 60 Minutes*

RADIO PROGRAMS   *All Things Considered*

MUSICAL COMPOSITIONS   Gershwin's *Porgy and Bess*

CHOREOGRAPHIC WORKS   Twyla Tharp's *Brief Fling*

WORKS OF VISUAL ART   Rodin's *The Thinker*

COMIC STRIPS   *Dilbert*

SOFTWARE   *WordPerfect, Acrobat Reader*

WEB SITES   *National Post Online, The Sports Network*

The titles of other works, such as short stories, essays, songs, and short poems, are enclosed in quotation marks. (See P6-d.)

NOTE: Do not use underlining or italics when referring to the Bible, titles of books in the Bible (Genesis, not *Genesis*), or titles of legal documents (the Constitution, not *Constitution*). Do not underline the title of your own paper.

M6-b Underline or italicize the names of spacecraft, aircraft, ships, and trains.

Challenger, Spirit of St. Louis, Queen Elizabeth II, Silver Streak

▶ The success of the Soviets' <u>Sputnik</u> galvanized the U.S. space

program.

M6-c Underline or italicize foreign words in an English sentence.

▶ Although Joe's method seemed to be successful, I decided to

establish my own <u>modus operandi</u>.

EXCEPTION: Do not underline or italicize foreign words that have become part of the English language — "laissez-faire," "fait accompli," "habeas corpus," and "per diem," for example.

M6-d Underline or italicize words, letters, and numbers mentioned as themselves.

▶ Tim assured us that the howling probably came from

his bloodhound, Hill Billy, but his <u>probably</u> stuck in our

minds.

▶ Sarah called her father by his given name, Johnny, but she was

unable to pronounce the J.

▶ A big 3 was painted on the door.

NOTE: Quotation marks may be used instead of underlining to set off words mentioned as words. (See P6-e.)

M6-e   Avoid excessive underlining or italics for emphasis.

Frequent underlining to emphasize words or ideas is distracting and should be used sparingly.

▶ Snowboarding is a sport that has become an addiction.

ON THE WEB

For an electronic exercise on using italics, go to
www.dianahacker.com/writersref

and click on ▶ **Electronic Grammar Exercises**
                        ▶ **Mechanics**
                                ▶ **E-ex M6–1**

R

Researching

Researching

Most college or university research assignments ask you to pose a question worth exploring, to read widely in search of possible answers, to interpret what you read, to draw reasoned conclusions, and to support those conclusions with valid, well-documented evidence.

Admittedly, the process takes time: time for researching and time for drafting, revising, and documenting the paper in the style recommended by your instructor (see the tabbed dividers marked MLA and APA/CMS). Before beginning a research project, you should set a realistic schedule of deadlines. For example, one student constructed the following schedule for a paper assigned on October 1 and due October 31.

SCHEDULE	FINISHED BY
1. Choose a possible topic.	October 2
2. Talk with a reference librarian and plan a search strategy.	3
3. Locate sources.	5
4. Read and take notes.	10
5. Decide on a tentative thesis and outline.	11
6. Draft the paper.	16
7. Visit the writing center to get help with ideas for revision.	17
8. Do further research if necessary.	20
9. Revise the paper.	25
10. Prepare a list of works cited.	26
11. Type and proofread the final draft.	28

R1

Conducting research

Throughout this tabbed section, you will encounter examples related to three sample research papers:

—A paper on the issue of whether to limit use of cell phones while driving, written by a student in an English composition class (see pp. 371–77). The student, Angela Daly, uses the MLA (Modern Language Association) style of documentation.

—A paper on a scientific controversy about the ability of apes to acquire language skills, written by a student in a psychology class (see pp. 408–17). The student, Karen Shaw, uses the APA (American Psychological Association) style of documentation.

—A paper on the extent to which Civil War general Nathan Bedford Forrest can be held responsible for the Fort Pillow massacre, written by a student in a history class (see pp. 439–43). The student, Ned Bishop, uses the CMS (*Chicago Manual of Style*) documentation system.

R1-a Pose possible questions worth exploring.

Working within the guidelines of your assignment, pose a few questions that seem worth researching. Here, for example, are some preliminary questions jotted down by students enrolled in a variety of classes in different disciplines.

—Can a government-regulated rating system for television shows curb children's exposure to violent programming?

—Which geological formations are the safest repositories for nuclear waste?

—Will a ban on human cloning threaten important medical research?

—What was Marcus Garvey's contribution to the fight for racial equality?

—How can governments and zoos help preserve China's endangered panda?

—Why was amateur archaeologist Heinrich Schliemann such a controversial figure in his own time?

As you formulate possible questions, make sure that they are appropriate lines of inquiry for a research paper. Choose questions that are narrow (not too broad), challenging (not too bland), and grounded (not too speculative).

Choosing a narrow question

If your initial question is too broad, given the length of the paper you plan to write, look for ways to restrict your focus. Here, for example, is how two students narrowed their initial questions.

TOO BROAD

—What are the hazards of fad diets?

—What causes homelessness?

NARROWER

— What are the hazards of liquid diets?

— How has deinstitutionalization of people with mental illnesses contributed to the problem of homelessness?

Choosing a challenging question

Your research paper will be more interesting to both you and your audience if you base it on an intellectually challenging line of inquiry. Avoid bland questions that fail to provoke thought or engage readers in a debate.

TOO BLAND

— What is obsessive-compulsive disorder?

— Where is wind energy being used?

CHALLENGING

— What treatments for obsessive-compulsive disorder show the most promise?

— Does investing in wind energy make economic sense?

You may well need to address a bland question in the course of answering a more challenging one. For example, if you were writing about promising treatments for obsessive-compulsive disorder, you would no doubt answer the question "What is obsessive-compulsive disorder?" at some point in your paper. It would be a mistake, however, to use the bland question as the focus for the whole paper.

Choosing a grounded question

Finally, you will want to make sure that your research question is grounded, not too speculative. Although speculative questions—such as those that address philosophical, ethical, or religious issues—are worth asking and may receive some attention in a research paper, they are inappropriate central questions. The central argument of a research paper should be grounded in facts; it should not be based entirely on beliefs.

TOO SPECULATIVE

— Is capital punishment moral?

— What is the difference between a just and an unjust law?

GROUNDED

—Does capital punishment deter crime?

—Should we adjust our laws so that penalties for possession of powdered cocaine and crack cocaine are comparable?

ON THE WEB

For an electronic exercise on choosing an appropriate research question, go to **www.dianahacker.com/writersref**

and click on ▶ **Electronic Research Exercises**
▶ **E-ex R1–1**

R1-b Map out a search strategy.

A search strategy is a systematic plan for tracking down sources. To create a search strategy appropriate for your research question, consult a reference librarian and perhaps take a look at your library's Web site, which will give you an overview of available resources.

Getting help

Reference librarians are information specialists who can save you time by steering you toward relevant and reliable sources. With the help of an expert, you can make the best use of electronic databases, Web search engines, and other reference tools.

When you ask a reference librarian for help, be prepared to answer a number of questions:

—What is your assignment?

—In which academic discipline are you writing?

—What is your tentative research question?

—How long will the paper be?

—How much time can you spend on the project?

It's a good idea to bring a copy of the assignment with you.

In addition to speaking with a reference librarian, you might log on to your library's Web site, which will typically include links to the library's catalogue and to a variety of databases and electronic sources. In addition, you may find links to other Web sites selected by librarians for their quality. The home page for Columbia University's library appears at the top of the following page.

LIBRARY HOME PAGE

@ Columbia University Libraries

Choosing an appropriate search strategy

There is no single search strategy that works for every topic. For some topics, it may be appropriate to search for information in newspapers, magazines, and Web sites. For others, the best sources might be found in scholarly journals and books and specialized reference works. Still other topics might be enhanced by field research—interviews, surveys, or direct observation, for example.

With the help of a reference librarian, each of the students mentioned on pages 295–96 constructed a search strategy appropriate for his or her research question.

ANGELA DALY   Angela Daly's topic, the dangers of using cell phones while driving, was so current that books were an unlikely source (by the time a book is published, it is already dated). To find up-to-date information on her topic, Daly decided to

— search a general database for articles in magazines, newspapers, and journals

— use Web search engines, such as *Google,* to locate relevant sites, online articles, and government publications

KAREN SHAW Karen Shaw's topic, the extent to which apes have learned language, has been the subject of psychological studies for many years, and it has been featured in the popular press (newspapers and magazines aimed at the general public). Thinking that both popular and scholarly works would be appropriate, Shaw decided to

— locate books through the library's online catalogue

— search a general database for popular articles

— search a specialized database, *PsycInfo,* for scholarly articles

NED BISHOP Ned Bishop's topic, the role played by Nathan Bedford Forrest in the Fort Pillow massacre, is an issue that has been investigated and debated by professional historians. Given the nature of his historical topic, Ned Bishop decided to

— locate books through the library's online catalogue

— search a specialized database, *America: History and Life,* for scholarly articles

— locate 1864 newspaper articles by using a print index

— search the Web for historical primary sources that have been posted online

R1-c To locate articles, search a database or consult a print index.

Most libraries subscribe to electronic databases (sometimes called *periodical databases*), which provide access to quality sources that are often not available free on the Web.

What databases offer

Your library's databases will lead you to articles in newspapers, magazines, and scholarly or technical journals. Many of the databases also give you access to other sources, such as scholarly monographs, e-journals, and dissertations. Though each library is unique, here are some databases you might find available:

> *InfoTrac.* A collection of databases, some of which index periodical articles.

> *ProQuest.* A database of periodical articles.

EBSCOhost. A database of periodical articles.

FirstSearch. A vast collection of specialized databases, including *WorldCat,* a database of library collections, and *ArticleFirst,* a database of journal articles.

Lexis-Nexis Academic Universe. A set of databases that are particularly strong in coverage of news, business and legal matters, and congressional information.

ERIC. An education database.

MLA Bibliography. A database of literary criticism.

PsycInfo. A database of psychology research.

Many databases include the full text of at least some articles; others list only citations or citations with short summaries called *abstracts.* When full text is not available, the citation will give you enough information to track down an article.

Refining keyword searches in databases and search engines

Although command terms and characters vary among electronic databases and Web search engines, some of the most commonly used functions are listed here.

— Use quotation marks around words that are part of a phrase: "Broadway musicals".

— Use AND to connect words that must appear in a document: Ireland AND peace. Some search engines require a plus sign instead: Ireland +peace.

— Use NOT in front of words that must not appear in a document: Titanic NOT movie. Some search engines require a minus sign (hyphen) instead: Titanic -movie.

— Use OR if only one of the terms must appear in a document: "mountain lion" OR cougar.

— Use an asterisk as a substitute for letters that might vary: "marine biolog*" (to find *marine biology* or *marine biologist,* for example).

— Use parentheses to group a search expression and combine it with another: (cigarettes OR tobacco OR smok*) AND lawsuits.

How to search a database

To find articles on your topic in a database, you will most likely start with a keyword search. If the first keyword you try results in no matches, experiment with other terms. If you retrieve too many matches, narrow your search by using one of the strategies listed in the chart on page 301.

For her paper on the dangers of using a cell phone while driving, Angela Daly conducted a keyword search in a general periodical database. She typed in *"cell phones AND driving"*; her search brought up thirty-six possible articles, some of which looked promising (see the screen on this page).

When to use a print index

If you want to search for articles published before the 1980s, you may need to turn to a print index. For example, Ned Bishop consulted the *New York Times Index* to locate newspaper articles written in April 1864, just after the battle at Fort Pillow. To find older magazine articles, consult the *Readers' Guide to Periodical Literature* or *Poole's Index to Periodical Literature* or ask a librarian for help.

DATABASE SCREEN: RESULTS OF A KEYWORD SEARCH

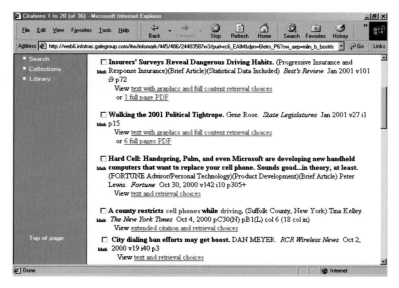

R1-d To locate books, consult the library's catalogue.

The books your library owns are listed in its computer catalogue, along with other resources such as videos. You can search the catalogue by author, title, or subject. Most of the time you will want to search by subject, using what is called a *keyword search*. A keyword search will not search the full text of books but only the title, subject headings, and sometimes tables of contents.

When a first search yields too few results, try searching by a broader topic. Then, once you find a book that looks on target, read the subject headings listed for it; they may be good search terms to try. When your search retrieves too many results, use the strategies for narrowing a search listed in the chart on page 301. Some catalogues also allow you to limit a search to books published after a certain date, a technique useful for excluding outdated books.

When Karen Shaw, whose topic was apes and language, entered the keyword search *apes and language* into the computer catalogue, she retrieved a list of twelve books. Below is the complete record for one of those books. She wrote down the call number—the book's address on the library shelves. As she worked, Shaw noticed that several books on her topic were shelved in the same area.

COMPUTER CATALOGUE SCREEN: COMPLETE RECORD FOR A BOOK

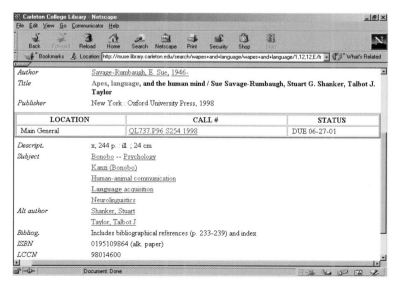

R1-e To locate a wide variety of sources, turn to the Web.

For some (but not all) topics, the Web is an excellent resource. For example, government agencies post information on the Web, and the sites of many organizations are filled with information about the issues they cover. Museums and libraries often post digital versions of primary sources, such as historical documents, on the Web. However, secondary sources, such as many scholarly articles and literary criticism, may not be available free on the Web; even online versions of many of these sources are accessible only to subscribers. (You may be able to access a library's subscription for free.)

Although the Web can be a rich source of information, some of which can't be found anywhere else, it lacks quality control. As you probably know, anyone can publish on the Web, so you'll need to evaluate online sources with special care (see R2-c).

This section describes the following Web resources: search engines, directories, archives, government and news sites, and online discussions.

ON THE WEB

For live links to the sources listed in this section, go to
www.dianahacker.com/writersref

and click on ▶ **Links Library**
▶ **Conducting Research**

Search engines

Search engines take your search terms and seek matches among millions of Web pages. Some search engines go into more depth than others, but none can search the entire Web. Often it is a good idea to try more than one search engine, since each locates sources in its own way.

For current information about search engines, visit *Search Engine Watch* at <http:/www.searchenginewatch.com>. This site classifies search engines, evaluates them, and provides updates on new search features. Following are some popular search engines:

AltaVista <http://www.altavista.com>

Google <http://www.google.com>

HotBot <http://www.hotbot.lycos.com>

All the Web <http://www.alltheweb.com>

In using a search engine, focus your search as narrowly as possible to prevent getting an impossible number of matches (or hits). You can sharpen your search by using many of the tips listed in the chart on page 301. For his paper on Nathan Bedford Forrest and the Fort Pillow massacre, Ned Bishop typed this into a search engine:

"Nathan Bedford Forrest" AND "Fort Pillow"

Of the resulting sixty-eight hits, several looked promising. In fact, the first source on the list, "Accounts of Fort Pillow," contained two useful primary sources: official reports of the incident by the Confederate and the Union commanders.

For her paper on using cell phones while driving, Angela Daly had difficulty restricting the number of hits. When she typed *cell phones* and *driving* into a search engine, she got over 40 000 matches. To narrow her search, Daly tried *cell phones while driving* and *accidents*. The result was 433 matches, still too many, so Daly clicked on Advanced Search. On the Advanced Search screen she restricted one of her next searches to government-sponsored sites

SEARCH ENGINE SCREEN: RESULTS OF AN ADVANCED SEARCH

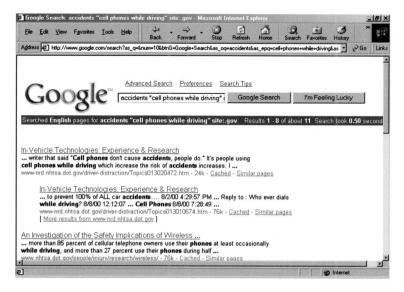

with URLs ending in *.gov.* The resulting list consisted of just 11 items, including promising sites sponsored by the National Highway Traffic Safety Administration (see the screen on p. 305).

Directories

Unlike search engines, which are powered by software known as *bots,* directories have a human touch. Directories are put together by information specialists who arrange sites by topic: education, health, public issues, and so on. Many search engines, such as *Google* and *Lycos,* offer a directory as an optional means of conducting a search.

Some directories are more selective and therefore more useful for scholarly research than the directories that typically accompany a search engine. For example, the directory for the *Scout Report Archives* was created with a research audience in mind; it includes annotations that are both descriptive and evaluative. The following list includes directories especially useful for scholarly research:

Infomine <http://infomine.ucr.edu>

Librarian's Index to the Internet <http://www.lii.org>

Scout Report Archives <http://scout.wisc.edu/archives/>

World Wide Web Virtual Library <http://www.vlib.org>

Archives

Archives contain the texts of poems, books, speeches, political cartoons, and historically significant documents such as the Canadian Constitution and the British North America Act. The materials in these sites are usually limited to older works because of copyright laws. The following online archives are impressive collections:

ArchiviaNet <http://www.archives.ca/02/0201_e.html>

Canadian Constitutional Documents <http://www.solon.org/Constitutions/Canada/English/index.html>

Electronic Text Center <http://etext.lib.virginia.edu>

Eurodocs <http://library.byu.edu/~rdh/eurodocs>

Internet History Sourcebooks <http://www.fordham.edu/halsall/>

National Archives of Canada <http://www.archives.ca/>

Government and news sites

For current topics, both government and news sites can prove useful. Many government agencies at every level provide online information. Government-maintained sites include resources such as legal texts, facts and statistics, government reports, and searchable reference databases. Here are just a few government sites (notice that the last one will lead you to others):

Statistics Canada <http://www.statcan.ca/start.html>

Strategis Canada <http://strategis.ic.gc.ca/>

Thomas Legislative Information <http://thomas.loc.gov>

2001 Census <http://www12.statcan.ca/english/census01>

United Nations <http://www.un.org>

Many news organizations offer up-to-date information on the Web. However, archived information may be available only for a fee; check with your library to see if it subscribes to a news archive that you can access at no charge. The following are some news sites on the Web:

Canoe <http://www.canoe.ca/>

CNN <http://www.cnn.com>

The Globe and Mail <http://www.theglobeandmail.com/>

National Post <http://www.canada.com/national/>

NewsLink <http://newslink.org>

Online discussions

The Web offers various ways of communicating with experts and others who share an interest in your topic. Some online discussions resemble voice mail: Messages are posted and retrieved at different times. Others are like talking on the phone: They take place in real time.

Discussions that do not take place in real time, known as *asynchronous communications,* include e-mail discussion lists (sometimes called LISTSERVs), Usenet newsgroups, Web forums (chat pages), and bulletin boards. To find publicly available lists, go to one of these Web sites:

CataList <http://www.lsoft.com/catalist.html>

Topica <http://www.liszt.com>

Tile.Net <http://tile.net/lists/>

Google Groups <http://groups.google.com/>

Real-time discussions, known as *synchronous communications,* include MUDs, MOOs, and chat rooms. Some are ongoing forums; others are set up to allow a group of people to communicate about a particular project or issue at a specific time.

NOTE: Be aware that many of the people you contact will not be experts on your topic. Although you are more likely to find serious and worthwhile commentary in moderated mailing lists and scholarly discussion forums than in more freewheeling newsgroups, it is difficult to guarantee the credibility of anyone you meet online.

R1-f Consider other search tools.

In addition to articles, books, and Web sources, you may want to consult reference works such as encyclopedias and almanacs. Bibliographies (lists of works written on a topic) and citations in scholarly works are other useful tools.

Reference works

The reference section of your library holds both general and specialized encyclopedias, handbooks, atlases, and biographical references. These sources are good places to find facts, statistics, and overviews of topics. Check with a reference librarian to see which works are most appropriate for your topic. A librarian will also be able to tell you which works are available in electronic format.

GENERAL REFERENCE WORKS   Here are a few frequently used general references that you might want to turn to:

The Canadian Encyclopedia

The Canadian Oxford Dictionary

Dictionary of Canadian Biography

National Atlas of Canada

The New Encyclopaedia Britannica

The Oxford English Dictionary

NOTE: Although general encyclopedias are often a good place to find background about your topic, you should rarely use them in your final paper. Most instructors expect you to rely on more specialized sources.

SPECIALIZED REFERENCE WORKS   Most specialized reference works contain material written by eminent scholars in the field. Works such as *The New Grove Dictionary of Music and Musicians,* the *McGraw-Hill Encyclopedia of Science and Technology,* and the *Encyclopedia of Bioethics* can provide solid overviews of topics within those subject areas.

ON THE WEB

For lists of specialized reference works, organized by academic discipline, go to **www.dianahacker.com/writersref**

and click on   ▶ **Research and Documentation Online**
                      ▶ **Finding Sources**

Bibliographies and scholarly citations

Bibliographies are lists of works written on a particular topic. They include enough information about each work (author's name, title, publication data) so that you can locate the book or article. In some cases bibliographies are annotated: They contain abstracts giving a brief overview of each work's contents.

In addition to stand-alone, book-length bibliographies, scholarly books and articles list the works the author has cited, usually at the end of an article or a book. These are useful shortcuts. For example, most of the scholarly articles Karen Shaw consulted contained citations to related research studies; through these citations, Shaw quickly located additional relevant sources on her topic, apes and language.

R1-g   Consider doing field research.

For a composition class, you might want to visit your local historical society to research a paper on some aspect of your town's early history, such as the role it played in the underground railroad. For a sociology class, you might decide to study campus trends in classroom participation: Which students are most, and least, involved in class discussions, and why? At work you might need to learn how food industry executives are responding to reports that their companies have cut portions of some food products while increasing prices. Projects like these may be enhanced by, and sometimes centred on, your own field research.

R2

Evaluating sources

With electronic search tools, you can often locate dozens or even hundreds of potential sources for your topic—far more than you will have time to read. Your challenge will be to home in on a reasonable number of quality sources, those truly worthy of your time and attention.

Later, once you have decided on some sources worth consulting, your challenge will be to read them with an open mind and a critical eye.

R2-a   Select sources worth your time and attention.

The chart on page 301 shows how to restrict the number of "hits" that come up in the library's book catalogue, in databases, and in search engines. This section shows how to scan through the lists of hits looking for those that seem most promising.

Scanning lists of hits in a book catalogue

The library's book catalogue will usually give you a fairly short list of hits. A book's title and date of publication will often be your first clues as to whether the book is worth consulting. If a title looks interesting, you can click on it for further information: the book's subject matter and its length, for example.

Scanning lists of hits in a database

Most databases, such as *ProQuest* and *Lexis-Nexis,* list at least the following information, which can help you decide if a source is relevant, current, scholarly enough, and neither too short nor too long for your purposes.

Title and brief description (How relevant?)

Date (How current?)

Name of periodical (How scholarly?)

Length (How extensive in coverage?)

For example, consider just a few of the hits Ned Bishop came up with when he consulted a general database in search of articles on the Fort Pillow massacre, using the search term *Fort Pillow.*

☐ **Black, blue and gray: the other Civil War; African-American soldiers, sailors and**
Mark **spies were the unsung heroes.** *Ebony* Feb 1991 v46 n4 p96(6)
　　View <u>text and retrieval choices</u>

☐ **The Civil War.** (movie reviews) Lewis Cole. *The Nation* Dec 3, 1990 v251 n19 p694(5)
Mark 　View <u>text and retrieval choices</u>

☐ **The hard fight was getting into the fight at all.** (black soldiers in the Civil War)
Mark Jack Fincher. *Smithsonian* Oct 1990 v21 n7 p46(13)
　　View <u>text and retrieval choices</u>

☑ **The Fort Pillow massacre: a statistical note.** John Cimprich, Robert C. Mainfort Jr..
Mark *Journal of American History* Dec 1989 v76 n3 p830(8)
　　View <u>extended citation and retrieval choices</u>

By scanning the titles, Bishop saw that only one contained the words *Fort Pillow.* This title and the name of the periodical—*Journal of American History*—suggested that the source was scholarly. The 1989 publication date was not a problem, since currency is not necessarily a key issue for historical topics. The article's length (eight pages) is given in parentheses at the end of the citation. While the article may seem short, the topic—a statistical note—is narrow enough to ensure adequate depth of coverage. Bishop decided the article was worth consulting.

Bishop chose not to consult the other sources. The first is a brief article in a popular magazine, the second is a movie review, and the third surveys a topic that is far too broad, "black soldiers in the Civil War."

Scanning lists of hits in a search engine

Anyone can publish on the Web, and unreliable sites often masquerade as legitimate sources of information. As you scan through a list of hits, look for the following clues about the probable relevance, currency, and reliability of a site—but be prepared to be disappointed, as the clues are by no means foolproof.

Title, keywords, and lead-in text (How relevant?)

A date (How current?)

An indication of the site's sponsor or purpose (How reliable?)

The URL, especially the domain name (How relevant? How reliable?)

The visual on this page shows a few of the hits that Karen Shaw retrieved after typing the keywords *apes* and *language* into a search engine; she limited her search to works with these words in the title.

Shaw rejected the first source because it was just a message in an online mailing list, and she skipped the third one because it sounded too promotional. The last source looked promising because of its university affiliation, though in fact it turned out to be a student paper.

Shaw was uncertain about the second hit, which was a commercial site, but she clicked on it. It was an impressive site, nicely designed, well written, and documented with footnotes and a bibliography; the only problem was that its author was nowhere to be found. Reluctantly, she decided not to use the information from the site in her paper.

LINGUIST List 7.144: Systemic-Functional WWW, **Apes** & **Language**
LINGUIST List 7.144. Tue Jan 30 1996. FYI: Systemic-Functional WWW,
Apes & **Language**. ... Message 2: **Apes** & **Language** syllabus. ...
www.linguistlist.org/issues/7/7-144.html - 11k - Cached - Similar pages

Can **Apes** Acquire **Language**?
Can **Apes** Acquire **Language**? Why have people embarked
on these Ape **language** studies? Some, it ...
www.fortunecity.com/greenfield/twyford/73/thoughts.html - 11k - Cached - Similar pages

YORK UNIVERSITY PROFESSOR'S BOOK PROVES **APES** CAPABLE OF ...
... to learn more about **language** in autistic and mentally handicapped children are
among those applauding the findings of **Apes**, **Language**, and the Human Mind. ...
www.yorku.ca/ycom/release/archive/080498.htm - 9k - Cached - Similar pages

Language in **Apes**
... Adams has some perceptive comments about "this business of trying to teach **apes language**"
(Adams & Carwardine 1993: 23). While sitting four feet away from a ...
Description: Introductory overview of ape **language** research, its history and its practice.
Category: Science > Social Sciences > Anthropology > Enculturated Apes
www.math.uwaterloo.ca/~dmswitze/apelang.html - 34k - Cached - Similar pages

---

R2-b Read with an open mind and a critical eye.

As you begin reading the sources you have chosen, keep an open mind. Do not let your personal beliefs prevent you from listening to new ideas and opposing viewpoints. Your research question—not a snap judgment about the question—should guide your reading.

When you read critically, you are not necessarily judging an author's work harshly; you are simply examining its assumptions, assessing its evidence, and weighing its conclusions.

Distinguishing between primary and secondary sources

As you begin assessing evidence in a text, consider whether you are reading a primary or a secondary source. Primary sources are original documents such as letters, diaries, legislative bills, laboratory studies, field research reports, and eyewitness accounts. Secondary sources are commentaries on primary sources. A primary source for Ned Bishop was Nathan Bedford Forrest's official report on the Battle of Fort Pillow. Bishop also consulted a number of secondary sources, some of which relied heavily on primary sources such as letters.

Although a primary source is not necessarily more reliable than a secondary source, it has the advantage of being a firsthand account. Naturally, you can better evaluate what a secondary source says if you have first read any primary sources it discusses.

Being alert for signs of bias

Both in print and online, some sources are more objective than others. If you were exploring the conspiracy theories surrounding John F. Kennedy's assassination, for example, you wouldn't look to a supermarket tabloid for answers. Even publications that are considered reputable can be editorially biased. For example, *Canoe,* the *National Post,* and *Maclean's* are all credible sources, but they are also likely to interpret events quite differently from one another. If you are uncertain about a periodical's special interests, check *Magazines for Libraries.* To check the reputation of a book, consult *Book Review Digest.* A reference librarian can help you locate these resources.

Like publishers, some authors are more objective than others. No authors are altogether objective, of course, since they are human beings with their own life experiences, values, and beliefs. But if you have reason to believe that an author is particularly biased, you will want to assess his or her arguments with special care. For a list of questions worth asking, see the chart on page 314.

Assessing the author's argument

In nearly all subjects worth writing about, there is some element of argument, so don't be surprised to encounter experts who disagree. When you find areas of disagreement, you will want to read your sources' arguments with special care, testing them with your own critical intelligence. Questions such as those in the chart on page 314 can help you weigh the strengths and weaknesses of each author's argument.

Evaluating all sources

CHECKING FOR SIGNS OF BIAS

— Does the author or publisher have political leanings or religious views that could affect objectivity?

— Is the author or publisher associated with a special-interest group, such as Greenpeace or the National Firearms Association, that might see only one side of an issue?

— How fairly does the author treat opposing views?

— Does the author's language show signs of bias?

ASSESSING AN ARGUMENT

— What is the author's central claim or thesis?

— How does the author support this claim — with relevant and sufficient evidence or with just a few anecdotes or emotional examples?

— Are statistics accurate? Have they been used fairly? (It is possible to "lie" with statistics by using them selectively or by omitting mathematical details.)

— Are any of the author's assumptions questionable?

— Does the author consider opposing arguments and refute them persuasively? (See C6-c.)

— Does the author fall prey to any logical fallacies? (See C6-a.)

R2-c Assess Web sources with special care.

As you have no doubt discovered, Web sources can be deceptive. Sophisticated-looking sites can be full of dubious information, and the identities of those who created a site are often hidden, along with their motives for having created it. Even hate sites may be cleverly disguised to look legitimate. In contrast, sites with reliable information can stand up to careful scrutiny. For a checklist on evaluating Web sources, see page 315.

In researching her topic on the dangers of using a cell phone while driving, Angela Daly encountered sites that raised her suspicions. In particular, some sites were sponsored by the wireless communications industry, which has an obvious interest in preventing laws restricting use of their products. Even a site sponsored by the Harvard Center for Risk Analysis seemed somewhat suspect, since the wireless industry funded the centre's study concluding that the risk of using a cell phone while driving is low compared with other risks.

Knowing that the creator of a site could be biased is not sufficient reason, however, to reject the site's information out of hand. For example, the Harvard Center for Risk Analysis offered evidence that was worth considering. Nevertheless, when you know something about the creator of a site and have a sense of a site's purpose, you will be in a good position to evaluate the likely worth of its information.

Evaluating Web sources

CAUTION: If the authorship and the sponorship of a site are both unclear, be extremely suspicious of the site.

AUTHORSHIP

— Is there an author? You may need to do some clicking and scrolling to find the author's name. Check the home page or an "about this site" link.

— Can you tell whether an author is knowledgeable and credible? Look for a home page, which may provide evidence of the author's expertise.

SPONSORSHIP

— Who, if anyone, sponsors the site? The sponsor of a site is often named and described on the home page.

— What does the domain name tell you? The domain name often specifies the type of group hosting the site: commercial (.com), educational (.edu), nonprofit (.org), Canadian government (.gc), Canadian (.ca), U.S. government (.gov), military (.mil), or network (.net).

PURPOSE AND AUDIENCE

— Why was the site created: To argue a position? To sell a product? To inform readers?

— Who is the site's intended audience?

CURRENCY

— How current is the site? Check for the date of publication or the latest update.

— How current are the site's links? If many of the links no longer work, the site may be too dated for your purposes.

┌───┐
ON THE WEB

For links to resources that will help you evaluate sources you find
on the Web, go to **www.dianahacker.com/writersref**

and click on ▶ **Links Library**
▶ **Conducting Research**
└───┘

R3

Managing information; avoiding plagiarism

An effective researcher is a good record keeper. Whether you decide
to keep records on paper or on your computer—or both—your
challenge as a researcher will be to find systematic ways of managing information. More specifically, you will need methods for maintaining a working bibliography (see R3-a), keeping track of source
materials (see R3-b), and taking notes without plagiarizing (steal-
ing from) your sources (see R3-c).

R3-a Maintain a working bibliography.

Keep a record of any sources you decide to consult. You will need
this record, called a *working bibliography,* when you compile the
list of works cited that will appear at the end of your paper. (The
format of this list depends on the documentation style you are
using. For MLA style, see MLA-4b; for APA style, see APA-4b; for
CMS style, see CMS-4c.) Your working bibliography will probably
contain more sources than you will actually use and put in your list
of works cited.

In the past, researchers recorded bibliographic information on
index note cards. Today, however, most researchers print out this
information from the library's computer catalogue, periodical databases, and the Web. The printouts usually contain all the information you need to create the list of works cited. That information is
given in the chart on the next page.

CAUTION: For Web sources, some bibliographic information may not
be available, but spend time looking for it before assuming that
it doesn't exist. Look especially for the author's name, the date of

Information for a working bibliography

For books

— All authors; any editors or translators
— Title and subtitle
— Edition (if not the first)
— Publication information: city, publisher, and date

For periodical articles

— All authors of the article
— Title and subtitle of the article
— Title of the magazine, journal, or newspaper
— Date and volume, issue, and page numbers, if relevant

For articles from electronic databases

— Publication information for the source
— Name of the database (and item number, if relevant)
— Name of the subscription service and its URL, if available
— Library where you retrieved the source
— Date you retrieved the source

For Web sources

— All authors, editors, or translators of the work
— Editor or compiler of the Web site, if relevant
— Title and subtitle of the source and title of the longer work (if applicable)
— Title of the site, if available
— Publication information for the source, if available
— Date of publication (or latest update), if available
— Any page or paragraph numbers
— Name of the site's sponsoring organization
— Date you visited the site and the site's URL

NOTE: For the exact bibliographic format to be used in the final paper, see MLA-4b, APA-4b, or CMS-4c.

publication (or latest update), and the name of any sponsoring organization. Such information should not be omitted unless it is genuinely unavailable.

R3-b   Keep track of source materials.

The best way to keep track of source materials is to photocopy them or print them out (except, of course, for books). Working with photocopies and printouts—as opposed to relying on memory or hastily written notes—has several benefits. It saves you time spent in the library. It allows you to highlight key passages, perhaps even colour-coding passages to reflect topics in your outline. And you can annotate the text in the margins and get a head start on the process of taking notes. Finally, working with hard copy reduces the chances of unintentional plagiarism, since you will be able to compare your use of a source in your paper with the actual source, not just with your notes (see R3-c).

NOTE: It's especially important to keep hard copies of Web sources, which may change or even become inaccessible. Make sure that your copy includes the site's URL and the date of access, information needed for your list of works cited.

When much of their material comes from the Web, some researchers prefer to organize their source material online—by downloading relevant material into files. This can be an efficient method of working, but it carries dangers. Although it is easy to patch information from downloaded files into your own paper, do so with caution. Some researchers have unwittingly plagiarized their sources because they lost track of which words came from sources and which were their own. To prevent unintentional plagiarism, put quotation marks around any text that you have patched into your own work. In addition, you might use a different colour for text from your source so it stands out unmistakably as someone else's (not your own) writing.

R3-c   As you take notes, avoid unintentional plagiarism.

You will discover that it is amazingly easy to borrow too much language from a source as you take notes. Do not allow this to happen. You are guilty of the academic offence known as *plagiarism* if you half-copy the author's sentences—either by mixing the author's phrases with your own without using quotation marks or by plugging your synonyms into the author's sentence structure. (For examples of this kind of plagiarism, see MLA-2, APA-2, and CMS-2.)

To prevent unintentional borrowing, resist the temptation to look at the source as you take notes—except when you are quoting. Keep the source close by so you can check for accuracy, but don't try to put ideas in your own words with the source's sentences in front of you.

There are three kinds of note taking: summarizing, paraphrasing, and quoting. As you take notes, be sure to include exact page references, since you will need the page numbers later if you use the information in your paper.

Summarizing without plagiarizing

A summary condenses information, perhaps reducing a chapter to a short paragraph or a paragraph to a single sentence. A summary should be written in your own words; if you use phrases from the source, put them in quotation marks.

Here is a passage from an original source read by John Garcia in researching a paper on mountain lions. Following the passage is Garcia's summary of the source.

ORIGINAL SOURCE

In some respects, the increasing frequency of mountain lion encounters in California has as much to do with a growing *human* population as it does with rising mountain lion numbers. The scenic solitude of the western ranges is prime cougar habitat, and it is falling swiftly to the developer's spade. Meanwhile, with their ideal habitat already at its carrying capacity, mountain lions are forcing younger cats into less suitable terrain, including residential areas. Add that cougars have generally grown bolder under a lengthy ban on their being hunted, and an unsettling scenario begins to emerge.

—Rychnovsky, "Clawing into Controversy," p. 40

SUMMARY

Source: Rychnovsky, "Clawing into Controversy"(40)

Encounters between mountain lions and humans are on the rise in California because increasing numbers of lions are competing for a shrinking habitat. As the lions' wild habitat shrinks, older lions force younger lions into residential areas. These lions have lost some of their fear of humans because of a ban on hunting.

Paraphrasing without plagiarizing

Like a summary, a paraphrase is written in your own words; but whereas a summary reports significant information in fewer words than the source, a paraphrase retells the information in roughly the same number of words. If you retain occasional choice phrases from the source, use quotation marks so you will know later which phrases are your own.

As you read the following paraphrase of the original source on page 319, notice that the language is significantly different from that in the original.

PARAPHRASE

Source: Rychnovsky, "Clawing into Controversy" (40)

Californians are encountering mountain lions more frequently because increasing numbers of humans and a rising population of lions are competing for the same territory. Humans have moved into mountainous regions once dominated by the lions, and the wild habitat that is left cannot sustain the current lion population. Therefore, the older lions are forcing younger lions out of the wilderness and into residential areas. And because of a ban on hunting, these younger lions have become bolder--less fearful of encounters with humans.

Using quotation marks to avoid plagiarizing

A quotation consists of the exact words from a source. In your notes, put all quoted material in quotation marks; do not trust yourself to remember later which words, phrases, and passages you have quoted and which are your own. When you quote, be sure to copy the words of your source exactly, including punctuation and capitalization. In the following example, John Garcia quotes from the original source on page 319.

QUOTATION

Source: Rychnovsky, "Clawing into Controversy" (40)

Rychnovsky explains that because the mountain lions' natural habitat can no longer sustain the population, older lions "are forcing younger cats into less suitable terrain, including residential areas."

R4

Choosing a documentation style

The various academic disciplines use their own editorial style for citing sources and for listing the works that are cited in a paper. *A Canadian Writer's Reference* describes three commonly used styles: MLA, APA, and CMS (see the appropriate tabbed sections). For a list of style manuals in a variety of disciplines, see R4-b.

R4-a Select a style appropriate for your discipline.

In researched writing, sources are cited for several reasons. First, it is important to acknowledge the contributions of others. If you fail to credit sources properly, you are guilty of plagiarism, a serious academic offence. Second, choosing good sources will add credibility to your work; in a sense, you are calling on authorities to serve as expert witnesses. The more care you have taken in choosing reliable sources, the stronger your case will be. Finally—and most importantly—you are helping to build knowledge by showing readers where they can pursue your topic in greater depth.

All of the academic disciplines cite sources for these same reasons. Why, then, do they use different styles for citing those sources? The answer lies in the intellectual goals, along with the values, of scholars in different disciplines.

MLA and APA in-text citations

The Modern Language Association (MLA) style and the American Psychological Association (APA) style both use citations in the text of a paper that refer to a list of works at the end of the paper. The systems work somewhat differently, however, because MLA style was created for scholars in English composition and literature, and APA style was created for researchers in the social sciences.

MLA IN-TEXT CITATION

Brandon Conran argues that the story is written from "a bifocal point of view" (111).

Leakey and Lewin (1992) argued that in ape brains "the cognitive foundations on which human language could be built are already present" (p. 244).

While MLA and APA styles work in a similar way, some basic disciplinary differences show up in these key elements:

—author's name

—date of publication

—page numbers

—verb tense in signal phrases

MLA style, which gives the author's full name on first mention, reflects the respect that English scholars have for authors of written words. APA style usually uses last names only, not out of disrespect but to lend an air of scientific objectivity. APA style, which gives a date after the author's name, reflects the social scientist's concern with the currency of experimental results. MLA style omits the date because English scholars are less concerned with currency; what someone had to say a century ago may be as significant as the latest contribution to the field.

Although both styles include page numbers for quotations, MLA style requires page numbers for summaries and paraphrases as well, whereas APA does not. English scholars place great value on written texts, and with a page number readers can easily find the exact passage that has been summarized or paraphrased. Social scientists are less concerned about page numbers because they value an article's ideas and research results more than its written text.

One final point about the differences between the two styles: MLA style uses the present tense (such as *argues*) to introduce cited material, whereas APA style uses the past or present perfect tense (such as *argued* or *have argued*). The present tense evokes the timelessness of a literary text; the past or present perfect tense emphasizes that an experiment was conducted in the past.

CMS footnotes or endnotes

Most historians and many scholars in the humanities use the style of footnotes or endnotes recommended by *The Chicago Manual of Style* (CMS). Historians base their work on a wide variety of primary and secondary sources, all of which must be cited. The CMS note system has the virtue of being relatively unobtrusive; even when a book or an article is thick with citations, readers will not be overwhelmed. In the text of the paper, only a raised number appears. Readers who are interested can consult the accompanying numbered note, which is given either at the foot of the page or on a separate page at the end of the paper.

TEXT

Historian Albert Castel quotes several eyewitnesses on both the Union and the Confederate sides as saying that Forrest ordered his men to stop firing.[7]

NOTE

7. Albert Castel, "The Fort Pillow Massacre: A Fresh Examination of the Evidence," *Civil War History* 4, no. 1 (1958): 44-45.

The CMS system gives as much information as the MLA or APA system, but less of that information is given in the text of the paper.

R4-b If necessary, consult a style manual.

Following is a list of style manuals used in a variety of disciplines.

BIOLOGY

Council of Biology Editors. *Scientific Style and Format: The CBE Manual for Authors, Editors, and Publishers.* 6th ed. New York: Cambridge UP, 1994.

BUSINESS

American Management Association. *The AMA Style Guide for Business Writing.* New York: AMACOM, 1996.

CHEMISTRY

Dodd, Janet S., ed. *The ACS Style Guide: A Manual for Authors and Editors.* 2nd ed. Washington: Amer. Chemical Soc., 1997.

ENGLISH AND THE HUMANITIES (SEE MLA-1 TO MLA-5.)

Gibaldi, Joseph. *MLA Handbook for Writers of Research Papers.* 6th ed. New York: MLA, 2003.

GEOLOGY

Bates, Robert L., Rex Buchanan, and Marla Adkins-Heljeson, eds. *Geowriting: A Guide to Writing, Editing, and Printing in Earth Science.* 5th ed. Alexandria: Amer. Geological Inst., 1995.

GOVERNMENT DOCUMENTS

Canada. Translation Bureau of Public Works and Government Services. *The Canadian Style: A Guide to Writing and Editing.* 2nd ed. Toronto: Dundurn, 1997.

HISTORY (SEE CMS-1 TO CMS-5.)

The Chicago Manual of Style. 15th ed. Chicago: U of Chicago P, 2003.

JOURNALISM

Buckley, Peter, ed. *CP Stylebook: A Guide for Writers and Editors.* 12th ed. Toronto: Canadian Press, 2002.

LAW

McGill Law Journal. *Canadian Guide to Uniform Legal Citation.* 5th ed. Toronto: Carswell, 2002.

LINGUISTICS

Linguistic Society of America. "LSA Style Sheet." Published annually in the December issue of the *LSA Bulletin.*

MATHEMATICS

American Mathematical Society. *The AMS Author Handbook: General Instructions for Preparing Manuscripts.* Rev. ed. Providence: AMS, 1996.

MEDICINE

International Committee of Medical Journal Editors. *Uniform Requirements for Manuscripts Submitted to Biomedical Journals.* Canadian Medical Association. 2003 <http://www.cma.ca/>.

MUSIC

Holoman, D. Kern, ed. *Writing about Music: A Style Sheet from the Editors of* 19th-Century Music. Berkeley: U of California P, 1988.

PHYSICS

American Institute of Physics. *Style Manual: Instructions to Authors and Volume Editors for the Preparation of AIP Book Manuscripts.* 5th ed. New York: AIP, 1995.

POLITICAL SCIENCE

American Political Science Association. *Style Manual for Political Science.* Rev. ed. Washington: APSA, 1993.

PSYCHOLOGY AND THE SOCIAL SCIENCES (SEE APA-1 TO APA-5.)

American Psychological Association. *Publication Manual of the American Psychological Association.* 5th ed. Washington: APA, 2001.

SCIENCE AND TECHNICAL WRITING

American National Standard for the Preparation of Scientific Papers for Written or Oral Presentation. New York: Amer. Natl. Standards Inst., 1979.

Microsoft Corporation. *Microsoft Manual of Style for Technical Publications.* 2nd ed. Redmond: Microsoft, 1998.

Rubens, Philip, ed. *Science and Technical Writing: A Manual of Style.* 2nd ed. New York: Routledge, 2001.

SOCIAL WORK

National Association of Social Workers. *Writing for the NASW Press: Information for Authors.* Rev. ed. Washington: Natl. Assn. of Social Workers Press, 1995.

MLA

MLA Papers

MLA Papers

Most English instructors and some humanities instructors will ask you to document sources with the Modern Language Association (MLA) system of citations described in section MLA-4. When writing an MLA paper that is based on sources, you face three main challenges in addition to documenting your sources: (1) supporting a thesis, (2) avoiding plagiarism, and (3) integrating quotations and other source material.

Examples in this tabbed section are drawn from research two students conducted on the use of cell phones while driving. Angela Daly's research paper on this topic appears on pages 371–77. Daly calls for legislation restricting use of cell phones while driving. Paul Levi's paper opposing such legislation appears on the companion Web site for *A Writer's Reference* (see p. 370 for the URL).

MLA-1

Supporting a thesis

Most research assignments ask you to form a thesis, or main idea, and to support that thesis with well-organized evidence.

MLA-1a Form a tentative thesis.

Once you have read a variety of sources and considered all sides of your issue, you are ready to form a tentative thesis: a one-sentence (or occasionally a two-sentence) statement of your central idea. In a research paper, your thesis will answer the central research question you posed earlier (see R1-a). Here, for example, is Angela Daly's research question and her tentative thesis statement.

DALY'S RESEARCH QUESTION

Should states regulate use of cell phones in moving vehicles?

DALY'S TENTATIVE THESIS

States should regulate use of cell phones on the road because many drivers are using the phones irresponsibly and causing accidents.

Once you have written a rough draft and perhaps done more reading, you may decide to revise your tentative thesis, as did Daly.

DALY'S REVISED THESIS

States must regulate use of cell phones on the road because drivers using phones are seriously impaired and because laws on negligent and reckless driving are not sufficient to punish offenders.

The thesis usually appears at the end of the introductory paragraph. To read Angela Daly's thesis in the context of her introduction, see page 371.

ON THE WEB

For an electronic exercise on thesis statements for a research paper, go to
www.dianahacker.com/writersref

and click on ▶ **Electronic Research Exercises**
▶ **E-ex MLA 1–1**

MLA-1b Organize your evidence.

The body of your paper will consist of evidence in support of your thesis. Instead of getting tangled up in a complex, formal outline, sketch an informal plan that organizes your evidence in bold strokes. Angela Daly, for example, used this simple plan to outline the structure of her argument:

— Drivers distracted by cellular phones are seriously impaired.

— Current laws on negligent and reckless driving are not adequate.

— In the United States, laws must be passed on the state level.

Once you have written a rough draft, a more formal outline can be a useful way to shape the complexities of your argument. See C1-d for an example.

MLA-2

Avoiding plagiarism

Your research paper is a collaboration between you and your sources. To be fair and ethical, you must acknowledge your debt to the writers of those sources. If you don't, you are guilty of plagiarism, a serious academic offence.

Three different acts are considered plagiarism: (1) failing to cite quotations and borrowed ideas, (2) failing to enclose borrowed language in quotation marks, and (3) failing to put summaries and paraphrases in your own words.

ON THE WEB

For electronic exercises on avoiding plagiarism, go to
www.dianahacker.com/writersref

and click on ▶ **Electronic Research Exercises**
▶ **E-ex MLA 2–1 and MLA 2–2**

MLA-2a Cite quotations and borrowed ideas.

You must of course cite all direct quotations. You must also cite any ideas borrowed from a source: summaries and paraphrases; statistics and other specific facts; and visuals such as cartoons, graphs, or diagrams.

The only exception is common knowledge — general information that your readers may know or could easily locate in any number of reference sources. For example, it is well known that Yann Martel won the Booker Prize in 2002 and that Emily Dickinson published only a handful of her many poems during her life. As a rule, when you have seen certain general information repeatedly in your reading, you don't need to cite it. However, when information has appeared in only a few sources, when it is highly specific (as with statistics), or when it is controversial, you should cite it.

The Modern Language Association recommends a system of in-text citations. Here, briefly, is how the MLA citation system usually works:

1. The source is introduced by a signal phrase that names its author.
2. The material being cited is followed by a page number in parentheses.
3. At the end of the paper, a list of works cited (arranged alphabetically according to authors' last names) gives complete publication information about the source.

IN-TEXT CITATION

According to Donald Redelmeier and Robert Tibshirani, "The use of cellular telephones in motor vehicles is associated with a quadrupling of the risk of a collision during the brief period of a call" (453).

ENTRY IN THE LIST OF WORKS CITED

Redelmeier, Donald A., and Robert J. Tibshirani. "Association between Cellular-Telephone Calls and Motor Vehicle Collisions." New England Journal of Medicine 336 (1997): 453-58.

Handling an MLA citation is not always this simple. For a detailed discussion of possible variations, see MLA-4.

MLA-2b Enclose borrowed language in quotation marks.

To show readers that you are using a source's exact phrases or sentences, you must enclose them in quotation marks unless they have been set off from the text by indenting (see p. 338). To omit the quotation marks is to claim—falsely—that the language is your own. Such an omission is plagiarism even if you have cited the source.

ORIGINAL SOURCE

Future cars will provide drivers with concierge services, web-based information, online e-mail capabilities, CD-ROM access, on-screen and audio navigation technology, and a variety of other information and entertainment services.

—Matt Sundeen, "Cell Phones and Highway Safety: 2000 State Legislative Update," p. 1

PLAGIARISM

Matt Sundeen points out that in cars of the future drivers will have concierge services, web-based information, online e-mail capabilities, CD-ROM access, on-screen and audio navigation technology, and a variety of other information and entertainment services (1).

BORROWED LANGUAGE IN QUOTATION MARKS

Matt Sundeen points out that in cars of the future drivers will have
"concierge services, web-based information, online e-mail capabilities,
CD-ROM access, on-screen and audio navigation technology, and a variety
of other information and entertainment services" (1).

MLA-2c Put summaries and paraphrases in your own words.

A summary condenses information from a source; a paraphrase repeats this information in about the same number of words. When you summarize or paraphrase, it is not enough to name the source; you must restate the source's meaning using your own language. (See also R3-c.) You are guilty of plagiarism if you half-copy the author's sentences—either by mixing the author's phrases with your own without using quotation marks or by plugging your synonyms into the author's sentence structure.

The first paraphrase of the following source is plagiarized—even though the source is cited—because too much of its language is borrowed from the original. The underlined strings of words have been copied word-for-word (without quotation marks). In addition, the writer has closely echoed the sentence structure of the source, merely plugging in some synonyms (*demonstrated* for *shown, devising* for *designing,* and *car* for *automotive*).

ORIGINAL SOURCE

The automotive industry has not shown good judgment in
designing automotive features that distract drivers. A classic
example is the use of a touch-sensitive screen to replace all
the controls for radios, tape/CD players, and heating/cooling.
Although an interesting technology, such devices require that
the driver take his eyes off the road.
                              —Tom Magliozzi and Ray Magliozzi,
                           Letter to a Massachusetts state senator, p. 3

PLAGIARISM: UNACCEPTABLE BORROWING

Radio show hosts Tom and Ray Magliozzi argue that <u>the automotive industry</u>
<u>has not</u> demonstrated <u>good judgment</u> in devising car <u>features that distract</u>
<u>drivers</u>. One feature is <u>a touch-sensitive screen</u> that replaces <u>controls for</u>
<u>radios, tape/CD players, and heating/cooling</u>. Although the technology is
interesting, <u>such devices require that</u> a driver look away from the road (3).

To avoid plagiarizing an author's language, resist the temptation to look at the source while you are summarizing or paraphrasing. Close the book, write from memory, and then open the book to check for accuracy. This technique prevents you from being captivated by the words on the page.

ACCEPTABLE PARAPHRASE

Radio show hosts Tom and Ray Magliozzi claim that motor vehicle manufacturers do not always design features with safety in mind. For example, when designers replaced radio, CD player, and temperature control knobs with touch-sensitive panels, they were forgetting one thing: To use the panels, drivers would need to take their eyes off the road (3).

MLA-3

Integrating sources

With practice, you will learn to integrate information from sources—quotations, summaries, paraphrases, and facts—smoothly into your own text.

ON THE WEB

For an electronic exercise on integrating quotations in MLA papers, go to **www.dianahacker.com/writersref**

and click on ▶ **Electronic Research Exercises**
▶ **E-ex MLA 3–1**

MLA-3a Use signal phrases to integrate quotations; limit your use of quotations.

Using signal phrases

Readers need to move from your own words to the words of a source without feeling a jolt. Avoid dropping quotations into the text without warning. Instead, provide clear signal phrases, usually including the author's name, to prepare readers for a quotation.

DROPPED QUOTATION

In 2000, the legislature of Suffolk County passed a law restricting drivers' use of handheld phones. "The bill prohibits the use of a cell phone while driving unless it is equipped with an earpiece or can act like a speakerphone, leaving the driver's hands free" (Kelley 1).

QUOTATION WITH SIGNAL PHRASE

In 2000, the legislature of Suffolk County passed a law restricting drivers' use of handheld phones. According to journalist Tina Kelley, "The bill prohibits the use of a cell phone while driving unless it is equipped with an earpiece or can act like a speakerphone, leaving the driver's hands free" (1).

To avoid monotony, vary both the language and the placement of your signal phrases. The models in the chart on page 336 suggest a range of possibilities.

When your signal phrase includes a verb, choose one that is appropriate in the context. Is your source arguing a point, making an observation, reporting a fact, drawing a conclusion, refuting an argument, or stating a belief? By choosing an appropriate verb, you can make your source's stance clear. See the chart for a list of verbs commonly used in signal phrases.

Limiting your use of quotations

Although it is tempting to insert many long quotations in your paper and to use your own words only for connecting passages, do not quote excessively. It is almost impossible to integrate numerous long quotations smoothly into your own text.

Except for certain legitimate uses of quotations, use your own words to summarize and paraphrase your sources and to explain your own ideas.

WHEN TO USE QUOTATIONS

—When language is especially vivid or expressive

—When exact wording is needed for technical accuracy

—When it is important to let the debaters of an issue explain their positions in their own words

—When the words of an important authority lend weight to an argument

—When language of a source is the topic of your discussion (as in an analysis or interpretation)

Varying signal phrases in MLA papers

MODEL SIGNAL PHRASES

In the words of researchers Redelmeier and Tibshirani, ". . ."

As Matt Sundeen has noted, ". . ."

Patti Pena, mother of a child killed by a driver distracted by a cell phone, points out that ". . ."

". . . ," writes Christine Haughney, ". . ."

". . . ," claims wireless spokesperson Annette Jacobs.

Radio hosts Tom and Ray Magliozzi offer a persuasive counterargument: ". . ."

VERBS IN SIGNAL PHRASES

acknowledges	comments	endorses	reasons
adds	compares	grants	refutes
admits	confirms	illustrates	rejects
agrees	contends	implies	reports
argues	declares	insists	responds
asserts	denies	notes	suggests
believes	disputes	observes	thinks
claims	emphasizes	points out	writes

It is not always necessary to quote full sentences from a source. To reduce your reliance on the words of others, you can often integrate a phrase from a source into your own sentence structure.

> Redelmeier and Tibshirani found that hands-free phones were not any safer in vehicles than other cell phones. They suggest that crashes involving cell phones may "result from a driver's limitations with regard to attention rather than dexterity" (456).

Using the ellipsis mark and brackets

Two useful marks of punctuation, the ellipsis mark and brackets, allow you to keep quoted material to a minimum and to integrate it smoothly into your text.

THE ELLIPSIS MARK   To condense a quoted passage, you can use the ellipsis mark (three spaced periods) to indicate that you have omitted words. What remains must be grammatically complete.

The University of North Carolina Highway Safety Research Center has begun a study assessing a variety of driver distractions. According to Allyson Vaughan, "The research . . . is intended to inject some empirical evidence into the debate over whether talking on wireless phones while driving leads to accidents" (1).

The writer has omitted the words *funded by the AAA Foundation for Traffic Safety,* which appeared in the source.

On the rare occasions when you want to omit one or more full sentences, use a period before the three ellipsis dots.

Redelmeier and Tibshirani acknowledge that their study "indicates an association but not necessarily a causal relation between the use of cellular telephones while driving and a subsequent motor vehicle collision. . . . In addition, our study did not include serious injuries . . ." (457).

Ordinarily, do not use an ellipsis mark at the beginning or at the end of a quotation. Your readers will understand that the quoted material is taken from a longer passage, so such marks are not necessary. The only exception occurs when words at the end of the final quoted sentence have been dropped. In such cases, put three ellipsis dots before the closing quotation mark and parenthetical reference, as in the previous example.

Obviously you should not use an ellipsis mark to distort the meaning of your source.

BRACKETS   Brackets allow you to insert your own words into quoted material. You can insert words in brackets to explain a confusing reference or to keep a sentence grammatical in your context.

According to economists Robert Hahn and Paul Tetlock, "Some studies say they [hands-free phones] would have no impact on accidents, while others suggest the reductions could be sizable" (2).

To indicate an error in a quotation, insert [sic] after the error.

Smith argues that "although the risk of driving while dialing has been exaggerated [sic], the dangers of driving while talking have not" (4).

Setting off long quotations

When you quote more than four typed lines of prose or more than three lines of poetry, set off the quotation by indenting it one inch (or ten spaces) from the left margin.

Long quotations should be introduced by an informative sentence, usually followed by a colon. Quotation marks are unnecessary because the indented format tells readers that the words are taken word-for-word from the source.

> Tom and Ray Magliozzi are not impressed by economists who conduct risk-benefit analyses of phone use by drivers:
>
>> Other critics [of regulation of cell phones]--some from prestigious "think tanks"--perform what appear to be erudite cost/benefit analyses. The problem here is that the benefits are always in units of convenience and productivity while the costs are in units of injuries and people's lives! (2)

Notice that at the end of an indented quotation the parenthetical citation goes outside the final mark of punctuation.

MLA-3b Use signal phrases to introduce most summaries and paraphrases.

Introduce most summaries and paraphrases with a signal phrase that names the author and places the material in context. Readers will then understand that everything between the signal phrase and the parenthetical citation summarizes or paraphrases the cited source.

Without the signal phrase (underlined) in the following example, readers might think that only the quotation at the end is being cited, when in fact the whole paragraph is based on the source.

> <u>Alasdair Cain and Mark Burris report that</u> research on traffic accidents and cell phone use has been inconclusive. Many factors play a role: for example, the type of phone (hands-free or not), the extent to which the conversation is distracting, and the demographic profile of the driver. Although research suggests that phoning in a moving vehicle affects driver performance, studies have failed to quantify the degree of driver impairment. Cain and Burris write that drivers using cell phones on the road "were anywhere from 34 percent to 300 percent more likely to have an accident" (1).

Reviewing an MLA paper: Use of sources

USE OF QUOTATIONS

— Is quoted material enclosed within quotation marks (unless it has been set off from the text)? (See MLA-2b.)

— Is quoted language word-for-word accurate? If not, do brackets or ellipsis marks indicate the changes or omissions? (See pp. 336–37.)

— Does a clear signal phrase (usually naming the author) prepare readers for each quotation? (See MLA-3a.)

— Does a parenthetical citation follow each quotation? (See MLA-4a.)

USE OF SUMMARIES AND PARAPHRASES

— Are summaries and paraphrases free of plagiarized wording—not copied or half-copied from the source? (See MLA-2c.)

— Are summaries and paraphrases documented with parenthetical citations? (See MLA-4a.)

— Do readers know where the material being cited begins? In other words, does a signal phrase mark the beginning of the cited material unless the context makes clear exactly what is being cited? (See MLA-3b.)

USE OF STATISTICS AND OTHER FACTS

— Are statistics and facts (other than common knowledge) documented with parenthetical citations? (See MLA-2a.)

— If there is no signal phrase, will readers understand exactly which facts are being cited? (See MLA-3c.)

There are times, however, when a signal phrase naming the author is not necessary. When the context makes clear where the cited material begins, you may omit the signal phrase and include the authors' last names in the parentheses: (Cain and Burris 1).

MLA-3c With statistics and other facts, a signal phrase may not be needed.

When you are citing a statistic or other specific fact, a signal phrase is often not necessary. In most cases, readers will understand that the citation refers to the statistic or fact (not the whole paragraph).

As of 2000, there were about ninety million cell phone users in the United States, with 85% of them using their phones while on the road (Sundeen 1).

There is nothing wrong, however, with using a signal phrase to introduce a statistic or other fact.

Matt Sundeen reports that as of 2000, there were about ninety million cell phone users in the United States, with 85% of them using their phones while on the road (1).

MLA-4

Documenting sources

In English and in some humanities classes, you will be asked to use the MLA (Modern Language Association) system for documenting sources, which is set forth in the *MLA Handbook for Writers of Research Papers,* 6th ed. (New York: MLA, 2003). MLA recommends in-text citations that refer readers to a list of works cited.

An in-text citation names the author of the source, often in a signal phrase, and gives the page number in parentheses. At the end of the paper, a list of works cited provides publication information about the source; the list is alphabetized by authors' last names (or by titles for works without authors). There is a direct connection between the in-text citation and the alphabetical listing. In the following example, that link is highlighted in red.

IN-TEXT CITATION

Matt Sundeen notes that drivers with cell phones place an estimated 98,000 emergency calls each day and that the phones "often reduce emergency response times and actually save lives" (1).

ENTRY IN THE LIST OF WORKS CITED

Sundeen, Matt. "Cell Phones and Highway Safety: 2000 State Legislative Update." National Conference of State Legislatures. Dec. 2000. 9 pp. 27 Feb. 2001 <http://ncsl.org/programs/esnr/cellphone.pdf>.

For a list of works cited that includes this entry, see page 377.

Directory to MLA in-text citation models

MLA-4a   MLA in-text citations

MLA in-text citations are made with a combination of signal phrases and parenthetical references. A signal phrase indicates that something taken from a source (a quotation, summary, paraphrase, or fact) is about to be used; usually the signal phrase includes the author's name. The parenthetical reference, which comes after the cited material, normally includes at least a page number.

IN-TEXT CITATION

One driver, Peter Cohen, says that after he was rear-ended, the guilty party emerged from his vehicle still talking on the phone (127).

Readers can look up the author's last name in the alphabetized list of works cited, where they will learn the work's title and other publication information. When readers decide to consult the source, the page number will take them straight to the passage that has been cited.

NOTE: If your cited material runs to more than one page, give the range of pages (such as 235–36 or 399–400).

Basic rules for print and electronic sources

The MLA system of in-text citations, which depends heavily on authors' names and page numbers, was created in the early 1980s with print sources in mind. Because some of today's electronic sources have unclear authorship and lack page numbers, they present a challenge. Nevertheless, the basic rules are the same for both print and electronic sources.

The models in this section (items 1–5) show how the MLA system usually works and explain what to do if your source has no author or page numbers.

■ **1. AUTHOR NAMED IN A SIGNAL PHRASE** Ordinarily, introduce the material being cited with a signal phrase that includes the author's name. In addition to preparing readers for the source, the signal phrase allows you to keep the parenthetical citation brief.

> Christine Haughney reports that shortly after Japan made it illegal to use a handheld phone while driving, "accidents caused by using the phones dropped by 75 percent" (A8).

The signal phrase—"Christine Haughney reports that"—names the author; the parenthetical citation gives the page number of the newspaper article in which the quoted words may be found.

Notice that the period follows the parenthetical citation. When a quotation ends with a question mark or an exclamation point, leave the end punctuation inside the quotation mark and add a period after the parentheses: ". . . ?" (8). (See also the note on p. 263.)

■ **2. AUTHOR NAMED IN PARENTHESES** If a signal phrase does not name the author, put the author's last name in parentheses along with the page number.

> Most states do not keep adequate records on the number of times cell phones are a factor in accidents; as of December 2000, only ten states were trying to keep such records (Sundeen 2).

Use no punctuation between the name and the page number.

■ **3. AUTHOR UNKNOWN** Either use the complete title in a signal phrase or use a short form of the title in parentheses. Titles of books are underlined; titles of articles and other short works are put in quotation marks.

> As of 2001, at least three hundred towns and municipalities had considered
> legislation regulating use of cell phones while driving ("Lawmakers" 2).

CAUTION: Before assuming that a Web source has no author, do some detective work. Often the author's name is available but is hard to find. For example, it may appear at the end of the source, in tiny print. Or it may appear on another page of the site, such as the home page.

NOTE: If a source has no author and is sponsored by a corporate entity, such as an organization or a government agency, name the corporate entity as the author (see item 9 on p. 345).

■ **4. PAGE NUMBER UNKNOWN** You may omit the page number if a work lacks page numbers, as is the case with many Web sources. Although printouts from Web sites usually show page numbers, printers don't always provide the same page breaks; for this reason, MLA recommends treating such sources as unpaginated.

> The California Highway Patrol opposes restrictions on the use of phones
> while driving, claiming that distracted drivers can already be prosecuted
> (Jacobs).

When the pages of a Web source are stable (as in pdf files), however, supply a page number in your in-text citation. (For example, the Web source by Sundeen cited on p. 340 has stable pages, so a page number is included in the citation.)

NOTE: If a Web source uses paragraph or section numbers, give the abbreviation "par." or "sec." in the parentheses: (Smith, par. 4).

■ **5. ONE-PAGE SOURCE** If the source is one page long, MLA allows (but does not require) you to omit the page number. Many instructors will want you to supply the page number because without it readers may not know where your citation ends or, worse yet, may not realize that you have provided a citation at all.

No page number given

> Milo Ippolito reports that the driver who struck and killed a two-year-old
> while using her cell phone got off with a light sentence even though she
> left the scene of the accident and failed to call 911 for help. In this and in
> similar cases, traffic offenders distracted by cell phones have not been
> sufficiently punished under current laws.

Page number given

Milo Ippolito reports that the driver who struck and killed a two-year-old while using her cell phone got off with a light sentence even though she left the scene of the accident and failed to call 911 for help (J1). In this and in similar cases, traffic offenders distracted by cell phones have not been sufficiently punished under current laws.

Variations on the basic rules

This section describes the MLA guidelines for handling a variety of situations not covered by the basic rules just given. Again, these rules on in-text citations are the same for both traditional print sources and electronic sources.

■ **6. TWO OR MORE TITLES BY THE SAME AUTHOR** If your list of works cited includes two or more titles by the same author, mention the title of the work in the signal phrase or include a short version of the title in the parentheses.

On December 6, 2000, reporter Jamie Stockwell wrote that distracted driver Jason Jones had been charged with "two counts of vehicular manslaughter ... in the deaths of John and Carole Hall" ("Phone" B1). The next day Stockwell reported the judge's ruling: Jones "was convicted of negligent driving and fined $500, the maximum penalty allowed" ("Man" B4).

Titles of articles and other short works are placed in quotation marks, as in the example just given. Titles of books are underlined.

In the rare case when both the author's name and a short title must be given in parentheses, separate them with a comma.

According to police reports, there were no skid marks indicating that the distracted driver who killed John and Carole Hall had even tried to stop (Stockwell, "Man" B4).

■ **7. TWO OR THREE AUTHORS** Name the authors in the signal phrase, as in the following example, or include their last names in the parenthetical reference: (Redelmeier and Tibshirani 453).

Redelmeier and Tibshirani found that "the risk of a collision when using a cellular telephone was four times higher than the risk when a cellular telephone was not being used" (453).

When three authors are named in the parentheses, separate the names with commas: (Alton, Davies, and Rice 56).

■ **8. FOUR OR MORE AUTHORS** Name all of the authors or include only the first author's name followed by "et al." (Latin for "and others"). Make sure that your citation matches the entry in the list of works cited (see also item 2 on p. 350).

> The study was extended for two years, and only after results were reviewed by an independent panel did the researchers publish their findings (Blaine et al. 35).

■ **9. CORPORATE AUTHOR** When the author is a corporation or an organization, name the corporate author either in the signal phrase or in the parentheses.

> Researchers at the Harvard Center for Risk Analysis found that the risks of driving while phoning were small compared with other driving risks (3-4).

In the list of works cited, the Harvard Center for Risk Analysis is treated as the author and alphabetized under *H*.

■ **10. AUTHORS WITH THE SAME LAST NAME** If your list of works cited includes works by authors with the same last name, include the author's first name in a signal phrase or first initial in the parentheses.

> Estimates of the number of accidents caused by distracted drivers vary because little evidence is being collected (D. Smith 7).

■ **11. INDIRECT SOURCE (SOURCE QUOTED IN ANOTHER SOURCE)** When a writer's or a speaker's quoted words appear in a source written by someone else, begin the citation with the abbreviation "qtd. in."

> According to Richard Retting, "As the comforts of home and the efficiency of the office creep into the automobile, it is becoming increasingly attractive as a work space" (qtd. in Kilgannon A23).

■ **12. ENCYCLOPEDIA OR DICTIONARY** Unless an encyclopedia or a dictionary has an author, it will be alphabetized in the list of works cited under the word or entry that you consulted—not under the title of the reference work itself (see item 13 on p. 353). Either in your text or in your parenthetical reference, mention the word or the entry. No page number is required, since readers can easily look up the word or entry.

The word crocodile has a surprisingly complex etymology ("Crocodile").

■ **13. MULTIVOLUME WORK** If your paper cites more than one volume of a multivolume work, indicate which volume you are referring to, followed by a colon and the page number in the parentheses.

Terman's studies of gifted children reveal a pattern of accelerated language acquisition (2: 279).

If your paper cites only one volume of a multivolume work, you will include the volume number in the list of works cited and will not need to include it in the parentheses.

■ **14. TWO OR MORE WORKS** To cite more than one source, separate the citations with a semicolon.

The dangers of mountain lions to humans have been well documented (Rychnovsky 40; Seidensticker 114; Williams 30).

■ **15. AN ENTIRE WORK** To cite an entire work, use the author's name in a signal phrase or a parenthetical reference. There is of course no need to use a page number.

Robinson succinctly describes the status of the mountain lion controversy in California.

■ **16. WORK IN AN ANTHOLOGY** Put the name of the author of the work (not the editor of the anthology) in the signal phrase or the parentheses.

In Susan Glaspell's "A Jury of Her Peers," Mrs. Hale describes both a style of quilting and a murder weapon when she utters the last words of the story: "We call it--knot it, Mr. Henderson" (302).

In the list of works cited, the work is alphabetized under Glaspell, not under the name of the editor of the anthology.

Literary works and sacred texts

Literary works and sacred texts are usually available in a variety of editions. Your list of works cited will specify which edition you are using, and your in-text citation will usually consist of a page number from the edition you consulted (see item 17).

However, MLA suggests that when possible you should give enough information — such as book parts, play divisions, or line numbers — so that readers can locate the cited passage in any edition of the work (see items 18–20).

■ **17. LITERARY WORKS WITHOUT PARTS OR LINE NUMBERS** Many literary works, such as most short stories and many novels and plays, do not have parts or line numbers that you can refer to. In such cases, simply cite the page number.

> At the end of Kate Chopin's "The Story of an Hour," Mrs. Mallard drops dead upon learning that her husband is alive. In the final irony of the story, doctors report that she has died of a "joy that kills" (25).

■ **18. VERSE PLAYS AND POEMS** For verse plays, MLA recommends omitting page numbers in the parenthetical citation. Instead, include act, scene, and line numbers that can be located in any edition of the work. Use arabic numerals, and separate the numbers with periods.

> In his famous advice to players, Shakespeare's Hamlet defines the purpose of theatre, "whose end, both at the first and now, was and is, to hold, as 'twere, the mirror up to nature" (3.2.21-23).

For a poem, cite the part (if there are a number of parts) and the line numbers, separated by a period.

> When Homer's Odysseus comes to the hall of Circe, he finds his men "mild / in her soft spell, fed on her drug of evil" (10.209-11).

For poems that are not divided into parts, use line numbers. For a first reference, use the word "lines": (lines 5-8). Thereafter use just the numbers: (12-13).

■ **19. NOVELS WITH NUMBERED DIVISIONS** When a novel has numbered divisions, put the page number first, followed by a semicolon, and then indicate the book, part, or chapter in which the passage may be found. Use abbreviations such as "bk." and "ch."

> One of Kingsolver's narrators, teenager Rachel, pushes her vocabulary
> beyond its limits. For example, Rachel complains that being forced to
> live in the Congo with her missionary family is "a sheer tapestry of
> justice" because her chances of finding a boyfriend are "dull and void"
> (117; bk. 2, ch. 10).

■ **20. SACRED TEXTS**   When citing a sacred text such as the Bible or the Koran, name the edition you are using in your works cited entry (see p. 354). In your parenthetical citation, give the book, chapter, and verse (or their equivalent), separated by periods. Common abbreviations for books of the Bible are acceptable.

> Consider the words of Solomon: "If your enemies are hungry, give them
> food to eat. If they are thirsty, give them water to drink" (<u>Holy Bible</u>,
> Prov. 25.21).

ON THE WEB

For electronic exercises on using MLA documentation style, go to
www.dianahacker.com/writersref

and click on ▶ **Electronic Research Exercises**
  ▶ **E-ex MLA 4–1 and MLA 4–2**

MLA-4b   MLA list of works cited

An alphabetized list of works cited, which appears at the end of your research paper, gives publication information for each of the sources you have cited in the paper. (For information about preparing this list, see pp. 369–70; for a sample list of works cited, see p. 377.)

NOTE: Unless your instructor asks for them, omit sources not actually cited in the paper, even if you read them.

Directory to MLA works cited models

General guidelines for listing authors

Alphabetize entries in the list of works cited by authors' last names (if a work has no author, alphabetize it by its title). The author's name is important because citations in the text of the paper refer to it and readers will be looking for it at the beginning of an entry in the alphabetized list.

NAME CITED IN TEXT

According to Matt Sundeen, . . .

BEGINNING OF WORKS CITED ENTRY

Sundeen, Matt.

The following examples show how to begin an entry for a work with a single author, multiple authors, a corporate author, an unknown author, and multiple works by the same author. (See items 1–5.) What comes after this first element of your citation will depend on the kind of source you are citing. (See items 6–56.)

NOTE: For a book, an entry in the works cited list will sometimes begin with an editor (see item 9 on page 352).

■ **1. SINGLE AUTHOR** For a work with one author, begin the entry with the author's last name, followed by a comma; then give the author's first name, followed by a period.

Tannen, Deborah.

■ **2. MULTIPLE AUTHORS** For works with two or three authors, name the authors in the order in which they are listed in the source. Reverse the name of only the first author.

Walker, Janice R., and Todd Taylor.

Wilmut, Ian, Keith Campbell, and Colin Tudge.

For a work with four or more authors, either name all of the authors or name the first author, followed by "et al." (Latin for "and others").

Sloan, Frank A., Emily M. Stout, Kathryn Whetten-Goldstein, and Lan Liang.

Sloan, Frank A., et al.

■ **3. CORPORATE AUTHOR** When the author of a print document or Web site is a corporation, a government agency, or some other organization, begin your entry with the name of the group.

Novartis.

Canada. Statistics Canada.

Canadian Automobile Association.

NOTE: Make sure that your in-text citation also treats the organization as the author (see item 9 on p. 345).

■ **4. UNKNOWN AUTHOR** When the author of a work is unknown, begin with the work's title. Titles of articles and other short works are put in quotation marks. Titles of books and Web sites are underlined. (For titles of works within Web sites, see item 28.)

Article
"Media Giants."

Book
Atlas of the World.

Web site
Caracol: The Official Website of the Caracol Archaeological Project.

Before concluding that the author of a Web source is unknown, check carefully (see the caution on p. 343). Also remember that an organization may be the author (see item 3 at the top of this page).

■ **5. TWO OR MORE WORKS BY THE SAME AUTHOR** If your list of works cited includes two or more works by the same author, use the author's name only for the first entry. For other entries use three hyphens followed by a period. The three hyphens must stand for exactly the same name or names as in the first entry. List the titles in alphabetical order.

Callwood, June, The Man Who Lost Himself. Toronto: McClellan, 2000.
---. The Sleepwalker. Toronto: Lester, 1990.

Books

Items 6–19 apply to print books. For online books, see page 359.

■ **6. BASIC FORMAT FOR A BOOK** For most books, arrange the information into three units, each followed by a period and one space: (1) the author's name; (2) the title and subtitle, underlined; and (3) the place of publication, the publisher, and the date.

```
  ┌─1─┐ ┌──────── 2 ────────┐ ┌──────── 3 ────────┐
Tan, Amy. The Bonesetter's Daughter. New York: Putnam, 2001.
```

Take the information about the book from its title page and copyright page. Use a short form of the publisher's name; omit terms such as *Press, Inc.,* and *Co.* except when naming university presses (McGill-Queen's UP, for example). If the copyright page lists more than one date, use the most recent one.

■ **7. AUTHOR WITH AN EDITOR** Begin with the author and title, followed by the name of the editor. The abbreviation "Ed." means "Edited by," so it is the same for one or multiple editors.

Kerouac, Jack. Atop an Underwood. Ed. Paul Marion. New York: Penguin, 2000.

■ **8. AUTHOR WITH A TRANSLATOR** Begin with the name of the author. After the title, write "Trans." (for "Translated by") and the name of the translator.

Allende, Isabel. Daughter of Fortune. Trans. Margaret Sayers Peden. New York:
    Harper, 2000.

■ **9. EDITOR** An entry for a work with an editor is similar to that for a work with an author except that the name is followed by a comma and the abbreviation "ed." for "editor" (or "eds." for "editors").

Craig, Patricia, ed. The Oxford Book of Travel Stories. Oxford: Oxford UP, 1996.

■ **10. WORK IN AN ANTHOLOGY** Begin with (1) the name of the author of the selection, not with the name of the editor of the anthology. Then give (2) the title of the selection; (3) the title of the anthology; (4) the name of the editor (preceded by "Ed." for "Edited by"); (5) publication information; and (6) the pages on which the selection appears.

```
  ┌─── 1 ───┐ ┌──── 2 ────┐ ┌──────── 3 ────────┐ ┌── 4 ──
Desai, Anita. "Scholar and Gypsy." The Oxford Book of Travel Stories. Ed. Patricia
    ──┐ ┌──────── 5 ────────┐ ┌─ 6 ─┐
    Craig. Oxford: Oxford UP, 1996. 251-73.
```

If you wish, you may cross-reference two or more works from the same anthology. Provide an entry for the anthology (see item 9 on p. 352). Then in separate entries list the author and title of each selection, followed by the last name of the editor of the anthology and the page numbers on which the selection appears.

Desai, Anita. "Scholar and Gypsy." Craig 251-73.

Malouf, David. "The Kyogle Line." Craig 390-96.

Alphabetize the entry for the anthology under the name of its editor (Craig); alphabetize the entries for the selections under the names of the authors (Desai, Malouf).

■ **11. EDITION OTHER THAN THE FIRST** If you are citing an edition other than the first, include the number of the edition after the title (or after the names of any translators or editors that appear after the title): 2nd ed., 3rd ed., and so on.

Auletta, Ken. The Underclass. 2nd ed. Woodstock, NY: Overlook, 2000.

■ **12. MULTIVOLUME WORK** Include the total number of volumes before the city and publisher, using the abbreviation "vols."

Conway, Jill Ker, ed. Written by Herself. 2 vols. New York: Random, 1996.

If your paper cites only one of the volumes, give the volume number before the city and publisher and give the total number of volumes after the date.

Conway, Jill Ker, ed. Written by Herself. Vol. 2. New York: Random, 1996.
    2 vols.

■ **13. ENCYCLOPEDIA OR DICTIONARY ENTRY** When an encyclopedia or a dictionary is well known, simply list the author of the entry (if there is one), the title of the entry, the title of the reference work, the edition number (if any), and the date of the edition.

Posner, Rebecca. "Romance Languages." The New Encyclopaedia Britannica:
    Macropaedia. 15th ed. 1987.

"Sonata." The American Heritage Dictionary of the English Language. 4th ed.
    2000.

Volume and page numbers are not necessary because the entries in the source are arranged alphabetically and therefore are easy to locate.

If a reference work is not well known, provide full publication information as well.

■ **14. SACRED TEXT** Give the title of the edition of the sacred text (taken from the title page), underlined; the editor's name (if any); and publication information.

Holy Bible: New Living Translation. Wheaton: Tyndale, 1996.

■ **15. FOREWORD, INTRODUCTION, PREFACE, OR AFTERWORD** Begin with the author of the foreword or other book part, followed by the name of that part. Then give the title of the book; the author of the book, preceded by the word "By"; and the editor of the book (if any). After the publication information, give the page numbers for the part of the book being cited.

Morris, Jan. Introduction. Letters from the Field, 1925-1975. By Margaret Mead.
    New York: Perennial-Harper, 2001. xix-xxiii.

If the book part being cited has a title, include it immediately after the author's name.

Ozick, Cynthia. "Portrait of the Essay as a Warm Body." Introduction. The Best
    American Essays 1998. Ed. Ozick. Boston: Houghton, 1998. xv-xxi.

■ **16. BOOK WITH A TITLE IN ITS TITLE** If the book contains a title normally underlined, neither underline the internal title nor place it in quotation marks.

Vanderham, Paul. James Joyce and Censorship: The Trials of Ulysses. New York:
    New York UP, 1997.

If the title within the title is normally put in quotation marks, retain the quotation marks and underline the entire title.

Faulkner, Dewey R., ed. Twentieth Century Interpretations of "The Pardoner's
    Tale." Englewood Cliffs: Prentice, 1973.

■ **17. BOOK IN A SERIES** Before the publication information, cite the series name as it appears on the title page, followed by the series number, if any.

Malena, Anne. The Dynamics of Identity in Francophone Caribbean Narrative.
　　Francophone Cultures and Lits. Ser. 24. New York: Lang, 1998.

■　**18. REPUBLISHED BOOK**　After the title of the book, cite the
original publication date, followed by the current publication information. If the republished book contains new material, such as an
introduction or afterword, include information about the new material after the original date.

Hughes, Langston. Black Misery. 1969. Afterword Robert O'Meally. New York:
　　Oxford UP, 2000.

■　**19. PUBLISHER'S IMPRINT**　If a book was published by an imprint (a division) of a publishing company, link the name of the
imprint and the name of the publisher with a hyphen, putting the
imprint first.

Truan, Barry. Acoustic Communication. Westport: Ablex-Greenwood, 2000.

Articles in periodicals

This section shows how to prepare works cited entries for articles
in magazines, scholarly journals, and newspapers. In addition to
consulting the models in this section, you will at times need to turn
to other models as well:

　—More than one author: see item 2 (p. 350)

　—Corporate author: see item 3 (p. 351)

　—Unknown author: see item 4 (p. 351)

　—Online article: see item 32 (p. 360)

　—Article from a subscription service: see item 31 (p. 360)

NOTE: For articles appearing on consecutive pages, provide the
range of pages, such as 121–29 or 298–310. When an article does
not appear on consecutive pages, give the number of the first page
followed by a plus sign: 32+.

■　**20. ARTICLE IN A MAGAZINE**　List, in order, separated by periods,
(1) the author's name; (2) the title of the article, in quotation
marks; and (3) the title of the magazine, underlined. Then give
(4) the date and the page numbers, separated by a colon. Abbreviate the names of the months except May, June, and July. If the
magazine is issued monthly, give just the month and year.

┌──── 1 ────┐ ┌──────── 2 ────────┐ ┌──── 3 ────┐ ┌──── 4 ────┐
Kaplan, Robert D. "History Moving North." Atlantic Monthly Feb. 1997: 21+.

If the magazine is issued weekly, give the exact date.

Lord, Lewis. "There's Something about Mary Todd." U.S. News and World Report
    19 Feb. 2001: 53.

■ **21. ARTICLE IN A JOURNAL PAGINATED BY VOLUME** Many scholarly journals continue page numbers throughout the year instead of beginning each issue with page 1; at the end of the year, the issues are collected in a volume. To find an article, readers need only the volume number, the year, and the page numbers.

Ryan, Katy. "Revolutionary Suicide in Toni Morrison's Fiction." African American
    Review 34 (2000): 389-412.

■ **22. ARTICLE IN A JOURNAL PAGINATED BY ISSUE** If each issue of the journal begins with page 1, you need to indicate the number of the issue. After the volume number, put a period and the issue number.

Wood, Michael. "Broken Dates: Fiction and the Century." Kenyon Review 22.3
    (2000): 50-64.

■ **23. ARTICLE IN A DAILY NEWSPAPER** Begin with the name of the author, if there is one, followed by the title of the article. Next give the name of the newspaper, the date, and the page number (including the section letter). Use a plus sign (+) after the page number if the article does not appear on consecutive pages.

Murphy, Sean P. "Decisions on Status of Tribes Draw Fire." Boston Globe 27 Mar.
    2001: A2.

If the section is marked with a number rather than a letter, handle the entry as follows:

Wilford, John Noble. "In a Golden Age of Discovery, Faraway Worlds Beckon." New
    York Times 9 Feb. 1997, late ed., sec. 1: 1+.

When an edition of the newspaper is specified on the masthead, name the edition after the date and before the page reference (eastern ed., late ed., natl. ed., and so on), as in the example just given.

■ **24. EDITORIAL IN A NEWSPAPER** Cite an editorial as you would an unsigned article, adding the word "Editorial" after the title.

"All Wet." Editorial. <u>Boston Globe</u> 12 Feb. 2001: A14.

■ **25. LETTER TO THE EDITOR** Name the writer, followed by the word "Letter" and the publication information for the periodical in which the letter appears.

Shrewsbury, Toni. Letter. <u>Atlanta Journal-Constitution</u> 17 Feb. 2001: A13.

■ **26. BOOK OR FILM REVIEW** Name the reviewer and the title of the review, if any, followed by the words "Rev. of" and the title and author or director of the work reviewed. Add the publication information for the publication in which the review appears.

Gleick, Elizabeth. "The Burdens of Genius." Rev. of <u>The Last Samurai</u>, by Helen
    DeWitt. <u>Time</u> 4 Dec. 2000: 171.

Denby, David. "On the Battlefield." Rev. of <u>The Hurricane</u>, dir. Norman Jewison.
    <u>New Yorker</u> 10 Jan. 2000: 90-92.

Electronic sources

MLA's guidelines for documenting electronic sources can be found in the *MLA Handbook for Writers of Research Papers* (6th ed., 2003). For more help with citing electronic sources in MLA style, see the list of frequently asked questions in the section "MLA Style" on MLA's Web site, <http://www.mla.org>.

> **ON THE WEB**
>
> For future updates to MLA style, go to MLA's Web site or go to
> **www.dianahacker.com/writersref**
>
> and click on ▶ **Research and Documentation Online**
> ▶ **Documenting Sources (MLA)**

NOTE: When a Web address in a works cited entry must be divided at the end of a line, MLA recommends that you break it after a slash. Do not insert a hyphen.

■ **27. AN ENTIRE WEB SITE** Begin with (1) the name of the author or corporate author (if known) and (2) the title of the site, underlined. Then give (3) the names of any editors, (4) the date of publication or last update, (5) the name of any sponsoring organization, (6) the date of access, and (7) the URL in angle brackets. Provide as much of this information as is available. In the following example, items 3 and 5 were not available.

With author

```
┌──── 1 ────┐ ┌──── 2 ────┐ ┌4┐ ┌── 6 ──┐
Peterson, Susan Lynn. The Life of Martin Luther. 1999. 9 Mar. 2001
         ┌──────────── 7 ────────────┐
         <http://pweb.netcom.com/~supeters/luther.htm>.
```

With corporate (group) author

United States. Environmental Protection Agency. Values and Functions of
    Wetlands. 25 May 1999. 24 Mar. 2001 <http://www.epa.gov-owow/
    wetlands/facts/fact2.html>.

Author unknown

Margaret Sanger Papers Project. 18 Oct. 2000. History Dept., New York U. 3 Apr.
    2001 <http://www.nyu.edu/projects/sanger/>.

With editor

Exploring Ancient World Cultures. Ed. Anthony F. Beavers. 1997. U of Evansville.
    12 Mar. 2001 <http://eawc.evansville.edu/index.htm>.

NOTE: If the site has no title, substitute a description, such as "Home page," for the title.

Block, Marylaine. Home page. 5 Mar. 2001. 12 Apr. 2001
    <http://www.marylaine.com>.

■ **28. SHORT WORK FROM A WEB SITE** Short works appear in quotation marks in MLA style: articles, poems, and other documents that are not book length. For a short work from a Web site, include as many of the following elements as apply and as are available: (1) author's name; (2) title of the work, in quotation marks; (3) title of the site, underlined; (4) date of publication or last update; (5) sponsor of the site (if not named as the author or given as the title of the site); (6) date you accessed the source; and (7) the URL in angle brackets.

Usually at least some of these elements will not apply or will be unavailable. In the following example, no sponsor or date of publication was available. (The date given is the date on which the researcher accessed the source.)

With author

```
 ┌── 1 ──┐ ┌──────── 2 ────────┐┌─ 3 ─┐ ┌── 6 ──┐
Shiva, Vandana. "Bioethics: A Third World Issue." NativeWeb. 15 Sept. 2001
      ┌──────────────── 7 ────────────────┐
      <http://www.nativeweb.org/pages/legal/shiva.html>.
```

Author unknown

"Media Giants." The Merchants of Cool. 2001. PBS Online. 7 Mar. 2001
    <http://www.pbs.org/wgbh/pages/frontline/shows/cool/giants>.

NOTE: When the URL for a short work from a Web site is very long, you may give the URL for the home page and indicate the path by which readers can access the source.

"Obesity Trends among U.S. Adults between 1985 and 2001." Centers for Disease
    Control and Prevention. 3 Jan. 2003. 17 Feb. 2003 <www.cdc.gov>. Path:
    Health Topics A-Z; Obesity Trends; U.S. Obesity Trends 1985 to 2001.

■ **29. ONLINE BOOK** When a book or a book-length work such as a play or a long poem is posted on the Web as its own site, give as much publication information as is available, your date of access, and the URL. (See also the models for print books on pp. 352–55.)

Rawlins, Gregory J. E. Moths to the Flame. Cambridge: MIT P, 1996. 3 Apr. 2001
    <http://mitpress.mit.edu/e-books/Moths/contents.html>.

■ **30. PART OF AN ONLINE BOOK** Place the part title before the book's title. If the part is a short work such as a poem or an essay, put its title in quotation marks. If the part is an introduction or other division of the book, do not use quotation marks.

Adams, Henry. "Diplomacy." The Education of Henry Adams. Boston: Houghton,
    1918. Bartleby.com: Great Books Online. 1999. 17 Feb. 2003
    <http://bartleby.com/159/8.html>.

Bryan, William S., and Robert Rose. Preface. A History of the Pioneer Families of
    Missouri. St. Louis: Bryan, 1876. University of Missouri Digital Library.
    2002. 20 Feb. 2003 <http://digital.library.umsystem.edu/cgi-bin/Ebind2h3/
    umkc3>.

Nineteenth-Century America. Ed. Ji-Hae Yoon and Natalia Smith. 1998. Academic

    Affairs Lib., U of North Carolina, Chapel Hill. 14 Mar. 2001

    <http://docsouth.unc.edu/jacobs/jacobs.html>.

■ **31. WORK FROM A SERVICE SUCH AS *INFOTRAC*** Libraries pay for access to databases through subscription services such as *InfoTrac.* For sources retrieved from such services, give as much of the following information as is available: (1) publication information for the source (see items 20–26); (2) the name of the database, underlined; (3) the name of the service; (4) the name and location of the library where you retrieved the article; (5) the date you accessed the source; and (6) the URL of the service.

The following models are for articles retrieved through three popular services: *InfoTrac, EBSCOhost,* and *ProQuest.* The first article is from a scholarly journal paginated by volume, the second from a bimonthly magazine, the third from a daily newspaper.

Johnson, Kirk. "The Mountain Lions of Michigan." Endangered Species Update

    19.2 (2002): 27+. Expanded Academic Index. InfoTrac. U of Michigan Lib.,

    Ann Arbor. 26 Nov. 2002 <http://infotrac.galegroup.com>.

Darnovsky, Marcy. "Embryo Cloning and Beyond." Tikkun July-Aug. 2002: 29–32.

    Academic Search Premier. EBSCOhost. Portland Community Coll. Lib.,

    Portland, OR. 1 Nov. 2002 <http://search.epnet.com>.

Kolata, Gina. "Scientists Debating Future of Hormone Replacement." New York

    Times 23 Oct. 2002: A20. ProQuest. Drew U Lib., Madison, NJ. 26 Nov. 2002

    <http://www.proquest.com>.

NOTE: When you access a work through a personal subscription service such as *America Online,* give the information about the source, followed by the name of the service, the date of access, and the keyword used to retrieve the source.

Conniff, Richard. "The House That John Built." Smithsonian Feb. 2001. America

    Online. 11 Mar. 2001. Keyword: Smithsonian Magazine.

■ **32. ARTICLE IN AN ONLINE PERIODICAL** When citing online articles, follow the guidelines for printed articles (see items 20–26), giving whatever information is available in the online source. End the citation with your date of access and the URL.

NOTE: In some online articles, paragraphs are numbered. For such articles, include the total number of paragraphs in your citation.

From an online scholarly journal

Belau, Linda. "Trauma and the Material Signifier." Postmodern Culture 11.2
(2001): 37 pars. 30 Mar. 2001 <http://jefferson.village.virginia.edu/
pmc/current.issue/11.2belau.html>.

From an online magazine

Morgan, Fiona. "Banning the Bullies." Salon.com 15 Mar. 2001. 2 Apr. 2001
<http://www.salon.com/news/feature/2001/03/15/bullying/index.html>.

From an online newspaper

Whillon, Phil. "Ready or Not." Los Angeles Times 2 Dec. 2001. 3 Dec. 2001
<http://www.latimes.com/news/la-foster-special.special>.

■ **33. CD-ROM** Treat a CD-ROM as you would any other source,
but name the medium before the publication information.

"Pimpernel." The American Heritage Dictionary of the English Language. 4th ed.
CD-ROM. Boston: Houghton, 2000.

Wattenberg, Ruth. "Helping Students in the Middle." American Educator 19.4
(1996): 2-18. ERIC. CD-ROM. SilverPlatter. Sept. 1996.

■ **34. E-MAIL** To cite an e-mail, begin with the writer's name
and the subject line. Then write "E-mail to" followed by the name of
the recipient. End with the date of the message.

O'Donnell, Patricia. "Re: Interview questions." E-mail to the author. 15 Mar. 2001.

■ **35. POSTING TO AN ONLINE LIST, FORUM, OR GROUP** Communications through e-mail discussion lists (often called LISTSERVs),
Web forums, and Usenet newsgroups do not take place in real time.
(For real-time online communications, see item 36.) When possible,
cite archived versions of postings; they are more permanent and
easier to retrieve. If you cannot locate an archived version, keep a
copy of the posting for your records.

Begin the entry with the author's name, followed by the title or
subject line; the words "Online posting"; the date of the posting; the
name of the list, forum, or newsgroup; and your date of access.
Then, for a discussion list, give the URL of the list if it is available;
otherwise give the e-mail address of the list moderator. For a Web
forum, give the network address. For a Usenet group, use the prefix
news: followed by the name of the newsgroup.

Discussion list posting (archived)

Edwards, David. "Media Lens." Online posting. 20 Dec. 2001. Media Lens Archives.

10 Apr. 2002 <http://groups.yahoo.com/group/medialens/message/25>.

Discussion list posting (not archived)

Woodbury, David. "Re: Johnston's Preparations." Online posting. 9 Apr. 2002.

American Civil War Western Theater Discussion Group. 10 Apr. 2002

<civilwarwest@yahoogroups.com>.

Web forum posting

Keirn, Kellie. "Evaluation Criteria." Online posting. 6 Feb. 2001 <http://

morrison.wsu.edu/ExchangeDetail.asp?i+274925>.

Newsgroup posting

Reedy, Tom. "Re: Macbeth an Existential Nightmare?" Online posting. 9 Mar. 2002.

8 Apr. 2002 <news:humanities.lit.authors.shakespe>.

■ **36. POSTING TO A MUD OR A MOO** MUDs and MOOs are forums that allow communication in real time. Include the writer's name (if relevant), a description and date of the event, the title of the forum, the date of access, and the electronic address, beginning with the prefix telnet://.

Carbone, Nick. Planning for the future. 1 Mar. 2001. TechRhet's Thursday night

MOO. 1 Mar. 2001 <telnet://connections.moo.mud.org:3333>.

If possible, cite an archived version of the posting.

Multimedia sources (including online versions)

Multimedia sources include visuals (such as works of art), audio works (such as sound recordings), audiovisuals (such as films), and live events (such as the performance of a play).

When citing multimedia sources that you retrieved online, consult the appropriate model in this section and give whatever information is available for the online source; then end the citation with your date of access and the URL. (See items 37, 40, and 44 for examples.)

■ **37. WORK OF ART** Cite the artist's name, followed by the title of the artwork, usually underlined, and the institution and city in which the artwork can be found. If you want to indicate the work's date, include it after the title. For a work of art you viewed online, end your citation with your date of access and the URL.

Constable, John. <u>Dedham Vale</u>. Victoria and Albert Museum, London.

van Gogh, Vincent. The Starry Night. 1889. Museum of Mod. Art, New York.
27 Feb. 2001 <http://www.moma.org/docs/collection/paintsculpt/c58.htm>.

■ **38. CARTOON** Begin with the cartoonist's name, followed by the title of the cartoon (if it has one) in quotation marks, the word "Cartoon," and the publication information for the publication in which the cartoon appears.

Rall, Ted. "Search and Destroy." Cartoon. Village Voice 23 Jan. 2001: 6.

■ **39. ADVERTISEMENT** Name the product or company being advertised, followed by the word "Advertisement." Give publication information for the source in which the advertisement appears.

Truth by Calvin Klein. Advertisement. Vogue Dec. 2000: 95-98.

■ **40. MAP OR CHART** Cite a map or chart as you would a book or a short work within a longer work. Add the word "Map" or "Chart" following the title.

"Presidential Election 2000." Map. National Atlas. 2001. US Dept. of the Interior
and US Geological Survey. 10 May 2002 <http://www.nationalatlas.gov/
elections/elect14.gif>.

Joseph, Lori, and Bob Laird. "Driving While Phoning Is Dangerous." Chart. USA
Today 16 Feb. 2001: 1A.

■ **41. MUSICAL COMPOSITION** Cite the composer's name, followed by the title of the work. Underline the title of an opera, a ballet, or a composition identified by name, but do not underline or use quotation marks around a composition identified by number or form.

Ellington, Duke. Conga Brava.

Haydn, Franz Joseph. Symphony no. 88 in G.

■ **42. SOUND RECORDING** Begin with the name of the person you want to emphasize: the composer, conductor, or performer. For a long work, give the title, underlined, followed by names of pertinent artists (such as performers, readers, or musicians) and the orchestra and conductor (if relevant). End with the manufacturer and the date.

Bizet, Georges. Carmen. Perf. Jennifer Laramore, Thomas Moser, Angela
Gheorghiu, and Samuel Ramey. Bavarian State Orch. and Chorus. Cond.
Giuseppe Sinopoli. Warner, 1996.

For a song, put the title in quotation marks. If you include the name of the album, underline it.

Chapman, Tracy. "Paper and Ink." Telling Stories. Elektra, 2000.

■ **43. FILM OR VIDEO** Begin with the title, underlined. For a film, cite the director and the lead actors or narrator ("Perf." or "Narr."), followed by the name of the distributor and the year of the film's release. For a videotape or DVD, add "Videocassette" or "DVD" before the name of the distributor.

Chocolat. Dir. Lasse Hallström. Perf. Juliette Binoche, Judi Dench, Alfred Molina,

Lena Olin, and Johnny Depp. Miramax, 2001.

High Fidelity. Dir. Stephen Frears. Perf. John Cusack, Iben Hjejle, Jack Black, and

Todd Louiso. 2000. Videocassette. Walt Disney Video, 2001.

■ **44. RADIO OR TELEVISION PROGRAM** Begin with the title of the radio segment or television episode (if there is one) in quotation marks, followed by the title of the program, underlined. Next give relevant information about the program's writer ("By"), director ("Dir."), performers ("Perf."), or host ("Host"). Then name the network, the local station (if any), and the date the program was broadcast.

"American Limbo." This American Life. Host Ira Glass. Public Radio Intl. WBEZ,

Chicago. 9 Feb. 2001.

"Live in 4A: Konstantin Soukhovetski." Performance Today. Natl. Public Radio.

2 May 2002. 10 May 2002 <http://www.npr.org/programs/pt/features/4a/

soukhovetski.02.html>.

If there is a series title, include it after the title of the program, neither underlined nor in quotation marks.

Mysteries of the Pyramids. On the Inside. Discovery Channel. 7 Feb. 2001.

■ **45. RADIO OR TELEVISION INTERVIEW** Begin with the name of the person who was interviewed, followed by the word "Interview." End with the information about the program as in item 44.

McGovern, George. Interview. Charlie Rose. PBS. WNET, New York. 1 Feb. 2001.

■ **46. LIVE PERFORMANCE** For a live performance of a play, a ballet, an opera, or a concert, begin with the title of the work performed. Then name the author or composer of the work (preceded by the word "By"), followed by as much information about the performance as is available: the director ("Dir."), choreographer ("Chor."), or conductor ("Cond."); the major performers ("Perf."); the theatre, ballet, or opera company; the theatre and its city; and the date of the performance.

Art. By Yasmina Reza. Dir. Matthew Warchus. Perf. Philip Franks, Leigh Lawson,
    and Simon Shephard. Whitehall Theatre, London. 3 Dec. 2001.

■ **47. LECTURE OR PUBLIC ADDRESS** Cite the speaker's name, followed by the title of the lecture (if any), the organization sponsoring the lecture, the location, and the date.

Cohran, Kelan. "Slavery and Astronomy." Adler Planetarium, Chicago. 21 Feb.
    2001.

■ **48. PERSONAL INTERVIEW** Begin with the name of the person you interviewed. Then write "Personal interview," followed by the date of the interview.

Shaikh, Michael. Personal interview. 22 Mar. 2001.

Other sources (including online versions)

This section includes a variety of traditional print sources not covered elsewhere. For sources obtained on the Web, consult the appropriate model in this section and give whatever information is available for the online source; then end the citation with the date on which you accessed the source and the URL. (See the second example under item 49.)

■ **49. GOVERNMENT PUBLICATION** Treat the government agency as the author, giving the name of the government followed by the name of the agency.

Canada. Industry Canada. A Guide to Patents. Ottawa: Canadian Intellectual
    Property Office, 2002.

United States. Natl. Council on Disability. Promises to Keep: A Decade of Federal
    Enforcement of the Americans with Disabilities Act. Washington: GPO, 2000.

For government documents published online, give as much publication information as is available and end your citation with the date of access and the URL.

United States. Dept. of Transportation. Natl. Highway Traffic Safety

Administration. An Investigation of the Safety Implications of Wireless

Communications in Vehicles. Nov. 1999. 20 May 2001

<http://www.nhtsa.dot.gov/people/injury/research/wireless>.

■ **50.** LEGAL SOURCE   For most legal documents, cite the name of
the document (without underlining or quotation marks), the article
and section numbers, and the year if relevant.

US Const. Art. 4, sec. 2.

For an act, include its Public Law number ("Pub. L."), the date
it was enacted, and its Statutes at Large number ("Stat.").

Electronic Freedom of Information Act Amendments of 1996. Pub. L. 104-418.

2 Oct. 1996. Stat. 3048.

■ **51.** PAMPHLET   Cite a pamphlet as you would a book.

Commonwealth of Massachusetts. Dept. of Jury Commissioner. A Few Facts about

Jury Duty. Boston: Commonwealth of Massachusetts, 1997.

■ **52.** DISSERTATION   Begin with the author's name, followed by
the dissertation title in quotation marks, the abbreviation "Diss.,"
the name of the institution, and the year the dissertation was
accepted.

Jackson, Shelley. "Writing Whiteness: Contemporary Southern Literature in Black

and White." Diss. U of Maryland, 2000.

For dissertations that have been published in book form, underline the title. After the title and before the book's publication
information, add the abbreviation "Diss.," the name of the institution, and the year the dissertation was accepted.

Damberg, Cheryl L. Healthcare Reform: Distributional Consequences of an

Employer Mandate for Workers in Small Firms. Diss. Rand Graduate School,

1995. Santa Monica: Rand, 1996.

■ **53.** ABSTRACT OF A DISSERTATION   Cite an abstract as you
would an unpublished dissertation. After the dissertation date, give
the abbreviation *DA* or *DAI* (for *Dissertation Abstracts* or *Dissertation Abstracts International*), followed by the volume number, the
date of publication, and the page number.

Chen, Shu-Ling. "Mothers and Daughters in Morrison, Tan, Marshall, and Kincaid."

Diss. U of Washington, 2000. <u>DAI</u> 61 (2000): 2289.

■ **54. PUBLISHED PROCEEDINGS OF A CONFERENCE** Cite published conference proceedings as you would a book, adding information about the conference after the title.

Kartiganer, Donald M., and Ann J. Abadie. <u>Faulkner at 100: Retrospect and</u>

<u>Prospect</u>. Proc. of Faulkner and Yoknapatawpha Conf., 27 July-1 Aug. 1997,

U of Mississippi. Jackson: UP of Mississippi, 2000.

■ **55. PUBLISHED INTERVIEW** Name the person interviewed, followed by the title of the interview (if there is one). If the interview does not have a title, include the word "Interview" followed by a period after the interviewee's name. Give publication information for the work in which the interview was published.

Renoir, Jean. "Renoir at Home: Interview with Jean Renoir." <u>Film Quarterly</u> 50.1

(1996): 2-8.

If the name of the interviewer is relevant, include it after the name of the interviewee.

Prince. Interview with Bilge Ebiri. <u>Yahoo! Internet Life</u> 7.6 (2001): 82-85.

■ **56. PERSONAL LETTER** Begin with the writer's name and add the phrase "Letter to the author," followed by the date.

Coggins, Christopher. Letter to the author. 6 May 2001.

MLA-4c MLA information notes (optional)

Researchers who use the MLA system of parenthetical documentation (see MLA-4a) may also use information notes for one of two purposes:

1. to provide additional material that might interrupt the flow of the paper yet is important enough to include
2. to refer readers to any sources not discussed in the paper

Information notes may be footnotes or endnotes. Footnotes appear at the foot of the page; endnotes appear on a separate page at the end of the paper, just before the list of works cited. For either style, the notes are numbered consecutively throughout the paper.

The text of the paper contains a raised arabic numeral that corresponds to the number of the note.

TEXT

Local governments are more likely than state governments to pass legislation against using a cell phone while driving.[1]

NOTE

[1] For a discussion of local laws banning cell phone use, see Sundeen 8.

MLA-5

Manuscript format; sample paper

MLA-5a Manuscript format

The following guidelines on formatting a paper and preparing a list of works cited are consistent with advice given in the *MLA Handbook for Writers of Research Papers,* 6th ed. (New York: MLA, 2003). For a sample MLA paper, see MLA-5b.

Formatting the paper

MLA papers should be formatted as follows.

MATERIALS   Use good-quality letter-sized white paper. Secure the pages with a paper clip. Unless your instructor suggests otherwise, do not staple or bind the pages.

TITLE AND IDENTIFICATION   MLA does not require a title page. On the first page of your paper, place your name, your instructor's name, the course title, and the date on separate lines against the left margin. Then centre your title. (See p. 371 for a sample first page.)

If your instructor requires a title page, ask for guidelines on formatting it. A format similar to the one on page 408 will most likely be acceptable.

PAGINATION   Put the page number preceded by your last name in the upper right corner of each page, one-half inch below the top edge. Use Arabic numerals (1, 2, 3, and so on).

MARGINS, LINE SPACING, AND PARAGRAPH INDENTS   Leave margins of one inch (2.5 cm) on all sides of the page. Do not justify (align) the right margin.

Double-space throughout the paper. Do not add extra lines of space above or below the title of the paper or between paragraphs.

Indent the first line of each paragraph one-half inch (1.25 cm or five spaces) from the left margin.

LONG QUOTATIONS   When a quotation is longer than four typed lines of prose or three lines of verse, set it off from the text by indenting the entire quotation a full inch (2.5 cm or ten spaces) from the left margin. Double-space the indented quotation, and don't add extra space above or below it.

Quotation marks are not needed when a quotation has been set off from the text by indenting. See page 338 for an example.

WEB ADDRESSES   When a Web address mentioned in the text of your paper must be divided at the end of a line, do not insert a hyphen (a hyphen could appear to be part of the address). For MLA rules on dividing Web addresses in your list of works cited, see page 370.

HEADINGS   MLA neither encourages nor discourages the use of headings and currently provides no guidelines for their use.

VISUALS   MLA classifies visuals as tables and figures (figures include graphs, charts, maps, photographs, and drawings). Label each table with an arabic numeral (Table 1, Table 2, and so on) and provide a clear caption that identifies the subject. The label and caption should appear on separate lines above the table, flush left. Below the table, give its source in a note like this one:

Source: John M. Violanti, "Cellular Phones and Fatal Traffic Collisions," Accident Analysis and Prevention 30 (1998): 521.

For each figure, place a label and a caption below the figure, flush left. They need not appear on separate lines. The word "Figure" may be abbreviated to "Fig." Include source information following the caption.

Visuals should be placed in the text, as close as possible to the sentences that relate to them unless your instructor prefers them in an appendix. See page 372 for an example of a visual in the text of a paper.

Preparing the list of works cited

Begin the list of works cited on a new page at the end of the paper. Centre the title Works Cited about one inch (2.5 cm) from the top of the page. Double-space throughout. See page 377 for a sample list of works cited.

ALPHABETIZING THE LIST   Alphabetize the list by the last names of the authors (or editors); if a work has no author or editor, alphabetize by the first word of the title other than *A, An,* or *The.*

If your list includes two or more works by the same author, use the author's name only for the first entry. For subsequent entries use three hyphens followed by a period. List the titles in alphabetical order. See also item 5 on page 351.

INDENTING   Do not indent the first line of each works cited entry, but indent any additional lines one-half inch (1.25 cm or five spaces). This technique highlights the names of the authors, making it easy for readers to scan the alphabetized list.

WEB ADDRESSES   Do not insert a hyphen when dividing a Web address at the end of a line. Break the line after a slash. Also, insert angle brackets around the URL.

If your word processing program automatically turns Web addresses into hot links (by underlining them and highlighting them in color), turn off this feature. For advice on how to do this, visit the MLA Web site at <http://www.mla.org> and consult the list of frequently asked questions.

MLA-5b   Sample MLA research paper

On the following pages is a research paper on the topic of cell phones and driving, written by Angela Daly, a student in a composition class. Daly's paper is documented with MLA-style in-text citations and list of works cited. Annotations in the margins of the paper draw your attention to features of special interest.

ON THE WEB

Another student, Paul Levi, has also written a paper on the topic of cell phones and driving; his paper takes the opposite stand from that taken by Angela Daly. To read Levi's paper, go to
www.dianahacker.com/writersref

and click on   ▶ **Model Papers**
              ▶ **MLA papers: Levi**

Daly 1

Angela Daly

Professor Chavez

English 101

14 March 2001

A Call to Action:

Regulate Use of Cell Phones on the Road

When a cell phone goes off in a classroom or at a concert, we

are irritated, but at least our lives are not endangered. When we are

on the road, however, irresponsible cell phone users are more than

irritating: They are putting our lives at risk. Many of us have

witnessed drivers so distracted by dialing and chatting that they

resemble drunk drivers, weaving between lanes, for example, or

nearly running down pedestrians in crosswalks. A number of bills to

regulate use of cell phones on the road have been introduced in

state legislatures, and the time has come to push for their passage.

Regulation is needed because drivers using phones are seriously

impaired and because laws on negligent and reckless driving are not

sufficient to punish offenders.

No one can deny that cell phones have caused traffic deaths

and injuries. Cell phones were implicated in three fatal accidents in

November 1999 alone. Early in November, two-year-old Morgan Pena

was killed by a driver distracted by his cell phone. Morgan's mother,

Patti Pena, reports that the driver "ran a stop sign at 45 mph, broad-

sided my vehicle and killed Morgan as she sat in her car seat." A

week later, corrections officer Shannon Smith, who was guarding

prisoners by the side of the road, was killed by a woman distracted

Title is centred.

Opening sentences
catch readers'
attention.

Thesis asserts
Angela Daly's
main point.

Daly uses a clear
topic sentence.

Signal phrase
names the author
of the quotation to
follow.

No page number
is available for this
Web source.

Daly 2

Author's name is given in parentheses; no page is available.

Page number is given when available.

Clear topic sentences like this one are used throughout the paper.

by a phone call (Besthoff). On Thanksgiving weekend that same month, John and Carole Hall were killed when a Naval Academy midshipman crashed into their parked car. The driver said in court that when he looked up from the cell phone he was dialing, he was three feet from the car and had no time to stop (Stockwell B8).

Expert testimony, public opinion, and even cartoons suggest that driving while phoning is dangerous. Frances Bents, an expert on the relation between cell phones and accidents, estimates that between 450 and 1,000 crashes a year have some connection to cell phone use (Layton C9). In a survey published by Farmers Insurance Group, 87% of those polled said that cell phones affect a driver's ability, and 40% reported having close calls with drivers distracted by phones. Many cartoons have depicted the very real dangers of driving while distracted (see Fig. 1).

Illustration has figure number, label, and source information.

"YEP... GOT MY *CELLPHONE*, MY *PAGER*, MY *INTERNET LINK*, MY *WIRELESS FAX*, AND THANKS TO THIS NIFTY *SATELLITE NAVIGATING SYSTEM*, I KNOW PRECISELY WHERE I AM AT ALL TIMES!"

Fig. 1. Chan Lowe, cartoon, Washington Post 22 July 2000: A21.

Daly 3

Scientific research confirms the dangers of using phones while

on the road. In 1997 an important study appeared in the New

England Journal of Medicine. The authors, Donald Redelmeier and

Robert Tibshirani, studied 699 volunteers who made their cell phone

bills available in order to confirm the times when they had placed

calls. The participants agreed to report any nonfatal collision in

which they were involved. By comparing the time of a collision with

the phone records, the researchers assessed the dangers of driving

while phoning. Here are their results:

> We found that using a cellular telephone was associated
>
> with a risk of having a motor vehicle collision that was
>
> about four times as high as that among the same drivers
>
> when they were not using their cellular telephones. This
>
> relative risk is similar to the hazard associated with
>
> driving with a blood alcohol level at the legal limit. (456)

In reports by news media, the latter claim was exaggerated ("similar

to" is not "equal to"), but the comparison with drunk driving is

startling nonetheless.

A 1998 study focused on Oklahoma, one of the few states to

keep records on fatal accidents involving cell phones. Using police

records, John M. Violanti of the Rochester Institute of Technology

investigated the relation between traffic fatalities in Oklahoma and

the use or presence of a cell phone. He found a ninefold increase in

the risk of fatality if a phone was being used and a doubled risk

simply when a phone was present in a vehicle (522-23). The latter

statistic is interesting, for it suggests that those who carry phones

Summary and
long quotation
are introduced
with a signal
phrase naming
the authors.

Long quotation is
set off from the
text; quotation
marks are omitted.

Summary begins
with a signal
phrase naming the
author and ends
with page numbers
in parentheses.

in their cars may tend to be more negligent (or prone to distractions of all kinds) than those who do not.

Some groups have argued that state traffic laws make legislation regulating cell phone use unnecessary. Sadly, this is not true. Laws on traffic safety vary from state to state, and drivers distracted by cell phones can get off with light punishment even when they cause fatal accidents. For example, although the midshipman mentioned earlier was charged with vehicular manslaughter for the deaths of John and Carole Hall, the judge was unable to issue a verdict of guilty. Under Maryland law, he could only find the defendant guilty of negligent driving and impose a $500 fine (Layton C1). Such a light sentence is not unusual. The driver who killed Morgan Pena in Pennsylvania received two tickets and a $50 fine--and retained his driving privileges (Pena). In Georgia, a young woman distracted by her phone ran down and killed a two-year-old; her sentence was ninety days in boot camp and five hundred hours of community service (Ippolito J1). The families of the victims are understandably distressed by laws that lead to such light sentences.

When certain kinds of driver behavior are shown to be especially dangerous, we wisely draft special laws making them illegal and imposing specific punishments. Running red lights, failing to stop for a school bus, and drunk driving are obvious examples; phoning in a moving vehicle should be no exception. Unlike more general laws covering negligent driving, specific laws leave little ambiguity for law officers and for judges and juries imposing punishments. Such laws have another important benefit: They leave no ambiguity for

---

Daly counters an opposing argument.

Facts are documented with in-text citations: authors' names and page numbers (if available) in parentheses.

Daly uses an analogy to justify passing a special law.

Daly 5

drivers. Currently, drivers can tease themselves into thinking they are using their car phones responsibly because the definition of "negligent driving" is vague.

As of December 2000, twenty countries were restricting use of cell phones in moving vehicles (Sundeen 8). In the United States, it is highly unlikely that legislation could be passed on the national level, since traffic safety is considered a state and local issue. To date, only a few counties and towns have passed traffic laws restricting cell phone use. For example, in Suffolk County, New York, it is illegal for drivers to use a handheld phone for anything but an emergency call while on the road (Haughney A8). The first town to restrict use of handheld phones was Brooklyn, Ohio (Layton C9). Brooklyn, the first community in the country to pass a seat belt law, has once again shown its concern for traffic safety.

Laws passed by counties and towns have had some effect, but it makes more sense to legislate at the state level. Local laws are not likely to have the impact of state laws, and keeping track of a wide variety of local ordinances is confusing for drivers. Even a spokesperson for Verizon Wireless has said that statewide bans are preferable to a "crazy patchwork quilt of ordinances" (qtd. in Haughney A8). Unfortunately, although a number of bills have been introduced in state legislatures, as of early 2001 no state law seriously restricting use of the phones had passed--largely because of effective lobbying from the wireless industry.

Despite the claims of some lobbyists, tough laws regulating phone use can make our roads safer. In Japan, for example, accidents

> Daly explains why U.S. laws need to be passed on the state level.

> Transition helps readers move from one paragraph to the next.

> Daly cites an indirect source: words quoted in another source.

> Daly counters a claim made by some opponents.

Daly 6

linked to cell phones fell by 75% just a month after the country

prohibited using a handheld phone while driving (Haughney A8).

Research suggests and common sense tells us that it is not possible

to drive an automobile at high speeds, dial numbers, and carry on

conversations without significant risks. When such behavior is regu-

lated, obviously our roads will be safer.

Because of mounting public awareness of the dangers of drivers

distracted by phones, state legislators must begin to take the prob-

lem seriously. "It's definitely an issue that is gaining steam around

the country," says Matt Sundeen of the National Conference of State

Legislatures (qtd. in Layton C9). Lon Anderson of the American Auto-

mobile Association agrees: "There is momentum building," he says,

to pass laws (qtd. in Layton C9). The time has come for states to

adopt legislation restricting the use of cell phones in moving

vehicles.

For variety Daly
places a signal
phrase after a
brief quotation.

The paper ends
with Daly's stand
on the issue.

Daly 7

Works Cited

Besthoff, Len. "Cell Phone Use Increases Risk of Accidents, but Users

Willing to Take the Risk." <u>WRAL Online</u>. 11 Nov. 1999. 12 Jan. 2001

<http://www.wral-tv.com/news/wral/1999/1110-talking-driving/>.

Farmers Insurance Group. "New Survey Shows Drivers Have Had 'Close

Calls' with Cell Phone Users." 8 May 2000. 12 Jan. 2001 <http://

www.farmersinsurance.com/news_cellphones.html>.

Haughney, Christine. "Taking Phones out of Drivers' Hands." <u>Washington</u>

<u>Post</u> 5 Nov. 2000: A8.

Ippolito, Milo. "Driver's Sentence Not Justice, Mom Says." <u>Atlanta Journal-</u>

<u>Constitution</u> 25 Sept. 1999: J1.

Layton, Lyndsey. "Legislators Aiming to Disconnect Motorists." <u>Washington</u>

<u>Post</u> 10 Dec. 2000: C1+.

Lowe, Chan. Cartoon. <u>Washington Post</u> 22 July 2000: A21.

Pena, Patricia N. "Patti Pena's Letter to Car Talk." <u>Cars.com</u>. Car Talk. 10 Jan.

2001 <http://cartalk.cars.com/About/Morgan-Pena/letter.html>.

Redelmeier, Donald A., and Robert J. Tibshirani. "Association between

Cellular-Telephone Calls and Motor Vehicle Collisions." <u>New England</u>

<u>Journal of Medicine</u> 336 (1997): 453-58.

Stockwell, Jamie. "Phone Use Faulted in Collision." <u>Washington Post</u> 6 Dec.

2000: B1+.

Sundeen, Matt. "Cell Phones and Highway Safety: 2000 State Legislative

Update." <u>National Conference of State Legislatures</u>. Dec. 2000. 9 pp.

27 Feb. 2001 <http://ncsl.org/programs/esnr/cellphone.pdf>.

Violanti, John M. "Cellular Phones and Fatal Traffic Collisions." <u>Accident</u>

<u>Analysis and Prevention</u> 30 (1998): 519-24.

Heading is centred.

The URL is broken after a slash. No hyphen is inserted.

List is alphabetized by authors' last names (or by title when a work has no author).

First line of each entry is at the left margin: extra lines are indented 1/2" (1.25 cm or five spaces).

Double-spacing is used throughout.

APA

APA Papers

CMS

Chicago Papers

APA/CMS Papers

This tabbed section shows how to document sources in psychology and other social science classes (APA style) and in history and some humanities classes (CMS style). It also includes discipline-specific advice on three important topics: supporting a thesis, avoiding plagiarism, and integrating sources. Examples are documented with the appropriate style.

NOTE: For cross-disciplinary advice on finding and evaluating sources and on managing information, see the tabbed section titled Researching.

APA PAPERS

Most writing assignments in the social sciences are either reports of original research or reviews of the literature written about a particular research topic. Often an original research report contains a "review of the literature" section that places the writer's project in the context of previous research.

Social science instructors will often ask you to document sources with the American Psychological Association (APA) system of in-text citations and references described in APA-4. In addition to documenting your sources, you face three main challenges when writing a social science paper that draws on written sources: (1) supporting a thesis, (2) avoiding plagiarism, and (3) integrating quotations and other source material.

APA-1

Supporting a thesis

Most assignments ask you to form a thesis, or main idea, and to support that thesis with well-organized evidence.

APA-1a Form a thesis.

A thesis, which usually appears at the end of the introduction, is a one-sentence (or occasionally a two-sentence) statement of your central idea. In a paper reviewing the literature on a topic, this thesis analyzes the often competing conclusions drawn by a variety of researchers.

Your paper will address a central research question, and your thesis will express a reasonable answer to that question, given the current state of research in the field. Here, for example, is a research question posed by a student in a psychology class, along with that student's thesis.

RESEARCH QUESTION

How and to what extent have the great apes—gorillas, chimpanzees, and orangutans—demonstrated language abilities akin to those of humans?

POSSIBLE THESIS

Researchers agree that apes have acquired fairly large vocabularies in American Sign Language and in artificial languages, but they have drawn quite different conclusions in addressing the following questions: (1) How spontaneously have apes used language? (2) How creatively have apes used language? (3) To what extent can apes create sentences? (4) What are some implications of the ape language studies?

ON THE WEB

For an electronic exercise on thesis statements for an APA paper, go to **www.dianahacker.com/writersref**

and click on ▶ **Electronic Research Exercises**
　　　　　　　▶ **E-ex APA 1–1**

APA-1b Organize your evidence.

The American Psychological Association encourages the use of headings to help readers follow the organization of a paper. For an original research report, the major headings often follow a standard model: Method, Results, Discussion. For a paper that reviews the literature on a research topic, headings will vary, depending on the topic. The student who wrote about apes and language used the four questions in her thesis as headings in her paper (see pp. 408–17).

APA-2

Avoiding plagiarism

Your research paper is a collaboration between you and your sources. To be fair and ethical, you must acknowledge your debt to the writers of those sources. If you don't, you are guilty of plagiarism, a serious academic offense.

Three different acts are considered plagiarism: (1) failing to cite quotations and borrowed ideas, (2) failing to enclose borrowed language in quotation marks, and (3) failing to put summaries and paraphrases in your own words.

ON THE WEB

For an electronic exercise on avoiding plagiarism in an APA paper, go to **www.dianahacker.com/writersref**

and click on   ▶ **Electronic Research Exercises**
              ▶ **E-ex APA 2–1**

APA-2a   Cite quotations and borrowed ideas.

You must of course cite all direct quotations. You must also cite any ideas borrowed from a source: summaries and paraphrases, statistics and other specific facts, and visuals such as cartoons, graphs, or diagrams.

The only exception is common knowledge—general information that your readers may know or could easily locate in any number of reference sources. For example, the approximate population of Canada is common knowledge among sociologists and economists, and psychologists are familiar with Freud's theory of the unconscious. As a rule, when you have seen certain general information repeatedly in your reading, you don't need to cite it. However, when information has appeared in only a few sources, when it is highly specific (as with statistics), or when it is controversial, you should cite it.

The American Psychological Association recommends an author-date style of citations. Here, very briefly, is how the author-date system often works. See APA-4 for a detailed discussion of variations.

1. The source is introduced by a signal phrase that includes the last names of the authors followed by the date of publication in parentheses.
2. The material being cited is followed by a page number in parentheses.
3. At the end of the paper, an alphabetized list of references gives publication information about the source.

IN-TEXT CITATION

Noting that apes' brains resemble those of our human ancestors, Leakey and Lewin (1992) argued that in ape brains "the cognitive foundations on which human language could be built are already present" (p. 244).

ENTRY IN THE LIST OF REFERENCES

Leakey, R., & Lewin, R. (1992). *Origins reconsidered: In search of what makes us human.* New York: Doubleday.

APA-2b Enclose borrowed language in quotation marks.

To show readers that you are using a source's exact phrases or sentences, you must enclose them in quotation marks. To omit the quotation marks is to claim—falsely—that the language is your own. Such an omission is plagiarism even if you have cited the source.

ORIGINAL SOURCE

No animal has done more to renew interest in animal intelligence than a beguiling, bilingual bonobo named Kanzi, who has the grammatical abilities of a 2½-year-old child and a taste for movies about cavemen. —Linden, "Animals," 1986, p. 57

PLAGIARISM

According to Linden (1986), no animal has done more to renew interest in animal intelligence than a beguiling, bilingual bonobo named Kanzi, who has the grammatical abilities of a 2-1/2-year-old child and a taste for movies about cavemen (p. 57).

BORROWED LANGUAGE IN QUOTATION MARKS

According to Linden (1986), "No animal has done more to renew interest in animal intelligence than a beguiling, bilingual bonobo named Kanzi, who has the grammatical abilities of a 2-1/2-year-old child and a taste for movies about cavemen" (p. 57).

NOTE: When quoted sentences are set off from the text by indenting, quotation marks are not needed (see p. 389).

APA-2c Put summaries and paraphrases in your own words.

A summary condenses information; a paraphrase reports information in about the same number of words. When you summarize or paraphrase, you must restate the source's meaning using your own language. You are guilty of plagiarism if you half-copy the author's sentences—either by mixing the author's well-chosen phrases without using quotation marks or by plugging your own synonyms into the author's sentence structure. The following paraphrases are plagiarized—even though the source is cited—because their language is too close to that of the source.

ORIGINAL SOURCE

If the existence of a signing ape was unsettling for linguists, it was also startling news for animal behaviorists.

—Davis, *Eloquent Animals,* 1976, p. 26

UNACCEPTABLE BORROWING OF PHRASES

Davis (1976) observed that the existence of a signing ape unsettled linguists and startled animal behaviourists (p. 26).

UNACCEPTABLE BORROWING OF STRUCTURE

Davis (1976) observed that if the presence of a sign-language-using chimp was disturbing for scientists studying language, it was also surprising to scientists studying animal behaviour (p. 26).

To avoid plagiarizing an author's language, set the source aside, write from memory, and consult the source later to check for accuracy. This strategy prevents you from being captivated by the words on the page.

ACCEPTABLE PARAPHRASE

Davis (1976) observed that both linguists and animal behaviourists were taken by surprise upon learning of an ape's ability to use sign language (p. 26).

APA-3

Integrating sources

By carefully integrating quotations and other source material into your own text, you help readers understand whose views they are hearing—yours or those of your sources. In addition, you show readers where cited material begins and where it ends.

NOTE: APA recommends using the past tense or the present perfect tense in phrases that introduce most sources: *Davis noted that* or *Davis has noted that* (not *Davis notes that*). Use the present tense, however, for discussing the results of an experiment (*the results show*) or explaining conclusions that are not in dispute (*researchers agree*).

It is generally acceptable in the social sciences to call authors by their last name only, even on a first mention. If your paper refers to two authors with the same last name, use initials as well.

ON THE WEB

For an electronic exercise on integrating quotations in APA papers, go to **www.dianahacker.com/writersref**

and click on ▶ **Electronic Research Exercises**
▶ **E-ex APA 3–1**

APA-3a Integrate quotations as smoothly as possible.

Readers need to move from your own words to the words of a source without feeling a jolt.

Using signal phrases

Avoid dropping quotations into the text without warning. Instead, provide clear signal phrases, usually including the author's name and the date of publication, to prepare readers for the quotation.

DROPPED QUOTATION

Even more significant is the pattern of combining symbols that Kanzi developed on his own. "When he gave an order combining two symbols for action--such as 'chase' and 'hide'--it was important for him that the first action--'chase'--be done first" (Gibbons, 1991, p. 1561).

QUOTATION WITH SIGNAL PHRASE

Even more significant is the pattern of combining symbols that Kanzi developed on his own. According to Gibbons (1991), "When he gave an order combining two symbols for action--such as 'chase' and 'hide'--it was important for him that the first action--'chase'--be done first" (p. 1561).

To avoid monotony, try to vary the language and placement of your signal phrases. The models in the chart on the next page suggest a range of possibilities.

When the signal phrase includes a verb, choose one that suits the context. Is your source arguing a point, making an observation, reporting a fact, refuting an argument, or suggesting a theory? By choosing an appropriate verb, you can make your source's stance clear. See the chart on the next page for a list of verbs commonly used in signal phrases.

Using the ellipsis mark

To condense a quoted passage, use the ellipsis mark (three spaced periods) to indicate that you have omitted words. What remains must be grammatically complete.

Eckholm (1985) reported that "a 4-year-old pygmy chimpanzee . . . has demonstrated what scientists say are the most humanlike linguistic skills ever documented in another animal" (p. A1).

The writer has omitted the words *at a research center near Atlanta,* which appeared in the original.

Varying signal phrases in APA papers

MODEL SIGNAL PHRASES

In the words of Terrace, ". . ."

As Davis has noted, ". . ."

The Gardners, Washoe's trainers, pointed out that ". . ."

". . . ," claimed linguist Noam Chomsky.

". . . ," wrote Eckholm, " . . ."

Psychologist H. S. Terrace has offered an odd argument for this view: ". . ."

Terrace answered these objections with the following analysis: ". . ."

VERBS IN SIGNAL PHRASES

admitted	contended	reasoned
agreed	declared	refuted
argued	denied	rejected
asserted	emphasized	reported
believed	insisted	responded
claimed	noted	suggested
compared	observed	thought
confirmed	pointed out	wrote

To omit a full sentence or more, use a period before the ellipsis dots.

> According to Wade (1980), the horse Clever Hans "could apparently count by tapping out numbers with his hoof. . . . Clever Hans owes his celebrity to his master's innocence. Von Osten sincerely believed he had taught Hans to solve arithmetical problems" (p. 1349).

Ordinarily, do not use an ellipsis mark at the beginning or at the end of a quotation. Readers will understand that the quoted material is taken from a longer passage.

Using brackets

Brackets (square parentheses) allow you to insert words of your own into quoted material, perhaps to explain a confusing reference or to keep a sentence grammatical in your context.

Seyfarth (1982) has written that "Premack [a scientist at the University of Pennsylvania] taught a seven-year-old chimpanzee, Sarah, that the word for 'apple' was a small, plastic triangle" (p. 13).

To indicate an error in a quotation, insert [*sic*] — italicized and in brackets — after the error.

Setting off long quotations

When you quote forty or more words, set off the quotation by indenting it one-half inch (or five spaces) from the left margin.

Long quotations should be introduced by an informative sentence, usually followed by a colon. Quotation marks are unnecessary because the indented format tells readers that the words are taken word-for-word from the source.

> Hart (1996) has described the kinds of linguistic signs and symbols used in the early ape language experiments:
>
>> Researchers attempted to teach individual signs derived from American Sign Language (ASL) to Washoe, a chimpanzee; Koko, a gorilla; and Chantek, an orangutan. Sarah, a chimpanzee, learned to manipulate arbitrary plastic symbols standing for words, and another chimpanzee, named Lana, used an early computer keyboard, with arbitrary symbols the researchers called lexigrams. (p. 108)

APA-3b Integrate summaries and paraphrases.

Summaries and paraphrases are written in your own words. As with quotations, you should introduce most summaries and paraphrases of a source with a signal phrase that mentions the author and the date of publication and places the material in context. Readers will then understand where the summary or paraphrase begins.

Without the signal phrase (underlined) in the following example, readers might think that only the last sentence is being cited, when in fact the whole paragraph is based on the source.

> Studies at the Yerkes Primate Center in Atlanta broke new ground. Researchers Greenfield and Savage-Rumbaugh (1990) reported that the pygmy chimp Kanzi seemed to understand simple grammatical rules about lexigram order. For instance, Kanzi learned that in two-word utterances

action precedes object, an ordering also used by human children at the two-word stage. What is impressive, noted Greenfield and Savage-Rumbaugh, is that in addition to being semantically related, most of Kanzi's lexigram combinations are original (p. 556).

There are times, however, when a signal phrase naming the author is not necessary. When the context makes clear where the cited material begins, you may omit the signal phrase and include the authors' names in the parentheses: (Greenfield & Savage-Rumbaugh, 1990, p. 556).

APA-3c Integrate statistics and other facts.

When you are citing a statistic or other specific fact, a signal phrase is often not necessary. In most cases, readers will understand that the citation refers to the statistic or fact (not the whole paragraph).

By the age of ten, Kanzi had learned to communicate about 200 symbols on his computerized board (Lewin, 1991).

There is nothing wrong, however, with using a signal phrase.

Lewin (1991) reported that by the age of ten, Kanzi had learned to communicate about 200 symbols on his computerized board.

APA-4

Documenting sources

In most social science classes, you will be asked to use the APA system for documenting sources, which is set forth in the *Publication Manual of the American Psychological Association,* 5th ed. (Washington: APA, 2001). APA recommends in-text citations that refer readers to a list of references.

An in-text citation names the author of the source (often in a signal phrase), gives the date of publication, and at times includes a page number in parentheses. At the end of the paper, a list of references provides publication information about the source; the list is alphabetized by authors' last names (or by titles for works without authors). There is a direct link between the in-text citation and the alphabetical listing. In the following example, that link is highlighted in red.

IN-TEXT CITATION

Rumbaugh (1995) reported that "Kanzi's comprehension of over 600 novel sentences of request was very comparable to Alia's; both complied with requests without assistance on approximately 70% of the sentences" (p. 722).

ENTRY IN THE LIST OF REFERENCES

Rumbaugh, D. (1995). Primate language and cognition: Common ground. *Social Research, 62,* 711-730.

Directory to APA in-text citation models

1. Basic format for a quotation, 392
2. Basic format for a summary or a paraphrase, 392
3. A work with two authors, 392
4. A work with three to five authors, 392
5. A work with six or more authors, 393
6. Unknown author, 393
7. Organization as author, 393
8. Two or more works in the same parentheses, 393
9. Authors with the same last name, 394
10. Personal communication, 394
11. An electronic document, 394
12. Indirect source, 395

APA-4a   APA in-text citations

The APA's in-text citations provide at least the author's last name and the date of publication. For direct quotations and some paraphrases, a page number is given as well.

NOTE: In the models that follow, notice that APA style requires the use of the past tense or the present perfect tense in signal phrases introducing material that has been cited: *Smith reported, Smith has argued.* (See also p. 386.)

■ **1. BASIC FORMAT FOR A QUOTATION** Ordinarily, introduce the quotation with a signal phrase that includes the author's last name followed by the date of publication in parentheses. Put the page number (preceded by "p.") in parentheses after the quotation.

> Hart (1996) wrote that some primatologists "wondered if apes had learned
> Language, with a capital *L*" (p. 109).

If the signal phrase does not name the author, place the author's name, the date, and the page number in parentheses after the quotation: (Hart, 1996, p. 109).

■ **2. BASIC FORMAT FOR A SUMMARY OR A PARAPHRASE** Include the author's last name and the date either in a signal phrase introducing the material or in parentheses following it. A page number is not required for a summary or a paraphrase, but include one if it would help readers find the passage in a long work (as in item 3).

> According to Hart (1996), researchers took Terrace's conclusions seriously,
> and funding for language experiments soon declined.

> Researchers took Terrace's conclusions seriously, and funding for language
> experiments soon declined (Hart, 1996).

■ **3. A WORK WITH TWO AUTHORS** Name both authors in the signal phrase or parentheses each time you cite the work. In the parentheses, use "&" between the authors' names; in the signal phrase, use "and."

> Greenfield and Savage-Rumbaugh (1990) have acknowledged that Kanzi's
> linguistic development was slower than that of a human child (p. 567).

> Kanzi's linguistic development was slower than that of a human child
> (Greenfield & Savage-Rumbaugh, 1990, p. 567).

■ **4. A WORK WITH THREE TO FIVE AUTHORS** Identify all authors in the signal phrase or parentheses the first time you cite the source.

> The chimpanzee Nim was raised by researchers who trained him in American
> Sign Language by molding and guiding his hands (Terrace, Petitto, Sanders,
> & Bever, 1979).

In subsequent citations, use the first author's name followed by "et al." in either the signal phrase or the parentheses.

Nim was able to string together as many as 16 signs, but their order appeared quite random (Terrace et al., 1979).

■ **5. A WORK WITH SIX OR MORE AUTHORS** Use the first author's name followed by "et al." in the signal phrase or parentheses.

The ape language studies have shed light on the language development of children with linguistic handicaps (Savage-Rumbaugh et al., 1993).

■ **6. UNKNOWN AUTHOR** If the author is unknown, mention the work's title in the signal phrase or give the first word or two of the title in the parenthetical citation. Titles of articles and chapters are put in quotation marks; titles of books and reports are italicized.

Chimpanzees in separate areas of Africa differ in a range of behaviours: in their methods of cracking nuts, for example, or in their grooming rituals. A team of researchers has concluded that many of these behaviours are cultural, not just responses to environmental factors ("Chimps," 1999).

NOTE: In the rare case when "Anonymous" is specified as the author, treat it as if it were a real name: (Anonymous, 2001). In the list of references, also use the name Anonymous as author.

■ **7. ORGANIZATION AS AUTHOR** If the author is a government agency or other corporate organization, name the organization in the signal phrase or in the parenthetical citation the first time you cite the source.

According to the Language Research Center (2000), linguistic research with apes has led to new methods of treating humans with learning disabilities such as autism and dyslexia.

If the organization has a familiar abbreviation, you may include it in brackets the first time you cite the source and use the abbreviation alone in later citations.

| **FIRST CITATION** | (National Institute of Mental Health [NIMH], 2001) |
| **LATER CITATIONS** | (NIMH, 2001) |

■ **8. TWO OR MORE WORKS IN THE SAME PARENTHESES** When your parenthetical citation names two or more works, put them in the same order that they appear in the reference list, separated by semicolons.

> Researchers argued that the apes in the early language experiments were merely responding to cues (Sebeok & Umiker-Sebeok, 1979; Terrace, 1979).

■ **9. AUTHORS WITH THE SAME LAST NAME** To avoid confusion, use initials with the last names if your reference list includes two or more authors with the same last name.

> Research by E. Smith (1989) revealed that . . .

■ **10. PERSONAL COMMUNICATION** Interviews, letters, e-mail, and other person-to-person communications should be cited as follows:

> One of Patterson's former aides, who worked with the gorilla Michael, believes that he was capable of joking and lying in sign language (E. Robbins, personal communication, January 4, 2001).

Do not include personal communications in your reference list.

■ **11. AN ELECTRONIC DOCUMENT** When possible, cite an electronic document as you would any other document (using the author-date style).

> R. Fouts and D. Fouts (1999) have explained one benefit of ape language research: It has shown us how to teach children with linguistic disabilities.

Electronic sources may lack authors' names or dates. In addition, they may lack page numbers (required in some citations). Here are APA's guidelines for handling sources without authors' names, dates, or page numbers.

Unknown author

If no author is named, mention the title of the document in a signal phrase or give the first word or two of the title in parentheses (see also item 6). (If an organization serves as the author, see item 7.)

> According to a BBC article, chimpanzees at sites in West Africa, Tanzania, and Uganda exhibit culture-specific patterns of behaviour when grooming one another ("Chimps," 1999).

Unknown date

When the date is unknown, APA recommends using the abbreviation "n.d." (for "no date").

Attempts to return sign-language-using apes to the wild have had mixed results (Smith, n.d.).

No page numbers

APA ordinarily requires page numbers for quotations, and it recommends them for summaries or paraphrases from long sources. When an electronic source lacks stable numbered pages, your citation should include—if possible—information that will help readers locate the particular passage being cited.

When an electronic document has numbered paragraphs, use the paragraph number preceded by the symbol ¶ or by the abbreviation "para.": (Hall, 2001, ¶ 5) *or* (Hall, 2001, para. 5). If neither a page nor a paragraph number is given and the document contains headings, cite the appropriate heading and indicate which paragraph under that heading you are referring to.

According to Kirby (1999), some critics have accused activists in the Great Ape Project of "exaggerating the supposed similarities of the apes [to humans] to stop their use in experiments" (Shared Path section, para. 6).

NOTE: Electronic files using portable document format (pdf) often have stable page numbers. For such sources, give the page number in the parenthetical citation.

■ **12. INDIRECT SOURCE** If you use a source that was cited in another source (a secondary source), name the original source in your signal phrase. List the secondary source in your reference list and include it in your parenthetical citation, preceded by the words "as cited in." In the following example, Booth is the secondary source.

Linguist Noam Chomsky has dismissed the studies on Kanzi with a flippant analogy: "To maintain that Kanzi has language ability is like saying a man can fly because he can jump in the air" (as cited in Booth, 1990, p. A3).

ON THE WEB

For electronic exercises on using APA documentation style, go to
www.dianahacker.com/writersref

and click on ▶ **Electronic Research Exercises**
▶ **E-ex APA 4–1 and APA 4–2**

APA-4b APA references

In APA style, the alphabetical list of works cited is titled "References." Following are models illustrating APA style for entries in the list of references. Observe all details: capitalization, punctuation, use of italics, and so on. For advice on preparing the list, see pages 406–07. For a sample reference list, see pages 416–17.

General guidelines for listing authors

Alphabetize entries in the list of references by authors' last names; if a work has no author, alphabetize it by its title. The first element of each entry is important because citations in the text of the paper refer to it and readers will be looking for it in the alphabetized list. The date of publication appears immediately after the first element of the entry.

NAME AND DATE CITED IN TEXT

Duncan (2001) has reported that . . .

BEGINNING OF ENTRY IN THE LIST OF REFERENCES

Duncan, B. (2001).

Items 1–4 show how to begin an entry for a work with a single author, multiple authors, an organization as author, and an unknown author. Items 5 and 6 show how to begin an entry when your list includes two or more works by the same author or two or more works by the same author in the same year.

What comes after the first element of your citation will depend on the kind of source you are citing (see items 7–31).

■ **1. SINGLE AUTHOR** Begin the entry with the author's last name, followed by a comma and the author's initial(s). Then give the date in parentheses.

Conran, G. (2001).

■ **2. MULTIPLE AUTHORS** List up to six authors by last names, followed by initials. Use an ampersand (&) instead of the word "and."

Walker, J. R., & Taylor, T. (1998).

Sloan, F. A., Stout, E. M., Whetten-Goldstein, K., & Liang, Lan. (2000).

Directory to APA reference list models

If there are more than six authors, list the first six and "et al." (meaning "and others") to indicate that there are others.

■ **3. ORGANIZATION AS AUTHOR** When the author is an organization, begin with the name of the organization.

American Psychiatric Association. (2000).

NOTE: If the organization is also the publisher, see item 28.

■ **4. UNKNOWN AUTHOR** Begin with the work's title. Titles of books are italicized. Titles of articles are neither italicized nor put in quotation marks. (For APA's rules on capitalization of titles, see p. 406.)

Oxford essential world atlas. (1996).

EMFs on the brain. (1995, January 21).

■ **5. TWO OR MORE WORKS BY THE SAME AUTHOR** Use the author's name for all entries. List the entries by year, the earliest first.

Schlechty, P. C. (1997).

Schlechty, P. C. (2001).

■ **6. TWO OR MORE WORKS BY THE SAME AUTHOR IN THE SAME YEAR** List the works alphabetically by title. In the parentheses, following the year, add "a," "b," and so on. Use these same letters when giving the year in the in-text citation. (See also p. 406.)

Kennedy, C. H. (2000a).

Kennedy, C. H. (2000b).

Articles in periodicals

This section shows how to prepare an entry for an article in a journal, a magazine, or a newspaper. In addition to consulting the models in this section, you may need to refer to items 1–6 (general guidelines for listing authors).

NOTE: For articles on consecutive pages, provide the range of pages at the end of the citation. When an article does not appear on consecutive pages, give all page numbers (see item 10 for an example).

■ **7. ARTICLE IN A JOURNAL PAGINATED BY VOLUME** Many professional journals continue page numbers throughout the year instead of beginning each issue with page 1; at the end of the year, the issues are collected in a volume. After the italicized title of the journal, give the volume number (also italicized), followed by the page numbers.

Morawski, J. (2000). Social psychology a century ago. *American Psychologist, 55,* 427-431.

■ **8. ARTICLE IN A JOURNAL PAGINATED BY ISSUE** When each issue of a journal begins with page 1, include the issue number in parentheses after the volume number. Italicize the volume number but not the issue number.

Scruton, R. (1996). The eclipse of listening. *The New Criterion, 15*(3), 5-13.

■ **9. ARTICLE IN A MAGAZINE** In addition to the year of publication, list the month and, for weekly magazines, the day. If there is a volume number, include it (italicized) after the title.

Raloff, J. (2001, May 12). Lead therapy won't help most kids. *Science News, 159,*
292.

■ **10. ARTICLE IN A NEWSPAPER** Begin with the name of the author,
followed by the exact date of publication. (If the author is unknown,
see also item 4.) Page numbers are introduced with "p." (or "pp.").

Haney, D. Q. (1998, February 20). Finding eats at mystery of appetite. *The
Oregonian,* pp. A1, A17.

■ **11. LETTER TO THE EDITOR** Letters to the editor appear in
journals, magazines, and newspapers. Follow the appropriate model
and insert the words "Letter to the editor" in brackets before the
name of the periodical.

Carter, R. (2000). New York, New York [Letter to the editor]. *Scientific American,*
238(1), 8.

■ **12. REVIEW** Reviews of books and other media appear in a variety of periodicals. Follow the appropriate model for the periodical.
For a review of a book, give the title of the review (if there is one),
followed by the words "Review of the book" and the title of the book
in brackets.

Gleick, E. (2000, December 14). The burdens of genius [Review of the book *The*
Last Samurai]. *Time, 156,* 171.

For a film review, write "Review of the motion picture," and for a TV
review, write "Review of the television program." Treat other media
in a similar way.

Books

In addition to consulting the items in this section, you may need to
turn to other models. See items 1–6 for general guidelines on listing
authors.

■ **13. BASIC FORMAT FOR A BOOK** Begin with the author's name,
followed by the date and the book's title. End with the place of publication and the name of the publisher.

Highmore, B. (2001). *Everyday life and cultural theory.* New York: Routledge.

■ **14. EDITORS** For a book with an editor but no author, begin
with the name of the editor (or editors) followed by the abbreviation
"Ed." (or "Eds.") in parentheses.

Duncan, G. J., & Brooks-Gunn, J. (Eds.). (1997). *Consequences of growing up poor.* New York: Russell Sage Foundation.

For a book with an author and an editor, begin with the author's name. Give the editor's name in parentheses after the title of the book, followed by the abbreviation "Ed." (or "Eds.").

Plath, S. (2000). *The unabridged journals* (K. V. Kukil, Ed.). New York: Anchor.

■ **15. TRANSLATION** After the title, name the translator, followed by the abbreviation "Trans.," in parentheses. Add the original date of the work's publication in parentheses at the end of the entry.

Singer, I. B. (1998). *Shadows on the Hudson* (J. Sherman, Trans.). New York: Farrar, Straus and Giroux. (Original work published 1957)

■ **16. EDITION OTHER THAN THE FIRST** Include the number of the edition in parentheses after the title.

Helfer, M. E., Keme, R. S., & Drugman, R. D. (1997). *The battered child* (5th ed.). Chicago: University of Chicago Press.

■ **17. ARTICLE OR CHAPTER IN AN EDITED BOOK** Begin with the author, year of publication, and title of the article or chapter. Then write "In" and give the editor's name, followed by "Ed." in parentheses; the title of the book; and the page numbers of the article or chapter in parentheses. End with the book's publication information.

Meskell, L. (2001). Archaeologies of identity. In I. Hodder (Ed.), *Archaeological theory today* (pp. 187-213). Cambridge, England: Polity Press.

■ **18. MULTIVOLUME WORK** Give the number of volumes after the title.

Wiener, P. (Ed.). (1973). *Dictionary of the history of ideas* (Vols. 1-4). New York: Scribner's.

Electronic sources

The following guidelines for electronic sources are based on the fifth edition of the *Publication Manual of the American Psychological Association* (2001). Any updates will be posted on the APA Web site, <http://www.apastyle.org>.

ON THE WEB

For future updates to APA style, go to the APA's Web site or to
www.dianahacker.com/writersref

and click on ▶ **Research and Documentation Online**
▶ **Documenting Sources (APA)**

■ **19. ARTICLE FROM AN ONLINE PERIODICAL** When citing online articles, follow the guidelines for printed articles (see items 7–12), giving whatever information is available in the online source. If the article also appears in a printed journal, a URL is not required; instead, include "Electronic version" in brackets after the title of the article.

Whitmeyer, J. M. (2000). Power through appointment [Electronic version].

Social Science Research 29(4), 535-555.

If there is no print version, include the date you accessed the source and the article's URL.

Ashe, D. D., & McCutcheon, L. E. (2001). Shyness, loneliness, and attitude

toward celebrities. *Current Research in Social Psychology, 6*(9). Retrieved

July 3, 2001, from http://www.uiowa.edu/~grpproc/crisp/crisp.6.9.htm

NOTE: When you have retrieved an article from a newspaper's searchable Web site, give the URL for the site, not for the exact source.

Cary, B. (2001, June 18). Mentors of the mind. *Los Angeles Times.* Retrieved July

5, 2001, from http://www.latimes.com

■ **20. ARTICLE FROM A DATABASE** Libraries pay for access to electronic databases such as *PsycINFO* and *JSTOR*, which are not otherwise available to the public. To cite an article from an electronic database, include the publication information from the source (see items 7–12). End the citation with your date of access, the name of the database, and the document number (if applicable).

Holliday, R. E., & Hayes, B. K. (2001, January). Dissociating automatic and

intentional processes in children's eyewitness memory. *Journal of*

Experimental Child Psychology, 75(1), 1-5. Retrieved February 21, 2001,

from Expanded Academic ASAP database (A59317972).

NOTE: Databases may be delivered in a variety of formats (via CD-ROM, university or library server, and the Web). You need not identify the specific format.

■ **21. NONPERIODICAL WEB DOCUMENT** To cite a nonperiodical Web document, such as a report, list as many of the following elements as are available.

> Author's name
>
> Date of publication (if there is no date, use "n.d.")
>
> Title of document (in italics)
>
> Date you accessed the source
>
> A URL that will take readers directly to the source

In the first model, the source has both an author and a date; in the second, the source lacks a date. If a source has no author, begin with the title and follow it with the date in parentheses.

Cain, A., & Burris, M. (1999, April). *Investigation of the use of mobile phones while driving*. Retrieved January 15, 2000, from http://www.cutr.eng.usf.edu/its/mobile_phone_text.htm

Archer, Z. (n.d.). *Exploring nonverbal communication*. Retrieved July 18, 2001, from http://zzyx.ucsc.edu/~archer

NOTE: If you retrieved the source from a university program's Web site, name the program in your retrieval statement.

Cosmides, L., & Tooby, J. (1997). *Evolutionary psychology: A primer*. Retrieved July 5, 2001, from the University of California, Santa Barbara, Center for Evolutionary Psychology Web site: http://www.psych.ucsb.edu/research/cep/primer.html

■ **22. CHAPTER OR SECTION IN A WEB DOCUMENT** Begin with the author, the year of publication, and the title of the chapter or section. Then write "In" and give the title of the document, followed by any identifying information in parentheses. End with your date of access and the URL for the chapter or section.

Heuer, R. J., Jr. (1999). Keeping an open mind. In *Psychology of intelligence analysis* (chap. 6). Retrieved July 7, 2001, from http://www.cia.gov/csi/books/19104/art9.html

■ **23.** E-MAIL   E-mail messages and other personal communications are not included in the list of references.

■ **24.** ONLINE POSTING   If an online posting cannot be retrieved (because the newsgroup or forum does not maintain archives), cite it as a personal communication in the text of your paper and do not include it in the list of references. If the posting can be retrieved from an archive, treat it as follows, giving as much information as is available.

Eaton, S. (2001, June 12). Online transactions [Msg 2]. Message posted to
    news://sci.psychology.psychotherapy.moderated

■ **25.** COMPUTER PROGRAM   Add the words "Computer software" in brackets after the title of the program.

Kaufmann, W. J., III, & Comins, N. F. (1998). Discovering the universe (Version
    4.1) [Computer software]. New York: Freeman.

Other sources

■ **26.** DISSERTATION ABSTRACT

Yoshida, Y. (2001). Essays in urban transportation (Doctoral dissertation, Boston
    College, 2001). *Dissertation Abstracts International, 62,* 7741A.

■ **27.** GOVERNMENT DOCUMENT

Industry Canada. (2002). *A guide to patents.* Ottawa: Canadian Intellectual
    Property Office.

■ **28.** REPORT FROM A PRIVATE ORGANIZATION   If the publisher is the author, give the word "Author" as the publisher. If the report has an author, begin with the author's name, and name the publisher at the end.

American Psychiatric Association. (2000). *Practice guidelines for the treatment of
    patients with eating disorders* (2nd ed.). Washington, DC: Author.

■ **29.** CONFERENCE PROCEEDINGS

Schnase, J. L., & Cunnius, E. L. (Eds.). (1995). *Proceedings of CSCL '95: The First
    International Conference on Computer Support for Collaborative Learning.*
    Mahwah, NJ: Erlbaum.

■ **30. MOTION PICTURE** To cite a motion picture (film, video, or DVD), list the director and the year of the picture's release. Give the title, followed by "Motion picture" in brackets, the country where it was made, and the name of the studio.

Soderbergh, S. (Director). (2000). *Traffic* [Motion picture]. United States: Gramercy Pictures.

■ **31. TELEVISION PROGRAM** To cite a television program, list the producer and the date it was aired. Give the title, followed by "Television broadcast" in brackets, the city, and the television network or service. For a television series, use the year in which the series was produced, and follow the title with "Television series" in brackets. For an episode in a series, list the writer and director and the year. After the episode title put "Television series episode" in brackets. Follow with information about the series.

Pratt, C. (Executive Producer). (2001, December 2). *Face the nation* [Television broadcast]. Washington, DC: CBS News.

Janows, J. (Executive Producer). (2000). *Culture shock* [Television series]. Boston: WGBH.

Loeterman, B. (Writer), & Gale, B. (Director). (2000). Real justice [Television series episode]. In M. Sullivan (Executive Producer), *Frontline*. Boston: WGBH.

APA-5

Manuscript format; sample paper

APA-5a Manuscript format

The American Psychological Association makes a number of recommendations for formatting a paper and preparing a list of references.

Formatting the paper

APA guidelines for formatting a paper are endorsed by many instructors in the social sciences.

MATERIALS AND TYPEFACE   Use good-quality letter-sized white paper. Avoid a typeface that is unusual or hard to read.

TITLE PAGE   The APA does not provide guidelines for preparing the title page of a college or university paper, but instructors may want you to include one. See page 408 for an example.

PAGE NUMBERS AND RUNNING HEAD   In the upper right-hand corner of each page, type a short version of your title, followed by five spaces and the page number. Number all pages, including the title page.

MARGINS AND LINE SPACING   Use margins of one inch (2.5 cm) on all sides of the page. Do not justify (align) the right margin. Double-space throughout the paper.

LONG QUOTATIONS   See page 389 for APA's guidelines for setting long quotations off from the text.

ABSTRACT   If your instructor requires one, include an abstract on its own page after the title page. Centre the word Abstract one inch (2.5 cm) from the top of the page.

An abstract is a 75-to-100-word paragraph that provides readers with a quick overview of your essay. It should express your main idea and your key points; it might also briefly suggest any implications or applications of the research you discuss in the paper.

HEADINGS   Although headings are not always necessary, their use is encouraged in the social sciences. For undergraduate papers, one level of heading will usually be sufficient.

In APA style, major headings are centred. Capitalize the first word of the heading, along with all words except articles, short prepositions, and coordinating conjunctions.

VISUALS   The APA classifies visuals as tables and figures (figures include graphs, charts, drawings, and photographs). Keep visuals as simple as possible. Label each table with an arabic numeral (Table 1, Table 2, and so on) and provide a clear title. The label and title should appear on separate lines above the table, flush left. Below the table, give its source in a note:

Note. From "Innovation Roles: From Souls of Fire to Devil's Advocates," by M. Meyer, 2000, *The Journal of Business Communication, 37,* p. 338.

For each figure, place a label and a caption below the figure, flush left. They need not appear on separate lines.

In the text of your paper, discuss the most significant features of each visual. Place the visuals as close as possible to the sentences that relate to them unless your instructor prefers them in an appendix.

Preparing the list of references

Begin your list of references on a new page at the end of the paper. Centre the title References about one inch (2.5 cm) from the top of the page. Double-space throughout. For a sample reference list, see pages 416–17.

INDENTING ENTRIES   APA recommends using a hanging indent: Type the first line of an entry flush left and indent any additional lines one-half inch (1.25 cm or five spaces), as shown in the list on pages 416–17.

ALPHABETIZING THE LIST   Alphabetize the reference list by the last names of the authors (or editors); when a work has no author or editor, alphabetize by the first word of the title other than *A, An,* or *The.*

If your list includes two or more works by the same author, arrange the entries by year, the earliest first. If your list includes two or more works by the same author in the same year, arrange them alphabetically by title. Add the letters "a," "b," and so on within the parentheses after the year. Use only the year for articles in journals: (2002a). Use the full date for articles in magazines and newspapers in the reference list: (2001a, July 7). Use only the year in the in-text citation.

AUTHORS' NAMES   Invert all authors' names and use initials instead of first names. With two or more authors, use an ampersand (&) before the last author's name. Separate the names with commas. Include names for the first six authors; if there are additional authors, end the list with "et al." (Latin for "and others").

TITLES OF BOOKS AND ARTICLES   Italicize the titles and subtitles of books; capitalize only the first word of the title and subtitle (and all proper nouns). Capitalize names of periodicals as you would capitalize them normally (see M3-c).

ABBREVIATIONS FOR PAGE NUMBERS   Abbreviations for "page" and "pages" ("p." and "pp.") are used before page numbers of newspaper articles and articles in edited books (see pp. 399 and 400) but not before page numbers of articles in magazines and journals (see pp. 398–99).

NOTE: The sample reference list (see pp. 416–17) shows how to type your list of references.

BREAKING A URL When a URL must be divided, break it after a slash or before a period. Do not insert a hyphen.

For information about the exact format of each entry in your list, consult the models on pages 396–404.

APA-5b Sample APA paper

Following is a research paper written by Karen Shaw, a student in a psychology class. Shaw's assignment was to write a "review of the literature" paper documented with APA-style citations and references.

In preparing her final manuscript, Shaw followed the APA guidelines. She did not include an abstract because her instructor did not require one.

ON THE WEB

For a downloadable version of Karen Shaw's paper, with marginal annotations, go to **www.dianahacker.com/writersref**

and click on ▶ **Model Papers**
　　　　　　　　　▶ **APA paper: Shaw**

Short title and
page number for
student papers.

Apes and Language   1

Full title, writer's
name, name and
section number of
course, instructor's
name, and date (all
centred).

Apes and Language:

A Review of the Literature

Karen Shaw

Psychology 110, Section 2

Professor Verdi

March 2, 2001

Apes and Language:

A Review of the Literature

Over the past 30 years, researchers have demonstrated that the

great apes (chimpanzees, gorillas, and orangutans) resemble humans

in language abilities more than had been thought possible. Just how

far that resemblance extends, however, has been a matter of some

controversy. Researchers agree that the apes have acquired fairly

large vocabularies in American Sign Language and in artificial lan-

guages, but they have drawn quite different conclusions in address-

ing the following questions:

    1. How spontaneously have apes used language?

    2. How creatively have apes used language?

    3. Can apes create sentences?

    4. What are the implications of the ape language studies?

This review of the literature on apes and language focuses on these

four questions.

How Spontaneously Have

Apes Used Language?

In an influential article, Terrace, Petitto, Sanders, and Bever

(1979) argued that the apes in language experiments were not using

language spontaneously but were merely imitating their trainers, re-

sponding to conscious or unconscious cues. Terrace and his col-

leagues at Columbia University had trained a chimpanzee, Nim, in

American Sign Language, so their skepticism about the apes' abilities

received much attention. In fact, funding for ape language research

Full title, centred.

The writer sets up her organization in her thesis.

Headings, centred, help readers follow the organization.

A signal phrase names all four authors and gives date in parentheses.

was sharply reduced following publication of their 1979 article "Can

an Ape Create a Sentence?"

In retrospect, the conclusions of Terrace et al. seem to have

been premature. Although some early ape language studies had not

been rigorously controlled to eliminate cuing, even as early as the

1970s R. A. Gardner and B. T. Gardner were conducting double-blind

experiments that prevented any possibility of cuing (Fouts, 1997,

p. 99). Since 1979, researchers have diligently guarded against

cuing.

Perhaps the best evidence that apes are not merely responding

to cues is that they have signed to one another spontaneously, with-

out trainers present. Like many of the apes studied, gorillas Koko

and Michael have been observed signing to one another (Patterson

& Linden, 1981). At Central Washington University the baby chim-

panzee Loulis, placed in the care of the signing chimpanzee Washoe,

mastered nearly fifty signs in American Sign Language without help

from humans. "Interestingly," wrote researcher Fouts (1997), "Loulis

did *not* pick up any of the seven signs that we [humans] used around

him. He learned only from Washoe and [another chimp] Ally"

(p. 244).

The extent to which chimpanzees spontaneously use language

may depend on their training. Terrace trained Nim using the behav-

iorist technique of operant conditioning, so it is not surprising that

many of Nim's signs were cued. Many other researchers have used a

conversational approach that parallels the process by which human

Because the author (Fouts) is not named in the signal phrase, his name and the date appear in parentheses, along with the page number.

An ampersand links the names of two authors in parentheses.

Brackets indicate words not in original source.

A page number is required for a quotation.

children acquire language. In an experimental study, O'Sullivan and
Yeager (1989) contrasted the two techniques, using Terrace's Nim as
their subject. They found that Nim's use of language was significantly more spontaneous under conversational conditions.

How Creatively Have

Apes Used Language?

There is considerable evidence that apes have invented
creative names. One of the earliest and most controversial examples
involved the Gardners' chimpanzee Washoe. Washoe, who knew signs
for "water" and "bird," once signed "water bird" when in the presence of a swan. Terrace et al. (1979) suggested that there was "no
basis for concluding that Washoe was characterizing the swan as a
'bird that inhabits water.'" Washoe may simply have been "identifying correctly a body of water and a bird, in that order" (p. 895).

Other examples are not so easily explained away. The bonobo
Kanzi has requested particular films by combining symbols on a computer in a creative way. For instance, to ask for *Quest for Fire,* a film
about early primates discovering fire, Kanzi began to use symbols for
"campfire" and "TV" (Eckholm, 1985). The gorilla Koko, who learned
American Sign Language, has a long list of creative names to her
credit: "elephant baby" to describe a Pinocchio doll, "finger
bracelet" to describe a ring, "bottle match" to describe a cigarette
lighter, and so on (Patterson & Linden, 1981, p. 146). If Terrace's
analysis of the "water bird" example is applied to the examples
just mentioned, it does not hold. Surely Koko did not first see an

The word "and"
links the names of
two authors in the
signal phrase.

When this article
was first cited, all
four authors were
named. In subse-
quent citations of
a work with three
to five authors,
"et al." is used after
the first author's
name.

The writer inter-
prets the evidence;
she doesn't just
report it.

elephant and then a baby before signing "elephant baby"--or a
bottle and a match before signing "bottle match."

Can Apes Create Sentences?

The early ape language studies offered little proof that apes
could combine symbols into grammatically ordered sentences. Apes
strung together various signs, but the sequences were often random
and repetitious. Nim's series of sixteen signs is a case in point: "give
orange me give eat orange me eat orange give me eat orange give me
you" (Terrace et al., 1979, p. 895).

More recent studies with bonobos at the Language Research
Center in Atlanta have broken new ground. Kanzi, a bonobo trained
by Savage-Rumbaugh, seems to understand simple grammatical rules
about word order. For instance, Kanzi learned that in two-word utter-
ances action precedes object, an ordering also used by human children at the two-word stage. In a major article reporting on their
research, Greenfield and Savage-Rumbaugh (1990) wrote that Kanzi
rarely "repeated himself or formed combinations that were semantically unrelated" (p. 556).

More important, Kanzi began on his own to create certain
patterns that may not exist in English but can be found among deaf
children and in other human languages. For example, Kanzi used his
own rules when combining action symbols. Symbols that involved an
invitation to play, such as "chase," would appear first; symbols that
indicated what was to be done during play ("hide") would appear
second. Kanzi also created his own rules when combining gestures

The writer draws
attention to an im-
portant article.

Apes and Language   6

and symbols. He would use the symbol first and then gesture, a practice often followed by young deaf children (Greenfield & Savage-
Rumbaugh, 1990, p. 560).

In a later study, Kanzi's abilities to understand spoken language were shown to be similar to those of a 2-1/2-year-old human,
Alia. Rumbaugh (1995) reported that "Kanzi's comprehension of over
600 novel sentences of request was very comparable to Alia's; both
complied with the requests without assistance on approximately 70%
of the sentences" (p. 722). A recent monograph provided examples of
the kinds of sentences both Kanzi and Alia were able to understand:

> For example, the word *ball* occurred in 76 different sentences,
> including such different requests as "Put the leaves in your
> ball," "Show me the ball that's on TV," "Vacuum your ball," and
> "Go do ball slapping with Liz." Overall, 144 different content
> words, many of which were presented in ways that required syn-
> tactic parsing for a proper response (such as "Knife your ball"
> vs. "Put the knife in the hat"), were utilized in the study.
> (Savage-Rumbaugh et al., 2000, pp. 101-102)

The researchers concluded that neither Kanzi nor Alia could have
demonstrated understanding of such requests without comprehending
syntactical relationships among the words in a sentence.

What Are the Implications of the Ape Language Studies?

Kanzi's linguistic abilities are so impressive that they may help
us understand how humans came to acquire language. Pointing out

The writer gives a
page number for
this summary
because the article
is long.

A quotation longer
than 40 words is
set off from the
text. Quotation
marks are not
used.

that 99% of our genetic material is held in common with the chimpanzees, Greenfield and Savage-Rumbaugh (1990) have suggested
that something of the "evolutionary root of human language" can be
found in the "linguistic abilities of the great apes" (p. 540). Noting
that apes' brains are similar to those of our human ancestors, Leakey
and Lewin (1992) argued that in ape brains "the cognitive foundations on which human language could be built are already present"
(p. 244).

The suggestion that there is a continuity in the linguistic abilities of apes and humans has created much controversy. Linguist
Noam Chomsky has strongly asserted that language is a unique
human characteristic (Booth, 1990). Terrace has continued to be
skeptical of the claims made for the apes, as have Petitto and Bever,
coauthors of the 1979 article that caused such skepticism earlier
(Gibbons, 1991).

Recently, neurobiologists have made discoveries that may
cause even the skeptics to take notice. Ongoing studies at the Yerkes
Primate Research Center have revealed remarkable similarities in the
brains of chimpanzees and humans. Through brain scans of live
chimpanzees, researchers have found that, as with humans, "the
language-controlling PT [*planum temporale*] is larger on the left side
of the chimps' brain than on the right. But it is not lateralized in
monkeys, which are less closely related to humans than apes are"
(Begley, 1998, p. 57).

The writer
presents a bal-
anced view of
the philosophical
controversy.

Apes and Language   8

Although the ape language studies continue to generate

controversy, researchers have shown over the past 30 years that the

gap between the linguistic abilities of apes and humans is far less

dramatic than was once believed.

The tone of the
conclusion is
objective.

List of references
begins on a new
page. Heading is
centred.

List is alphabetized
by authors' last
names.

The first line of an
entry is at the left
margin; subse-
quent lines indent
½″ (1.25 cm or five
spaces).

Double-spacing is
used throughout.

References

Begley, S. (1998, January 19). Aping language. *Newsweek, 131,*
56-58.

Booth, W. (1990, October 29). Monkeying with language: Is chimp
using words or merely aping handlers? *The Washington Post,*
p. A3.

Eckholm, E. (1985, June 25). Kanzi the chimp: A life in science.
The New York Times, pp. C1, C3.

Fouts, R. (1997). *Next of kin: What chimpanzees have taught me
about who we are.* New York: William Morrow.

Gibbons, A. (1991). Déjà vu all over again: Chimp-language wars.
Science, 251, 1561-1562.

Greenfield, P. M., & Savage-Rumbaugh, E. S. (1990). Grammatical
combination in *Pan paniscus:* Processes of learning and inven-
tion in the evolution and development of language. In S. T.
Parker & K. R. Gibson (Eds.), *"Language" and intelligence in
monkeys and apes: Comparative developmental perspectives*
(pp. 540-578). Cambridge: Cambridge University Press.

Leakey, R., & Lewin, R. (1992). *Origins reconsidered: In search of
what makes us human.* New York: Doubleday.

O'Sullivan, C., & Yeager, C. P. (1989). Communicative context and
linguistic competence: The effect of social setting on a chimpanzee's conversational skill. In R. A. Gardner, B. T. Gardner,
& T. E. Van Cantfort (Eds.), *Teaching sign language to chimpanzees* (pp. 269-279). Albany: SUNY Press.

Patterson, F., & Linden, E. (1981). *The education of Koko.* New York:

Holt, Rinehart & Winston.

Rumbaugh, D. (1995). Primate language and cognition: Common

ground. *Social Research, 62,* 711-730.

Savage-Rumbaugh, E. S., Murphy, J. S., Sevcik, R. A., Brakke, K. E.,

Williams, S. L., Rumbaugh, D. M., et al. (2000). *Language*

comprehension in ape and child: Monograph. Atlanta, GA:

Language Research Center. Retrieved January 6, 2000, from the

Language Research Center Web site: http://www.gsu.edu/

~wwwlrc/monograph.html

Terrace, H. S., Petitto, L. A., Sanders, R. J., & Bever, T. G. (1979).

Can an ape create a sentence? *Science, 206,* 891-902.

CMS (*CHICAGO*) PAPERS

Most assignments in history and other humanities classes are based to some extent on reading. At times you will be asked to respond to one or two readings, such as essays or historical documents. At other times you may be asked to write a research paper that draws on a wide variety of sources.

Most history instructors and some humanities instructors require you to document sources with footnotes or endnotes based on *The Chicago Manual of Style* (CMS), 15th ed. (Chicago: U of Chicago P, 2003). (See CMS-4.) When you write a paper using sources, you face three main challenges in addition to documenting your sources: (1) supporting a thesis, (2) avoiding plagiarism, and (3) integrating quotations and other source material.

CMS-1

Supporting a thesis

Most assignments ask you to form a thesis, or main idea, and to support that thesis with well-organized evidence.

CMS-1a Form a thesis.

A thesis is a one-sentence (or occasionally a two-sentence) statement of your central idea. Usually your thesis will appear at the end of the first paragraph (as in the example on p. 440), but if you need to provide readers with considerable background information, you may place it in the second paragraph.

The thesis of your paper will be a reasoned answer to the central research question you pose, as in the following example.

RESEARCH QUESTION

To what extent was Confederate Major General Nathan Bedford Forrest responsible for the massacre of Union troops at Fort Pillow?

POSSIBLE THESIS

Although we will never know whether Nathan Bedford Forrest directly ordered the massacre of Union troops at Fort Pillow, evidence suggests that he was responsible for it.

Notice that the thesis expresses a view on a debatable issue—an issue about which intelligent, well-meaning people might disagree. The writer's job is to convince such readers that this view is worth taking seriously.

ON THE WEB

For an electronic exercise on thesis statements for a CMS research paper, go to **www.dianahacker.com/writersref**

and click on ▶ **Electronic Research Exercises**
▶ **E-ex CMS 1–1**

CMS-1b Organize your evidence.

The body of your paper will consist of evidence in support of your thesis. Instead of getting tangled up in a complex, formal outline, sketch an informal plan that organizes your evidence in bold strokes. The student who wrote about Fort Pillow used a simple list of questions as the blueprint for his paper. In the paper itself, these became headings that helped readers follow the writer's line of argument.

What happened at Fort Pillow?

Did Forrest order the massacre?

Can Forrest be held responsible for the massacre?

CMS-2

Avoiding plagiarism

Your research paper is a collaboration between you and your sources. To be fair and ethical, you must acknowledge your debt to the writers of those sources. If you don't, you are guilty of plagiarism, a serious academic offense.

Three different acts are considered plagiarism: (1) failing to cite quotations and borrowed ideas, (2) failing to enclose borrowed language in quotation marks, and (3) failing to put summaries and paraphrases in your own words.

ON THE WEB

For an electronic exercise on avoiding plagiarism in CMS papers,
go to **www.dianahacker.com/writersref**

and click on ▶ **Electronic Research Exercises**
▶ **E-ex CMS 2–1**

CMS-2a Cite quotations and borrowed ideas.

You must of course cite all direct quotations. You must also cite any
ideas borrowed from a source: summaries and paraphrases, statistics and other specific facts, and visuals such as cartoons, graphs, or
diagrams.

The only exception is common knowledge—general information that your readers may know or could easily locate in any number of reference sources. For example, the approximate population
of Canada is common knowledge among sociologists and economists, and historians are familiar with facts such as the date of the
British North America Act. As a rule, when you have seen certain
general information repeatedly in your reading, you don't need to
cite it. However, when information has appeared in only a few
sources, when it is highly specific (as with statistics), or when it is
controversial, you should cite it.

CMS citations consist of numbered notes in the text of the
paper that refer readers to notes with corresponding numbers
either at the foot of the page (footnotes) or at the end of the paper
(endnotes).

TEXT

Governor John Andrew was not allowed to recruit black soldiers from out of
state. "Ostensibly," writes Peter Burchard, "no recruiting was done outside
Massachusetts, but it was an open secret that Andrew's agents were working
far and wide."[1]

NOTE

1. Peter Burchard, *One Gallant Rush: Robert Gould Shaw and His Brave
Black Regiment* (New York: St. Martin's, 1965), 85.

For detailed advice on using CMS notes, see CMS-4. When you
use footnotes or endnotes, you will usually need to provide a bibliography as well (see CMS-4b).

CMS-2b Enclose borrowed language in quotation marks.

To show readers that you are using a source's exact phrases or sentences, you must enclose them in quotation marks. To omit the quotation marks is to claim — falsely — that the language is your own. Such an omission is plagiarism even if you have cited the source.

ORIGINAL SOURCE

For many Southerners it was psychologically impossible to see a black man bearing arms as anything but an incipient slave uprising complete with arson, murder, pillage, and rapine.
— Dudley Taylor Cornish, *The Sable Arm: Negro Troops in the Union Army, 1861–1865,* p. 158

PLAGIARISM

According to Civil War historian Dudley Taylor Cornish, for many Southerners it was psychologically impossible to see a black man bearing arms as anything but an incipient slave uprising complete with arson, murder, pillage, and rapine.[2]

BORROWED LANGUAGE IN QUOTATION MARKS

According to Civil War historian Dudley Taylor Cornish, "For many Southerners it was psychologically impossible to see a black man bearing arms as anything but an incipient slave uprising complete with arson, murder, pillage, and rapine."[2]

NOTE: When quoted sentences are set off from the text by indenting, quotation marks are not needed (see pp. 425–26).

CMS-2c Put summaries and paraphrases in your own words.

A summary condenses information; a paraphrase reports information in about the same number of words. When you summarize or paraphrase, you must restate the source's meaning using your own language. In the following example, the paraphrase is plagiarized — even though the source is cited — because too much of its language is borrowed from the source without quotation marks. The underlined phrases have been copied word-for-word. In addition, the writer has closely followed the sentence structure of the original source, merely plugging in some synonyms (such as *fifty percent* for *half* and *savage hatred* for *fierce, bitter animosity*).

ORIGINAL SOURCE

Half of the force holding Fort Pillow were Negroes, former slaves now enrolled in the Union Army. Toward them Forrest's troops had the fierce, bitter animosity of men who had been educated to regard the colored race as inferior and who for the first time had encountered that race armed and fighting against white men. The sight enraged and perhaps terrified many of the Confederates and aroused in them the ugly spirit of a lynching mob.

—Albert Castel, "The Fort Pillow Massacre," pp. 46–47

PLAGIARISM: UNACCEPTABLE BORROWING

Albert Castel suggests that much of the brutality at Fort Pillow can be traced to racial attitudes. Fifty percent of the troops holding Fort Pillow were Negroes, former slaves who had joined the Union Army. Toward them Forrest's soldiers displayed the savage hatred of men who had been taught the inferiority of blacks and who for the first time had confronted them armed and fighting against white men. The vision angered and perhaps frightened the Confederates and aroused in them the ugly spirit of a lynching mob.[3]

To avoid plagiarizing an author's language, set the source aside, write from memory, and consult the source later to check for accuracy. This strategy prevents you from being captivated by the words on the page.

ACCEPTABLE PARAPHRASE

Albert Castel suggests that much of the brutality at Fort Pillow can be traced to racial attitudes. Nearly half of the Union troops were blacks, men whom the Confederates had been raised to consider their inferiors. The shock and perhaps fear of facing armed ex-slaves in battle for the first time may well have unleashed the fury that led to the massacre.[3]

CMS-3

Integrating sources

By carefully integrating quotations and other source material into your own text, you help readers understand whose views they are hearing—yours or those of your sources. In addition, you show readers where cited material begins (your note shows where it ends).

NOTE: As a rule, use the present tense or present perfect tense in phrases that introduce quotations or other source materials: *Foote points out that* or *Foote has pointed out that* (not *Foote pointed out that*). If you have good reason to emphasize that the author's language or opinion was articulated in the past, however, the past tense is acceptable.

The first time you mention an author, use the full name: *Shelby Foote argues. . . .* When you refer to the author again, you may use the last name only: *Foote raises an important question.*

ON THE WEB

For an electronic exercise on integrating quotations in CMS papers, go to **www.dianahacker.com/writersref**

and click on ▶ **Electronic Research Exercises**
　　　　　　　　▶ **E-ex CMS 3–1**

CMS-3a Integrate quotations as smoothly as possible.

Readers should be able to move from your own words to the words you quote from a source without feeling a jolt.

Using signal phrases

Avoid dropping quotations into the text without warning. Instead, provide clear signal phrases, usually including the author's name, to prepare readers for the source.

DROPPED QUOTATION

Those testifying on the Union and Confederate sides recalled events at Fort Pillow quite differently. Unionists claimed that their troops had abandoned their arms and were in full retreat. "The Confederates, however, all agreed that the Union troops retreated to the river with arms in their hands."[4]

QUOTATION WITH SIGNAL PHRASE

Those testifying on the Union and Confederate sides recalled events at Fort Pillow quite differently. Unionists claimed that their troops had abandoned their arms and were in full retreat. "The Confederates, however," writes historian Albert Castel, "all agreed that the Union troops retreated to the river with arms in their hands."[4]

Varying signal phrases in CMS papers

MODEL SIGNAL PHRASES

In the words of historian James M. McPherson, ". . ."

As Dudley Taylor Cornish has argued, ". . ."

In a letter to his wife, a Confederate soldier who witnessed the massacre wrote that ". . ."

". . . ," claims Benjamin Quarles.

". . . ," writes Albert Castel, ". . ."

Shelby Foote offers an intriguing interpretation of these events: ". . ."

VERBS IN SIGNAL PHRASES

admits	compares	insists	rejects
agrees	confirms	notes	reports
argues	contends	observes	responds
asserts	declares	points out	suggests
believes	denies	reasons	thinks
claims	emphasizes	refutes	writes

To avoid monotony, try to vary both the language and the placement of your signal phrases. The models in the chart above suggest a range of possibilities.

When the signal phrase includes a verb, choose one that is appropriate in the context. Is your source arguing a point, making an observation, reporting a fact, refuting an argument, or suggesting an interpretation? By choosing an appropriate verb, you can make your source's stance clear. See the chart above for a list of verbs commonly used in signal phrases.

Using the ellipsis mark

To condense a quoted passage, you can use the ellipsis mark (three spaced periods) to indicate that you have omitted words. The sentence that remains must be grammatically complete.

> Union surgeon Fitch's testimony that all women and children had been evacuated from Fort Pillow before the attack conflicts with Forrest's report: "We captured . . . about 40 negro women and children."[5]

The writer has omitted several words not relevant to the issue at hand: *164 Federals, 75 negro troops, and.*

When you want to omit a full sentence or more, use a period before the three ellipsis dots. For instance, see the example at the top of page 426.

Ordinarily, do not use the ellipsis mark at the beginning or at the end of a quotation. Readers will understand that the quoted material is taken from a longer passage.

Using brackets

Brackets allow you to insert words of your own into quoted material, perhaps to explain a confusing reference or to keep a sentence grammatical in your context.

> According to Albert Castel, "It can be reasonably argued that he [Forrest] was justified in believing that the approaching steamships intended to aid the garrison [at Fort Pillow]."[6]

NOTE: Use [*sic*] to indicate that an error in a quoted sentence appears in the original source. (An example appears at the top of p. 426.) However, if a source is filled with errors, as is the case with many historical documents, this use of [*sic*] can become distracting and is best avoided.

Setting off long quotations

The Chicago Manual of Style allows some leeway in deciding whether to set off a quotation or run it into your text. For emphasis you may want to set off a quotation of more than four or five lines of text; almost certainly you should set off quotations of eight lines or more. To set off a quotation, indent it one-half inch (1.25 cm or five spaces) from the left margin.

Long quotations should be introduced by an informative sentence, usually followed by a colon. Quotation marks are unnecessary because the indented format tells readers that the words are taken word-for-word from the source.

> In a letter home, Confederate officer Achilles V. Clark recounted what happened at Fort Pillow:
>
> > Words cannot describe the scene. The poor deluded negroes would run up to our men fall upon their knees and with uplifted hands scream for mercy but they were ordered to their feet and then shot down. The

whitte [*sic*] men fared but little better. . . . I with several others tried to stop the butchering and at one time had partially succeeded, but Gen. Forrest ordered them shot down like dogs, and the carnage continued.[7]

CMS-3b Integrate summaries and paraphrases.

Summaries and paraphrases are written in your own words. As with quotations, you should introduce most summaries and paraphrases of a source with a signal phrase that mentions the author and places the material in context. Readers will then understand that everything between the signal phrase and the numbered note summarizes or paraphrases the cited source.

Without the signal phrase (underlined) in the following example, readers might think that only the last sentence is being cited, when in fact the whole paragraph is based on the source.

According to Kenneth Davis, official Confederate policy was that black soldiers were to be treated as runaway slaves; in addition, the Confederate Congress decreed that white Union officers commanding black troops be killed. Confederate Lieutenant General Kirby Smith of Mississippi boldly announced that he would kill all captured black troops. Smith's policy never met with strong opposition from the Richmond government.[8]

When the context makes clear where the cited material begins, however, you may omit the signal phrase.

CMS-3c Integrate statistics and other facts.

When you are citing a statistic or other specific fact, a signal phrase is often not necessary. In most cases, readers will understand that the citation refers to the statistic or fact (not the whole paragraph).

Of the 295 white troops garrisoned at Fort Pillow, 168 were taken prisoner. Black troops fared much worse, with only 58 of 262 men being taken into custody and most of the rest presumably killed or badly wounded.[9]

There is nothing wrong, however, with using a signal phrase.

Shelby Foote notes that of the 295 white troops garrisoned at Fort Pillow, 168 were taken prisoner but that black troops fared much worse, with only

58 of 262 men being taken into custody and most of the rest presumably killed or badly wounded.[9]

CMS-4

Documenting sources

Professors in history and some humanities courses often require footnotes or endnotes based on *The Chicago Manual of Style*. When you use CMS notes, you will usually be asked to include a bibliography at the end of your paper (see CMS-4b).

TEXT

A Union soldier, Jacob Thomas, claimed to have seen Forrest order the killing, but when asked to describe the six-foot-two general, he called him "a little bit of a man."[10]

FOOTNOTE OR ENDNOTE

10. Brian Steel Wills, *A Battle from the Start: The Life of Nathan Bedford Forrest* (New York: HarperCollins, 1992), 187.

BIBLIOGRAPHY ENTRY

Wills, Brian Steel. *A Battle from the Start: The Life of Nathan Bedford Forrest.* New York: HarperCollins, 1992.

CMS-4a Give a full note for a first reference to a source; abbreviate notes for subsequent references.

The first time you cite a source, the note should include publication information for that work as well as the page number on which the passage being cited may be found.

1. Peter Burchard, *One Gallant Rush: Robert Gould Shaw and His Brave Black Regiment* (New York: St. Martin's, 1965), 85.

For subsequent references to a source you have already cited, give only the author's last name, a short form of the title, and the page or pages cited. A short form of the title of a book is italicized; a short form of the title of an article is put in quotation marks.

8. Burchard, *One Gallant Rush,* 31.

When you have two consecutive notes from the same source, you may use "Ibid." and the page number for the second note. Use "Ibid." alone if the page number is the same.

9. Ibid., 61.

ON THE WEB

For electronic exercises on using the CMS documentation system, go to **www.dianahacker.com/writersref**

and click on ▶ **Electronic Research Exercises**
▶ **E-ex CMS 4–1 and CMS 4–2**

CMS-4b   Include a bibliography if one is required.

A bibliography, which appears at the end of your paper, lists every work you have cited in your notes; in addition, it may include works that you consulted but did not cite. For advice on constructing the list, see page 438. A sample bibliography appears on page 443.

CMS-4c   Note and bibliography models

The following models are consistent with guidelines set forth in *The Chicago Manual of Style,* 15th ed. For each type of source, a model note appears first, followed by a model bibliography entry. The model note shows the format you should use when citing a source for the first time. For subsequent citations of a source, use shortened notes (as described in CMS-4a).

Directory to CMS note and bibliography models

BOOKS
1. Basic format for a book, 429
2. Two or three authors, 429
3. Four or more authors, 429
4. Unknown author, 430
5. Edited work without an author, 430
6. Edited work with an author, 430
7. Translated work, 430
8. Edition other than the first, 430
9. Volume in a multivolume work, 430

Books

1. BASIC FORMAT FOR A BOOK

1. William H. Rehnquist, *The Supreme Court: A History* (New York: Knopf, 2001), 204.

Rehnquist, William H. *The Supreme Court: A History.* New York: Knopf, 2001.

2. TWO OR THREE AUTHORS

2. Michael D. Coe and Mark Van Stone, *Reading the Maya Glyphs* (London: Thames & Hudson, 2002), 129-30.

Coe, Michael D., and Mark Van Stone. *Reading the Maya Glyphs.* London: Thames & Hudson, 2002.

3. FOUR OR MORE AUTHORS

3. Lynn Hunt and others, *The Making of the West: Peoples and Cultures* (Boston: Bedford/St. Martin's, 2001), 541.

Hunt, Lynn, Thomas R. Martin, Barbara H. Rosenwein, R. Po-chia Hsia, and
Bonnie G. Smith. *The Making of the West: Peoples and Cultures.* Boston:
Bedford/St. Martin's, 2001.

■ **4.** UNKNOWN AUTHOR

4. *The Men's League Handbook on Women's Suffrage* (London, 1912), 23.

The Men's League Handbook on Women's Suffrage. London, 1912.

■ **5.** EDITED WORK WITHOUT AN AUTHOR

5. Jack Beatty, ed., *Colossus: How the Corporation Changed America* (New
York: Broadway Books, 2001), 127.

Beatty, Jack, ed. *Colossus: How the Corporation Changed America.* New York:
Broadway Books, 2001.

■ **6.** EDITED WORK WITH AN AUTHOR

6. Ted Poston, *A First Draft of History,* ed. Kathleen A. Hauke (Athens:
University of Georgia Press, 2000), 46.

Poston, Ted. *A First Draft of History.* Edited by Kathleen A. Hauke. Athens:
University of Georgia Press, 2000.

■ **7.** TRANSLATED WORK

7. Sergei Nikolaevich Bulgakov, *Philosophy of Economy: The World as
Household,* trans. Catherine Evtuhov (New Haven: Yale University Press, 2000),
167.

Bulgakov, Sergei Nikolaevich. *Philosophy of Economy: The World as Household.*
Translated by Catherine Evtuhov. New Haven: Yale University Press, 2000.

■ **8.** EDITION OTHER THAN THE FIRST

8. Andrew F. Rolle, *California: A History,* 5th ed. (Wheeling, IL: Harlan
Davidson, 1998), 243.

Rolle, Andrew F. *California: A History.* 5th ed. Wheeling, IL: Harlan Davidson, 1998.

■ **9.** VOLUME IN A MULTIVOLUME WORK

9. James M. McPherson, *Ordeal by Fire,* vol. 2, *The Civil War* (New York:
McGraw-Hill, 1993), 205.

McPherson, James M. *Ordeal by Fire.* Vol. 2, *The Civil War.* New York: McGraw-Hill, 1993.

■ **10.** WORK IN AN ANTHOLOGY

10. Zora Neale Hurston, "From *Dust Tracks on a Road,*" in *The Norton Book of American Autobiography,* ed. Jay Parini (New York: Norton, 1999), 336.

Hurston, Zora Neale. "From *Dust Tracks on a Road.*" In *The Norton Book of American Autobiography,* edited by Jay Parini, 333-43. New York: Norton, 1999.

■ **11.** LETTER IN A PUBLISHED COLLECTION

11. Thomas Gainsborough to Elizabeth Rasse, 1753, in *The Letters of Thomas Gainsborough,* ed. John Hayes (New Haven: Yale University Press, 2001), 5.

Gainsborough, Thomas. Letter to Elizabeth Rasse, 1753. In *The Letters of Thomas Gainsborough,* edited by John Hayes, 5. New Haven: Yale University Press, 2001.

■ **12.** WORK IN A SERIES

12. R. Keith Schoppa, *The Columbia Guide to Modern Chinese History,* Columbia Guides to Asian History (New York: Columbia University Press, 2000), 256-58.

Schoppa, R. Keith. *The Columbia Guide to Modern Chinese History.* Columbia Guides to Asian History. New York: Columbia University Press, 2000.

■ **13.** ENCYCLOPEDIA OR DICTIONARY ENTRY

13. *Encyclopaedia Britannica,* 15th ed., s.v. "Monroe Doctrine."

NOTE: The abbreviation "s.v." is for the Latin *sub verbo* ("under the word").

Reference works are usually not included in the bibliography.

■ **14.** SACRED TEXT

14. Matt. 20.4-9 (Revised Standard Version).

References to sacred texts are usually not included in the bibliography.

Articles in periodicals

For articles in periodicals, a footnote or endnote should cite an exact page number. In the bibliography entry, include the page range for the entire article.

NOTE: If you accessed an article through an online database such as *ProQuest,* see also item 24.

■ **15.** ARTICLE IN A JOURNAL PAGINATED BY VOLUME

15. Virginia Guedea, "The Process of Mexican Independence," *American Historical Review* 105, no. 1 (2000): 120.

Guedea, Virginia. "The Process of Mexican Independence." *American Historical Review* 105, no. 1 (2000): 116-31.

■ **16.** ARTICLE IN A JOURNAL PAGINATED BY ISSUE

16. Jonathan Zimmerman, "Ethnicity and the History Wars in the 1920s," *Journal of American History* 87, no. 1 (2000): 101.

Zimmerman, Jonathan. "Ethnicity and the History Wars in the 1920s." *Journal of American History* 87, no. 1 (2000): 92-111.

■ **17.** ARTICLE IN A MAGAZINE

17. Joy Williams, "One Acre," *Harper's,* February 2001, 62.

Williams, Joy. "One Acre." *Harper's,* February 2001, 59-65.

■ **18.** ARTICLE IN A NEWSPAPER

18. Dan Barry, "A Mill Closes, and a Hamlet Fades to Black," *New York Times,* February 16, 2001, sec. A.

Barry, Dan. "A Mill Closes, and a Hamlet Fades to Black." *New York Times,* February 16, 2001, sec. A.

■ **19.** UNSIGNED ARTICLE

19. *Boston Globe,* "Renewable Energy Rules," August 11, 2003, sec. A.

Boston Globe. "Renewable Energy Rules." August 11, 2003, sec. A.

■ **20. BOOK REVIEW**

20. Nancy Gabin, review of *The Other Feminists: Activists in the Liberal Establishment,* by Susan M. Hartman, *Journal of Women's History* 12, no. 3 (2000): 230.

Gabin, Nancy. Review of *The Other Feminists: Activists in the Liberal Establishment,* by Susan M. Hartman. *Journal of Women's History* 12, no. 3 (2000): 227-34.

Electronic sources

■ **21. WEB SITE** Include as much of the following information as is available: author, title of the site, sponsor of the site, and the site's URL. When no author is named, treat the sponsor as the author.

21. Kevin Rayburn, *The 1920s,* http://www.louisville.edu/~kprayb01/1920s.html.

Rayburn, Kevin. *The 1920s.* http://www.louisville.edu/~kprayb01/1920s.html.

■ **22. SHORT DOCUMENT FROM A WEB SITE** Short works are those that appear in quotation marks: articles and other documents that are not book length. (For online books, see item 23.)

When citing a short work, include as many of the following elements as are available: author's name, title of the short work, title of the site, sponsor of the site, and the URL. Many Web documents are not marked with page numbers; when possible, give the text division instead. In the following example, "Origins and Inspiration" is a heading breaking up the text of the article being cited.

With author

22. Sheila Connor, "Historical Background," *Garden and Forest,* Library of Congress, http://lcweb.loc.gov/preserv/prd/gardfor/historygf.html, Origins and Inspiration.

Connor, Sheila. "Historical Background." *Garden and Forest.* Library of Congress. http://lcweb.loc.gov/preserv/prd/gardfor/historygf.html.

Author unknown

22. PBS Online, "Media Giants," *Frontline: The Merchants of Cool,* http://www.pbs.org/wgbh/pages/frontline/shows/cool/giants.

PBS Online. "Media Giants." *Frontline: The Merchants of Cool.* http://www.pbs.org/wgbh/pages/frontline/shows/cool/giants.

■ **23. ONLINE BOOK** When a book or a book-length work is posted on the Web, give as much publication information as is available, followed by the URL.

23. Heinz Kramer, *A Changing Turkey: The Challenge to Europe and the United States* (Washington, DC: Brookings Press, 2000), 85, http://brookings.nap.edu/books/0815750234/html/index.html.

Kramer, Heinz. *A Changing Turkey: The Challenge to Europe and the United States.* Washington, DC: Brookings Press, 2000. http://brookings.nap.edu/books/0815750234/html/index.html.

■ **24. DOCUMENT FROM A DATABASE** For an article accessed through a database service such as *EBSCOhost,* include a URL after the publication information. If the document is paginated, give a page number in the note and a page range in the bibliography. For unpaginated documents, page references are not possible.

24. Eugene F. Provenzo Jr., "Time Exposure," *Educational Studies* 34, no. 2 (2003): 266, http://search.epnet.com.

Provenzo, Eugene F. Jr. "Time Exposure." *Educational Studies* 34, no. 2 (2003): 266-67. http://search.epnet.com.

■ **25. ELECTRONIC JOURNAL ARTICLE** Electronic journals are published online. Their articles are often unpaginated.

25. Linda Belau, "Trauma and the Material Signifier," *Postmodern Culture* 11, no. 2 (2001): par. 6, http://www.iath.virginia.edu/pmc/text-only/issue.101/11.2belau.txt.

Belau, Linda. "Trauma and the Material Signifier." *Postmodern Culture* 11, no. 2 (2001). http://www.iath.virginia.edu/pmc/text-only/issue.101/11.2belau.txt.

■ **26. E-MAIL MESSAGE** Refer to e-mail messages in your text or in a note. E-mail messages are not included in the bibliography.

26. Kathleen Veslany, e-mail message to author, January 25, 2003.

■ **27. ONLINE POSTING** If an online posting has been archived, include a URL. Do not include online postings in the bibliography.

27. Janice Klein, posting to State Museum Association discussion list, June 19, 2003, http://listserv.nmmnh-abq.mus.nm.us/scripts/wa.exe?A2=ind0306c&L=sma-l&F=lf&S=&P=81.

Other sources

■   **28.** GOVERNMENT DOCUMENT

28. Industry Canada, *A Guide to Patents* (Ottawa: Canadian Intellectual Property Office, 2002), 59.

Industry Canada. *A Guide to Patents*. Ottawa: Canadian Intellectual Property Office, 2002.

■   **29.** UNPUBLISHED DISSERTATION

29. Stephanie Lynn Budin, "The Origins of Aphrodite (Greece)" (Ph.D. diss., University of Pennsylvania, 2000), 301-2.

Budin, Stephanie Lynn. "The Origins of Aphrodite (Greece)." Ph.D. diss., University of Pennsylvania, 2000.

■   **30.** PERSONAL COMMUNICATION

30. Sara Lehman, letter to author, August 13, 2000.

Personal communications are not included in the bibliography.

■   **31.** INTERVIEW

31. Ron Haviv, interview by Charlie Rose, *The Charlie Rose Show,* Public Broadcasting System, February 12, 2001.

Haviv, Ron. Interview by Charlie Rose. *The Charlie Rose Show*. Public Broadcasting System, February 12, 2001.

■   **32.** VIDEO OR DVD

32. *The Secret of Roan Inish,* DVD, directed by John Sayles (1993; Culver City, CA: Columbia Tristar Home Video, 2000).

The Secret of Roan Inish. DVD. Directed by John Sayles. 1993; Culver City, CA: Columbia Tristar Home Video, 2000.

■   **33.** SOUND RECORDING

33. Gustav Holst, *The Planets,* Royal Philharmonic, André Previn, Telarc compact disc 80133.

Holst, Gustav. *The Planets*. Royal Philharmonic. André Previn. Telarc compact disc 80133.

■ **34. SOURCE QUOTED IN ANOTHER SOURCE**

34. Adam Smith, *The Wealth of Nations* (New York: Random House, 1965), 11, quoted in Mark Skousen, *The Making of Modern Economics: The Lives and the Ideas of the Great Thinkers* (Armonk, NY: M. E. Sharpe, 2001), 15.

Smith, Adam. *The Wealth of Nations,* 11. New York: Random House, 1965. Quoted in Mark Skousen, *The Making of Modern Economics: The Lives and the Ideas of the Great Thinkers* (Armonk, NY: M. E. Sharpe, 2001), 15.

ON THE WEB

To check for possible updates to CMS style, go to
www.dianahacker.com/writersref

and click on ▶ **Research and Documentation Online**
▶ **Documenting Sources (CMS)**

CMS-5

Manuscript format; sample pages

CMS-5a Manuscript format

The following guidelines for formatting a CMS paper and preparing its endnotes and bibliography are based on *The Chicago Manual of Style,* 15th ed. For pages from a sample paper, see CMS-5b.

Formatting the paper

CMS manuscript guidelines are fairly generic, since they were not created with a specific type of writing in mind.

TITLE PAGE   Include the full title of your paper, your name, the course title, the instructor's name, and the date. Do not number the title page but count it in the manuscript numbering; that is, the first page of the text will be numbered 2. See page 439 for a sample title page.

PAGINATION   Using Arabic numerals, number all pages except the title page in the upper right corner.

MARGINS AND LINE SPACING   Leave margins of at least one inch (2.5 cm) at the top, bottom, and sides of the page. Double-space the text of the manuscript, including long quotations that have been set off from the text. (For line spacing in notes and the bibliography, see the bottom of this page and p. 438.)

LONG QUOTATIONS   See pages 425–26 for CMS guidelines for setting long quotations off from the text.

VISUALS   *The Chicago Manual* classifies visuals as tables and illustrations (illustrations, or figures, include drawings, photographs, maps, and charts). Label each table with an Arabic numeral (Table 1, Table 2, and so on) and provide a clear title that identifies the subject. The label and title should appear on separate lines above the table, flush left. Below the table, give its source in a note like this one:

Source: Edna Bonacich and Richard P. Appelbaum, *Behind the Label* (Berkeley: University of California Press, 2000), 145.

For each figure, place a label and a caption below the figure, flush left. The label and caption need not appear on separate lines. The word "Figure" may be abbreviated to "Fig."

Preparing the endnotes

Begin the endnotes on a new page at the end of the paper. Centre the title Notes about one inch from the top of the page, and number the pages consecutively with the rest of the manuscript. See page 442 for an example.

INDENTING AND NUMBERING   Indent the first line of each entry one-half inch (1.25 cm or five spaces) from the left margin; do not indent additional lines in an entry. Begin the note with the Arabic numeral that corresponds to the numbered note in the text. Put a period after the number.

LINE SPACING   Single-space each note and double-space between notes (unless your instructor prefers double-spacing throughout).

Preparing the bibliography

Typically, the notes in CMS papers are followed by a bibliography, an alphabetically arranged list of all the works cited or consulted (see p. 443 for an example). Centre the title Bibliography about one inch (2.5 cm) from the top of the page. Number bibliography pages consecutively with the rest of the paper.

ALPHABETIZING THE LIST   Alphabetize the bibliography by the last names of the authors (or editors); when a work has no author or editor, alphabetize by the first word of the title other than *A, An,* or *The.*

If your list includes two or more works by the same author, use three hyphens instead of the author's name in all entries after the first. You may arrange the entries alphabetically by title or chronologically; be consistent throughout the bibliography.

INDENTING AND LINE SPACING   Begin each entry at the left margin, and indent any additional lines one-half inch (1.25 cm or five spaces). Single-space each entry and double-space between entries (unless your instructor prefers double-spacing throughout).

CMS-5b Sample pages from a CMS paper

Following are sample pages from a research paper by Ned Bishop, a student in a history class. Bishop was asked to document his paper using CMS endnotes and a bibliography. In preparing his manuscript, Bishop also followed CMS guidelines.

ON THE WEB

To read Ned Bishop's entire paper with marginal annotations, go to
www.dianahacker.com/writersref

and click on   ▶ **Model Papers**
                ▶ **CMS paper: Bishop**

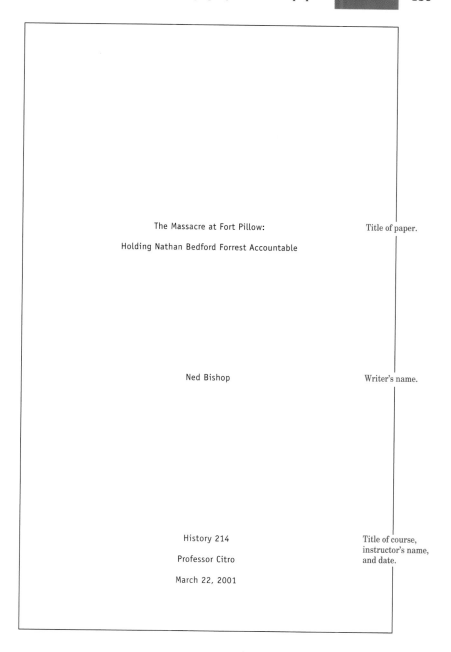

The Massacre at Fort Pillow:

Holding Nathan Bedford Forrest Accountable

Title of paper.

Ned Bishop

Writer's name.

History 214

Professor Citro

March 22, 2001

Title of course,
instructor's name,
and date.

Bishop 2

Although Northern newspapers of the time no doubt exaggerated some of the Confederate atrocities at Fort Pillow, most modern sources agree that a massacre of Union troops took place there on April 12, 1864. It seems clear that Union soldiers, particularly black soldiers, were killed after they had stopped fighting or had surrendered or were being held prisoner. Less clear is the role played by Major General Nathan Bedford Forrest in leading his troops. Although we will never know whether Forrest directly ordered the massacre, evidence suggests that he was responsible for it.

Thesis asserts writer's main point.

What happened at Fort Pillow?

Headings help readers follow the organization.

Fort Pillow, Tennessee, which sat on a bluff overlooking the Mississippi River, had been held by the Union for two years. It was garrisoned by 580 men, 292 of them from the Sixth United States Colored Heavy and Light Cavalry, 285 from the white Thirteenth Tennessee Cavalry. Nathan Bedford Forrest's troops numbered about 1,500 men.[1]

Statistics are cited with an endnote.

The Confederates attacked Fort Pillow on April 12, 1864, and had virtually surrounded the fort by the time Forrest arrived on the battlefield. At 3:30 P.M., Forrest displayed a flag of truce and sent in a demand for unconditional surrender of the sort he had used before: "The conduct of the officers and men garrisoning Fort Pillow has been such as to entitle them to being treated as prisoners of war. . . . Should my demand be refused, I cannot be responsible for the fate of your command."[2] Union Major William Bradford, who had replaced Major Booth, killed earlier by sharpshooters, asked for an hour to

Quotation is cited with an endnote.

consult. Forrest, worried that vessels in the river were bringing in more troops, shortened the time to twenty minutes. Bradford refused to surrender, and Forrest quickly ordered the attack.

The Confederates charged across the short distance between their lines and the fort, helping one another scale the parapet, from which they fired into the fort. Victory came quickly, with the Union forces running toward the river or surrendering. Shelby Foote describes the scene like this:

> Some kept going, right into the river, where a number drowned and the swimmers became targets for marksmen on the bluff. Others, dropping their guns in terror, ran back toward the Confederates with their hands up, and of these some were spared as prisoners, while others were shot down in the act of surrender.[3]

In his own official report, Forrest makes no mention of the massacre. He does make much of the fact that the Union flag was not taken down, saying that if his own men had not taken down the flag, "few if any, would have survived unhurt another volley."[4] However, as Jack Hurst points out and Forrest must have known, in this twenty-minute battle, "Federals running for their lives had little time to concern themselves with a flag."[5]

The federal congressional report on Fort Pillow, which charged the Confederates with appalling atrocities, drew much criticism from Southern writers, and even respected writer Shelby Foote, who does

Long quotation is set off from text by indenting. Quotation marks are omitted.

Quotations are introduced with signal phrases.

The complete text of the paper appears on the companion Web site for *A Writer's Reference.* See page 438 for the address.

Notes

First line of each note is indented ½″ (1.25 cm or 5 spaces).

1. John Cimprich and Robert C. Mainfort Jr., "Fort Pillow Revisited: New Evidence about an Old Controversy," *Civil War History* 28, no. 4 (1982): 293-94.

2. Brian Steel Wills, *A Battle from the Start: The Life of Nathan Bedford Forrest* (New York: HarperCollins, 1992), 182.

Note number is not raised and is followed by a period.

3. Shelby Foote, *The Civil War, a Narrative: Red River to Appomattox* (New York: Vintage, 1986), 110.

4. Nathan Bedford Forrest, "Report of Maj. Gen. Nathan B. Forrest, C. S. Army, Commanding Cavalry, of the Capture of Fort Pillow," *Shotgun's Home of the American Civil War,* http://www.civilwarhome.com/forrest.htm.

Authors' names are not inverted.

5. Jack Hurst, *Nathan Bedford Forrest: A Biography* (New York: Knopf, 1993), 174.

Last name and brief title refer to an earlier note by the same author.

6. Foote, *Civil War,* 111.

7. Cimprich and Mainfort, "Fort Pillow," 305.

8. Ibid., 299.

9. Foote, *Civil War,* 110.

10. Wills, *Battle from the Start,* 187.

Notes are single-spaced, with double-spacing between notes. (Some instructors may prefer double-spacing throughout.)

11. Albert Castel, "The Fort Pillow Massacre: A Fresh Examination of the Evidence," *Civil War History* 4, no. 1 (1958): 44-45.

12. Cimprich and Mainfort, "Fort Pillow," 300.

13. Hurst, *Nathan Bedford Forrest,* 177.

14. Ibid.

15. Dudley Taylor Cornish, *The Sable Arm: Black Troops in the Union Army, 1861-1865* (Lawrence, KS: University Press of Kansas, 1987), 175.

16. Foote, *Civil War,* 111.

17. Cimprich and Mainfort, "Fort Pillow," 304.

Bibliography

Castel, Albert. "The Fort Pillow Massacre: A Fresh Examination of the Evidence." *Civil War History* 4, no. 1 (1958): 37-50.

Cimprich, John, and Robert C. Mainfort Jr. "Fort Pillow Revisited: New Evidence about an Old Controversy." *Civil War History* 28, no. 4 (1982): 293-306.

Cornish, Dudley Taylor. *The Sable Arm: Black Troops in the Union Army, 1861-1865.* Lawrence, KS: University Press of Kansas, 1987.

Foote, Shelby. *The Civil War, a Narrative: Red River to Appomattox.* New York: Vintage, 1986.

Forrest, Nathan Bedford. "Report of Maj. Gen. Nathan B. Forrest, C. S. Army, Commanding Cavalry, of the Capture of Fort Pillow." *Shotgun's Home of the American Civil War.* http://www.civilwarhome.com/forrest.htm.

Hurst, Jack. *Nathan Bedford Forrest: A Biography.* New York: Knopf, 1993.

McPherson, James M. *Battle Cry of Freedom: The Civil War Era.* New York: Oxford University Press, 1988.

Wills, Brian Steel. *A Battle from the Start: The Life of Nathan Bedford Forrest.* New York: HarperCollins, 1992.

Entries are alphabetized by authors' last names.

First line of entry is at left margin; additional lines are indented ½" (1.25 cm or 5 spaces).

Entries are single-spaced, with double-spacing between entries. (Some instructors may prefer double-spacing throughout.)

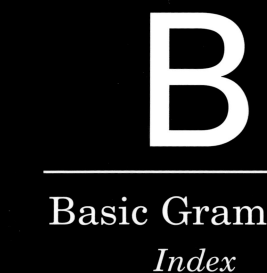

B

Basic Grammar
Index

B

Basic Grammar

B1

Parts of speech

The parts of speech are a system for classifying words. There are eight parts of speech: noun, pronoun, verb, adjective, adverb, preposition, conjunction, and interjection. Many words can function as more than one part of speech. For example, depending on its use in a sentence, the word *paint* can be a noun (*The paint is wet*) or a verb (*Please paint the ceiling next*).

ON THE WEB

For electronic exercises on parts of speech, go to
www.dianahacker.com/writersref

and click on ▶ **Electronic Grammar Exercises**
　　　　　　▶ **Basic Grammar**
　　　　　　　▶ **E-ex B1–1 through B1–7**

B1-a Nouns

A noun is the name of a person, place, thing, or an idea. Nouns are often but not always signalled by an article (*a, an, the*).

> N　　　N　　　　　　　N
> The cat in gloves catches no mice.

> N　　　　　　　　　　N　　　N
> Repetition does not transform a lie into truth.

Nouns sometimes function as adjectives modifying other nouns.

> 　　　　　N/ADJ　　　　　　　N/ADJ
> You can't make a silk purse out of a sow's ear.

Nouns are classified for a variety of purposes. When capitalization is the issue, we speak of *proper* versus *common* nouns (see M3-a). If the problem is one of word choice, we may speak of *concrete* versus *abstract* nouns (see W5-b). Most nouns come in *singular* and *plural* forms; *collective* nouns may be either singular or plural (see G1-f and G3-a). *Possessive* nouns require an apostrophe (see P5-a).

B1-b Pronouns

A pronoun is a word used in place of a noun. Usually the pronoun substitutes for a specific noun, known as its *antecedent*.

When the *wheel* squeaks, *it* is greased.

Although most pronouns function as substitutes for nouns, some can function as adjectives modifying nouns.

PN/ADJ
This hanging will surely be a lesson to me.

Most of the pronouns in English are listed in this section.

PERSONAL PRONOUNS   Personal pronouns refer to specific persons or things.

Singular: I, me, you, she, her, he, him, it

Plural: we, us, you, they, them

POSSESSIVE PRONOUNS   Possessive pronouns indicate ownership.

Singular: my, mine, your, yours, her, hers, his, its

Plural: our, ours, your, yours, their, theirs

INTENSIVE AND REFLEXIVE PRONOUNS   Intensive pronouns emphasize a noun or another pronoun (The senator *herself* met us at the door). Reflexive pronouns name a receiver of an action identical with the doer of the action (Paula cut *herself*).

Singular: myself, yourself, himself, herself, itself

Plural: ourselves, yourselves, themselves

RELATIVE PRONOUNS   Relative pronouns introduce subordinate clauses functioning as adjectives (The man *who robbed us* was never caught). In addition to introducing the clause, the relative pronoun, in this case *who,* points back to a noun or pronoun that the clause modifies (*man*). (See B3-e.)

who, whom, whose, which, that

INTERROGATIVE PRONOUNS   Interrogative pronouns introduce questions (*Who* is expected to win the election?).

who, whom, whose, which, that

DEMONSTRATIVE PRONOUNS   Demonstrative pronouns identify or point to nouns. Frequently they function as adjectives (*This* chair is my favourite), but they may also function as noun equivalents (*This* is my favourite chair).

this, that, these, those

INDEFINITE PRONOUNS   Indefinite pronouns refer to nonspecific persons or things. Most are singular (*everyone, each*); some are plural (*both, many*); a few may be singular or plural (see G1-e).

all, another, any, anybody, anyone, anything, both, each, either, everybody, everyone, everything, few, many, neither, nobody, none, no one, nothing, one, several, some, somebody, someone, something

RECIPROCAL PRONOUNS   Reciprocal pronouns refer to individual parts of a plural antecedent (We helped *each other*).

each other, one another

NOTE: Pronouns cause a variety of problems for writers. See Pronoun-antecedent agreement (G3-a), Pronoun reference (G3-b), Distinguishing between pronouns such as *I* and *me* (G3-c), and Distinguishing between *who* and *whom* (G3-d).

B1-c Verbs

The verb of a sentence usually expresses action (*jump, think*) or being (*is, become*). It is composed of a main verb (MV) possibly preceded by one or more helping verbs (HV).

MV
The best fish swim near the bottom.

HV   MV
A marriage is not built in a day.

Notice that words can intervene between the helping and the main verb (*is* not *built*).

Helping verbs

Helping verbs in English include forms of *have, do,* and *be,* which may also function as main verbs; and verbs known as modals, which function only as helping verbs. The verbs *have, do,* and *be* change form to indicate tense; the modals do not.

FORMS OF *HAVE, DO,* AND *BE*
have, has, had
do, does, did
be, am, is, are, was, were, being, been

MODALS
can, could, may, might, must, shall, should, will, would, ought to

Main verbs

A main verb changes form if put into the following test sentences. When both the past-tense and past-participle forms end in *-ed,* the verb is regular; otherwise, the verb is irregular. (See G2-a.)

BASE FORM	Usually I (*walk, ride*).
PAST TENSE	Yesterday I (*walked, rode*).
PAST PARTICIPLE	I have (*walked, ridden*) many times before.
PRESENT PARTICIPLE	I am (*walking, riding*) right now.
-S FORM	Usually he/she/it (*walks, rides*).

If a word doesn't change form when slipped into these test sentences, you can be certain that it is not a main verb. For example, the noun *revolution,* though it may seem to suggest an action, can never function as a main verb. Just try to make it behave like one (*Today I revolution . . . Yesterday I revolutioned . . .*) and you'll see why.

The verb *be* is highly irregular, having eight forms instead of the usual five: the base form *be;* the present-tense forms *am, is,* and *are;* the past-tense forms *was* and *were;* the present participle *being;* and the past participle *been.*

NOTE: Some verbs are followed by words that look like prepositions but are so closely associated with the verb that they are a part of its meaning. These words are known as *particles.* Common verb-particle combinations include *bring up, call off, drop off, give in, look up, run into,* and *take off.*

A lot of parents *pack up* their troubles and *send* them *off* to camp.

—Raymond Duncan

NOTE: Verbs cause many problems for writers. See Subject-verb agreement (G1); Other problems with verbs, including verb forms, tense, and mood (G2); ESL problems with verbs (T2); and Active verbs (W3).

B1-d Adjectives and articles

An adjective is a word used to modify, or describe, a noun or pronoun. An adjective usually answers one of these questions: Which one? What kind of? How many?

ADJ
the lame elephant [Which elephant?]

ADJ   ADJ
valuable old stamps [What kind of stamps?]

ADJ
sixteen candles [How many candles?]

Adjectives usually precede the words they modify. However, they may also follow linking verbs, in which case they describe the subject. (See B2-b.)

ADJ
Good medicine always tastes bitter.

Articles, sometimes classified as adjectives, are used to mark nouns. There are only three: the definite article *the* and the indefinite articles *a* and *an.*

ART   ART
A country can be judged by the quality of its proverbs.

NOTE: Writers sometimes misuse adjectives (see G4). Speakers of English as a second language may have trouble placing adjectives correctly (see T3-e); they may also encounter difficulties with articles (see T1).

B1-e Adverbs

An adverb is a word used to modify a verb (or verbal), an adjective, or another adverb. It usually answers one of these questions: When? Where? How? Why? Under what conditions? To what degree?

ADV

Pull gently at a weak rope. [Pull how?]

ADV

Read the best books first. [Read when?]

Adverbs modifying adjectives or other adverbs usually intensify or limit the intensity of the word they modify.

ADV   ADV

Be extremely good, and you will be very lonesome.

The negators *not* and *never* are classified as adverbs.

NOTE: Writers sometimes misuse adverbs (see G4). Speakers of English as a second language may have trouble placing adverbs correctly (see T3-e).

B1-f Prepositions

A preposition is a word placed before a noun or pronoun to form a phrase modifying another word in the sentence. The prepositional phrase nearly always functions as an adjective or as an adverb. (See B3-a.)

P   P

The road *to hell* is paved *with good intentions.*

To hell functions as an adjective modifying the noun *road; with good intentions* functions as an adverb modifying the verb *is paved.*

There are a limited number of prepositions in English. The most common are included in the following list.

about	beside	in	past	unlike
above	besides	inside	plus	until
across	between	into	regarding	unto
after	beyond	like	respecting	up
against	but	near	round	upon
along	by	next	since	with
among	concerning	of	than	within
around	considering	off	through	without
as	despite	on	throughout	
at	down	onto	till	
before	during	opposite	to	
behind	except	out	toward	
below	for	outside	under	
beneath	from	over	underneath	

Some prepositions are more than a word long. *Along with, as well as, in addition to, instead of, next to,* and *up to* are common examples.

NOTE: Except for certain idiomatic uses (see W5-d), prepositions cause few problems for native speakers of English. For second-language speakers, however, prepositions can cause considerable difficulty (see T2-d and T4-b).

B1-g Conjunctions

Conjunctions join words, phrases, or clauses, and they indicate the relation between the elements joined.

COORDINATING CONJUNCTIONS Coordinating conjunctions connect grammatically equal elements. (See S1-b and S6.)

and, but, or, nor, for, so, yet

CORRELATIVE CONJUNCTIONS Correlative conjunctions are pairs of conjunctions that connect grammatically equal elements. (See S1-b.)

either . . . or, neither . . . nor, not only . . . but also, whether . . . or, both . . . and

SUBORDINATING CONJUNCTIONS Subordinating conjunctions introduce subordinate clauses and indicate their relation to the rest of the sentence. (See B3-e.)

after, although, as, as if, because, before, even though, if, in order that, rather than, since, so that, than, that, though, unless, until, when, where, whether, while

CONJUNCTIVE ADVERBS Conjunctive adverbs are adverbs used to indicate the relation between independent clauses. (See P3-b.)

accordingly, also, anyway, besides, certainly, consequently, conversely, finally, furthermore, hence, however, incidentally, indeed, instead, likewise, meanwhile, moreover, nevertheless, next, nonetheless, otherwise, similarly, specifically, still, subsequently, then, therefore, thus

NOTE: The ability to distinguish between conjunctive adverbs and coordinating conjunctions will help you avoid run-on sentences and make punctuation decisions (see G6, P1-a, and P3-b). The ability to recognize subordinating conjunctions will help you avoid sentence fragments (see G5).

B1-h Interjections

Interjections are words used to express surprise or emotion (*Oh! Hey! Wow!*).

B2

Parts of sentences

Most English sentences flow from subject to verb to any objects or complements. *Predicate* is the grammatical term given to the verb plus its objects, complements, and modifiers.

ON THE WEB

For electronic exercises on parts of sentences (subjects, objects, and complements), go to **www.dianahacker.com/writersref**

and click on ▶ **Electronic Grammar Exercises**
              ▶ **Basic Grammar**
                 ▶ **E-ex B2–1 through B2–5**

B2-a Subjects

The subject of a sentence names who or what the sentence is about. The simple subject is always a noun or a pronoun; the complete subject consists of the simple subject (SS) and all of its modifiers.

> ┌ SS ┐
> *The purity of a revolution* usually lasts about two weeks.

> ┌ SS ┐
> *Historical books that contain no lies* are extremely tedious.

> ┌ SS ┐
> In every country, *the sun* rises in the morning.

To find the complete subject, ask Who? or What?, insert the verb, and finish the question. What usually lasts about two weeks? *The purity of a revolution.* What are extremely tedious? *Historical books that contain no lies.* What rises in the morning? *The sun* [not *In every country, the sun*].

To find the simple subject, strip away all modifiers in the complete subject. This includes single-word modifiers such as *the* and *historical,* phrases such as *of a revolution,* and subordinate clauses such as *that contain no lies.*

A sentence may have a compound subject containing two or more simple subjects joined with a coordinating conjunction such as *and* or *or.*

┌── ss ──┐   ┌── ss ──┐
Much industry and little conscience make us rich.

In imperative sentences, which give advice or commands, the subject is an understood *you.*

[*You*] Hitch your wagon to a star.

Although the subject ordinarily comes before the verb, occasionally it does not. When a sentence begins with *There is* or *There are* (or *There was* or *There were*), the subject follows the verb. The word *There* is an expletive in such constructions, an empty word serving merely to get the sentence started.

┌── ss ──┐
There is *no substitute for victory.*

Sometimes a writer will invert a sentence for effect.

┌─ ss ─┐
Happy is *the nation that has no history.*

In questions, the subject may appear before the verb, after the verb, or between parts of the verb.

s ┌── v ──┐
Who will take the first step?

v ┌──── s ────┐
Why is the first step so difficult?

HV S MV
Will you take the first step?

NOTE: The ability to recognize the subject of a sentence will help you edit for a variety of problems such as sentence fragments (G5), faulty subject-verb agreement (G1), and misuse of pronouns such as *I* and *me* (G3-c). If English is not your native language, see also T3-a and T3-b.

B2-b Verbs, objects, and complements

Section B1-c explains how to identify verbs. A sentence's verb(s) may be classified as linking, transitive, or intransitive, depending on the kinds of objects or complements the verb can (or cannot) take.

Linking verbs and subject complements

Linking verbs (v) take subject complements (sc), words or word groups that complete the meaning of the subject (s) by either re-naming it or describing it.

```
┌──────────── s ────────────┐ ┌─ v ─┐┌─ sc ─┐
The handwriting on the wall may be a forgery.
```

```
 s   v  sc
Love is blind.
```

When the simple subject complement renames the subject, it is a noun or pronoun, such as *forgery;* when it describes the subject, it is an adjective, such as *blind.*

Linking verbs are usually a form of *be: be, am, is, are, was, were, being, been.* Verbs such as *appear, become, feel, grow, look, make, prove, remain, seem, smell, sound,* and *taste* are linking when they are followed by a word group that names or describes the subject.

Transitive verbs and direct objects

A transitive verb takes a direct object (DO), a word or word group that completes the meaning of the verb by naming a receiver of the action.

```
┌──── s ────┐  v  ┌─────── DO ───────┐
The little snake studies the ways of the big serpent.
```

The simple direct object is always a noun, such as *ways,* or a pronoun.

Transitive verbs usually appear in the active voice, with the subject doing the action and a direct object receiving the action.

Active-voice sentences can be transformed into the passive voice, with the subject receiving the action instead.

ACTIVE VOICE   The early bird sometimes catches the early worm.

PASSIVE VOICE   The early worm is sometimes caught by the early bird.

What was once the direct object (*the early worm*) has become the subject in the passive-voice transformation, and the original subject appears in a prepositional phrase beginning with *by*. The *by* phrase is frequently omitted in passive-voice constructions: *The early worm is sometimes caught.* (See also W3-a.)

Transitive verbs, indirect objects, and direct objects

The direct object of a transitive verb is sometimes preceded by an indirect object (IO), a noun or pronoun telling to whom or for whom the action of the sentence is done.

> S   V   IO ┌ DO ┐   S┌── V ──┐   IO ┌── DO ──┐
> You show [to] me a hero, and I will write [for] you a tragedy.

Transitive verbs, direct objects, and object complements

The direct object of a transitive verb is sometimes followed by an object complement (OC), a word or word group that completes the direct object's meaning by renaming or describing it.

> ┌── S ──┐ V ┌ DO ┐ ┌────── OC ──────┐
> Some people call a spade an agricultural implement.

> S   V   ┌── DO ──┐ OC
> Love makes all hard hearts gentle.

When the object complement renames the direct object, it is a noun or pronoun, such as *implement*. When it describes the direct object, it is an adjective, such as *gentle*.

Intransitive verbs

Intransitive verbs take no objects or complements. They may or may not be followed by adverbial modifiers.

> S   V
> Money talks.

    s   v
All roads lead to Rome.

Nothing receives the actions of talking and leading in these sentences, so the verbs are intransitive. Intransitive verbs are often followed by adverbial modifiers. In the above sentence, for example, *to Rome* is a prepositional phrase functioning as an adverb modifying *lead.*

NOTE: The dictionary will tell you whether a verb is transitive or intransitive. Some verbs have both transitive and intransitive functions.

TRANSITIVE   Sandra flew her Cessna over the canyon.

INTRANSITIVE   A bald eagle flew overhead.

In the first example, *flew* has a direct object that receives the action: *her Cessna.* In the second example, the verb is followed by an adverb (*overhead*), not by a direct object.

B3

Subordinate word groups

Subordinate word groups cannot stand alone. They function only within sentences, usually as adjectives, adverbs, or nouns.

ON THE WEB

For electronic exercises on subordinate word groups (prepositional phrases, verbal phrases, and subordinate clauses), go to
www.dianahacker.com/writersref

and click on ▶ **Electronic Grammar Exercises**
　　　　　　　▶ **Basic Grammar**
　　　　　　　▶ **E-ex B3–1 through B3–9**

B3-a Prepositional phrases

A prepositional phrase begins with a preposition such as *at, by, for, from, in, of, on, to,* or *with* (see B1-f) and ends with a noun or a noun equivalent called its *object.*

Prepositional phrases function as adjectives or adverbs. When functioning as an adjective, a prepositional phrase usually appears right after the noun or pronoun it modifies.

Variety is the spice *of life.*

Adjective phrases answer one or both of the questions Which one? and What kind of? If we ask Which spice? or What kind of spice? we get a sensible answer: *the spice of life.*

Adverbial prepositional phrases modifying the verb can appear nearly anywhere in a sentence.

Do not judge a tree *by its bark.*

Tyranny will *in time* lead to revolution.

To the ant, a few drops of rain are a flood.

Adverb phrases usually answer one of these questions: When? Where? How? Why? Under what conditions? To what degree?

Do not judge a tree *how? By its bark.*

Tyranny will lead to revolution *when? In time.*

A few drops of rain are a flood *under what conditions? To the ant.*

B3-b Verbal phrases

A verbal is a verb form that does not function as the verb of a clause. Verbals include infinitives (the word *to* plus the base form of the verb), present participles (the *-ing* form of the verb), and past participles (the form of the verb usually ending in *-d, -ed, -n, -en,* or *-t*) (see G2-a).

Verbals can take objects, complements, and modifiers to form verbal phrases. These phrases are classified as participial, gerund, and infinitive.

Participial phrases

Participial phrases always function as adjectives. Their verbals are either present participles, always ending in *-ing,* or past participles, frequently ending in *-d, -ed, -n, -en,* or *-t* (see G2-a).

Participial phrases frequently appear right after the noun or pronoun they modify.

Truth *kept in the dark* will never save the world.

Unlike other adjectival word groups, however, participial phrases can precede the word they modify or appear at some distance from it.

Being weak, foxes are distinguished by superior tact.

History is something that never happened, *written by someone who wasn't there.*

Gerund phrases

Gerund phrases are built around present participles (verb forms ending in *-ing*), and they always function as nouns: usually as subjects, subject complements, direct objects, or objects of the preposition.

Justifying a fault doubles it.

Kleptomaniacs can't help *helping themselves.*

Infinitive phrases

Infinitive phrases, usually constructed around *to* plus the base form of the verb (*to call, to drink*), can function as adjectives, adverbs, or nouns. When functioning as a noun, an infinitive phrase usually plays the role of subject, subject complement, or direct object.

We do not have the right *to abandon the poor.*

He cut off his nose *to spite his face.*

To side with truth is noble.

B3-c Appositive phrases

Appositive phrases describe nouns or pronouns. In form they are nouns or noun equivalents.

> Politicians, *acrobats at heart,* can sit on a fence and yet keep both ears to the ground.

B3-d Absolute phrases

An absolute phrase modifies a whole clause or sentence, not just one word. It consists of a noun or noun equivalent usually followed by a participial phrase.

> *His words dipped in honey*, the senator mesmerized the crowd.

B3-e Subordinate clauses

Subordinate clauses are patterned like sentences, having subjects and verbs and sometimes objects or complements, but they function within sentences as adjectives, adverbs, or nouns. They cannot stand alone as complete sentences.

Adjective clauses

Adjective clauses modify nouns or pronouns, usually answering the question Which one? or What kind of? They begin with a relative pronoun (*who, whom, whose, which,* or *that*) or a relative adverb (*when* or *where*).

The arrow *that has left the bow* never returns.

In addition to introducing the clause, the relative pronoun points back to the noun that the clause modifies.

The fur *that warms a monarch* once warmed a bear.

Relative pronouns are sometimes "understood."

The things [*that*] *we know best* are the things [*that*] *we haven't been taught.*

The parts of an adjective clause are often arranged as in sentences (subject/verb/object or complement).

S   V   DO

We often forgive the people *who bore us.*

Frequently, however, the object or complement appears first, violating the normal order of subject/verb/object.

DO   S   V

We rarely forgive those *whom we bore.*

NOTE: For punctuation of adjective clauses, see P1-e and P2-e. If English is not your native language, see T3-c for a common problem with adjective clauses.

Adverb clauses

Adverb clauses modify verbs, adjectives, or other adverbs, usually answering one of these questions: When? Where? Why? How? Under what conditions? To what degree? They begin with a subordinating conjunction (*after, although, as, as if, because, before, even though, if, in order that, rather than, since, so that, than, that, though, unless, until, when, where, whether, while*).

When the well is dry, we know the worth of water.

Venice would be a fine city *if it were only drained.*

Noun clauses

Noun clauses function as subjects, objects, or complements. They usually begin with one of the following words: *how, that, which, who, whoever, whom, whomever, what, whatever, when, where, whether, whose, why.*

────── s ──────

Whoever gossips to you will gossip of you.

────── DO ──────

We will never forget *where we buried the hatchet.*

The word introducing the clause may or may not play a signifi-cant role in the clause. In the preceding example sentences, *Who-ever* is the subject of its clause, but *where* does not perform a func-tion in its clause.

As with adjective clauses, the parts of a noun clause may ap-pear out of their normal order (subject/verb/object).

DO S V

Talent is *what you possess.*

The parts of a noun clause may also appear in their normal order.

S V DO

Genius is *what possesses you.*

B4

Sentence types

Sentences are classified in two ways: according to their structure (simple, compound, complex, and compound-complex) and accord-ing to their purpose (declarative, imperative, interrogative, and exclamatory).

ON THE WEB

For an electronic exercise on sentence types, go to
www.dianahacker.com/writersref

and click on ▶ **Electronic Grammar Exercises**
▶ **Basic Grammar**
▶ **E-ex B4–1**

B4-a Sentence structures

Depending on the number and types of clauses they contain, sentences are classified as simple, compound, complex, or compound-complex.

Clauses come in two varieties: independent and subordinate. An independent clause contains a subject and predicate, and it either stands alone or could stand alone. A subordinate clause also contains a subject and predicate, but it functions within a sentence as an adjective, an adverb, or a noun; it cannot stand alone.

SIMPLE SENTENCE A simple sentence is one independent clause with no subordinate clauses.

┌─────────── INDEPENDENT CLAUSE ───────────┐
Without music, life would be a mistake.

COMPOUND SENTENCE A compound sentence is composed of two or more independent clauses with no subordinate clauses. The independent clauses are usually joined with a comma and a coordinating conjunction (*and, but, or, nor, for, so, yet*) or with a semicolon.

┌── INDEPENDENT CLAUSE ──┐   ┌── INDEPENDENT CLAUSE ──┐
One arrow is easily broken, but you can't break a bundle of ten.

COMPLEX SENTENCE A complex sentence is composed of one independent clause with one or more subordinate clauses.

    SUBORDINATE
┌── CLAUSE ──┐
If you scatter thorns, don't go barefoot.

COMPOUND-COMPLEX SENTENCE A compound-complex sentence contains at least two independent clauses and at least one subordinate clause. The following sentence contains two independent clauses, each of which contains a subordinate clause.

┌── IND CLAUSE ──┐   ┌── IND CLAUSE ──┐
  ┌ SUB CLAUSE ┐   ┌ SUB CLAUSE ┐
Tell me what you eat, and I will tell you what you are.

B4-b Sentence purposes

Writers use declarative sentences to make statements, imperative sentences to issue requests or commands, interrogative sentences to ask questions, and exclamatory sentences to make exclamations.

DECLARATIVE	The echo always has the last word.
IMPERATIVE	Love your neighbour.
INTERROGATIVE	Are second thoughts always wisest?
EXCLAMATORY	I want to wash the flag, not burn it!

Index

In addition to giving you page numbers, this index shows you which tabbed section to flip to. For example, the entry for *a* vs. *an* directs you to section **W** (Word Choice), pages 111–12, and to section **T** (ESL Trouble Spots), page 211. Just flip to the appropriate tabbed section and then track down the exact pages you need.

B

J

O

P

ESL Menu

A complete section on major ESL problems:

ESL notes in other sections:

Revision Symbols

Letter-number codes refer to sections of this book.

abbr	faulty abbreviation **M4**	*p*	error in punctuation
ad	misuse of adverb or adjective **G4**	$\hat{;}$	comma **P1**
add	add needed word **S2**	*no ,*	no comma **P2**
agr	faulty agreement **G1, G3-a**	;	semicolon **P3**
appr	inappropriate language **W4**	:	colon **P4**
art	article **T1**	$\overset{,}{v}$	apostrophe **P5**
awk	awkward	" "	quotation marks **P6**
cap	capital letter **M3**	. ? !	period, question mark, exclamation point,
case	error in case **G3-c, G3-d**	— ( )	dash, parentheses,
cliché	cliché **W5-e**	[ ] . . .	brackets, ellipsis mark,
coh	coherence **C4-d**	/	slash **P7**
coord	faulty coordination **S6-b**	*pass*	ineffective passive **W3**
cs	comma splice **G6**	*pn agr*	pronoun agreement **G3-a**
dev	inadequate development **C4-b**	*proof*	proofreading problem **C3-c**
dm	dangling modifier **S3-e**	*ref*	error in pronoun reference **G3-b**
-ed	error in *-ed* ending **G2-d**	*run-on*	run-on sentence **G6**
emph	emphasis **S6**	*-s*	error in *-s* ending **G2-c**
ESL	ESL trouble spot **T1, T2, T3, T4**	*sexist*	sexist language **W4-e**
exact	inexact language **W5**	*shift*	distracting shift **S4**
frag	sentence fragment **G5**	*sl*	slang **W4-c**
fs	fused sentence **G6**	*sp*	misspelled word **M1**
gl/us	see Glossary of Usage **W1**	*sub*	faulty subordination **S6-c, S6-d**
hyph	error in use of hyphen **M2**	*sv agr*	subject-verb agreement **G1, G2-c**
idiom	idioms **W5-d**	*t*	error in verb tense **G2-f**
inc	incomplete construction **S2**	*trans*	transition needed **C4-d**
irreg	error in irregular verb **G2-a**	*usage*	see Glossary of Usage **W1**
ital	italics (underlining) **M6**	*v*	voice **W3**
jarg	jargon **W4-a**	*var*	sentence variety **S6-b, S6-c, S7**
lc	lowercase letter **M3**	*vb*	verb error **G2**
mix	mixed construction **S5**	*w*	wordy **W2**
mm	misplaced modifier **S3-b**	*//*	faulty parallelism **S1**
mood	error in mood **G2-g**	∧	insert
nonst	nonstandard usage **W4-c**	*x*	obvious error
num	error in use of numbers **M5**	*#*	insert space
om	omitted word **S2**	⌒	close up space
¶	new paragraph **C4**		

Detailed Menu